# SECRETS OF COLD WAR TECHNOLOGY

## Project HAARP and Beyond

# Gerry Vassilatos

Bayside, California

COPYRIGHT 1996 © Gerry Vassilatos

All rights reserved. No part of this publication may be reproduced, stored in a retrieval system or transmitted in any form or by any means, electronic, mechanical, photocopying, recording or otherwise without the prior permission of the publisher or author except for brief passages quoted in critical articles and reviews.

Published by:

BORDERLAND SCIENCES RESEARCH FOUNDATION
P.O. Box 220,
Bayside, CA 95524 USA

ISBN 0-945685-17-3

Library of Congress Catalog Number: 96-78764

10  9  8  7  6  5  4  3  2  1

Published in the United States of America

First Edition

Cover Design by Michael Theroux and Ion Graphix

# CONTENTS

| | | |
|---|---|---|
| *Prologue* | Symbols and Models | 5 |
| Chapter 1 | Nikola Tesla and Radiant Energy | 19 |
| Chapter 2 | Marquese Guglielmo Marconi and Wave Radio | 95 |
| Chapter 3 | Superior Directives and Privatized Military Research | 125 |
| Chapter 4 | Nuclear Weaponry and Nuclear Hybrids | 141 |
| Chapter 5 | Radar EMP and Ionoscatter Technology | 194 |
| Chapter 6 | Military VLF and ELF Technology | 219 |
| Chapter 7 | Auroral Energy Research | 247 |
| Chapter 8 | Orbital Reconnaissance and Radiation Technology | 277 |
| Bibliography | | 308 |
| Index | | 322 |

# PROLOGUE
## *Symbols and Models*

### FOCUS

Much concern has recently been focussed upon the military managed project known as HAARP. This excessive concern is the result of misunderstood facts basic to the nature of radio technology and the means by which superior control dictates, manages, and directs technological themes. Thus, while appearing to be military generated efforts, most recent projects are actually the direct result of demands which emanate from points of origin entirely independent of Industry. Deeper study in the history of these technological ventures reveals an astounding labyrinth of bureaucracy which has been created to mask and benefit individuals who exercise singular dynastic roles in the world. Such individuals have clearly been dictating the themes which the Governmental and the Military hierarchate is absolutely compelled to obey.

By its many morbid conspiratist devotees, HAARP has been called the very apex of Twentieth Century military technology. But, though HAARP has been managed by military authority, it has done so under the cover of an industrial directive. Moreover, that industrial directive is not one originating in Government Authority. There are those who have cited HAARP as an effort which has been completely managed by industry. But this is not completely true. In this specific Project, industries have been covering a far superior and central agency whose purpose and intentions have little to do with scientific pursuits. Deeper examination reveals that industrial organizations are receiving directives from a superior command centre, not easily discerned. It is only after deliberate and methodic penetration of the historical facts germane to HAARP and all related technologies, that one reaches conclusions which are far more astounding and shocking than the reports shared by many conspiracy writers.

HAARP and its other brethren projects are not recent developments. They are the most recent representatives in a research effort whose history stretches out before the last Century. Before we presume to dissect and interpret HAARP, we require historical familiarity with the documented hardware, phenomena, and original rationale for the deployment of these projects. It is curious and unfortunate that conspiracy writers are often the very first to introduce topics which should become part of the social dialogue on those subjects. Though these individuals demonstrate a first rate ability in discovering covert initiatives, they unfortunately do not develop their findings into scholarly themes. The result is almost invariably an hysterical response to what has been discovered, and not a factually based analysis.

Because we cannot be sure of statements made by such "conspiratists", we are driven into a comprehensive study of the topic area in question. All the pertinent histories and facts must be massed together and studied. Only a thorough and scholarly examination of related study matter can obtain for us the answers to questions posed by the existence of projects such as HAARP. Toward these scholarly goals, I have applied the utmost diligence. Nevertheless, credit must go to another as initiator of the effort which has produced this text. I am very much indebted to Mr. Michael Theroux of Borderland Science Research Foundation for his role. In both initiating and stimulating these dialogues concerning the HAARP question, I was ultimately moved toward the discoveries which form the present thesis. Through his diligent and scholarly pursuit of the HAARP question, a vital collection of files and narratives on the topic was first made available to me.

## SYMBOLISTS

The unfortunate mishandling of a few military technologies by conspiratist writers has flooded society with unfounded suspicions and rumors. In such a fear-ruled atmosphere there can be no true objectivity, no serious scientific discussion. In order to allay the fundamental fears which have been incited by all too numerous and over enthused writers, this text on military technologies has been composed. As what we require is factual clarification, this commentary contains only the historical facts pertinent to the development of certain weapons and communications technologies.

It is imperative that we establish a very clear separation between the new conspiracy literature and real scholarly science bibliographies. The growing list of "pop" books and essays on HAARP are absolutely inadequate as scientific sources. Repetitious and locked into a very specific kind of inspiration, such writers have more recently blended HAARP topics with the available entourage of hysteria; the general undercurrent of conspiracy scenarios. This thematic connectedness is taken by aficionadi of this genre and woven into a synthetic theme which covers the eyes. In these turbid waters, we perceive the workings of a deeper malevolent energy, one whose nature has been successfully and necessarily repressed throughout the millennia. Though verbose and often well stocked with bibliographic references, conspiratist texts are not without the insidious attribute of fear. From the topical perspective of scientific scholarship, such convolutions would ordinarily evidence a lack of formal training. But the essential observation which allows us to comprehend the true source from which conspiracy books emerge cites the excessive and hysterical fear itself; the overwhelming mood which permeates every such text.

Closer examination of the vacuous, though verbose, content in conspiracy books explains why such books cannot provide scientific answers to the questions which are posed. One cannot judge them on the basis of scholarly deficiencies. Ill-informed, ill-poised, and illogical from every standpoint, the recent pop-writing collective has evidenced a shocking unfamiliarity with the most basic of radio engineering principles. In this we do not refer merely to their unpreparedness in the alternative science category, but to old fundamentals in pedantic conventional science. Cited as with absolute authority, their misunderstandings do not complete any cohesive thesis other than that which their hysteria yields. Such books do not sustain even the scrutiny of those who, through devoted study, have made themselves thoroughly familiar with both scientific convention and esoteric alternatives. Immersed in the turbid emotional waters through which they write, their hapless readers are soon pulled down in an undertow of vague inferences. But apart from these criticisms, one perceives the real reason why such writers could not formulate a real and cohesive theme among their many discussions. Their hysteria alone is evidence that these books emerge from another inspiration altogether.

Drawn down through the confusion and into paranoia, the essential structural material of the subconscious, conspiracy writers serve as hapless mediums of a submerged and incoherent flood of emotions. Such a stream, when written in the language of consciousness, successfully evokes hysteria. The emotional white water of these kinds of books has blocked true scientific realization concerning HAARP. The frequent topic of those whose inspiration is both submerged and fundamentally subconscious, an hysterical tone is being projected into society. In addition, because these texts do not emerge from the conscious mind, they cannot supply conscious coherence to their readers. Such books then become an effective source of extended social ignorance on the topic area. While hysteria fears the devastation of ecological systems by a fully operational IRI, the most powerful effect of HAARP has already made its first impact. It has done so in the very deepest visceral part of humanity. HAARP has impacted the inscrutable and irresistible, that monstrous thing that hides in its lair. The Id and its entourage of misperceptions. Some say that conspiracy writers are sensitives who have somehow vocalized the subconscious undercurrents now prevalent in all of society. If this is true, then we can forgive their writing style. If at all, we may only comprehend the murky message in conspiracy books as the writings of symbolists. But as symbolic expressions, these books are incapable of granting scientific insights. Thus, by their very nature, such books are useless in satisfying those having engineering pursuits. The quest of young minds is often completely and effectively diverted by the available conspiracy literature. Minds devoted to such literature remain entirely ineffective as a corporate force for social improvement.

Having its inspiration entirely in the subconscious, conspiracy books do not represent science. Conspiracy books are not scientific works. They are each excellent examples of verbalized symbolic art. They represent the serpentine reactions of the negative subconscious to perceived external threats. These are usually technological provocations, which the negative subconscious both hates and seeks to destroy. If there is some truth in the murky and nightmarish phantasmata with which they move, these symbols are warning our world of an impending crisis far deeper than anything technology can supply. The very emergence of these anti-technological symbols is the danger. The subconscious mind, which hates technology and is intent on driving society down into its own murky waters, has already begun its assault on society. Demanding total attention, the subconscious wishes to dominate and destroy technological society. But these are topics for another thesis, the most fascinating discussions concerning the energy of consciousness itself.

It has become very obvious that those who spew such vociferous volumes of hysteria begin, not in the solid record of the past, but in their own fears. Inferences thus derived release the negative subconscious into the greater seas of the reading public. As these manuscripts wend their way through society, a free flow of emotive energy rather than conscious thought, it effectively accretes vitality. Vitality is drained from those who read the manuscripts. Those who read these books, to the exclusion of all other technical literature, expose themselves to a deceptive source of hopelessness. Conspiracy themes never offer an escape hatch to the reader. One is soon caught in the halls of the Labyrinth without the silken thread of Ariadne! Acquiring and accreting fragmentary facts, the subconscious stream represented by these books, tugs already weakened minds further away from truth.

The factual fragments comprising conspiracy books and their invariable accompanying cassettes and videos are designed to bait the reader into forming specialized conclusions. These almost invariably satisfy the personal needs of readers who are actively seeking a conspiracy. The writers of these books carry no burden of proof. Theirs is the role of provocateur, irresponsible activators and promoters of social malaise without solution. The public now seems to require the services of innumerable writers and spokespersons who make their money by selling the fear and hysteria which a metaphoric stream of subconscious symbols evokes. A populace whose innermost sentiment expects nothing but disappointment thrives on the nightmarish symbols and fragmentary messages written by conspiracy symbolists. One nevertheless finds that a continual flood of such symbol-laden manuscripts are finding their way into the new conspiratist genre.

Being collections of murky symbols and subconscious expressions, these books are expected to contain mutually contradicting statements and opinions. Conspiracy books are never the scientific reports which they purport to be. Nevertheless, it becomes obvious that certain very popular writers are in serious need of self-examination and of fundamental study, each in their topic area. One reads through several examples of these texts with growing boredom. Each verifies the inner observation that such books are made to be sold, not to convey facts. Filled as they are with the turbid waters of hysteria, this publications assault has succeeded only in confusing readers everywhere.

Conspiracy books are not clear water pools in which to quench a serious scientific thirst. Misunderstood and misused, many students nevertheless seek out these books of symbols, servants of the subconscious, while hoping to find answers to scientific questions. Being thus produced by negative subconscious energy, conspiracy books are incapable of serving us with more information than the fear which they transmit. The murky world of nightmarish fantasies and horrifying figures is not the world from which archetypes and other uplifting symbols emerge, the superconscious world of vision and revelation.

Very unfortunately, these inferior publications do not contain the real answers, the real models, which a waiting public expects. The only service which conspiracy books seem to provide is the magnification of paranoid undercurrents. Conspiracy books are then psychosocial expressions of an energy-minimizing substratum, one which drains the vitality away from those who continue reading them. These books themselves are evidence that a new foray of subconscious energies are actively reaching up from the depths, and connectively linking susceptible people together in unhealthy aggregates. Too few appreciate the power of such undercurrents, or the inherent energy working therein. This aspect of the subconscious is deadly to societies who indulge its expressions, a possible explanation for those cultures which quickly rose and fell.

## CONVOLUTIONS

Why would the discovery of a project such as HAARP stimulate some into a dialogue with the subconscious at all? Why would otherwise reasonably good narrative writers engage the symbols of fear and hysteria, and not seek liberating emergence into the surface world? Such discussions have thematic content which addresses the problem of perception and interpretation, the differences between symbols and models of reality. The choice between these two opposites will determine our ability to make accurate and informed judgements of the things which perplex us. In light of such a premise, we find ourselves walking the narrow way between symbol and model. These are two very opposed systems of interpretation, the difference between which readers do not always comprehend. Symbols do not represent the conscious world, they represent the manner in which the subconscious interprets the world, making expressive commentary on what it perceives from its lowly and undeveloped perspective. But models are the conscious means which we use to comprehend what we consciously perceive the conscious world of actions.

The topics which we will discuss throughout this book are the result of a model-making process. Indeed, the themes which form the thesis are the result of several overlaying models which seem to fit together too neatly for coincidence. Why are models necessary? Why are we unable to make experiential judgements of our direct perceptions concerning issues germane to military topics? Because of secrecy. Secrecy blocks us from making those direct perceptions which we so desire to secure. The need to know experiences restriction, prevented from reaching its fulfillments. Ruling social structures in which we have little or no direct perception, actually provoke the necessary construction of models which we make to explain what we cannot directly perceive and know. These notions are especially true when considering the social structure in which we are constrained to live. In the absence of extensive perception concerning the entirety of structures which rule our lives, we discover the absolute need for devising very accurate models. This model making process is predicated on the need to know, the need to extend beyond our perimeters, the need to know why we experience the things we experience.

These are matters central to the "philosophis thematon", the philosophic theme. It is that theme which questions the more immediate and obvious presentations made by the world upon our lives. Why are certain social classes constrained to live under the rulership which both governs and restricts their lives? To whom do these frames and structures belong? Who truly rules the structures themselves? Why are bureaucratic demands directed toward lower social levels, and never up toward the rulers? How democratic are democratic republics? All these questions preface any discussion of technology and military projects. They form the broad tapestry within which technology and invention arrive, fresh from an incorruptible source of dreams and visions. The necessary imperative to know the answers to such questions marks the scholarly quest. Were this a mere discussion of technology in its own right, we would not necessitate such a digression. While engineering aspects of technology do and can be treated within the scholarly vacuum of analysis, we have decided to reveal the world scope into which technology is launched.

In truth, technology cannot be discussed without taking account of much larger considerations. The Geopolitical considerations. Technology does not exist in its own vacuum. It is an expression as structured and powerful as those social structures which rule. Because of this, technology represents an element of challenge, a conundrum whose every revolutionary manifestation comes as a repetitive and unexpected reminder that a far superior command exists in the world ruling structure. Technology enters the real world, where actions and reactions cannot always be scientifically and stringently assessed. Indeed one finds the absolute need to predicate the entire discussion with a necessary model which makes the treatments of technology, within the social setting, more nearly comprehensible. Technology modifies the world into which it comes. It generates an unexpected power. This power appears to emerge from the lowest level of the superstructure. The world of rulership moves around and over technologies, engaging it in a dynamic manner. The relationship between the ruling structure and technology is not a simple and scientific issue, it is an issue of power and of authority.

This is precisely why we must be prepared toward these comprehensions with some familiarity of the difference between symbols and models. To know each their significance and differences is to begin a liberating process of understanding. Models and model making are the necessary craft of those who, resisted by the very secretive and privatized nature of ruling structures, are compelled in the pursuit of specific knowledge. We seek knowledge of why the world structure behaves toward technology in each of the ways in which history has declared it to behave. Why do ruling structures quake when technologies emerge? In the absence of direct answers, those seemingly elusive gems which structures never supply in explanation for their overt actions, we are literally compelled to the model making process.

## MODELS

Models are not the world realities themselves, they are substitutions for realities which remain for us inaccessible, restricted, and unknown. Much of the social structure which rules us is thus best described. It is in the absence of direct perception and knowledge that we devise our models. Why this has been a perpetual theme of those who study rulership and the structure of world rule is the very obvious result of secretization and privatization. Ruling structures, whose mandates affect our lives in sometimes repressive and demanding ways, remain for us an impervious megalith. We find ourselves observing bureaucratic machinations and receiving the consequential processes whose impersonal demands do not match the reality of the observed machinations. A few strokes of the pen in a distant, unseen office, and we find ourselves overlaboring in order to pay the increased taxes which have thus been decreed. And so we and our families will labor, never having seen the person who wrote the decree, or the reason given for the increase. We, the recipients of such actions, are yet denied direct viewing access as well as direct participation in that higher process.

The social structures which history has built are not so exceedingly complex, convoluted, and inaccessible as we would be led to believe. They are simple, the engineworks of simple and fundamental ambitions. Nevertheless, because of the secretization of its machinations, one requires an interpretation of what one perceives occurring in society. Were the ruling structure permeable and accessible we would have direct perception, and therefore direct knowledge of what energetic exchanges are transpiring in the halls of rulership. Indeed, the ruling structures form an organismic whole. The mysterious power which moves through them makes them live, and very unfortunately, make us labor toward the proliferation of repressive policies. Discovering the real nature of that power which enlivens ruling structures is as difficult a task as that delivered to qualitative scientists who search for apologetic proofs that the vital force exists! Nevertheless, the ruling structures do act, and move, and have their being, however low we may consider their consciousness. And their life force can be easily isolated.

But since social structures of world power and their subordinate bureaucratic organizations are labyrinthine in the internal dynamics, we are rendered incapable of directly viewing the exact causes and effects of their internal workings. The only covert reality of the world power system is the combined haze which entraps sight, mind, and life within its predetermined structure. Indeed, peering up through the centuries-old Babylonian Tapestry, one sees only complexities. The world dynamic, the world power system, is not complex. It only appears to be complex. It is one whose dictates and functions entrap the life of those who seek to penetrate its true personalities and their directives. It is a consciousness entrapping structure, as hose who seek to penetrate its bureaucracies well find. In addition, it is a life entrapping structure. Therefore, once we see this structure of world system rule, we pleasantly discover that world movements and world actions are very simple. Simple because they are based on nothing less than human directives; incredibly wealthy, powerful, and adept humans, whose aristocratic prowess is surrounded by advisement...but nonetheless, human. Indeed each war, each "conflict", each "operation" represents and extends the human attributes of greed and ambition in all too many gauche ways. Evidence is overwhelming that human ambitions move the governments from a much higher place of earthly power.

Since we are part of a process in which these structures dynamically interact, recipients of their demands and punishments, it is imperative that we comprehend their dynamics. This need to know now evidences far more than a philosophic fancy. It is, much rather, a need to know which is based on personal survival. Because we are the direct recipients of movements which work within the social engines, movements in which we are not at first directly engaged, we desire some access to those processes and innermost workings. But there is resistance in the structure, by which we are prevented both from participating and from knowing too much. Knowing precedes action. Knowing precedes participation. If participation in the structures themselves be restricted, then participation will commence at lower and more powerful levels in the social caste system. Technology and invention is the most accessible means for refocusing power within the superstructure, the accessible means for liberating consciousness.

The distance placed between ourselves and the social engines represent a unknown, a divorcing factor which stimulates the need for reaching that understanding with all the more veracity. Moreover, because we do not see, and cannot see what moves within the engineworks, we interpret the alienating refusal to allow us to see as a sign that something malicious is at work. The gap which exists between the vagrant dictates of rulership and the enforcement of command represents another area of investigation. We cannot even say that we know why the commands delivered to us carry the greatest burden of imperative. Because of the alienating nature of representative bureaucracies at higher structural levels, we become the helpless observers and recipients of dynamics over which we have neither participation or control. Because we do not see the exact movements of power within the structures which rule our lives, we are again forced to interpret what we experience from external appearances. The external appearances of changes, evidently originating in the structure, betray somewhat of the invisible inner workings of those engines. Though there is a defined perception gap between origins of command and commands delivered to us, we can yet assess the rationales for certain movements of power at these high levels by taking simple notice of superficial manifestations. These provide vital bits of information, not easily distorted by public relations methodology.

The initiating energies of the ruling social structure also represent unknowns, which are disjunct from the final demands placed upon our lives. Because we receive life restrictive commands from those engines, and cannot reasonably comprehend the exact nature or rationale for those commands, we are again forced to interpret what we experience. There is therefore a gap between what we are commanded to do, and the reasons given to us for the necessity of those commands. Since these engines have so configured our lives, and continue to place demands upon us, we are compelled more than ever by that internal imperative which demands facts. Why are certain classes selected as the recipients of these disjunct energies, originating from higher social levels which we never see? If we cannot address such simple and more immediate personal issues, then we are not in a position knowledgeable enough to determine the power or fate of technologies which enter such a world of structures, demands, and power.

The distance of perception, the distance of trust, the distance of reason and demand, each of these is the result of a social engine whose very reason for existing represents the more fundamental mystery. The social structures which rule our lives remain as essentially unknown, synthetic systemologies whose lifespan continues long after we have died under their rule. Although we have been given certain degrees of education concerning "civic" and bureaucratic structures, it is more honest to admit that we perceive the smallest and most insignificant parts of those machines. Despite our so limited perception, experience has repeatedly taught us that what we are told is not always what is. Within these same structures then, we have learned that the distance between truth and falsehood is perpetually varying. Extending these realizations to the whole working of the social engine, one derives a conception of the otherwise hidden machine which is not favorable. There is a perception gap between what movements are said to occur, and what actually has occurred. Within those well hidden engine houses are many secrets we shall never know.

We live in a ruling structure whose very existence is arbitrary, whose appearance is mirage-like, whose machinations are privatized, and whose very motivations are questionable. In all of these considerations, there are the numerous contradictions which the ruling structure delivers to us on a regular basis. Our lives are filled with the contradictory expectations of the ruling structure. But the very contradictions of our experience in these regards provide us with the best kind of evidence. Those strenuous exertions and other bureaucratic machinations are working to keep us precisely where we are in the social mold. Because of all these distances, these divorcements, these alienations, these contradictions, these perception gaps, we find reason for designing accurate models which will enable better understanding our dilemma. Think of the models as maps which will grant us aid in escaping the mazeworks of delusion. In these matters, ours is a philosophic exercise having a specific purpose.

To summarize, we must say that, in the absence of direct perception there can be no accurate and no exact knowledge. Observers caught in this quandary must rely on interpolations and interpretations of what they perceive is actually occurring in their lives. This condition so suffuses world power structures that analysts are forced to rely completely on their own interpolations and interpretations for clarified understanding of events and the significance of certain powerful movements. And here is precisely where contaminating influences can produce skewed interpretations. For if we yield to our suspicions, so powerfully provoked by the alienating machinations of social structure, then we fall into a reliance on symbol and not on fact. We acquire facts at a certain level in our research process. After that however, we rely on interpolations and interpretations; the materials from which accurate models of the superstructure are fabricated.

In the absence then of direct perception, of direct knowledge, of direct access, one must construct models in order to gain some measure of survivalistic understanding. To know is to have the ability to better survive. To know is the power to exert force for change. To know is the ability to direct changing influences with precision into the social structure. Other than this kind of knowledge, we can neither know our own positions, the power and threat of technology, or the manner in which ruling structures will be changed by technology. As concerns the dynamic tension into which we have been thrown, whether we cannot directly see and whether will not be permitted to see, makes no real difference. We feel and respond. With every impact on our lives, set by decrees originating in those structures, we are informed of significant movements. Like riding a tiger. One does not need to anatomy before recognizing how the beast responds to stimuli. Survival in such a circumstance is the rationale for tenaciously holding to one's objectives and learning how to steer the tiger.

Models are the similacræ of the large systems and machinations which we cannot directly see. When we lack complete and direct perception, models are the maps to guide our vision and our understanding. Furthermore, accurate models are not the result of extending thought into symbolic realms; a process which we are cautioned not to engage. Some condemn and eliminate the model making process because of this potential for error and delusion. This is especially true when analysts examine the seemingly complex structures of bureaucracies and governments. The criticism derives from the notion that complexity introduces random features, phantom structures, the chance coherence from otherwise chaotic activity. There are those who refuse to accept what clearly presents itself as order, refusing to endorse the models which those ordered patterns reveal. Others refuse to accept the realities which they consider to be phantoms, the result of ephemeral orders.

Indeed, many believe that models concerning world structure and world rulerships are derived as a result of micropatterns in an otherwise chaotic system. Many say that these micropatterns are misperceived as order by the naive. If so, then the connectivity among such micropatterns is indeed extraordinary, a result of equally random coherence. We cannot accept, endorse, or proliferate that self-deceptive claim which insists that subjective observations are projections, the result of externalized desires and other misperceptions. In this very schema, much of what actually occurs in the world structure is cloaked.

In the absence of abundant technical bibliographies, and without familiarity in the pertinent themes taught in these bibliographies, one cannot indeed forge the formidable barriers which prevent delusional reliance on symbols rather than facts. Nonetheless, accurate models can be drawn by observing ruling world structures simply because the ambitions and movements within those structures are directed by humans, and not by demigods. Models can sometimes predict an outcome, when information leaks permit. One can also add refined features which derive from reliable information leaks. One balances these "leaked' pieces of information against a wide framework of experience and observation, deriving and perfecting a model on which to make tests. One tests a model to judge its accuracy, modifying its features to match in some more accurate way what reality is revealing. In this way, models are refined until they most nearly match the unknown reality.

The development of models is the necessary process when confronting an unknown, whether natural or social. Experience and factual bases are materials from which reliable model making finds its start. The simplicity of directives, of commands, of demands, and indeed of all the machinations so strenuously exercised in the channels where power flows are simple human responses. These preclude all random coherence effects, and permit the designing of truly simple models which so accurately describe the behaviors which we observe in the world that they cannot be erroneous. The models which we will present function well on several different concern levels with precision. They also hold up with reasonably sharp precision when different event scenarios are applied to them. Thus, the comprehension of large bureaucratic complexities can be primitively modelled on the basis of personal experiences. One can not always predict, but one can interpret.

## SHROUDS

Each serious endeavor to penetrate and comprehend the covert atmosphere enshrouding HAARP has demanded nothing less than a thorough familiarity with technological history. In this regard, only a special familiarity with military developments in radio and communications arts deployment can empower the inquiring scholar to reach reasonable conclusions. The central question concerns itself with the huge array which Raytheon has constructed in Gakona, Alaska. We know what the Ionospheric Research Instrument actually is. But what does it do? For what reason does it exist at all? The mystery has done more than tantalize informed thought. It has revealed the abysmal lack of knowledge among writers who do not know their topic area, and yet will not stop writing. The "problem" which this project has presented to concerned civilians is one of classification, there seeming to be no reasonable explanation for the presence of the IRI at all. Those who have attempted its classification do so without a cohesive model from which to make reasonable assessments. Closer scrutiny reveals the function and purpose of the device without further need for speculation. Accurate models of action hold up under various logical applications, each plausible HAARP scenario being weighed against all the facts and historical documentation.

More sensitive persons have referred to HAARP as the modern ultimate in human technological arrogance. Those who very clearly sense the absolute separation of military and citizen know that military intentions are the result of superior commands, directives which come down to military through bureaucratic power channels. The arrogant separation existing between government, military, and civilian sectors is evidence of an alienating secrecy. This policy requires absolute obedience to an authority which maintains absolute secrecy. The law abiding citizen is therefore required to render respect to an authority which keeps the population in the shadow of ignorance. The permeating alienation which has so thoroughly characterized our time is the direct result of a ruling structure which seeks the absolute domination of every bureaucracy, every technology, and every conscious state, were that possible. The rulership of which we speak exists above the halls of government, in control centers having nothing at all to do with bureaucratic or democratic process.

Radio History provides a stranger walk than fiction or the subconscious can convolute. But here too, one must not simply make speculative comment on scattered inferences. This useless and futile tautology has been the achievement of several supposed technical writers who very obviously have not spent time thinking about what they say. We must have facts on which to base any such strong assertions. Indeed, the ignorance concerning past technology is a tragic legacy of our time. Having forgotten the past discoveries, there are those who now presume to analyze both the present and future. The Victorian Bibliography, which too few popular writers cherish, contains wonders which we have only begun to suspect. This bibliography remains a monument, a treasury of anomalous discoveries entrusted to our time by trustworthy experimenters.

The true interpreter of problematic and questionable military research reads through patents and articles thoroughly before drawing out possible inferences. Trustworthy inferences are composed only after lengthy study in the topic area, a radio science bibliography which now spans the whole Twentieth Century. The acquisition of such a bibliography requires hundreds of consecutive hours of unremitting deep and committed research, with an equal expenditure of several thousand dollars. Certain dedicated individuals have already undertaken this task, a labor which is pleasurably never ending. In truth, the storehouse of lost treasures is inexhaustible. There are, in fact, very few individuals with whom I am able to speak on such levels. In this respect I am very fortunate to know a pure and independent researcher, an experimenter in the great tradition. Mr. William Lehr is one of my vital links in the continuity, the unbroken chain of scholars. Our discussions have been a reference frame and source of the very deepest inspiration.

Those who seek truth often do meet on the great plains of knowledge. One must plow deep in the rocky soils before picking up the trail. The most remarkable experience meets us when we make first contact with vital references and documents. The degree and pursuit of work which culminates in such a personal event is excessive, the expenditures of scholarly passion. There are those whose passionless love of comfort derides those of us whose eyes sometimes dizzy with the rapid flickers of passing microfilm. Persons such as this should never dare speak when in the presence of scholarship, much less to acquire collections of researchers for purposes of self-aggrandizement.

## SECRETS

The unexamined bibliography contains a mountain of factual gems and secrets which few value. But only a logical and thorough recapitulation of all of the developmental roads leading into and beyond HAARP must be aggressively engaged. The conclusions drawn from this bibliography are indeed provocative and controversial. This publication therefore contains only historical facts pertinent to the military management and development of ELF, VLF, SHF, and other technologies. Beyond this, I have made every effort to present a thoroughly researched chronicle of Cold War and SDI projects. The actual state of military technological art is a great deal more advanced than we are led to believe. The patent record alone proves it. In addition, a very great deal of time has been spent agonizing over each hypothesis in the chain which leads to the conclusions of my last chapters. But how indeed have some 75 years of privatized Military Research succeeded in producing, establishing, and using such a completely new and superior superradiant communications technology capable of rendering all present communications arts obsolete?

It was in the last twenty years of military developments that the successful deployment of such technology made its appearance. If in fact this is true, if there are indeed revolutionary new technologies, why then are military groups stating their reliance on older systems? Moreover, if this be true, then why have these obsolescent systems required staffing, energy, and funding at all? The two contradictions mutually neutralize, while the truth emerges from the smoke screens. I have underscored my assertions. I am convinced that, while citizens of the 1950's were thrilling to science fiction themes and dreaming of a bright future world, military researchers had already directed the creation of amazing radiation technologies which have been used ever since. This technology is even now so far in advance of any known system that a trained mind is troubled by its inherent implications. Can it be believed that a technology, entirely operated through gamma ray energies, whose potentials could completely change the face of our world as we know it, had already been registered and dispatched by 1960? Apart from a flash of insight, coupled with an accidental patent discovery, who would ever have vaguely suspected such a thing? Currently and routinely utilized, the interrelated advanced systems which we will report have remained, for decades, the best well guarded "open secret".

# CHAPTER 1
## Nikola Tesla and Radiant Energy

### ANOMALY

Deep in the heart of many conspiratist topics sits a desperate desire to rediscover the lost magic of Nature. It was with this lost magic, this qualitatively accessed communion with Nature, that late Victorian researchers were all too familiar. Their numerous accounts cannot often be rationalized against the wall of academic regulation which prides itself in explaining all natural phenomena through simple mechanisms, the reductions of natural phenomena to meaningless force-chains. But even the journals of that day reveal a scientific world absolutely awash in discoveries and anomalous phenomena, portraying energies and dynamics which defy mechanistic explanation. The lost magic of vital energy! Developments which came with our present century represent empirical discoveries which yet have no theoretical precedent. In the very midst of that marvelous Epoch stand several personages who must forever remain as legends of Qualitative Science. One of these is Nikola Tesla. But why is Tesla the shadow which yet so haunts and provokes military researchers? Furthermore, why can it be said that the name of Nikola Tesla represents the "absolute rule" by which to comprehend each of the successive military projects, seemingly separate and unconnected experimental ventures observed throughout the Twentieth Century?

Why are the various achievements of Tesla so often quoted in military hardware articles, proposals which seem to attract the greatest interest only after mentioning both his name and some aspect of his work? Since they most certainly have not been able to duplicate Teslian Technology, why then do we continually find that military project committees are forever yet attempting to approximate Teslian Technology? Every professional Tesla aficionado secretly knows that Tesla electrical energies were more like luminous beams of gaseous light than radiowaves or electrified particles. What they do not know is how he produced the energies. This simple but profound process represents a most fundamental natural principle which could never have been predicted. Having been the result of accidental empirical discovery, so few suspect it can exist. The blinding influence of mathematically precise models serves only to block awareness that other realities can or do exist. However basic and simple, Tesla Technology contains the secret of a power revolution which each knows would have changed the world. In his lifetime, the once famous Tesla became the target of dubious financial intrigues, failed death attempts, and outrageous deprivations and deprecations. The fear which surrounded this rare genius seemed to heighten with his every announcement, a thing which greatly amused him throughout the years of his self-exile. It is the persistence of this fear which so provokes military agencies the world over to make attempts in this essential research.

*Nikola Tesla*

The central effort of each Cold War project tells the tale of seemingly separate themes. But once again, only a complete familiarity with each stage of technical achievement in this progressive advancement can enable an informed comprehension of such themes. From a singular vantage point alone do we see each of these separate themes merge, intertwine, and become coherent. Themes germane to comprehending Cold War Technology were each the result of private attempts at reproducing the achievements of a single individual, one whose work has now positively haunted the scientific and military world in excess of a century. Why indeed is it also very obvious that, with the exception of one very simple discovery, neither military nor private developers have yet successfully duplicated any part of true Teslian Technology? In order to best appreciate the sheer frustration of radio and military engineers, whose consistent failure to reproduce the effects reported by Nikola Tesla troubles their fundamental theoretical base, we must study something of Tesla and his own work.

The technical themes relevant to understanding of all advanced technologies necessarily begins with Tesla. Because of a long-standing network of misinformation and the resultant skewed academic perceptions, Teslian Impulse Technology has never been openly legitimized or endorsed as a viable threat to either military or industrial agencies. This gloss is of course a complete fabrication. The most diligent examination of Tesla lectures and other lost Tesla publications, coupled with access to corroborative experimental work which vindicates most of Tesla's own findings, has made the following chapter possible. In these few pages, you will therefore receive a summary review of the essential Teslian principles. These are absolutely necessary before we proceed with our central theme. My simple request is that you patiently read through this section, keeping in mind that all of the information will be completely applicable to each subsequent chapter.

It is only through the window of Teslian Impulse Technology that we can comprehend the progression of projects industrial and military throughout the entire Century. Learning each lesson carefully will best help appreciate the scope of this present theme in all of its deep implications. Here you will find factual information otherwise difficult, if not impossible, to obtain. One learns quickly that "things Teslian" are much more than they appear to be. Tesla was a classical lover of conundrums and enigmas, and knew how to use them to encrypt his meanings. When Tesla spoke, everyone listened intently. But few persons understood his meaning. To know Teslian Technology, one must be willing to suspend conventional knowledge, listening only to the descriptions and cunning understatements by which Tesla craftily concealed his priority discoveries. Confusion over a surprising few distinctions has proved to be the only stumbling block keeping professional engineering communities from achieving the Teslian agenda.

It is for many young aspiring scholars an astounding revelation to find that the degree of revolutionary thought engaged before the Century's turn went further than modern technology now dares to dream. The more established academes consistently rejected Teslian hypotheses as a matter of habit. Tesla was nothing less than a Jules Verne character, who stepped out of a visionary world and worked wonders in the world. What Tesla achieved could not have been made possible without his extraordinary sensitivity and keen awareness of his own perceptions. In the absence of physical evidence, Tesla all too often worked his way toward natural truth. In this manner he discovered what theoreticians would never seek.

Most who pursue things Teslian know the sundry details of his early work in Polyphase, and his subsequent discovery of high frequency alternating current. Few however manage to isolate, identify, and comprehend his most important single discovery, the phenomenon through which all of his supposed outlandish claims were actually made possible. The discovery has not been adequately described among those who claim to know something beyond the initiatory facts concerning his work. Those who believe that only experimentation will reveal the truth concerning Tesla may be in for a sad defeat. Indeed, those who undertake the reproduction of Teslian transformers know the disappointment and subsequent disinterest which has followed so many others before.

Few are honest enough to admit the possibility that their own failed experimental reproductions are entirely due to their own misunderstanding. Those who publish the plans for such designs have already contaminated the process with a fundamental and failure-prone misunderstanding. Old electrical experimenter's texts are no better. By the end of the last Century, so much misinformation concerning the essential Teslian component, the Tesla Transformer, had brought a complete and devastating chaos to the field. When experimental results therefore contradict statements made by Tesla, the usual conclusions find soured agreement with the low opinions of Tesla which academicians hold. In the rare instance that they are able to manage a positive remark, usually one of mock indulgence, the accolades address his early work with Polyphase. Other than these occasional smug comments, most academicians view Tesla as a "poet-scientist" who made too much of standard phenomena. Nothing can be further from the truth.

After completing his initial work in Polyphase and High Frequency Alternating Currents, Tesla made a singular discovery which forever altered the course and nature of his experimental research. Whether purposefully or inadvertently, this singular discovery has been completely overlooked even by those who claim to know his work best. A single article and statements made in several of his Lectures absolutely affirm the conviction that Tesla, while working with violently abrupt electrical discharges, discovered a new force.

Indeed, it was through the development and application of this new physical agency, his greatest discovery, that Tesla encountered unexpected and devastating hostility throughout both the academic and the financial worlds. The monstrous social forces which drove him into self-exile did not, however, stop him from continuing his most important applications of this energetic species. Living in New York City until his passing in 1943, Nikola Tesla continued to conduct small experiments in applications which recall his discovery of radiant electrical energy. Few of his experiments were conducted without an accompanying assortment of reliable witnesses.

Throughout his lifetime in New York City there were many notables who observed these developments with greatest fascination. Among those who were awestruck by the things they saw were Samuel Clemens, Marguerite Merington, Robert Underwood Johnson, Edward Hewitt, Kolman Czito, Fritz Lowenstein, George Scherff, Dr. John Hammond, Lee de Forest, and Dr. Anton Kammela, Several mysterious professionals who assisted Tesla in his actual tests runs were simply referred to as "Mr. Uhlmann, Mr. Ailey, and Mr. Myers". Apart from this scant information, we do not know more of these witnesses to his works. Along with these personages were a number of his private machinists. His secretaries, a number including Dorothy Skerritt and Muriel Arbus, bore witness to his persistent experimentation. The office at 8 E.40th Street off Fifth Avenue also served as a small laboratory workshop. All of this was moved to the Hotel New Yorker in his later years. Thus whether on the large scale, by which his younger years of experimenting were performed, or on the small scale, which characterized his last years, there are several witnesses to his continuous exertions and successes. What Tesla stated in the press, throughout his career, were always supported by a great number of experimental proofs.

## VORTEX

    Tesla spent his student years in the Polytechnic Institute at Graz, Austria. While thoroughly engrossed in deep study of the "electrical mysteries", young Nikola Tesla observed the operation of an alternating current generator in a lecture hall demonstration. This was the high frontier of his day, and he was very much impressed with the apparent efficiency of this design. When compared with the older Gramme machines, this alternating current generator was a true engineering marvel. The complete absence of commutator bands in the housing allowed the complete elimination of sparking losses, a greatly increased efficiency in output current being the result. The AC generator did not sizzle as it turned, it hummed. The problem was in the form of current which emerged. It alternated with a regular tempo, first surging one way, and then the other. Used for every application save one, motors, the AC generator outperformed any device which formerly comprised the electrical arsenal of apparatus.

    Slowly, methodically, young Tesla began developing a conceptual model for a new system of power distribution based on alternating current. Consumers could be given a superior electrical supply, one which would replace every Edisonian model then so much the revolution. The Tesla systems could supply power for most electrical appliances. Most, but not all. Motors proved to be the problem. How to manage the continuous rotation of a motor operated by an alternating current proved too taxing for any other mind. Tesla himself was completely baffled for a time with this perplexing problem, but not because he could not solve it. Tesla knew he already had the answer, a familiar experience for one who received inspiration through vision. Tesla was awaiting the moment when the revelation would flash before his eyes. Ready for that instant, he would simply write down what he perceived in the ecstasy of his visions.

    This vision proved nearly impossible to release until, while strolling in a park, he chanced to behold a beautiful sunset. Moved to emotion, Tesla began quoting a melodious poem written by his favored author, Goethe. During this dramatic rendition, Tesla suddenly became enraptured with the vision of a swirling vortex in the very heart of the sun. In this momentary episode, Tesla demonstrated both his absolute reliance on vision and his ability to materialize the same. The use of several superimposed alternating currents managed the formation of a swirling magnetic vortex, one in whose grip an armature was forcibly and continuously dragged around upon its axle. Tesla Polyphase revolutionized the world. Tesla became a multimillionaire literally overnight. Together with George Westinghouse, he harnessed Niagara Falls, establishing forever the hydroelectric resource. Tesla continued seeking new ways to improve his Polyphase system, developing means for raising the frequency of current alternations into new and formerly unknown levels. He designed and tested a few new high frequency alternators, high speed rotating machines which produced up to 30,000 alternations per second. Tesla also found it possible to send such high frequency alternations through a single wire.

At this time, Tesla unfortunately attracted the monopolistic dreams of one J. P. Morgan. The contact, established through Morgan's associates, was one which had more the atmosphere of a threat. Politely refused by the young Tesla on several occasions, the continual visits by Morgan associates became something of a humorous charade. Tesla had observed the results of yielding to these forays, while working with Thomas Edison in New Jersey. Morgan, who worked his way into the Edison Company, eventually became the primary stockholder. Enunciating his impossible demands on Edison, the aged inventor was reduced to an callous and embittered shell. Tesla, who kept politely refusing Morgan, was finally threatened. Powerline technology had been monopolized by Morgan who, on the strength of this monopoly, strongly suggested that Tesla might not be able to export his Polyphase Power to any consumers. Without Morgan-owned powerlines there would be no Tesla-Westinghouse Company. Tesla informed Morgan that means had already be found to eliminate the need for powerlines, a statement which appeared the very height of desperation. Morgan believed he had sufficiently leaned on Tesla to acquire his company. But these attempts to force Tesla to yield failed. Tesla proved more indomitable than even the imposing Morgan and, when the silence was broken, Tesla demonstrated before Morgan associates a new means for transmitting high frequency alternations through both the ground and the air in absence of powerlines. Morgan was literally thunderstruck by this premise, and sought opportunities against Tesla at every turn.

Students are taught that Tesla developed non-rotating high frequency generators, systems employing sparks and capacitors. The name of Tesla is inexorably and tragically equated only with alternating currents. It is in this essential error that academes, engineers, young students, and avid experimenters have too long remained. Though engineers still erroneously equate Tesla only with high frequency alternating current, a recent and prolific experimenter has proven all these suppositions to be fraudulent. While Tesla was in fact the first to discover the high frequency alternating current realm, there was a more important discovery which is rarely outlined. The truth of this second great discovery remains unrecognized and unappreciated.

But what was the critical event which few recognize, and which fewer still have the patience to extract from Tesla literature? When did this event occur, and how does Tesla address the finding? Except for the consummate achievements of engineer Eric Dollard, undoubtedly the most brilliant expositor of Teslian Technology in the world today, we too would have believed the error. What Mr. Dollard has successfully demonstrated is the absolute separation between Tesla's Polyphase period and the Impulse Technology which explains his fifty years of experiments conducted until his passing. Mr. Dollard experimentally vindicated most of Tesla's basic and seemingly outlandish claims. In a series of experimental demonstrations, exact reproductions of Tesla systems, Mr. Dollard shows us evidence that post-Polyphase Teslian Technology relied entirely upon a strange and special electroradiant phenomenon. But how did Tesla arrive at this new and revolutionary development, and how do engineers perceive this phase of his work?

## SHOCKWAVES

James Clark-Maxwell predicted the possibility that electromagnetic waves might exist. In theoretical discussions designed to more thoroughly explain his mathematical descriptions, Maxwell asked his readers to consider two different kinds of electrical disturbance possibly existing in Nature. The first consideration dealt with longitudinal electric waves, a phenomenon which required alternating concentrations of electrostatic field lines. This densified and rarefied pulsation of electrostatic fields necessarily demanded a unidirectional field, one whose vector was fixed in a singular direction. The only variable permitted in generating longitudinal waves was the concentration of the field. Subsequent propagation along the electrostatic field lines would produce pulsating thrusts on charges, pulsations moving in a single direction. These "electrical soundwaves" were rejected by Maxwell, who concluded that such a condition was impossible to achieve.

His second consideration dealt with the existence of transverse electromagnetic waves. These required the rapid alternation of electrical fields along a fixed axis. Space spreading electrical lines would supposedly "bend to and fro" under their own momentum, while radiating away at the speed of light from the alternating source. Corresponding forces, exact duplicates of the alternations produced at the source, would be detected at great distances. He encouraged that experimenters seek this waveform, suggesting possible means for achieving the objective. And so the quest to find electromagnetic waves began.

In 1887, Heinrich Hertz announced that he had discovered electromagnetic waves, an achievement at that time of no small import. In 1889, Nikola Tesla attempted the reproduction of these Hertzian experiments. Conducted with absolute exactness in his elegant South Fifth Avenue Laboratory, Tesla found himself incapable of producing the reported effects. No means however applied would produce the effects which Hertz claimed. Tesla began experimenting with abrupt and powerful electric discharges, using oil filled mica capacitors charged to very high potentials. He found it possible to explode thin wires with these abrupt discharges. Dimly perceiving something of importance in this experimental series, Tesla abandoned this experimental series, all the while pondering the mystery and suspecting that Hertz had somehow mistakenly associated electrostatic inductions or electrified shockwaves in air for true electromagnetic waves. In fact, Tesla visited Hertz and personally proved these refined observations to Hertz who, being convinced that Tesla was correct, was about to withdraw his thesis. Hertz was truly disappointed, and Tesla greatly regretted having to go to such lengths with an esteemed academician in order to prove a point.

But while endeavoring toward his own means for identifying electrical waves, Tesla was blessed with an accidental observation which forever changed the course of his experimental investigations. Indeed, it was an accident which forever changed the course of his life and destiny. In his own attempts to achieve where he felt Hertz had failed, Tesla developed a powerful method by which he hoped to generate and detect real electromagnetic waves. Part of this apparatus required the implementation of a very powerful capacitor bank. This capacitor "battery" was charged to very high voltages, and subsequently discharged through short copper bus-bars. The explosive bursts thus obtained produced several coincident phenomena which deeply impressed Tesla, far exceeding the power of any electrical display he had ever seen. These proved to hold an essential secret which he was determined to uncover.

The abrupt sparks, which he termed "disruptive discharges", were found capable of exploding wires into vapor. They propelled very sharp shockwaves, which struck him with great force across the whole front of his body. Of this surprising physical effect, Tesla was exceedingly intrigued. Rather like gunshots of extraordinary power than electrical sparks, Tesla was completely absorbed in this new study. Electrical impulses produced effects commonly associated only with lightning. The explosive effects reminded him of similar occurrences observed with high voltage DC generators. A familiar experience among workers and engineers, the simple closing of a switch on a high voltage dynamo often brought a stinging shock, the assumed result of residual static charging.

This hazardous condition only occurred with the sudden application of high voltage DC. This crown of deadly static charge stood straight out of highly electrified conductors, often seeking ground paths which included workmen and switchboard operators. In long cables, this instantaneous charge effect produced a hedge of bluish needles, pointing straight away from the line into the surrounding space. The hazardous condition appeared briefly, at the very instant of switch closure. The bluish sparking crown vanished a few milliseconds later, along with the life of any unfortunate who happened to have been so "struck". After the brief effect passed, systems behaved as designed. Such phenomena vanished as charges slowly saturated the lines and systems. After this brief surge, currents flowed smoothly and evenly as designed.

The effect was a nuisance in small systems. But in large regional power systems where voltages were excessive, it proved deadly. Men were killed by the effect, which spread its deadly electrostatic crown of sparks throughout component systems. Though generators were rated at a few thousand volts, such mysterious surges represented hundreds of thousands, even millions of volts. The problem was eliminated through the use of highly insulated, heavily grounded relay switches. Former engineering studies considered only those features of power systems which accommodated the steady state supply and consumption of power. It seemed as though large systems required both surge and normal operative design considerations. Accommodating the dangerous initial "supercharge" was a new feature. This engineering study became the prime focus of power companies for years afterward, safety devices and surge protectors being the subject of a great many patents and texts.

Tesla knew that the strange supercharging effect was only observed at the very instant in which dynamos were applied to wire lines, just as in his explosive capacitor discharges. Though the two instances were completely different, they both produced the very same effects. The instantaneous surge supplied by dynamos briefly appeared super-concentrated in long lines. Tesla calculated that this electrostatic concentration was several orders in magnitude greater than any voltage which the dynamo could supply. The actual supply was somehow being amplified or transformed. But how?

The general consensus among engineers was that this was an electrostatic "choking" effect. Many concluded it to be a "bunching" action, where powerfully applied force was unable to move charge quickly through a system. Mysterious, the combined resistance of such systems seemed to influence the charge carriers before they were able to move away from the dynamo terminals! Like slapping water with a rapid hand, the surface seemed solid. So also it was with the electrical force, charges meeting up against a seemingly solid wall. But the effect lasted only as long as the impact. Until current carriers had actually "caught up" with the applied electrical field, the charges sprang from the line in all directions. A brief supercharging effect could be expected until charges were distributed, smoothly flowing through the whole line and system. The dynamo itself thus became the brief scene of a minor shockwave. He began wondering why it was possible for electrostatic fields to move more quickly than the actual charges themselves, a perplexing mystery. Was the field itself an entity which simply drove the more massive charges along? If this was true, then of what was the electrostatic field itself "composed"? Was it a field of smaller particles? The questions were wonderfully endless.

Despite the wonderful ideas which this study stimulated, Tesla saw a practical application which had never occurred to him. Consideration of the dynamo supercharging effect suggested a new experimental apparatus. It was one which could greatly outperform his capacitor battery in the search to find electrical waves. A simple high voltage DC generator provided his electric field source. Tesla understood that the resistance of lines or components, viewed from the dynamo end, seemed to be an impossible "barrier" for charge carriers to penetrate. This barrier caused the "bunching" effect. Electrostatic charges were literally stopped and held for an instant by line resistance, a barrier which only existed during the brief millisecond interval in which the power switch was closed. The sudden force application against this virtual barrier squeezed charge into a density impossible to obtain with ordinary capacitors. It was the brief application of power, the impact of charge against the resistance barrier, which brought this abnormal electro-densified condition. This is why the conductive wires in his present experiment often exploded.

The analogy to steam power and steam engines was unmistakable. Large steam engines had to be valved very carefully. This required the expertise of old and well-experienced operators who knew how to "open up" an engine without rupturing the vessels and causing a deadly explosion. Too suddenly valved, and even a large steam engine of very high capacity could explode. Steam also had to be admitted into a system gently, until it began smoothly and gradually flowing into every orifice, conduit, and component. Here too was the mysterious "choking" effect, where a large capacity system seemed to behave like an uncommonly high resistance to any sudden and sustained application of force. Tesla learned that he could literally shape the resultant discharge, by modifying certain circuit parameters. Time, force, and resistance were variables necessary to producing the phenomenon.

## PERMEATIONS

The academic world of experimenters was yet fixated on his former discovery of high frequency alternating currents. It seemed that Tesla alone now exclusively studied these impulse discharges. He was producing explosive impulses which had not been observed in laboratories. Every component was carefully insulated, himself implementing insulator rods and rubberized regalia to insure complete safety. Tesla had observed electrostatic machines whose ability to charge insulated metals was potent, but this demonstration exceeded the mere charging of wire by the instantaneous switch closure. This effect produced "springing" charge, phenomena like no other before witnessed by

Tesla for its sheer strength. Whatever the conditions observed in previous systems, he had now learned how to maximize the effect. Balancing voltage and resistance against capacity, Tesla learned to routinely produce supercharge states which no existing device could equal.

Empirical observation had long taught that ordinary capacitor discharges were oscillating currents, spark currents which literally "bounced" between each capacitor plate until their stored energy was wasted away. The high voltage of the dynamo exerted such an intense unidirectional pressure on the densified charges that alternations were impossible. The only possible backrushes were oscillations. In this case, charges surged and stopped in a long series until the supercharge was wasted away. All parameters which forced such oscillations actually limited the supercharge from manifesting its total energetic supply, a condition Tesla strove to eliminate. Indeed he spent an excessive time developing various means to block every "backrush" and other complex current echo which might forced the supercharge to prematurely waste its dense energy. Here was an effect demanding a single unidirectional super pulse. With both the oscillations and alternations eliminated, new and strange effects began making their appearance. These powerful and penetrating phenomena were never observed when working with high frequency alternations.

The sudden quick closure of the switch now brought a penetrating shockwave throughout the laboratory, one which could be felt both as a sharp pressure and a penetrating electrical irritation. A "sting". Face and hands were especially sensitive to the explosive shockwaves, which also produced a curious "stinging" effect at close range. Tesla believed that material particles approaching the vapor state were literally thrust out of the wires in all directions. In order to better study these effects, he poised himself behind a glass shield and resumed the study. Despite the shield, both shockwaves and stinging effects were felt by the now mystified Tesla. This anomaly provoked a curiosity of the very deepest kind, for such a thing was never before observed. More powerful and penetrating than the mere electrostatic charging of metals, this phenomenon literally propelled high voltage charge out into the surrounding space where it was felt as a stinging sensation. The stings lasting for a small fraction of a second, the instant of switch closure. But Tesla believed that these strange effects were a simple effect of ionized shockwaves in the air, rather like a strongly ionized thunderclap.

Tesla devised a new series of experiments to measure the shockwave pressure from a greater distance. He required an automatic "trip switch". With this properly arranged, a more controlled and repetitious triggering of the effect was possible. In addition, this arrangement permitted distant observations which might cast more light on the shied-permeating phenomenon. Controlling the speed of the high voltage dynamo controlled the voltage. With these components properly adjusted, Tesla was able to walk around his large gallery spaces and make observations. Wishing also to avoid the continuous pressure barrage and its stinging sparks, Tesla shielded himself with several materials. The arrangement of rapidly interrupted high voltage direct currents resulted in the radiation of stinging rays which could be felt at great distances from their super-sparking source. In fact, Tesla felt the stings right through the shields! Whatever had been released from the wires during the instant of switch closure, successfully penetrated the shields of glass and of copper. It made no difference, the effect permeated each substance as if the shield were not there at all. Here was an electrical effect which communicated directly through space without material connections. Radiant electricity!

In these several new observations, the phenomenon was violating electrostatic charge principles experimentally established by Faraday. Projected electrostatic charges normally spread out over the surface of metallic shield, they do not penetrate metal. This effect had certain very non-electrical characteristics. Tesla was truly mystified by this strange new phenomenon, and searched the literature for references to its characteristics. No such reference was found, except in the surreptitious observations of two experimenters. In one case, Joseph Henry observed the magnetization of steel needles by a heavy spark discharge. The extraordinary feature of this observation (1842) lay in the fact that the Leyden Jar, whose spark apparently produced the magnetizations, stood on the upper floor of an otherwise electrically impervious building. Brick walls, thick oak doors, heavy stone and iron flooring, tin ceilings. Moreover, the steel needles were housed in a vault in the cellar. How did the spark affect such a change through such a natural barrier? Dr. Henry believed that the spark had released special "light-like rays", and these were the penetrating agencies responsible for the magnetizations.

A second such account (1872) occurred in a high school building in Philadelphia. Elihu Thomson, a physics instructor, sought to make the sparks of a large Ruhmkorrf Spark Coil more visible for his next lecture. Attaching one pole of the coil to a cold water pipe, and reactivating the coil, Thomson was thrilled to find that the nature of the spark had changed from blue to white. Wishing to amplify this effect, Thomson attached the other pole to a large metal tabletop. Again reactivating the coil produced a shrieking silver-white spark, entirely visible to any who sat in the last row. Wishing to show this to a colleague, Edwin Houston, Thomson made for the door and was abruptly stopped. Touching the brass knob on the otherwise insulated oak door, Thomson received an unexpected sizzling shock. Turning off the Ruhmkorrf Coil, Thomson found it possible to stop the effect. Calling for Edwin, he summarized what had occurred. Then turning the unit back on again, the stinging charge effects returned. The two gentlemen ran throughout the huge stone, oak, and iron building with insulated metal objects now. Each touch of a penknife or screwdriver to anything metallic, however distant from the coil or insulated from the floor, produced long and continuous white sparks. The account was written up as a short article in Scientific American later in the same year.

In studying each of these two prior observations, events each separated by some thirty years, Tesla perceived an essential unity with that of his own discovery. Each observation was perhaps a slight variant of the very same phenomenon. Somehow accidentally, each experimenter had managed to produce the explosive super-charging effect. In the case of Dr. Henry, the explosive bursts occurred in a single flash, electrostatic machines being used to accumulate the initial charge. The second case was peculiar, since it evidenced the sustained and continuous production of super-charging effects. The effect was rare because it obviously required very stringent electrical parameters. Tesla deduced this from the simple fact that the effect was so infrequently observed by experimenters the world over. In addition, he was quick to remark concerning the anomalous attributes attached to the phenomenon. Tesla knew that, despite the extremely penetrating effects in each case, he had secured the only means for achieving the "complete" and maximum manifestation of supercharging. His was an apparatus with no equal, capable of releasing an aspect of the electrostatic field which others very apparently had not.

Though discovered by Tesla in 1889, the preliminary observation of this effect was published after an intensive battery of investigations. The "Dissipation of Electricity", published just prior to Christmas of 1892, is the pivotal Tesla lecture. This is the departure point in which Tesla abandons research and development of high frequency alternating current. Divorcing himself from that field entirely, Tesla describes the shockwaves and other effects of IMPULSES. In addition to those physical sensations which he describes in characteristic understatements, Tesla also enlarges upon the "gaseous" aspects associated with the phenomena. He observed that the abruptly charged wires in his experiments projected a strange gaseous stream when immersed in an oil bath. A phenomenon which he once thought due entirely to wire-adsorbed gases, he found that the effect could be so continuously produced from a single wire that no volume of ordinary adsorbed gas could supply the flow. Indeed, he was able to produce streams of this kind in oil which so powerfully projected from charged wire ends that they visibly depressed the oil into a hole, some two inches in depth! Tesla began to realize the true nature of the fine issuing "gas" which projected from wire ends immersed in oil.

He now prepared an extensive series of tests in order to determine the true cause and nature of these shocking air pulses. In his article, Tesla describes the shield-permeating shocks as "soundwaves of electrified air". Nevertheless, he makes a remarkable statement concerning the sound, heat, light, pressure, and shock which he sensed passing directly through copper plates. Collectively, they "imply the presence of a medium of gaseous structure, that is, one consisting of independent carriers capable of free motion". Since air was obviously not this "medium", to what then was he referring? Further in the article he clearly states that "besides the air, another medium is present".

## RADIANT ELECTRICITY

Through successive experimental arrangements, Tesla discovered several facts concerning the production of his effect. First, the cause was undoubtedly found in the abruptness of charging. It was in the switch closure, the very instant of "closure and break", which thrust the effect out into space. The effect was definitely related to time, IMPULSE time. Second, Tesla found that it was imperative that the charging process occurred in a single impulse. No reversal of current was permissible, else the effect would not manifest. In this, Tesla made succinct remarks describing the role of capacity in the spark-radiative circuit. He found that the effect was powerfully strengthened by placing a capacitor between the disrupter and the dynamo. While providing a tremendous power to the effect, the dielectric of the capacitor also served to protect the dynamo windings. Not yet sure of the process at work in this phenomenon, Tesla sought the empirical understanding required for its amplification and utilization. He had already realized the significance of this unexpected effect. The idea of bringing this strange and wondrous new phenomenon to its full potential already suggested thrilling new possibilities in his mind. He completely abandoned research and development of alternating current systems after this event, intimating that a new technology was about to unfold.

The effect could also be greatly intensified to new and more powerful levels by raising the voltage, quickening the switch "make-break" rate, and shortening the actual time of switch closure. Thus far, Tesla employed rotating contact switches to produce his unidirectional impulses. When these mechanical impulse systems failed to achieve the greatest possible effects, Tesla sought a more "automatic" and powerful means. He found this "automatic switch" in special electrical arc dischargers. The high voltage output of a DC generator was applied to twin conductors through his new arc mechanism, a very powerful permanent magnet sitting crosswise to the discharge path. The discharge arc was automatically and continually "blown out" by this magnetic field.

Imperative toward obtaining the desired rare effect, the capacitor and its connected wire lines had to be so chosen as to receive and discharge the acquired electrostatic charge in unidirectional staccato fashion. The true Tesla circuit very much resembles a pulse jet, where no back pressure ever stops the onrushing flow. Electrostatic charge rises to a maximum, and is discharged much more quickly. The constant application of high voltage dynamo pressure to the circuit insures that continual successions of "charge-rapid discharge" are obtained. It is then and only then that the Tesla Effect is observed. Pulses literally flow through the apparatus from the dynamo. The capacitor, disrupter, and its attached wire lines, behave as the flutter valve.

The high voltage dynamo remains the true electrostatic source in the apparatus. This was a fact well appreciated by Tesla, who disliked the painful radiant effects proceeding into space. It was evident that the dynamo had somehow been modified by the addition of these "pulsing valve" circuits. The dynamos being used provided deadly voltages, capable of killing a man. The valve circuits were forcing a strange radiance of those deadly field energies. Somehow, the dynamo energy was being expanded into space with dangerous and painful force. But how? By what mysterious and provocative means was this condition established? The result of this experimental series fixed a new concept in Tesla's mind. Tesla had of course realized the implications of his mysterious shocking-field effect. This was radiant electricity. With this phenomenon, Tesla could develop a far better world-changing technology than Polyphase. Moreover, this radiant electric effect could replace powerlines.

The Tesla Research Laboratory was a four story structure which stood at 33-35 South Fifth Avenue in New York City. Buildings such as the Tesla Laboratory may yet be found in the Soho section of Manhattan. Each is large in size, amply supplied with several floors of immense gallery halls and upper floor studios. He was thus afforded the space to perform several critical experiments in broadcast electrical power techniques. Tesla first conducted elaborate and extensive investigations in order to comprehend the exact nature of this new electrical effect. Tesla realized that this strange "shocking field" actually radiated through space from the impulse apparatus. If this was electrostatic energy, it was more intense and more penetrating than any electrostatic field he had ever observed. If this was merely a "stuttered" electrostatic field, why then was its strength so very intensified? Tesla began to believe that he had discovered a new electrical force, not simply a treatment of an existing force. It is for this reason that he often described the effect as "electrodynamic" or "more electrostatic".

By properly adjusting the inherent circuit parameters, Tesla learned how to produce an extremely rapid series of unidirectional impulses on demand. When the impulses were short, abrupt, and precise in their successions, Tesla found that the shocking effect could permeate very large volumes of space with apparently no loss of intensity. He also found that the shocking effect penetrated sizable metal shields and most insulators with ease. Developing a means for controlling the number of impulses per second, as well as the intermittent time intervals between each successive impulse, he began discovering a new realm of effects. Each impulse duration gave its own peculiar effects. Able to feel the stinging shocks, though shielded at a distance of nearly fifty feet from his apparatus, Tesla recognized at once that a new potential for electrical power transmission had been revealed to him. Tesla was first to understand that electrical shock waves represented a new means for transforming the world.

Even as his Polyphase had done, Tesla fully intended to disclose his discoveries to the world at large. Radiant electricity had special characteristics of which the scientific world had no knowledge. If released with sufficient power, radiant electrical broadcasts could kill. His initial experiments were sufficiently potent enough to cause severe and painful stings. Here was a lethal system requiring control and development. What was intended to be a great benefit to humanity could be misconstrued as the greatest detriment. Working with a simple but powerful embodiment of his original apparatus, Tesla found that radiant electricity could induce powerful electrical effects at a distance. These effects were not alternations, not alternating waves. They were longitudinal waves, composed of successive shocking waves. The advance of each shocking wave, followed by short neutral zones together comprised the radiant field. Vectorial components of these shockwave successions were always unidirectional. The stuttering shockwaves were capable of forcing charges in the direction of their propagation.

Objects placed near this device became powerfully electrified, retaining a singular charge sign for many minutes after the magnetic discharger had been deactivated. Tesla found it possible to amplify these single charge effects by a simple asymmetrical alignment of the magnetic discharger. By placing the magnetic discharger closer to one or the other side of the charging dynamo, either force positive or force negative vectors could be selected and projected. Thus, charge could be projected into or drawn from any object in the field space. Introducing objects into the radiant space gave spectacular effects, becoming surrounded by crowns of white sparks. Objects charged by this apparatus evidenced a powerful and permeating charge action like no other seen before. This was a new electrical force. Tesla realized more than ever that he was in unknown territory. The fact that these radiant forces travelled as light-like rays distinguished them from the electromagnetic waves of Maxwell. The waves were weak, but these rays were strong. Uncommonly strong

Directional effects could obtained by shaping the wire lines which radiated the shocking waves. The condition which best radiated evenly in all directions required that each line be semi-circular, the entire apparatus being circularly disposed. How far did this field extend, and what was the effect of distance on the intensity of the radiant field? Tesla found it impossible to measure a diminution in radiant force at several hundred yards. In comparison, he recalled that Hertz found it relatively easy to measure notable inverse square diminutions within the confines of his laboratory in Bonn. Tesla suspected that these effects were coherent, not subject to inverse laws other than those due to ray divergence. If he wished to broadcast power to a neighborhood, it would be critical that all radiant energy be focussed in receivable directions.

Also, Tesla wished to determine the effect of gradually decreased impulse durations required greatest skill and precaution. Tesla knew that he would be exposing himself to mortal danger. Controlling the rapidity of current blowout in the magnetic DC arc, Tesla released a new spectrum of light-like energies throughout his large gallery space. These energetic species were like no other which the world has since seen. Tesla found that impulse duration alone defined the effect of each succinct spectrum. These effects were completely distinctive, endowed with strange additional qualities never purely experienced in Nature. Moreover, Tesla observed distinct color changes in the discharge space when each impulse range had been reached or crossed. Never before seen discharge colorations did not remain a mystery for long. Trains of impulses, each exceeding 0.1 millisecond duration, produced pain and mechanical pressures. In this radiant field, objects visibly vibrated and even moved as the force field drove them along. Thin wires, exposed to sudden bursts of the radiant field, exploded into vapor. Pain and physical movements ceased when impulses of 100 microseconds or less were produced. These latter features suggested weapon systems of frightful potentials.

With impulses of 1.0 microsecond duration, strong physiological heat was sensed. Further decreases in impulse brought spontaneous illuminations capable of filling rooms and vacuum globes with white light. At these impulse frequencies, Tesla was able to stimulate the appearance of effects which are normally admixed among the electromagnetic energies inherent in sunlight. Shorter impulses produced cool room penetrating breezes, with an accompanying uplift in mood and awareness. There were no limits in this progression toward impulses of diminished duration. None of these impulse energies could be duplicated through the use of high frequency harmonic alternations, those which Sir Oliver Lodge popularized, and which later was embodied in Marconi Wave Radio. Few could reproduce these effects because so few understood the absolute necessity of observing those parameters set by Tesla. These facts have been elucidated by Eric Dollard, who also successfully obtained the strange and distinct effects claimed by Tesla.

## TRANSFORMER

By 1890, after a period of intense experimentation and design development, Tesla summarized the components necessary for the practical deployment of a radiant electrical power distribution system. Tesla had already discovered the wonderful fact that impulse durations of 100 microseconds or less could not be sensed and would do no physiological harm. He planned to use these in his power broadcast. Furthermore, shocking waves of 100 microsecond duration passed through all matter, a fitting form of electrical energy to broadcast throughout the stone, steel, and glass of a power-needy city. Tesla would not expect distortions with specially adjusted energy fields, vectors which permeated matter without interactive effects.

Tesla made a most startling discovery the same year, when placing a long single-turn copper helix near his magnetic disrupter. The coil, some two feet in length, did not behave as did solid copper pipes and other objects. The thin-walled coil became ensheathed in an envelope of white sparks. Undulating from the crown of this coil were very long and fluidic silvery white streamers, soft discharges which appeared to have been considerably raised in voltage. These effects were greatly intensified when the helical coil was placed within the disrupter wire circle. Inside this "shockzone", the helical coil was surrounded in a blast which hugged into its surface, and rode up the coil to its open end. It seemed as though the shockwave actually pulled away from surrounding space to cling to the coil surface, a strange attractive preference. The shockwave flowed over the coil at right angles to the windings, an unbelievable effect. The sheer length of discharges leaping from the helix crown was incomprehensible. With the disrupter discharge jumping 1 inch in its magnetic housing, the white flimmering discharges rose from the helix to a measured length of over two feet. This discharge equalled the very length of the coil itself! It was an unexpected and unheard transformation.

Here was an action more nearly "electrostatic" in nature, although he knew that academes would not comprehend this term when used in this situation. Electrostatic energy did not fluctuate as did his shockwaves. The explosive shockwave had characteristics unlike any other electrical machine in existence. Yet Tesla stated that the shockwave, during the brief instant in which it made its explosive appearance, more nearly resembled an electrostatic field than any other known electrical manifestation. Just as in electrostatic friction machines, where current and magnetism are negligible, a very energetic field component fills space in radiating lines. This "dielectric" field normally launches through space in a slow growth as charges are gathered. Here was a case where a DC generator provided the high voltage. This voltage charged an insulated hoop of copper, growing to its maximum value. If all values in the circuit were properly balanced, in the manner prescribed by Tesla, a sudden charge collapse would then occur. This collapse was necessarily very much shorter than the interval required to charge the hoop. The collapse comes when the magnetic disrupter extinguishes the arc. If the circuit is properly structured, no backrush alternations ever occur.

This unidirectional succession of charge-discharge impulses causes a very strange field to expand outward, one which vaguely resembles a "stuttering" or "staccato" electrostatic field. But these terms did not satisfactorily describe the conditions actually measured around the apparatus, a powerful radiant effect exceeding all expectable electrostatic values. Actual calculation of these discharge ratios proved impossible. Implementing the standard magneto-inductive transformer rule, Tesla was unable to account for the enormous voltage multiplication effect. Conventional relationships failing, Tesla hypothesized that the effect was due entirely to radiant transformation rules, obviously requiring empirical determination. Subsequent measurements of discharge lengths and helix attributes provided the necessary new mathematical relationship.

He had discovered a new induction law, one where radiant shockwaves actually auto-intensified when encountering segmented objects. The segmentation was the key to releasing the action. Radiant shockwaves encountered an helix and "flashed over" the outer skin, from end to end. This shockwave did not pass through the windings of the coil at all, treating the coil surface as an aerodynamic plane. The shockwave pulse auto-intensified exactly as gas pressures continually increase when passing through Venturi tubes. A consistent increase in electrical pressure was measured along the coil surface. Indeed, Tesla stated that voltages could often be increased at an amazing 10,000 volts per inch of axial coil surface. This meant that a 24 inch coil could absorb radiant shockwaves which initially measured 10,000 volts, with a subsequent maximum rise to 240,000 volts! Such transformations of voltage were unheard with apparatus of this volume and simplicity. Tesla further discovered that the output voltages were mathematically related to the resistance of turns in the helix. Higher resistance meant higher voltage maxima.

He began referring to his disrupter line as his special "primary", and to the helical coil placed within the shockzone, as his special "secondary". But he never intended anyone to equate these terms with those referring to magneto-electric transformers. This discovery was indeed completely different from magneto-induction. There was a real and measurable reason why he could make this outlandish statement. There was an attribute which completely baffled Tesla for a time. Tesla measured a zero current condition in these long copper secondary coils. He determined that the current which should have appeared was completely absent. Pure voltage was rising with each inch of coil surface. Tesla constantly referred to his "electrostatic induction laws", a principle which few comprehended. Tesla called the combined disrupter and secondary helix a "Transformer".

Tesla Transformers are not magnetoelectric devices, they use radiant shockwaves, and produce pure voltage without current. No university High Frequency Coil must ever be called a "Tesla Coil", since the devices usually employed in demonstration halls are the direct result of apparatus perfected by Sir Oliver Lodge and not by Nikola Tesla. The Tesla Transformer is an impulse apparatus, and cannot be as easily constructed except by strict conformity with parameters which Tesla enunciated. Tesla Transformers produce extraordinary white impulse discharges of extreme length and pressure, which exceed the alternating violet spark displays of Lodge Coils. This is illustrated by noting the manner in which Tesla Transformers are actually constructed. While looking and seeming the same, each system actually performs very different functions. Lodge Coils are alternators. Tesla Transformers are unidirectional impulses.

The most efficient Tesla Transformations were obtained only when the disruptive radiating wire line equalled the mass of the helical coil. The empirical determination proved that a mysterious and simple mass-to-mass correspondence necessarily existed between the disrupter apparatus and the secondary coil. Tesla learned that a simple balance beam could be used to best design his Transformers. Metal line or thick metal strapping would be cut and placed on one side of the balance. Thin copper wire would be unwound from a spool and hung on the other balance beam end. When the balance was even, when the masses were identical, Tesla cut the thin wire. Transformers made in this mass-to-mass ratio consistently provided the most powerful transformations. Each Transformer conducted a specific impulse duration with special force. Therefore each had to be "tuned" by adjusting the disrupter to that specific impulse duration. Adjustments of arc distance provided this control factor. Once each transformer was tuned to its own special response rate, impulses could flow smoothly through the system like gas flowing in a pipe.

Finding that gas-dynamic analogies and applications indeed provided him with a consistent record of successful assessments in these regards, Tesla began considering whether or not the white flame discharges, so different from anything he had ever seen, might not be a gaseous manifestation of electrostatic force. There were certainly abundant experimental instances in which a purely gaseous nature, so unlike anything electrical, was being clearly made manifest. The manner in which the radiant shockwave travelled over the wire coilings in white flimmering laminar streams, brought a new revolution in thought. Voltage pulses traversed the secondary surface like a gas pulse under increasing constriction. Until reaching the free end of the coil, these gaseous pulses flowed over the copper surface rather than through it. Tesla referred to this specific manifestation as the "skin effect". In this the discharge greatly resembled the manner of gases in motion over surfaces.

Furthermore, whenever a metal point was connected to the upper terminal of one of his Transformers, the stream became more directive. It behaved just like a stream of water in a pipe. When the white flimmering stream was directed at distant metal plates, it produced electronic charges. This charge production could be measured as amperage, "current", at the reception site. In transit however, no such amperage existed. Amperage appeared only when intercepted. Eric Dollard has stated that the space surrounding Tesla Impulse Transformers so surges with these streams that the "interception current" can reach several hundred or even thousands of amperes. But of what was this mysterious stream composed? Tesla struggled with the doubt that these discharge phenomena might be ordinary electricity behaving in extraordinary ways. But did electricity indeed have a smooth, soft, and flimmering nature? The electricity with which he was familiar was shocking, hot, burning, deadly, piercing, stinging, all the attributes of an irritant. But this discharge phenomenon was, whether cool or warm to the touch, soft and gentle. It would not kill.

Even the manner in which the pulse exploded as bright white discharges of greatly transformed voltage, suggested the way in which gases behave when released from their confinements under pressure. These reflective meditations convinced Tesla that this effect was not purely electrical in nature. Closely examining the white flames, Tesla realized why there was no measurable "electrical current" at the crown of these activated coils. The normal heavy charge carriers, electrons, could not travel as quickly as the radiant pulse itself. Choked in the metallic lattice of the coil, electrons became immobile. No electron current moved through the coil at all. The radiant pulse which moved over the coil surface, was therefore not electronic in nature.

Additionally, Tesla discovered an amazing phenomenon which removed all doubt concerning the true nature of energetic carriers at work in his apparatus. Tesla arranged a very heavy a U-shaped copper bus-bar, connecting both legs directly to his disrupter primary. Across the legs of this U-shaped busbar were placed several incandescent lamps. The arrangement was a very evident short circuit. The lamps were illuminated to a brilliant cold white light, while being shorted by a heavy copper shunt. Uncharacteristic of particulate current electricity, the bright but cold lamps revealed that another energetic current was indeed flowing through the "short-circuits".

Those who observed this experiment did not expected it to perform any function save the incineration of the disrupter circuit and possibly of the dynamo itself. Instead of this, witnesses beheld a marvel. The lamps lit to an uncommon brightness. In this simple demonstration, Tesla was illustrating but one of his many evidences. Electronic charges would prefer the least resistant circuit, rejecting the incandescent bulbs for the copper path. The current in this situation chose to conform with a contradictory principle. Perhaps this was true because the currents were not electrical. Tesla repeatedly used this demonstration to evidence the "fractionation" of currents electronic, from currents neutral.

## LUMINIFEROUS ÆTHER

A single question remained, the answer to which would provide him with the essential information needed to create a new technology. What so separated or "fractioned" the diverse mobile carriers in his Transformer? It was the geometric configuration of the coil which inadvertently separated each component. Electrons were blocked from flowing through the wire length, while the radiant pulse was released over the coil surface as a gaseous pulse. Electrons should have drifted through the wire but, during each impulse period, were blocked by the line resistance. Thus, the gaseous mobile carriers were released to flow outside the wire, a pulse which travelled along the outer coil surface from end to end.

Here then was evidence that electrical discharges were indeed composed of several simultaneous mobile species. Tesla now comprehended why his first high frequency alternating currents never evidenced these powerful actions. It was the abruptness, the violence of the impulsive discharge, which gave free mobility to this unsuspected "gaseous" component. Impulses, unidirectional impulses, were the only means by which these potentials could be unlocked. Alternations were absolutely useless in this regard. Moreover, because alternations could not unleash the second gas-dynamic component, it remained an unusable and pitifully weak means. Tesla forever viewed his high frequency alternating devices as failed projects. This has great bearing on his highly critical views of Marconi and all the others like him who pursued high frequency alternating wave radio. Tesla began to study a topic which has found more enemies and critics than any this century. Tesla, with greatest interest now, began researching "the æther".

Victorian Science came to believe that space, all of space, was absolutely permeated with an ultrafine gas which they termed "æther". It was in this gaseous atmosphere that light was said to be transmitted through space. In fact, space was not viewed as a pure vacuum, æther filled that vacuum. Some Victorians stated that the æther could, at times, be visibly seen. The golden haze which often fills spaces within buildings were said to be manifestations of æther gas. These displays could be seen in conditions of minimal humidity and in the absence of aerial dust. Others mentioned the colorations often seen with the eyes opened, in a dark room or against a ganzfeld, as evidence of ætheric luminations (Reichenbach). In order to satisfy all of the physical dynamics which eventually became attached to the concept, æther gas acquired several mutually contradictory attributes.

Lodge stated that æther gas necessarily existed in a density comparable to that of steel, yet behaved as a fluid. Æther gas was also capable of passing through most substances, a permeating substance having no terrestrial equal. When an experiment designed to measure "æther drift" with light beam interferometry failed, most repudiated the existence of this gaseous space filling atmosphere altogether. Just before this moment in science history however, a wonderful theoretical abstract was published explaining the reality of the æther in chemical terms. If not for the author and his credibility, few would appreciate the import of his assertions.

A comprehensive analysis of these contradictory attributes was engaged by Professor Dmitri Mendeleev, "father" of the Periodic Table. Just before the turn of the Century, Dr. Mendeleev produced a wonderful theoretical view which elegantly satisfied each of the reigning contradictions of his day. His work was published years later in a small booklet entitled "A Chemical Conception of The Ether" (1904). Herein, he treated the æther gas as an interstellar atmosphere composed of at least two lighter-than-hydrogen elements. These were produced by violent bombardments in stars, the sun being the most prolific neighboring source. According to Dr. Mendeleev, æther gas was an atmosphere probably composed of several different elemental species. He anticipated that the two gases would be found. Although these pre-hydrogen elements remained yet unknown, Mendeleev placed them in his Periodic Table just as he did when composing the Table in 1869.

These gases were placed in a special "zero group" preceding the Noble gases. The inertness of these æther gases explained their elusive "non-reactive" character. The nearly massless state of these different ætheric gases explained their ability both to permeate all matter without chemically interacting with it, and the high apparent density of æther. The lightest and first æther gas was assigned a theoretical atomic weight one hundred millionth that of hydrogen. The kinetic velocity of this first gas was calculated at 2.5 million meters per second. Such a highly mobile and vanishing ætheric mass could be rarefied and yet "appear" extremely dense. Dr. Mendeleev fully anticipated that these gaseous elements would someday be found through extraordinary apparatus. Others felt that, in this physical analysis, Dr. Mendeleev had not glimpsed the real æther at all. Many Victorian claimed that æther was extremely dense, like a flood of matter which could be felt as a pressure and seen as a multicolored radiance. Tesla ascribed to both of these views.

Tesla applied these principles in explaining the actions so visibly at work in his newest apparatus. Macroscopically, radiant shockwaves behaved as a gaseous impulse having electrical characteristics. This was no ordinary gas however. This "gaseous" component was not atmospheric in the ordinary sense. It was not the result of adsorbed gases on the copper coil surface. This gas pulse travelled over the coil surfaces with super-luminal velocity. Mr. Dollard utilized line interferometry to measure and compare both components in a real Tesla Impulse Transformer, and has proven the vast velocity differences between both. Moreover, the mysterious surface-riding component was found to travel at a super-luminal velocity. Those experimental measurement successfully vindicated the claim of Tesla in this regards in 1985. When referring to these discharges and their strange attributes and effects, Tesla always used gas-dynamic terms and gas-dynamic analogues. Throughout his use of such terminology, Tesla was inferring that something unlike normal electricity was flowing through short electrical impulses. That something was indeed behaving like a gas. The gas-dynamic components which rode the outer coil surface required aerodynamically smooth surfaces.

Tesla came to believe that dielectric fields were actually composed of æther streams. Theoretically then, one could derive limitless energy by trapping and conducting a naturally occurring dielectric field line. The problem was that no ordinarily accessible material could resist the æther enough to derive any momentum from it. With a stream so rare as to pass through all known materials, the kinetic energy inherent in dielectric field lines would remain an elusive energy source. Tesla believed he may have found the secret to tapping this energy, but it would not require an ordinary kind of matter. Tesla viewed voltage as streams of æther under various states of pressure. Raising these stresses could produce enormous æther streams, where the observed voltages would then be extremely high and luminous. This was the very condition which Tesla had come to believe had been established in his Transformers.

In fact, Tesla repeatedly stated that his Transformers effected powerful movements in the æther. In one truly mystifying experiment indicative of these comprehension, Tesla describes the production of very rapid impulse trains with a subsequent production of "cool misty white streamers extending a yard into space". These were cool to the touch, and harmless. If electrical in nature, they would necessarily have been several million volts in potentials. Their harmlessness is coupled with their sinuous nature, one completely unlike electrical currents. Michael Theroux successfully duplicated Teslian experiments with an apparatus whose secondary was no more than 2 feet in length, with a width of 1 foot. When charged with a powerful electrostatic disruptive device of his own design and construction, Mr. Theroux succeeded in producing fluidic white streamers, sometimes exceeding 12 feet in length! These streamers continually grew in size, reaching the far wall of a cellar laboratory. Sinuous in their twisting manner, he reports that the ends of these branched with lobate ends, an unlikely characteristic for ordinary electricity. Contrasted against the discharges produced by Wimhurst Machines and other Electrostatic devices alone, these white and highly vibrant displays lacked the blue and stark jaggedness commonly associated with sparks termed "electric". In the light of experimental achievements such as these, and their attendant phenomena, we are required to review our theoretical base and reassess our most fundamental conventions.

Indeed, to understand Tesla Technology one must eliminate the notion that electrons are the "working fluid" in his radiant energy designs. With the lower coil end connected directly to the dynamo, high voltage æther streamers were projected from the upper terminal. When describing each of his relevant patents in this new technology, Tesla forever spoke of "light-like rays" and "the natural medium". The first term refers to the tightly constricted æther streams which are propelled from his Transformers along infinitesimal ray lines, and the latter refers to the all-pervading æther atmosphere in which his technology operated.

Tesla now understood why the coloration of discharges varied so with various impulse durations. Each gas of the ætheric atmosphere was being stimulated to luminescence. Tesla repeatedly produced discharge colorations which had no equivalent in the common gas spectra prevalent in the terrestrial atmosphere. Colors of blood-red, and sky blue, of peach, and white were each described in detail by Nikola Tesla. Although sharing certain characteristics with electricity, ætheric energy was a totally different expression. Ætheric energy held a potential which more nearly matched the expectations of those who dream and wish, a mystery realm. Tesla perceived this kinship between thought and ætheric energy with keenest intrigue, already planning the several necessary investigations before approaching this potential psychotronic technology. He often exposed himself to the very shortest of æther impulse radiance, discovering the mind-elevating effects grew with time. Ætheric energy demonstrated growth characteristics which Tesla noted with amazement.

It is impossible to comprehend Teslian Technology apart from the controversial topic concerning the æther. Many analysts will reject the concept without first seeking out and discovering the proofs which have been established by experimenters such as Eric Dollard. Nevertheless, the overwhelming evidence proves that Tesla had indeed been first to identify the gases which Dr. Mendeleev had so long predicted. Tesla addressed the notion that æther streams were being pulled through his Transformers, drawn in at higher natural pressure, and accelerated in the sharp electrical discharge. As electrical systems, Tesla apparatus cannot completely be understood or explained. One must view Teslian Technology as an æther gas technology, one capable of being explained only through gas-dynamic analogues.

It was now easy to understand how such projected rays, æther gas streams under high pressure, could penetrate metals and insulators alike. These powerful rays often could penetrate certain materials with inexplicable efficiency. Electricity did not perform these wonders. Tesla also now understood why these discharge streams produced their smoothly hissing sounds, visibly appearing like gas jets under high pressure. Æther gas under pressure. But what of the other characteristics of this gaseous component? Here was a new world of forces and dynamics vaguely glimpsed by researchers such as Luigi Galvani who, in order to release the more vitalizing components observed in metals which were aerially disposed or grounded, persistently sought the elimination of electronic charge. Tesla was completely mystified. He had successfully released the mystery current, normally suppressed and bound in electronic charge carriers. Unidirectional impulsive discharges of high voltage and abrupt durations released them. What other potentials would æther gas technology release?

## BROADCAST POWER

The original cylindrical coils were quickly replaced with cone shaped coils. With these bizarre geometries, Tesla was able to focus the gas-dynamic component, which now rose up like a jet of hissing white light from the coil tip. Tesla recognized that these discharges, while spectacular and awe inspiring, actually represented lost power. A power broadcast station had to evenly disperse the energetic radiance in all directions. Flame-like discharges caused the available power to undulate in space. This would produce unpredictable power drops at great distances. Consumers would not receive a reliable and consistent stream of energy. If his Power Transformer was to operate with highest broadcast efficiency, these flame-like discharges necessarily had to be suppressed. But suppressing these excessive æther jets proved problematic.

Tesla found that the white flimmering streams were absorbed in large capacity volumes, masses in which the streams were absorbed, filtered, and expelled. The use of copper spheres atop his Transformers forced the streams sufficiently apart to suppress the white flame. Power was now evenly dispersed throughout space as required. But a new problem appeared. The copper spheres, being impacted by the high voltage streams which they were forced to now conduct, expelled electronic components. These appeared along with the radiance, producing truly dangerous conditions. The problem was stimulated by conduction, a case where the spherical copper ball was impacted throughout its volume. The white flimmering streams permeated the copper and expelled electrons. These contaminants concentrated their escape from the system as harmful, blue stinging dartlets. By comparison, the white flame-like discharge was a smooth and harmless glow.

Comparing the two species, Tesla recognized the difference in charge carriers. Tesla was once nearly killed when one such dartlet jumped three feet through the air and struck him directly over the heart. The copper spheres had to be removed and replaced by another dispersion component. Metals were apparently of no utility in this case, being natural reservoirs of electrons. Tesla eventually suggested that metals manufactured electrons when impacted with these special flame-white currents, the carriers in the white flames becoming concentrated within the metallic lattice. This concept was later developed into an amazing theory by Tesla, one which thoroughly explains natural radioactivity as the result of impact.

While developing new lamps for his power system, Tesla discovered that gas-filled globes could provide more efficient suppression capacity for flaring æther streams, and promptly directed that his transformers be surmounted with such globes. The absence of metal mass eliminated the possibility that æther impulses could impact the metal lattice and expel electronic charges. These gas-globe terminals dispersed only the pure ætheric stream, a perfect solution for his original dilemma. Tesla now found himself in possession of components necessary to establishing his Power Broadcast System on a commercial basis.

He had already observed how the very air near these Transformers could be rendered strangely self-luminous. This was a light like no high frequency coil ever could produce, a corona of white brilliance which expanded to ever enlarging diameters. The light from Tesla Transformers continually expands. Tesla described the growing column of light which surrounds any elevated line which has been connected to his Transformers. Unlike common high frequency alternations, Tesla radiant energy effects grow with time. Tesla recognized the reason for this temporal growth process. There were no reversals in the source discharges, therefore the radiant energy would never remove the work performed on any space or material so exposed. As with the unidirectional impulse discharges, the radiant electric effects were additive and accumulative. In this respect, Tesla observed energy magnifications which seemed totally anomalous to ordinary engineering convention.

It was easy to control the brilliance of a room by controlling the voltage in his transformers. The light from this sort of illumination was curiously bright to human perception, but nearly impossible to photograph on film. Tesla found it necessary to make long time exposures of his discharges before the faintest sort of streamers could be made visible. This strange inability to register photographically was contrasted against the brilliance perceived in the eyes, one which required delicate control. Tesla also designed, built, and utilized large globe lamps which required only a single external plate for receiving the radiant energies. However distantly placed from the radiant source, these lamps became brilliantly illuminated. Theirs was a brilliance approaching that of an arc lamp, and exceeding any of the conventional Edison filament lamps by several factors. It was also easy for Tesla to control the heat of any space. By controlling both the voltage and impulse duration of energy in his Transformers, Tesla could heat up a room. Cool breezes could also be arranged by appropriately setting the impulse duration.

Tesla was amazed by the fact that mass ratios governed the efficient operation of his æther Transformers. The wonderful fact that mass ratios provided the most efficient transaction of broadcast energy was the mystifying reminder that these energies were not electrical. No electrical law existed in just such a bizarre format, not even when describing inductions between high frequency alternators. The original gas-dynamic implication inherent in this strange ratio requirement was confirmed. Now Tesla designed receiving apparatus for his future consumers. The mass of home receiving coils had to match the equivalent mass of the central transmitting coils of the broadcast center. Tesla matched coils and capacitors to produce this equivalent mass ratio, satisfying the natural requirements of the ætheric radiance. An elevated ball-like terminal would receive the broadcast energy, conveying it down into a central home-distribution apparatus. Here, the ætheric energy would be rebroadcast throughout the household without wires. Appliances could simply be moved to where they were needed, and turned on. Nothing could be more simple.

While Tesla's models were made with technological objectives in mind, he was not without an appreciation of fine art and the beauty of artistic elegance. In certain respects, Tesla's tastes were extravagant, a luxury which he could certainly yet afford. He was certain that each component of his system would be redesigned by artists and made more appealing for the consumer. The "look" of these appliances carried with them an aire of the future. In fact, Tesla invented an astounding collection of futuristic-looking appliances. Motors now appeared in an amazing variety, requiring no wire connections, save the small metal plates held on opposite ends of the motor housing. Placed in any position, the motors powerfully spun when the radiant field was on. Here was motive energy for home and industry alike.

Tesla performed outdoor experimental tests of broadcast power in the northernmost reaches of Manhattan by night. Sending metallized balloons aloft, he raised conductive lines. These were connected to the terminals of his Transformers, and activated. When properly adjusted, the white luminous columns began covering the vertical aerial line and expanded by the second. Enveloping Tesla, his assistants, and the surrounding trees, this strange white luminosity moved out into the countryside to an enormous volume of space. Tesla described this phenomenon in several of his power transmission patents, the obvious artifact of a non-electrical energy. His Transformer was now behaving as originally visualized. Now it was a true Transmitter, a Transmitter of ætheric energy. Appliances were disposed at various distances from this temporary central broadcast station on the meadows, absorbing energy from the ætheric radiance and performing to full efficiency. Lamps brilliant, motors humming, heaters radiating. The small radiant system worked with a rare power.

More highly energetic, exceeding the mobility of ionic charges, and overpowering any field inductions by several thousand orders, only ætheric energy could have accomplished this feat. Tesla had all of the components now. Broadcast power, once a visionary dream, had become a working system. There appeared to be no limit to the potential of this technological marvel. Tesla discovered a fact which later developed into a later regime of thought. He found to his amazement that single connections from impulse transmitter to ground produced greatly intensified responses in his distant appliances. This principle was applied to the appliances as well, resulting in an unprecedented increase in their overall performance. The single ground connection suddenly produced new and anomalous efficiencies in the system, an extraordinary excess of energy which his impulse transmitter was providing. Tesla was familiar with the natural growth process of ætheric streams, but why would ground connections so magnify the brilliance of lamps and the output of motors in this way?

This observation stimulated perplexing thoughts. How was ætheric energy, a supposed aerial dynamic, tunneling through the ground? Why were the magnification effects noticed when his appliances were ground connected? What self-magnifying capabilities were possibly stimulated when operating in conjunction with the ground connection? Was the earth itself a vast reservoir of æther gas? Furthermore, in what condition was this gas, was it under pressure? The phenomenon stimulated a revolution in his mind. For in this, Tesla perceived an unexpected power source.

## ÆTHERIC CURRENT

The key to producing all ætheric action was to secure a means for actually effecting ætheric deviations, the very thing now possessed by Tesla alone. Sir

Oliver Lodge stated that the only means for "getting at the æther" was "an electrical means", but not one member of the Royal Society had been able to achieve this feat with the rare exception of Sir William Crookes. The Tesla method used æther to modify æther! The secret was separating the contaminants from the æther current at the very source of generation, a feat which he had achieved in his Transformers. But how? How, with the apparatus made available to him through his creative abilities, did he achieve what military groups today cannot?

Tesla used the violence of magnetically disrupted arc discharges to chaoticize electronic and ætheric carriers in metal conductors. Breaking the agglomerations which bind them together, each component was free to separate. This condition could not be achieved in arc discharges where currents were allowed to alternate. In such apparatus, the electronic carriers overwhelmed the release of æther and, while æther was present in the discharge, could never be separated from the composite current. This is the fundamental reason why experimenters in England could never reproduce these effects, finally concluding that Tesla was "paraphrasing physical reality". Typically understated, the prevailing attitude toward Tesla found its real source in an inability among researchers to truly comprehend the elegance of what had been discovered. Thus, although shown these things in repeated demonstrations by Tesla himself, the inability which prevailed among these highly esteemed personages revealed the real source of error.

The Tesla method began with the "disruptive discharge". This disruptive discharge was more like an explosive charge, a blast whose effects lasted for a controllable time increment. Successions of these blasts were possible only when sufficient disruption was maintained. The Tesla magnetic arc disrupter was the chief tool of this process, a heavy duty discharge device which yet finds its use in military power applications. This gap could be adjusted, and was held apart at a distance of several inches. The large polished spheres were often made of steel. Other models featured heavy curved horns, often bimetallic. With one made of carbon and the other of copper, the bimetallic combination maintained a rectified condition in the applied current. This effectively blocked any possible backrush possibly induced by the capacitor discharge. Tesla originally used atmospheric pressure to resist the instantaneous formation of arcs across the heavy gap space of this component. He later experimented with various high pressures and different gases. Each experiment provided new and unexpected disruption effects.

Victorian researchers such as Sir John Rayleigh discovered the truly strange behavior of nitrogen gas when electrified. Tubes filled with nitrogen retained their electrified state for a long time after the current source had been removed. Glowing with a strange peach colored light, many wondered whether this might not be a natural ætheric process in action. Tesla investigated nitrogen gas as an atmosphere for his disrupter because it seemed to contain an essential secret. Perhaps it would release a more uncontaminated ætheric current for his primaries. The extraordinary efficiency of the magnetic arc disrupter in developing ætheric currents derived from several principles. Tesla saw that electrical current was really a complex combination of æther and electrons. When electricity was applied to the disrupter a primary fractioning process took place. Electrons were forcibly expelled from the gap by the strong magnetic influence. The æther streams, neutral in charge, remained flowing through the circuit however. The magnetic disrupter was his primary means for fractionating the electrons from the æther particles.

In his later developments, Tesla described arc radiopower devices which employed pure nitrogen plasmas. Electrified with the power of a high voltage DC generator, these magnetic ducted devices fired explosive blasts of nitrogen plasma. To this day, no vacuum tube radiogenerator can ever approach the pure power obtained through such high powered nitrogen arc disrupters. Applying this kind of "blast" to circuitry produced a host of unexpected effects. When the blast was applied to thick copper strapping, stray electrons were apparently thrust out of the current flow. These plasma blasts often leaped up to a height of twenty feet, a violent and totally unexpected response. In some cases this disrupter produced bluewhite lightning like discharges, an action which proved the expulsion of electronic currents from the primary circuit (Lehr). Yet, within the gap could be seen a dense stream of whitefire; a stream of purified æther gas.

There was a reason why nitrogen worked best in this capacity. It was an electron "absorber". Electronic charge was best absorbed and carried out of the current when nitrogen gas was employed. Magnetic thrusting drove the electronic charge away, the cause of bluish lightning-like bolts, Copper produced far too much electronic charge, the discharges difficult to restrain. There had to be a material which would pass æther without adding electrons through bombardment. Tesla found that the use of carbon was well-suited to this purpose. Carbon proved to have the greatest effect in maintaining a purified æther state in the "cleansed" streams. Tesla replaced all the copper with carbon, finding that the unmanageable lightning bolts were substantially reduced in size. This potent device utilized two large ball-shaped carbon electrodes which were highly polished (Lehr).

Magnetically cleansed of their accompanying electron populations, Tesla began to discover the phenomena accompanying ætheric currents. Here was renewed evidence that electrical current was indeed a complex mixture of particles. Once a well expressed and well endorsed theory, the notion of current as a complex combination of streaming particles, was not limited to electrons. In fact, no one knew exactly what electrical carriers were. In this lack of definition, many anomalous such discoveries ensued; a study absolutely required for those who would claim to be qualitative researchers.

Furthermore, this view explained all "action at a distance". The "tension" in space between electrostatically charged objects was viewed as a literal streaming flow of æther particles from positive to negative. The static charges themselves were thought to be "constrictions" through which space flowing æther could be automatically directed. Electrostatic charge was equated with æther pressures. Electrostatic fields were viewed as rectified streams of æther. The "dielectric field", the "dielectricity" of which so many now speak, was once held to be a streaming of æther particles among charged bodies. But no one knew how to release that æther stream from the adhesive electron sheaths in which æther remained naturally imprisoned. Luigi Galvani had intimated the "atmosphere" or "aura" of metals when, in 1620, he found that large metal plates could exert powerfully penetrating effects on the heart and respiration, as well as induce sleep or vitality. These effects were greatly magnified when grounded or elevated above ground. In these early discoveries, there remained new mysteries.

Being that æther streams flowed so powerfully between strong electrostatic charges, some posited the possibility of deriving energy from the flow. All attempts however at interrupting and sufficiently resisting such directed streams proved hopeless. Æther was very obviously able to be stopped by no natural material! Tesla began to believe that it was only the lack of appropriate materials and systems which prevented the pure use of this momentum stream; a puzzle which baffled Dr. Joseph Henry and Michael Faraday. Because their available materials, metals, were capable only of operating on the more gross electrons, technology had been shaped and limited.

Magneto-induction was the result of limits imposed by existing technology. Magneto-induction used electrons and not æther to effect force exchanges. Because electrons were not ultimate particles, not the ultimate particles generated in Nature, they could not supply an endless source of momentum. These induction devices had to be moved to produce motion! Tesla already saw the directions in which his technology could move. The elimination of electrons from æther currents already provided him with uncommon activities. Uncommon at least from the standpoint of pure "electric" or "electrical" phenomena, here were effects which could find no resolution in electrical science. This was æther physics, the foundation of an unknown and unexplored realm. Tesla knew that the resultant technology from this realm would change the world in more ways than even he could yet realize.

New and more powerful expressions of this ætheric streaming action were produced in his nitrogen supplied magnetic disrupter. The abrupt high voltage discharge applied by his dynamo managed to first expand the electron-constricted æther streams beyond their normal cross-section. The nascent electrons were made to pass in a burst through a magnetic field, to which they powerfully responded. Æther is neutral. Tesla saw that electrical currents were actually streams of æther and its surrounding "twist" of electrons. In this regards, the chief attribute of nitrogen in the magnetic disrupter seemed to be the absorption and removal of electrons from the stream. It was obvious that this system effectively and forcefully separated electrons from the neutral æther particles inherent in the dynamo-supplied current. Once the æther stream had been cleared of its too constricting electronic envelope, it could flow freely.

The current remaining in the disrupter was a purified ætheric stream. It was this stream which was visible, flowing a bright silver-white light between the electrodes. This stream continued flowing through the thick copper strap. Bursts of æther were thus applied to any object within the copper strap, an exposure which produced uncommon effects. Tesla sought the elimination of copper from his transformers. Tesla designed a hollow tubular glass Transformer which was to utilize a special gas medium in place of the copper wire. Tesla believed that this design would produce the most purified ætheric streams imaginable. The elimination of copper would prevent any subsequent electronic manufacture capable of contaminating his magnetically purified æther streams. It is in fact probable that he did experiment with these designs.

The magnetic nitrogen gas disrupter was developed well beyond even this stage. Until well into the 1930's, Tesla continued to speak of the device capable of producing intense rays. It was an open ended tube, one which surrounded an electrified terminal with a streaming jet of "suitable fluid". Through such means, Tesla claimed the release of collimated rays having "transcendent intensity". Tesla therefore appropriated means by which electrons were eliminated from currents, while ætheric components were accelerated and released. Tesla was no longer working with "electricity". Tesla worked with æther currents.

New and startling effects could be obtained when once the separation process, the fractioning process, had been engaged. Tesla found that æther streams, though harmless to the body, were often devastating for more metallic things. Passage through various kinds of matter always produced new and strange effects. To illustrate the fact that these currents were not electrical, not some new manifestation of electronic current, Tesla often publicly performed a very strange demonstration. He grasped the upper terminal of one of his large Transformers with one hand, while in the other hand holding a thick metal bar. Æther current flowed through carbonaceous and watery media without harm. Nevertheless, Tesla dramatically proved the strange bombarding power of these non-electronic currents as the metal in his hand either melted or exploded. The reaction of materials was entirely due to the bombardment effect of æther on the matter. But matter alone was not the only variable which could effect new ætheric phenomena. Geometries also shaped the phenomena.

Highly segmented geometries fractioned electronic charge from æther by resisting and blocking the electrons normally constrained to move through the wire length. Blocked by the high resistant because of impulsive applications of current, æther was free to surge over the segments fluidically. Tesla now saw that the ability of æther to pass over segmented metallic surfaces, such as his helical and spiral Transformers, was only a fortuitous attribute. It was accidental that he observed this phenomenon at all. But Tesla found numerous other attributes of this energetic stream, attributes which manifested themselves only when æther interacted with certain materials and laboratory components. All important to these responses of æther, among the symmetries of metals and insulators, was the impulse duration applied in generating the stream. It was the brevity of each impulse in the projected train which stimulated each response.

Ætheric streams could be projected in extremely parallel paths by solid sheets of polished metal. Concave mirrors focussed the streams. Cone shaped hoods focussed the streams. Placing gas filled spheres in copper cylinders produced potent and directed rays. Tesla investigated the various aspects of rays which his transmitters now projected with great interest. His radiant system was like no other. This projective radiance bore all the characteristics of light, yet was invisible. Tesla called these manifestations "dark rays" and "dark light". He found that they could be reflected when both their impulse rate was a specific interval, and when appropriate metal surfaces were intercepted.

Tesla observed that shadowgraphs could be made by his beam projectors when intercepted by photographic films. He accidentally discovered the effect while using light from his beam projectors to photograph himself and several friends. The developed image was one which revealed far more than the portrait itself. Tesla found that "dark rays" could pass through walls, producing images on fluorescent screens. The effects were not X-Rays, being reflected from thick metal walls. With the simple first such projectors, Nikola Tesla found it possible to wirelessly illuminate lamps at great distances, push objects, charge objects, and burn holes through objects. In short, any amount of power could be delivered along the beamray channels.

In this we glimpse subatomic particle streams not completely electronic in nature. The abrupt disruption of current stimulates an energetic release, the result of violence done to matter. Tesla found it possible to focus and beam these rays, effects which many have sought to reproduce. But despite the repeated failure of academes and well-intentioned experimenters to reproduce these effects, one individual dominates the scene. In these most important demonstrations, vindications of Teslian Technology, it must be mentioned that Eric Dollard successfully reproduced several of these effects and made the results available in a series of videocassettes. In these, Mr. Dollard demonstrates the charging of capacitors by the radiant emission of impulse-supplied vacuum lamps. This charging action occurred across a small space between the side of these lamps and the blunt face of a high voltage capacitor. This anomalous feat was also followed by a remarkable demonstration of mass-repulsion, and another of mass-attraction. In addition, while using gaseous projector tubes as Tesla prescribes, Mr. Dollard demonstrated the transmission of pulsating æther across the laboratory, with the subsequent absorption and conversion of the same into a measurable current.

Tesla discussed the possibility of beaming energy directly into the night sky, causing the very air to fluoresce. In such discussions, he suggested that night illumination of the sky could be used by ocean going vessels as a feature of safety. In connection with these topics, he stimulated much exciting thought on the notion that energy could be obtained from the sky, once a "world system" of beamray transmitters was established. No doubt, those whose fortunes relied on fuel and powerlines did not appreciate these candid talks. It was well appreciated that Tesla could achieve the seemingly impossible things of which he so openly spoke.

## RADIANT ENERGY

All of these empirical discoveries brought Tesla into the fascinating examination of æther stream behavior in matter in 1891. Æther behaved in strange ways when forced to tunnel through metals, gases, stone, glasses, jewels. In its fundamental principles, Teslian Technology involves impact and force exchange. In methodic succession, Tesla found which metals and organic substances ætheric streams penetrate without resistance. He also determined which materials offered considerable resistance to the streams, a valuable piece of information. The fact that æther streams could be substantially deformed in passing through certain such materials indicated the degree to which such materials were internally arranged. When æther streams were compelled to flow through given metals, usually good electrical conductors such as silver and copper, the particulate impacts released new species. These often appeared as darting sparks of various colorations, contaminating the pure ætheric flow. Æther particles were extremely mobile, virtually massless when compared with electrons, and could therefore pass through matter with very little effort. Electrons could not "keep up" with either the velocity or the permeability of ætheric particles. According to this view, æther particles were infinitesimals, very much smaller than electrons themselves.

The ætheric carriers contained momentum. Their extreme velocity matched their nearly massless nature, the product of both becoming a sizable quantity. They moved with superluminal velocity, a result of their incompressible and massless nature. Whenever a directed radiant matter impulse begins from some point in space, an incompressible movement occurs instantly through space to all points along that path. Such movement occurs as a solid ray, an action defying modern considerations of signal retardations in space. Incompressible raylines can move through any distance instantly. Should the path be 300,001 kilometers long, the impulse at the source end will each that point as quickly as at all other points. This is superluminal velocity. Radiant matter behaved incompressibly. In effect, this stream of radiant matter, virtually massless and hydrodynamically incompressible, was a pure energy! Radiant Energy.

In addition to this inherent momentum, æther streams would actually interact with matter only with the proper conductive materials were stressed with the proper impulse intervals. This understanding provided an essential clue to the real nature of matter and energy, a foundation which was empirically pioneered by Tesla and theoretically developed by Dr. Gustav Le Bon. The interchange of energy into matter and matter into energy presupposed a fundamental "materium". Victorians considered the ætheric gases to be this materium. One could theoretically pass a concentrated æther stream through any material and produce new elements and energetic emanations. These transitions occurred as a continuum which lacked any fixed "stations" of mass or of energy. For Victorians, the progressive passage from matter into energy or from energy to matter did not occur in fixed "quanta". Tesla had the first experimental evidence that this was indeed possible. His statements concerning material generation and transmutation were perceived as ravings.

Opinions be damned. Superior technology affords a very few researchers with access to deeper than conventional realities. Nature reveals levels which form the infrastructure to things observable through available scientific means. Deeper infrastructures require a succession of superior technologies, the gantries of Nature being thus reveled to equipped human explorers. Regardless of opinion, Tesla found all too numerous facts which later contradicted the emerging science of quantum physics. Despite its promoted openness to skeptical analysis, academic science has always demonstrated its unfortunate tendency to universalize every theory which offers some explanation for a part of natural phenomena. In this we perceive an essential and knowledge-devastating flaw. Enlarging the microscopic issues to encompass the whole is worse than a tragic myopic lapse. In the bold face of plentiferous natural contradictions, it is laughable evidence of stubborn pride at academic levels supposedly incapable of exercising such base human sentiments. All too flawed and all too human. Be sure of this, Nature cannot be codified in the simplistic dynamics of moving matter and energetic exchanges. Nature is far more integrated and articulate, endowed with potentials not now thought scientific.

Indeed in the ætheric continuum, there are none of the graphic details concerning quanta. There are no structured levels, no quanta, in which ætheric energy is constrained. Quantum physics applies to a very specific realm of energetic transactions, one whose properties are entirely bound up in considerations of inertia. The physics of the ætheric continuum knows no such limitations, details, or rigorous fixtures. Incompressible, infinitesimal in cross sections, æther gases permeate matter. Tesla stated that all kinetic energy was ultimately traceable directly back to the ætheric atmosphere. Ætheric movements provoke the "inertia" in Nature. In exploring the ultra-gaseous ætheric medium, Tesla produced a method for bombarding various materials with intensely concentrated ætheric streams. This first began with his search for a superior ætheric lamp, one which required only an ætheric supply to produce an intense brilliance.

Supported on a single lead wire, these bulbs produced then-unheard effects. Tesla placed jewels, light metals, heavy metals, non-metals, and radioactive materials in these globes. He immersed these materials in various gaseous atmospheres. He finally tried hard vacuum. Æther streams exploded through the various crystalline lattices placed atop the single electrode. Each unidirectional impulse passed directly through the material and out into surrounding space. Electrode matter was simply evaporated, converted to æther and other particles. The hardest, most refractory materials simply vanished away after several seconds of this treatment. Tesla said that impulses acted as tiny "hammers", passing from within the substance itself out to space. Here was proof that æther was converting matter into pure energy. Tesla noted that the radiant expulsions actually passed through the globes. In many cases they left only a faint metallic stain. Soon, continued exposure to the æther streams drove even these stains away.

Radiant Energy was not thermionic emission, as others have tried to rationalize the phenomenon. Thermionic electrons do not pass through glass envelopes of the thickness Tesla employed. Here was a distinct phenomenon, one which did not in fact manifest with other than impulse applications. Tesla alternately called these pure ætheric expulsions "radiant matter" and "radiant energy". Neutral in charge and infinitesimal in both mass and cross-section, Radiant Energy was unlike any light seen since his work was concluded. If asked whether Radiant Energy can be compared with any existing physical item today, one would have to decline. We cannot draw parallels between Radiant Energy and the light energies with which science has long been preoccupied. But if light-like at all, Radiant Energy is possessed of qualities unlike any light which we have learned to generate. And this is precisely the problem. Tesla Technology is Impulse Technology. Without the disruptive, unidirectional IMPULSE, there are no Radiant Energy effects. Generating this Radiant Energy requires special energetic applications, applications of succinct and brief impulses. These impulses must be generated through the explosive agency of a disruptive discharge just as Tesla prescribed.

The problem Tesla faced in obtaining purified Radiant Energy currents was found to be the very conductive media which he was forced to use as conductors. Materials appropriate to the release of contaminant-free emanations could no longer be the familiar copper or even silver. Conductors now were necessarily the very light metals. For this purpose, Tesla relied on metals such as magnesium, aluminum, and even beryllium. With these metals as conductors, electrodes, targets, and windows, Tesla produced a series of long vacuum tubes. Made specifically for beaming ætheric streams, each of these beamray tubes employed a single concave electrode in one end. In many cases there was a thin metallic window, usually aluminum or beryllium, at the opposite end. The large and heavy-walled glass tube was encased in a lead shield to protect the operator from inadvertent dangerous emissions. When activated by the disrupter, an intensely focussed ætheric stream was projected from the free end. This beam took the form of a tight thready ray. Tesla had initial difficulty insulating the applications end of this beamray tube. Preventing the wild arcing of supply line energy was problematic, premature æther discharges often darting around the tube rather than flowing through it. This problem was solved by enclosing the tube with a second glass jacket, and pumping mineral oil through the outer sleeve.

The pressure within these bulbs became anomalous and high. Despite the hard vacuum which Tesla had first provided, these bulbs often exploded. In certain modern reproductions of these experiments, conducted by the renown Eric Dollard, vacuum bulbs so activated actually ruptured in tiny holes, and yet continued to produce their "vacuum" discharges! Mr. Dollard and the witnesses of these experiments reported hearing a hissing issuance which emerged from the glass rupture holes. Once the activating energy was removed, the globes simply imploded. Here is evidence of a radiant material emission, whose powerful streams exert great pressure.

## BEAMRAYS

Tesla found that these globe-expelled streams manifested strange effects beyond the glass containers. He was able to charge capacitors to dangerous charge levels at great distances by focussing the light from these globes. Their light was electrified! In bombardments, æther did more than eject quanta. In this special light, Tesla saw that æther streams were manufacturing electrons and other detritus. This provoked his study of quanta, particles which he considered tightly constricted streams of æther. Deformed by material passage into ultramicroscopic foci, Tesla believed that particles could be "undone" by appropriate means. This would release the ætheric contents, an insignificant amount of energy per particle. The stability of particulate matter depended only upon the fixed movements of æther particles in their constricted radii. Particulate charges, charge carriers themselves, demonstrated a remarkable consistency in either projecting or absorbing æther streams. In this phenomenon, Tesla perceived an ultimate æther energy source. In his later years, he would seek means to release a purified ætheric energy.

Tesla experimented with ruby, zirconia, diamond, sapphire, carborundum, each producing a brilliant light until disintegration. He simply could not find a refractory material which could withstand the passage of this radiant flux without vaporizing. The lamps which Tesla finally succeeded in developing, carbon button vacuum globes, did not require an "amperage". These lamps gave off intensely brilliant light approaching the intensity and quality of true sunshine. The reason for his reliance on carbon was truly intriguing. Used in latter stages of his Transformers, metals could become deadly producers of electron dartlets. Ætheric bombardments manufactured electrons in copper terminals. These contaminated the otherwise smooth and harmless æther streams. Tesla sought a material whose response to æther bombardment would not result in

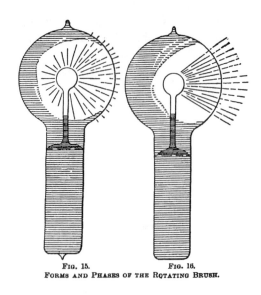

Fig. 15.  Fig. 16.
FORMS AND PHASES OF THE ROTATING BRUSH.

the introduction of electrons or any other free ionic charge. Carbon performed well in permitting a smooth and unhindered flow of æther, one which remained essentially unchanged. In fact, it was with his carbon button lamps that Tesla made some of the greatest strides in æther technology (see figure).

The streams proceeding from within these lamps could be so adjusted, by means of an adjusted rapidity in the impulse rate, so as to appear rainbow colored, flame-like, brush-like, or intensely white. These descriptions are not to be taken as the common varieties of brush or flame discharges. Indeed, ordinary electrical flame discharges require DC or low frequency alternations. True Tesla flame-like discharges require highest impulse rates. Experiments have successfully duplicated these effects, the result of work accomplished nearly a decade ago by Eric Dollard. The flimmering streams are like no other electrical discharge ever produced by familiar means. When properly adjusted, these discharges closely approximate the true appearance of the aurora borealis. Their colorations change unpredictably from second to second, a phenomenon not observed with ordinary electrical discharges. But at special impulse rates, these white discharges disappear, and a "dark light" emanation is powerfully produced: a "very special radiation". It is neutral, penetrating, and not of a species identified with Ultraviolet, X-Ray, or Gamma Ray, or neutron streams.

By 1893, Tesla had designed and operated signalling systems which used such globes to flash telegraphic signals across space without apparent loss to their receivers. These ætheric signalling systems required no amplifiers, being powerful and static-free. From his South Fifth Avenue Laboratory, Tesla had already been sending loud æther ray signals up and down the Hudson River for years with little more than small ball antennas. He was the first to develop radio circuits and components. Tesla discovered that substances such as selenium behaved as soft receptors of ætheric energies. Poised in solid copper cones, uncharacteristic of even shortwave radio signalling systems, Tesla demonstrated both broadcast and directed beam signalling apparatus. Boxed in beautiful mahogany with brass trims, his ætheric signalling system was compact and powerful. Tesla found that very low powered radiant lamp transmitters had effect on the ætheric atmosphere of the earth. Modulating this dynamic æther envelope effected very long range communications in excess of the normal line-of-sight limitations. These developments came several years before Marconi ever appeared on the scene with his concoction of plagiarized equipment. The Tesla Radio System used potent ætheric streams, not weak waves. Tesla illustrated this fact in later years, when Marconi wave radio began evidencing all of its inefficiencies and failed potentials.

Tesla Radio did not operate in the electrical wave continuum, nor was it reliant on waves. Tesla Radio operated in the ætheric atmosphere, and utilized "dark light rays" of real force. Ætheric rays, thin thready ætheric streams, exceeded the power and penetrability of waves by an incalculable degree. Tesla Radio receiving circuitry used the power in the transmitted radiance to power the little compact receiving stations, an unlikely possibility with weak wave radio. Tesla soon adopted these systems for telephonic modes of operation. An onboard battery was provided for the transmit circuit of his portable radios. These power requirements were indeed minimal, a marvel for those who very later on were compelled by court action to examine the contents of Tesla Radios. Power was provided by a mere dry cell or at most, a very small storage battery.

When examined closely by court officers years later, his patents in these regards often raised dubious expressions in the faces of his unenlightened critics. In both size and effectiveness, their transmissions were exceedingly powerful, an anomalous condition by all existing standards of the day. Those who knew nothing of the power inherent in ætheric streams could not conceive of a passive receiving system which claimed to exchange telephonic signals without excessive componentry, or an active transmitting circuit which used such little power to reach the claimed great distances.

But his curiosity did not stop with this success. Later vacuum tubes were tremendously modified and arranged so that æther streams would impinge upon special targets. Some of these tubes poised the targets entirely within the tube. Others placed the materials at one end of the tubes, windows through which streamed æther and detrital components.

Researcher and author Jorge Resines has obtained information on the various remarkable tubes which Tesla produced throughout these years, an astounding collection. In a recent publication, Mr. Resines produced drawings of these, a remarkable assortment resembling modern military radiopower tubes. Tesla made extensive use of uranium, thorium, and radium as targets. It is probable that Tesla began his research in compact æther power generators when these latter varieties were employed. Tesla found that the heavier metals produced an amazing variety of contaminating particulate emissions. It was the resistance of elements and other materials which produced so many well known, and other new energetic species when bombarded by ætheric streams. Academes who limited themselves to catalogues of fixed photon and particle species were not observing the most fundamental dynamics, contenting themselves only with the by-products produced in resistive interactions with ætheric streams. If the electron-rich emissions from his original copper sphere terminals were life-hazardous discharges, the emissions from these tubes were far more dangerous.

Tesla discovered the varieties of energetic species emerging from the target windows long before Roentgen announced the discovery of X-rays. Tesla had already catalogued the existence of these and other æther-contaminating emissions. His conception of radioactivity included the notion that "space impinging" æther streams were bombarding matter of appropriate atomic cross-section. Those densely packed lattices, capable of intercepting and diffracting incoming æther, manifested a continual outward expulsion of particles and energetic emissions. It was from experimental examples such as these that Tesla drew analogues, explaining natural radioactivity. Besides citing the large nuclear cross-section of heavy atoms and their usual radioactivity, Tesla also believed that special atomic symmetries could diffract or deflect incoming æther streams sufficiently enough to produce radioactive emissions in lighter metals.

The projected æther streams could be directed through very long distances without the slightest sign of divergence. They were intensely powerful. Indeed these rays seemed to self-constrict, a nature unknown in the electromagnetic spectrum. Soon Tesla began examining the possibility of beaming æther streams between special towers, a powerline analogue which substituted æther beams for powerlines. In this manner, power would not be wasted away in all directions as he had originally planned to do. Now, a much improved system would permit the conservation and concentration of æther energy along tight thready beams. Power could be distributed to neighborhoods from such central tower receivers along horizontal radii to consumers. The entire distribution system resembled a neurological network. Beamed from tower to tower throughout the countryside, ætheric energy streams from central stations could thus be distributed everywhere without substantial loss (see figure).

The ætheric beams had other, more deliberate applications, which startled Tesla and all those who witnessed his many experiments. These beams could

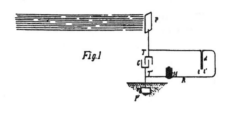

*Fig.1*

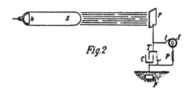

*Fig.2*

be focussed to a tiny pinpoint and directed into metals. The streams simply sprayed over the surfaces. But when the impulse durations were carefully adjusted, the spray became a needle which easily pierced the plate. In this permeating stream of force, metal plates simply melted. In some cases they exploded. Tesla found it possible to burn diamond with such pinpoints of force. Indeed by such results, his concept of "force" had been completely revolutionized. What he had both observed and learned in these issues were cunningly preserved by him in numerous press interviews. His pre-planned statements had as their intention a provocation of the deepest kind. Toward whom were these principally aimed? Toward all those who, while not interested or excited enough about his findings to learn more, yet maintained their distant and aloof luxury of criticism and slander. Only one person maintained the closest and almost fatherly bond with him throughout these years. That person was Sir William Crookes, Tesla's hero and mentor. Their continuous and sincere correspondence remained one of the only sources of human solace upon which Tesla could both seek and rely.

While experimenting with his vacuum globes, Tesla observed the linearity of the expelled streams. When projected from small spherical electrodes, these ætheric rays travelled in sharp radii from the center. So infinitesimal were the carriers of this ætheric stream that they were able to reveal the inner atomic lattice of crystalline matter. Small crystals of metal or gemstones produced characteristic point patterns on the surface of the globes. It was apparent that æther particles, the neutral sub-electronic particles that Tesla termed "Radiant Energy", actually passed through the material which were poised on the electrodes "from the inside out". That is, they passed through the atomic lattices of those materials and, in so doing, carried information in the stream. What sort of information? Nuclei diffracted these infinitesimals on their rapid journeys up through the electrode nuclei. In doing so, their otherwise uniform density was deformed. That the particles of this Radiant Energy could pass through the atomic lattices at all gave proof that these were neutral particles. For Tesla, thy were the result of extreme bombardments, where matter is absolutely sheared beyond its subatomic conditions. Tesla, along with Dr. Le Bon, adhered to the notion that a smooth transition existed between energy and matter. A whole spectrum of materializations could therefore exist when appropriate bombarding matter was secured. Tesla believed he had found the most powerful agency for such bombardments, an agency released only through the explosive successions of his Transformer.

## TELEVISION

Because these streams could carry such detailed information, Tesla began to imagine a means for transmitting visual information. The additional characteristic by which æther streams maintained their strict rectilinear paths in transit, stimulated Tesla to hypothesize that broad æther streams could carry pictorial imagery. Projected from broad plates, and forming densely "parallel" streams, such a system could carry images to any distance.

Potent and penetrating, ætheric rays provided a new kind of light for an equally new kind of communications system. Tesla stated that whole images could be projected through such invisible radiant matter rays. Such a visual exchange system would be as simple as a slide projector, though obviously more potent. In this, Tesla early conceived of a television system which, yet today, remains revolutionary.

Striking in its analogue to the "magick lanterns" of the Victorian Epoch, Tesla produced a design lacking the complex scanning mechanisms which plagued all later picture transmission systems. Invisibly travelling through walls, ætheric streams could be captured and resolved by using special sensitive plates, on which live images could be focussed. Image loaded ætheric streams would be projected from central broadcast stations at impulse rates which would simply pass through all material obstacles. Invisible in their transit through intervening spaces, such whole image transmissions could be received and translated back into visibility through the imposition of special phosphor-coated plates. Images would travel through space as a whole block. These images could be beamed directly from source to receiver. Signals would be strong, requiring no amplification or additional energy supply. Signals would be noise free, the dense ætheric continuum being completely different that the harsh electromagnetic continuum. Dark light projection through walls! Tesla described a means by which several such signals could be superimposed without mutual interference. A simple tuning mechanism in the receiver would select the images desired. Tesla related that such superimposition could accommodate thousands of simultaneous signals, thousands of channels. Whole

image transmission of extreme definition, without a scanning mechanism, was made possible by the ætheric stream. It would be years later, in 1917, that Tesla described a modification of this system of whole image television. In a subsequent interview, Tesla described a system by which distant objects could be whole-imaged. His design incorporated all of the components planned for his commercial television system. His modified system was a remote-locating device. Again lacking the complexity of scanning systems and other heavy support components, any ship equipped with his fluorescent screens could "image" a distant ship or submarine by projecting a ray beam through air, fog, rain, or even water. The rays were unstoppable, being reflected whenever they intercepted a metallic hood or hull.

Tesla's shipborne beamray projector would pulse ætheric streams, of very specific intervals, out across a horizontal plane. Tesla stated that this "electric ray", when encountering any obstacle, would be reflected back to the source point. Here, the otherwise invisible beam would be visually resolved by the same special phosphor-coated plates as planned for the commercial television system. In this announcement, Tesla leaked a secret concerning the essential nature of his æther beamrays. Apparently, through the application of very specific impulses at the source, æther streams could actually be reflected from matter. The Tesla range-locator, a system designed to spot submarines or battleships alike, was simple, potent, failproof, and effective. Here again, Tesla made use of the extreme definition provided through the beamed projection of ultra-infinitesimal "Radiant Energy". Here again was evidence that neutral Radiant Energy could be made to interact with matter simply by varying the pulsed projection interval. The military was not interested at the time.

## ÆTHER DRIFT

Once initiated and maintained, the space flowing currents from a beamray tube could not be extinguished. Difficult at first to believe, but the æther currents from such devices for a time continued. Tesla found it possible to produce long lasting currents which persisted throughout his laboratory and demonstration spaces. All he needed to do was turn on a beamray tube to stimulate the space flow. Tesla found that the removal of æther currents from a space in which they had been directed, was not easy. No, æther currents were not easily extinguished. Radiant Energy did not behave as all other familiar energy forms. Here were artificial "æther drifts", a topic which represented a deep mystery. Momentum. The momentum of æther currents was sufficient to maintain their continuous passage through any space for a time. An initiatory period was required to establish the current. Æther responded to pressure changes. Any strong currents in the æther would gather other energy from the surrounding ætheric atmosphere. Once started, these would continue for an hour or more.

Tesla demonstrated this principle of action. Lamps remained brightly lit long after power had been withdrawn. When merely placed in the paths where æther currents had been directed, lamps could be reignited. This condition persisted for several minutes, evidence that æther currents kept flowing long after the beamray tube was extinguished. Tesla very casually mentioned this fact when describing a process by which he could "obtain energy for hours" after his impulse transmitters were disconnected. Tesla described this "ionized" condition in the ambient medium. He also described the nature of strange discharges obtained from organic materials. Clothes, hair, and wooden objects produced soft white, gossamer sparks for an equivalent hour or more. These were long, very clingy, and thready. Strange gossamer! Such discharges do not sound familiar. They are certainly not electrical phenomena, being the very obvious result of an intense bombardment in a far deeper natural realm of energy. From any electrical vantage alone, all of these phenomena sounded absolutely ridiculous and overdone, the "poetic" fabrications of a madman.

In addition, Tesla found that space-traversing currents gained extra power from the surrounding ætheric supply. This extra supply was pulled into the current channel, guided only by its own momentum. This was why æther power did not diminish as other energetic manifestations. Æther, possessed of momentum, did not suffer from frictional losses either. Æther beams remained rigidly fixed in their position, flowing on and on until the gradual diminution process finally brings them to a halt. An experimenter, Mr. Gregory Hodowanec, has conducted experiments in this fascinating field. He has successfully corroborated these claims of Tesla, showing in a most remarkable and simple manner that any impulse, movement, or stimulation in the ætheric atmosphere "continues to flow" in place for hours at a time. Along with the gravitic waves with which he is principally concerned, Mr. Hodowanec employs capacitors to detect ætheric impulses in space. Most remarkably, he has extended the science of æther into an exploration of gravitation.

Quite obviously, Tesla Transformers were able to stimulate strong flow lines in the ætheric atmosphere. These surged through his special vacuum tubes along any direction in which they were aimed. He found himself, like his mentor Sir William Crookes, searching through laboratory space for evidence of atmospheric æther drifts. Sir William had predicted that "ectoplasmic disturbances" in the ætheric continuum might be detected with special high vacuum discharge globes of his own early design. Used as a scrying telescope for peering into the spectral world, he had hoped that it would reveal a new dimension. Toward this and other ends, Dr. Crookes continually made tests with his large globular discharge devices, carefully unpacking them from their special velvet-lines boxes in old English estates. There in large darkened rooms, while peering into the mirrored concave electrodes covered over in white flimmering radiance, the whimsical bespectacled man with the twinkling smile eagerly sought ghosts.

Another "detail" which Tesla discovered dealt with the "pliant" nature of the æther. When appropriately stimulated by his methods, æther could be made to execute strange convolutions. Æther was incredibly responsive to pressure changes anywhere along its path. The slightest effective exertion on such a stream produced an instantaneous corresponding movement throughout the whole flow. Ætheric streams behaved in a "stiff" way, much like high pressure jets of water fired through pinholes. They were not always visible in transit, producing a white streaming light only near the point of their departure from his special high vacuum tubes. These beams were not composed of electrons, X-Rays, or Gamma Rays. Once released and directed ætheric beams did not diverge or bend unless striking into appropriate materials.

Tesla forever maintained that natural radioactivity was the weak by-product of a powerful, but unmeasurable dielectric flux whose source was space æther. Focussing into dense nuclei, æther was diverted and blocked. This concentrated bombardment produced particulate and photonic emanations through "spallation", divergent energetic impacts between particles. But using dielectric energy would be using the very source of these radioactive manifestations. It was curious that æther, being the far greater power source, was so very soft in its natural state. One could stand exposed to an æther stream and never become ill. Tesla found to his delight that æther streams of specific impulse were beneficial, and exposed himself to their streams daily for periods of an hour or more as desired. Tesla inferred that æther particles passed through the body as if it were transparent. The only time they interacted was when the pulsations were such that physiology began to pulsate in rhythmic successions with the incoming æther pulses. In his use of ætheric streams, Tesla found a remarkable resultant elevation in both sensation and consciousness. Ideas seemed to emerge and visions clarify during these exposures. Interactions of bio-organic matter with æther pulsations became the source of vitalizing influences. Æther was neutral, and did not ionize matter unless focussed and delivered as a short duration impulse train.

Tesla learned that he could actually impress an ætheric stream with changes from the reception site, a true anomaly. Æther was so responsive to manipulations from the received end of a stream that cascade reactions would quickly spread along the stream back to its source. Thus, a receiver could literally force the æther source to feed it wherever it moved! This was the result of pressure laws, superluminal speeds, and ætheric density. Any rarefaction in the æther flow would instantly tug æther into the lower pressure volume. Æther responses occurred with superluminal velocity, conditions being established and strengthened after a small such manipulation of the flow. Tesla saw that he could literally "shape" the æther flow within certain degrees of freedom. Most engineers simply failed to comprehend how anyone could exert a powerful such effect on a gaseous atmosphere which was supposedly inaccessible!

Additionally, beams of æther acquired extra power in transit across any long space, an essential anomaly. This is why beamrays of Radiant Energy never weakened after being projected for long distances. This was an unheard condition, where otherwise "lost energy" maintains and gathers strength after being expended across space. Obviously, Radiant Energy was finding a mysterious energetic supply while in transit. None of the expectable energy laws of natural diminution applied to Radiant Energy. This was because the æther was everpresent, a ready and undiminished supply of energy. Æther was a gaseous radiance, often invisible to the eye, but a powerful pressure source. Along with several colleagues of the day, Tesla firmly ascribed to the ætheric theory of gravitation. Gravitation was evidence that a groundward ætheric pressure was at work, permeating mass and producing fixed relationships of attraction with respect to the earth proper. The apparent constant acceleration of different falling masses was accordingly calculated as a function of density and cross-section. Theoretically, the concept remains a curiously flawless explanation of gravitation. Perhaps the recent scientific world too much resembles the world of "pop" art and music, where fickle fads and novelties are more important than expressions of excellence.

It seemed confirmed that æther, Radiant Energy, was indeed possessed of strange responses to external action. It actually interacted with receivers of its penetrating force. If allowed to strike distant targets for example, a strange

transformation in the otherwise straight path lines could take place. Beams would become tightly constricted at the target, self-focussing themselves into the material. But subsequent movements in targeted matter would cause deflections and undulations in the otherwise straight beam. The influence of the recipient, of the target, could very often work its way back to the source and force a deflection! Æther beams were thus extremely sensitive, and could "track" a target (see figure).

Despite every twist or turn, once an æther beam had constricted into a material target, there was no escaping it. These dynamics were later viewed in a series of celebrated illustrations which Tesla directed and approved. One sees flying craft and ocean vessels drawing power from the one of the World Broadcast Stations, the bright beam "tracking" each target and supplying it with motive power. In this, it was evident that æther streams were ruled by pressure principles, and responded to pressure changes instantaneously. But pressures in what atmosphere?

Additionally, while it was possible for Tesla to direct such beams of æther in any direction, these were not the most powerful manifestations of æther flow in the environment. Tesla had indeed found certain very defined natural ætheric drifts, angles along which æther streams seemed to last much, much longer than usual. It was as if some additional power had been added to the beamrays which he launched. He observed the times required for these artificial æther currents to gradually fade out. Though initially strong when launched, their effects did fade eventually. Regardless of their remarkable continuance, a persistence due to ætheric pliancy and momentum, æther currents anywhere directed did not continue forever. They evidenced a diminution, and this suggested an interfering source. Where was it?

Tesla now perceived a much larger vista. He comprehended the successful operation of his first Transformers in the absence of formal ground connections. In these modes, Impulse Transformers were shunting space sourced æther from aerial routes through aerial routes. These modes exchanged æther streams largely in a horizontal plane. This now was not viewed by Tesla as the most powerful embodiment of the system. Complete efficiency, maximum power, was obtained only in connection with the ground. This arrangement placed the apparatus in conformance with natural processes, vast systems whose dominating activities demanded technological conformity. Tesla had discovered a system which had to be geophysical in order to be efficient, a revolutionary concept for the day. This notion hailed back to archane knowledge which placed technology in subservience to natural process. Unlike the mechanistic science which began with the Eighteenth Century, and which challenged Natural Order with a supposed autonomous technology, Tesla had stumbled onto a great and forgotten truth. Here was a technology which could tap a virtually eternal natural process.

Many other ætheric drifts were measured. Shifting and wandering, these could be measured with changes in seasons and weather patterns. Tesla perceived that whorls, eddies, and laminar flow lines revealed a dynamic æther. This was a theme not widely discussed since Descartes drew his conceptual maps of ætheric whirlpools in space. Here then was not a simple and "homogeneous continuum", as Victorian Science believed, whose streams smoothly and effortlessly flowed through the terrestrial environment. Tesla discovered the detail which these theories lacked, through the empirical method which so often corrects and finalizes our knowledge. In this quest, he was indebted to his senses, an absolute reliance on the Qualitative Method which affirmed the greater sensitivity of human perceptions. Tesla placed first emphasis always on the inestimable value of perception and the humanly valuable knowledge which it so often brought.

# SPACE ÆTHER

He again recalled the light from his vacuum bulbs and their strong resemblance to natural sunlight. The mere light from these lamps was filled with a component which produced strong pressure effects and additionally, could charge capacitors. So complete were the electrostatic states of capacitors charged in this manner that mica dielectrics often ruptured under the strain. Tesla knew that ætheric particles, his "Radiant Energy", were being expelled from his single terminal lamps. This produced the pressures felt on the face when exposed to the brilliant light. Entering the metallic layers of the capacitor, these æther particles were manufacturing electrons. This what brought about the electrostatic strain capable of rupturing the dielectrics. There was no electricity in the æther stream per se, the electricity appeared when resisted by appropriate elements. Metals, the good electroconductors, were obviously some of these elements.

But sunshine had these attributes as well. Sunlight contained an ætheric component, previously described by researchers such as Baron Karl von Reichenbach, Gustav Le Bon, and George S. White. Metals in sunlight evidenced absorptions in varieties of response to ætheric penetrations. Dr. Le Bon spoke of his experiments with metals which had been exposed to focussed sunlight, experiments which produced radio activities far in excess of those produced by radium itself. Indeed, there had been those cases where roofing copper, after years of exposure to intense sunlight and natural process, became quite radioactive (Lehr). Exposure to sunlight æther produced bombardments capable of transmuting elements. Additionally, exposure to sunlight produced the same pressure effects as observed in his æther-pulsed vacuum lamps. One often sensed that some energetic component was actually completely penetrating the skin. On the skin surface, academes measured "infrared" and "ultraviolet", the manufactured products of æther streams passing through bio-organic matter.

When Tesla began publishing his thoughts on ætheric particles from space, what he first termed "cosmic rays", the academic derision was unbridled and caustic. One of the chief voices in this assault on Tesla was one young Robert Millikan, who had apparently learned that art of "creative skeptical mockery" to gain favor from his mentors. In later years when academic doldrums required some new creative turn, Dr. Millikan now claimed credit for having discovered "cosmic rays". Had he bothered to read the articles which Tesla had written, and against which he had so very much to say, Millikan would not have been satisfied with his own so-called discoveries. Tesla stated that true cosmic rays were like Radiant Energy, not at all the heavy ions, and gamma rays which Millikan was detecting. In speaking of the prodigious quantities of æther forcibly expelled by the sun and stars, academes of his day thought him quite mad.

Nevertheless, Tesla continued to teach that these radiant particles were undetectable by normal means. Those like Millikan, who succeeded in detecting charged particles from space, and not identified these primary radiant particles. Tesla stated that the so-called "cosmic rays" of the conventional lexicon were tertiary and even quaternary residues, the splattered by-products of collisions stimulated by Radiant Energy. He claimed the means by which he had successfully detected these before the turn of the Century. More than this, Tesla was now about to harness the "eternal wheelworks of Nature".

The ætheric volumes which came to the earth from the space was an incalculable volume, a power source of eternal consequence. It arrived to earth under extreme pressure, a value which Tesla calculated in the range of several "hundred million volts". Tesla stated that the ætheric atmosphere, though often a "dark light", floods the earth at all times with its great power. Tesla stated that both the geointernal radioactive elements and the native heat of the earth was a direct result of ætheric bombardment from space. Although the sun was a dominant source of Radiant Energy, Tesla stated that it was not the only supplier of ætheric particles. Æther was expelled from all points in interstellar space, a constant supply of natural Radiant Energy. Such energy was released by stellar processes. Since the sun was a local æther source, it figured in the total æther supply. The normal space influx was therefore augmented during the daytime by the additional solar supply. Bombarding the earth from all directions, Radiant Energy entered the earth. Once having passed through the crust, it was sufficiently slowed to lodge deep within the mantle. After passing through these miles of rock, the highly pressured and kinetically energetic æther transferred its prodigious energies to the deeper material of the earth itself.

Sunlight. Starlight. Space. Radiant Energy. The connections were too direct to be misleading, the concept too direct to be erroneous. Here was an inescapable probability awaiting application. Just as his æther stream projectors had power to push matter and charge certain metals, so too did sunlight have this inherent potential. Only a means for fully tapping this enormous flow prevented humanity from harnessing the true and most formidable energy in sunlight. Conceiving of the sun, its æther flow, and the earth itself, Tesla recognized that a vast ætheric exchange system was here represented. This system was the self-generative natural source from which energy could simply be absorbed and used. No fuel needed ever be consumed again.

The notion that æther could be resisted by certain materials, was new to the theory of æther. Formerly, this theory ascribed unreal characteristics to æther. Tesla now had empirical facts against which to form a realistic model. Specific matter could deflect ætheric streams. Electrostatic fields as well demonstrated their ability to distort ætheric streams. Here were special facts, having special technological implications. To be empowered in the quest of developing ætheric technology was to be on the very threshold of achieving wonders. In several experimental instances, researchers discovered the complete annihilation of gravitic effects due to extreme positive electrostatic charge. George Piggot showed that it was possible to suspend large beads of silver within a positive monopolar field. Dr. Francis Nipher also demonstrated the complete reversal of gravitational attraction in a modified Cavendish balance. Here too it was found that strong positive electrostatic charge, though completely shielded in Faraday cages, successfully repelled neutral matter. These could only be the result of ætheric interactions.

Tesla now understood why certain geological regions were most "energetic" and conducive to the juncture of electrical communication systems. Old telegraphers and telephone linesmen knew the difference between "good ground" ad "bad ground". This lesson was again being learned by those who had chosen the pursuit of wave radio. Only certain ground sites were acceptable as sites from which exceptionally strong signals could be launched out into space. While Tesla disdained those who so pursued Marconi and his weak reproductions of Hertzian research, he also understood why the geological sites worked in their efficient manner. Most practical engineers simply equated these geological sites with "better conductivity". This simplistic explanation was, very unfortunately, untrue. It was found that such "good ground" did not always conform with geological features at all. Furthermore, it was impossible to rely on geological patterns for the accurate selection of radio station sites. Tesla perceived that space sourced æther streams were responsible for "good ground", focussing and flowing into the ground for reasons much deeper than geology alone. Perhaps it was the ætheric flow which caused the geology!

Tesla inferred that locales in which æther had been resisted caused such intense bombardment that radioactive minerals had there been generated. Æther streams were modified by existed geological structures, focussing or dispersing throughout each region. Perhaps also these were the reasons why certain locations demonstrated distorted gravitational and perceptual behaviors. This bombardment from space was energetic enough to produce the observed natural georadioactivity and geothermal heat. In this view, gravitation itself was a direct result of ætheric bombardment from space. Tesla viewed the earth itself as a gigantic stone lens, focussing all incoming æther particles. In this manner, geothermal heat would be localized within a given subterranean horizon. Heat would be continually released throughout the earth, being most intense within its horizon. There were other geophysical consequences of this focussed bombardment. Indeed, the æther flow from space was an overwhelming supply. Tesla often became ecstatic just to imagine or speak of it.

Æther was entering the earth from space continuously! Tesla began making connections from this knowledge into those mysteries which presently occupied the scientific preoccupations of his day. This wonderful ætheric flow from space manifested itself in a host of unexplained electrical phenomena with which science had long been baffled. Many explanations rushed together.

Now Tesla was able to understand that sunlight contained an ætheric component, one which drove itself in endless streams from space into the ground. This was the process responsible for the generating the natural dielectric field of the earth, responsible for the spontaneous charging of aerial terminals or grounded capacitors, responsible for natural electric displays, and so forth.

The terrestrial electric field, problematic from every explanatory perspective, could be explained by ætheric principles alone. A technology which worked entirely in the ætheric realm would provide undreamed potentials for humanity. In truth the ætheric realm lay too close to the very realms of sensation and consciousness for coincidence, a parallel which Tesla had long pondered. Perhaps the formation of deserts was caused by excessive such bombardments. The subsequent loss of life and water vapor from such regions evidenced the dangerous conditions that could be produced by a technological system which used æther. He would necessarily have to seek out places which were already desertified, a site whose elevation was great. He began to plan his great experiment in order to determine the exact parameters needed to establish a truly commercial æther power system.

Tesla observed these pulsations and chose a range within which to operate his æther engine. The incoming æther waves would supply a continual supply of enormous power. If his impulse transmitter could be made to accommodate the exact incoming pulsations which he had chosen, a valving action would be established. The impulse transmitter could then appropriate the incoming energetic pulsations, entering into the natural geoætheric flow. Once this condition was established, one which Tesla referred to as "impulse resonance", a host of possibilities would then present themselves. Tesla could arrange to rebroadcast these æther pulses at more rapid rates, to be absorbed at higher rates by distant ground connected appliances.

Tesla now apprehended the fact that incoming æther so bombarded the ground that electronic charge was actually produced therein. These spontaneously manufactured electrons distributed themselves through slow conduction process throughout the ground. Of course, there were geo-related inconsistencies to this conductive process, electrons bunching in certain places and causing continual electrostatic phenomena (Corliss) .Here then was the mysterious source of terrestrial dielectric fields. Apart from the daytime deformations caused by the sun, the orientation of this dielectric field remained constant day and night. While only mildly deformed during the day, the field was a remarkably resilient natural feature of the environment, one whose very presence could not truly be understood. From where did this field originate?

What was the source of the excess electronic charge constantly emerging from the ground, whose electrostatic field reached out into space? Tesla had learned that ætheric bombardments of certain matter ejected, and at times manufactured electrons. Æther particles often condensed within atomic nuclei, the manufacture process being evidence by an excess of negative charge in laboratory bombardment experiments. The very light of his vacuum lamps was sufficiently charged with neutral Radiant Energy to charge capacitors. If this served as an example of natural principles, then Radiant Energy from space was the real source of the terrestrial electronic charges.

Bombarding the atmosphere, and plowing into the upper crust on their way toward the mantle, the primary ultra-infinitesimal æther particles manufactured electrons. These drifted up to the surface and distributed themselves more or less uniformly, a constantly manufactured supply of undiminished quantity. This was why the dielectric field of the earth remained so clock-constant. Just as the Radiant Energy from his vacuum lamps steadily charged capacitors across a room, so also did the Radiant Energy from space steadily charge the earth. This powerful natural æther flow, from space to ground, flooded the environment. The conversion of æther into electrons within the rocky crust continually produces an excess population of negative charge which has never found satisfactory explanation.

It was apparent that, while the sun was the most "local" terrestrial æther source, a vast reservoir of densely concentrated æther was indeed coming in from all other parts of space at all times undiminished. The sun did not dominate the ætheric supply, it augmented the supply. This reception process was endless, a constant stream of unsuspected energy which entered the earth day and night. For Tesla this revealed a whole dynamic in which ætheric flow directed and guided all processes electrical. Æther was the superior, electricity the inferior. What æther did, electrical phenomena followed. This single principle became for him a rule of unparalleled use. Tesla consistently stated that æther was being condensed into electrons at a specific rate, by which the terrestrial electric field was being manufactured. Physicists derided this notion, claiming that the excess electrons came from space "already made". Science remains bound in numerous tautologies encompassing geomagnetism, solar wind, geo-thermoelectric process, and so on. Each of these hypotheses represent failed attempts at maintaining the "ionic balance".

None of the bookkeeping techniques explains the excess of negative charge however. Later theories tried to show that these electrons arrived in a solar wind, the expelled debris from the solar thermonuclear reaction. But, all natural effects being balanced, no such "excess" of negative charge should be claimed for a solar wind hypothesis. The solar wind is a plasma, a neutral population. Tesla realized that academic science had been measuring the weak transition of æther into electrons, and calling the process a mystery. Not comprehending the invisible cause of the effect they measured, academes could not discover the source of excess negative charge! What Tesla greatly desired was the extraction of energy, free energy, from the natural æther flow.

Several pieces of essential information had been working their magick in Tesla's mind for months. Since his outdoor experiments with his preliminary broadcast power system, Tesla pondered the mystery of ground connections and their strangely increased efficiency. How had the ground applied impulses from the Transmitter somehow inexplicably accumulated power in traversing the ground toward the grounded appliances? He had found that a single elevated terminal greatly intensified the "energy magnification" effect. Many confused this arrangement with the ordinary aerial-ground components being developed at the time for wave radio applications. Misunderstanding the ætheric prime motivator of these transmitters, most would have viewed the various models of Tesla power systems in this conventional way. Indeed, examining the patents reveals no especially unusual components. The only attributes which differ in Tesla Patents are his descriptions, purposefully precise and perplexing in their assertions. In fact, the descriptions teach that efficient performance occurs with terminals which are largely capacitive. According to wave radio principles, these systems should never operate. Those who attempt to analyze Tesla impulse transmitters from the wave radio perspective walk away either baffled or critical. One cannot rationalize Tesla Patent texts when viewed in a conventional vein.

Æther was more highly concentrated in the ground, but it flowed from space into that ground. Since the stream was directed groundward, the only possible means for absorbing extra æther energy was to forcefully drive an æther current down! With the applied flow directed into the ground, incoming æther from space would be given a resistance-free path to follow. The impulse transmitter would be acting as a pump. The immense space reservoir would be drawn down through the system. With the parameters very strictly controlled, space æther would prefer the elevated terminal to the natural geology, a more resistant an inhomogeneous surface. Accelerated by this downward flow, æther streams would very quickly turn toward the impulse transmitter from outlying volumes of space. The impulse transmitter would be a source of almost eternal energy. But there were a few more facts to learn and a few more problems to solve before a practical æther engine could be built and operated. Were there additional characteristics in the natural flow which would require special systems accommodations?

Tesla used gas-dynamic and hydro-dynamic analogues in developing apparatus toward this remarkable objective. In his outdoor tests, the ground connection had revealed something of the process which he would now engage. Tesla had already learned that his impulse transmitters could absorb "extra energy" when grounded. Appliances too, when grounded, would produce uncharacteristic magnified performances. He should have known! This was early evidence that a natural æther supply was already present between sky and ground. In some inexplicable way, his impulse transmitters had entered the æther absorption process of Nature. Through some simple "pumping" action, an additional energy flow had made its appearance in his power broadcast. This now made sense. The creation of an "æther pump" would necessarily conform with the prevailing natural æther flow, one which poured down from space to the earth. The relatively small applications of his impulse transmitter was being given an enormous "boost" by the natural downpour!

Discovering more details about the space æther was now more than intriguing. It was a technological necessity. In the absence of any such knowledge, the pursuit of excellence had been a slow and methodic succession of discoveries in which he was left alone. His numerous publications and press conferences consistently highlighted the potentials of a future technology which would change the world system. Having already demonstrated the fact that Polyphase could undo an "institution" as American as Thomas Edison, his former employee, many financiers had become concerned when Tesla described wireless power transmission. Heavily invested in Polyphase, the general feeling of security was by far too shaken by his now numerous and detailed announcements. It was very obvious to all who knew him, for he was well known in such social circles, that he had perfected the broadcast power system to a degree which could put them all out of business. Here were the first confrontations of finance and technology, meeting in the person of Nikola Tesla. Concerned enough to meet the impending crisis which seemed so imminent at the hands of Tesla, a select and powerful consortium of financiers arranged a formal reply to Tesla's many overtures.

In the early morning hours of March 13, 1895 at 2:00 AM, the magnificent Tesla Research Laboratory at 33-35 South Fifth Avenue exploded and burned. Floor upon floor fell until the building was nothing but a swirling wind of ash. The devastation was unprecedented, the very obvious work of hired saboteurs. Dynamite charges destroyed the very building foundation, a death trap which could not fail. Unknowing to them, and breaking his normal nightly routine that particular evening, Tesla had quietly slipped out through a concealed stairwell for an extended dinner at Delmonico's. Tesla returned with his frantic assistant, Mr. Czito, and watched the ashes drift down the avenue until dawn. He vanished for two weeks to the great concern of his closest and dearest friends.

The message of his return left his shadowy enemies thunderstruck. Tesla was still alive! His next public announcement was divisive and deliberate. Every press interview for the remainder of his life took a new turn. He was no longer opened and candid. This mystique drove intrigued enthusiasts toward his every statement. He was now planning the broadcast of power on a worldwide scale, and requested funding from the very ones he clearly knew were the guilty parties. It was well known by the public that certain such individuals had long threatened Tesla with the hostile takeover of his Polyphase amalgamation with Westinghouse. Fearful of public accusations in the all too obvious foiled death attempt, the guilty parties crawled out of the woodwork with philanthropic donations which Tesla absorbed with relish. He played this game with the same parties all of their remaining lives, until none of them were left to extort "philanthropic donations". The hurt and the loss, nevertheless remained. He was purposed now to achieve what he had set out to do. Overturning the financial stronghold which he perceived taking root in the world, would be brought down at all costs. Energy, fuel, financial power, and regulation, these several principles would be reversed by the social response which his new technology would exact. The demand? Absolute freedom from the tyranny of regulators.

Into these fields he continually strove, his technology the threshing tool. In his new laboratory at 40 West Houston Street, Tesla conducted a number of very revealing experiments with grounded impulse transmitters. He had conducted sufficient experiments in this new laboratory to acquire certain basic information necessary to the construction of a large-scale test station, a remarkable ability to perform small scale tests with a view toward subsequent enlargements. Pumping the local area with æther streams, Tesla discovered an amazing and essential fact which he had not previously realized. His ground pumping impulse transmitters operated with peak efficiency only when specific pulsations were applied. He also noted that the timing of applied such pulsations would produce zero reading or maximum readings on the output side. This meant only one thing: the strongest incoming pulsations were clock-regular. Instances where he received "zero outputs" were instances where the impulse transmitter was completely out of phase. Instances where he received strongest outputs were instances where the transmitters were completely in phase with the incoming pulsations. Of course there were those instances where a moderate output was gained, instances where the pumping action may have preceded or followed the incoming pressures just a bit. In order to absorb these natural pulsations with greatest efficiency, he had to find a simple way to synchronize the Transmitter with them exactly.

The pulsations themselves represented a natural process which Tesla had never suspected. Here was evidence that space æther did not in fact flow from space smoothly. The earth as whole was somehow modulating parts of the æther flow. Tesla monitored and charted this complex and fascinating natural phenomenon, an exciting display of mysterious origin. There were slow pulses whose ultraslow periods exceeded his ability to record them. Others required hours to express themselves, yet others a few minutes each. The æther pulsation spectrum had no lower limits and certainly no upper ones. Here were ample natural "channels" to use for power and other applications. In order to build a functioning æther engine, he would have to select one of these strong natural pulsations.

Tesla found that an amazing sequence of pulsations coexisted in this incoming flood. These came as pressure waves, never reversing direction, and were interspersed by relaxation intervals having specific duration. Therefore, the incoming æther came as complex superimposed pulsations, each having their own periods of pressure and relaxation. There was no upper or lower limit to these. Many of these pulse trains were very powerful, not just a few. Those powerful pulsations obviously differed in cause and source. Some were solar stimulated, others had more mysterious origins in outer space. He correctly surmised the source of the more powerful pulsations. The sun played its greatest role in this pulsation process. Because it represented an æther source so close to the earth, its streams did not arrive with the uniform distribution of the space æther supply. The proximity stimulated the strong pulsations which were found to occur at fixed rates and in a specific range of pulsations. Pulsation groups were found, those groups each having singular source. Whether in the sun, the stars, the influence of planets, or mysterious causes in space, each group represented an available pulsation spectrum for utility.

The source of all these pulsations had several causes. Space sourced æther entered the earth at pulsation rates related to the mysterious processes occurring in deepest space. Many of their pulsations were the result of those space processes, having nothing to do with earth. Others yet had to do with process in space we may never properly comprehend. These represent the native properties of space and so forth. Yet there existed a class of pulsations definitely related to the proximal sun and the earth as a resistive body. The rocky earth represents a resistance to the otherwise smooth and continuous flow of æther from space.

Resistance in the crust brought an æther intensification process into play. The self-collimating self-magnifying property which he had observed, while experimenting in countless other applications, was suddenly appreciated on a terrestrial scale. Resisted æther focussed into the resistant medium, producing intense bombardments with subsequent explosive particle emissions. One principle emission was electronic in nature. Electrons appeared in the rocky resistant matter, a contaminant which often choked the pure ætheric flow. The electron conversion process retarded the ætheric flow. On the terrestrial scale, such effects were enormous in scope. The incoming space æther stream was not such a smooth flow after all, an unexpected fact. Tesla saw the native pulsation properties of space sources. These did not result from contact with earth resistance at all. But because the earth itself resisted the various incoming supplies in various degrees, special group pulsations had long ago been initiated in the groundward æther efflux. These group pulse effects were produced on a vast scale. The incoming æther pulsated into and over the surface of the ground, in some places smoothly, in others with greater difficulty. Certain geological locales had been the historically persistent site where prodigious lightning activity had been the familiar local attribute.

This retardation in the natural absorption of æther yet occurs on a vast terrestrial scale. The already pulsating streams encounter resistance, first in the atmosphere, and then in the crust. Space streams, however pulsing, are slowed from the otherwise superluminal velocities as a group by crustal resistance and the electron conversion process. The condition had existed for aeons. Momentum in the æther supply maintained the incoming group pulsations. The growth and establishment of this pulsation process was unstoppable. Æther pulses in, is converted into electrons, relaxes, and comes in again. In addition, the proximity of the sun played its part in another class of group pulsations. The sun was not homogeneous in its bombardment of the whole earth surface. Solar æther drove a vector over and through the earth. Several group pulsations were the result of this passage. There were geological modifications and magnifications of these effects. A whole class of æther pulsations were solar related. This pulsation train was unidirectional, æther passed into the earth, flowed around it, and went off into interplanetary space.

Streaming æther would have, in fact, been problematic in this effort. Pulsations offered the possibility of an increased engine efficiency. The impulse transmitter would be so synchronized as the apply its groundward æther blasts at the exact instant in which a space pulse arrived. It would rest with the arrival of the natural relaxation interval. Arranging a highly resistive condition had been the work of engineers for countless centuries. This discovery and situation, revolutionary and futuristic from every aspect, required the opposite engineering conditions. Tesla had long experimented with the use of liquid air to refrigerate his systems. He was first to find that zero-resistance could actually be established in cryogenically cooled circuit components. Non-resistance was the key. The key to extracting momentum, power from the æther!

## ÆTHER ENGINES

In order to fully utilize the groundward space ætheric flow, one simply had to conform with its natural pulsations. Tesla Transmitter stations had to accommodate these incoming pulsations with least resistivity. Tesla designed systems to accommodate cryogenic liquids for this purpose. Side branch circuits would appropriate the pressures from this main flux, applying them for broadcast purposes at quicker impulse rates. Tesla believed it was possible to arrange the parameters of his system to best enable earth absorption of greater-than-normal ætheric quantities. The large aerial terminal would focus in æther streams, beneath the station, a very deep and considerably broad ground system would spread out this concentrated flux into the earth, where it would find its way through to the upper core. Establishing the initial "power draw" required a special function which Tesla had already worked out.

The station would therefore operate in a fixed "pumping cycle", drawing æther down into the ground in strong pulsations. Space æther flowed into the ground in a smooth flood. When his impulse transmitters accelerated the downward æther flow, large pulsations flooded the ground. On the surface, this appeared as growing power pulsations. The pulsations actually passed downward into and through the ground as body waves. These travelled with superluminal velocity within the subterranean depths. Æther impelled as pulsations of this kind did not cease moving. Indeed, a flow had been established which, once induced, would not stop moving.

The impulse synchronization was the key to receiving and securing the natural æther flow. That impulse rate had to be exact and had to match the incoming pulsations. After this low-resistance condition had been established for the incoming pulsations, voltage was the key toward drawing in the space æther. Tesla calculated that a value of 100,000,000 Volts would be necessary to stimulate a sufficient influx. Superhigh æther pressures would therefore be applied into the ground, pulling on the elevated terminal. This powerful depressurizing pull on the normal incoming æther flow above the station would draw æther in from the entire overlying space. Æther streams would gradually bend into the elevated terminal. The system would accommodate the normal space process by offering a non-resistant path for each incoming pulse. The selected pulse range was designed to appropriate the natural influx. A synchronized ætheric pulse train was to be "driven", by an application of station energy, into the ground. This pulse train would be provided at the rate of 150,000 pulses per second, impulses each being followed by a specific relaxation period.

The pulsation range which Tesla chose was one permitting maximum energy absorption for an attainable large size. The transmitter would be built to produce 150,000 æther pulsations per second, each impulse lasting for approximately (.0062 milliseconds). Calculations showed Tesla that this assembly volume would indeed bring in enough energy to demonstrate industrial potential. Besides proving that æther energy could literally drive the station, providing an eternal flow of power into the earth under controlled conditions, Tesla planned to show the distant reception of æther energy from his station. Receivers would be established at various long distances from the site, each being a model home or industrial plant. Tesla would prove to his antagonists, who incidentally were providing him with funds for the experiment, that æther power would replace fuel oil.

The first requirement Tesla demanded for an experimental station of this kind was elevation. He need to place his experimental station at a height far above any intervening natural structures. The second requirement was isolation. He needed absolute separation from cities and towns, indeed from all human life. This latter feature was a precaution against possible "accidents". Tesla inferred that an uncontrollable process could develop during the experiment which he planning to undertake. Tesla was initially frightened that such a vast increase in local æther flux might have dire consequences if strict control features could not be found. His concern reached extreme levels, when calculations showed him the possible results of his intended "experiment". The highly focussed æther streams which he was intending on drawing down would also bring increased bombardments of the local geology, and subsequent phenomenal effects which might get beyond his control. What effects? Tesla fully anticipated that the artificially intensified ætheric flow might cause disturbances in the ground, bombardments whose released heat and electrical discharges might trigger rock shearing. Should he lose control of the ætheric influx, through inadvertent inability to moderate its unpredictable growth factor, the atmosphere might begin to "burn".

What Tesla meant by this had nothing to do with chemical burning. He meant that the ætheric bombardment would begin a process of elemental dissolution, where atmospheric gases would be quickly converted into æther and other by-products. In such a nightmarish scenario, the atmosphere would be driven into the growing æther column, a mounting avalanche without control. He feared that, should such a sudden surge remove control from his hands, the station would, be destroyed. But this would not stop the cascading ætheric column, which would self-intensify itself to world-devastating potentials. He often published these intimations, mentioning the possibility that such a sudden flux could "split the earth in half". It was toward averting these fearful scenarios that he now applied his mind's best efforts. He declared that the experiment would not be undertaken should no natural control process appear.

Tesla realized that the flow of æther through his Transmitter would meet with a gradually increasing degree of resistance, when electrons began forming along the otherwise smooth path. This would soon choke the æther flow, causing an avalanche of electron manufacture. If not adequately handled, the growing electron flux would moderate and quench the reaction. While limiting the efficiency of his "æther engine", other dangers could ensue. The ultimate result of this electron manufacture process would be a dangerous electrostatic condition which could kill. Once this process began, a charge-forming avalanche was inevitable. The accumulation of these charges could destroy the Transmitter itself. Should a means not be engineered to eliminate them from the area, the electron manufacture process would multiply itself quite rapidly and unpredictably. With unpredictably increased æther flow, the formation of dangerous blue-white electric sparks would begin discharging from the terminals and all parts of the Transmitter.

Thus, before he undertook the large-scale experiment, he had already glimpsed his "control factor". He had already found the very means for "moderating" the reaction. It was electricity itself! Electricity, the retarding factor in his every experiment with pure ætheric energy, would provide the moderating influence. The "moderator" which Tesla so desperately sought, the blessing and the curse, was electrical charge itself. How ironic that the very substance which he had so successfully eliminated in his circuitry, now returned as an agent of moderation to prevent a world catastrophe!

The problem demanded that a special automatic leakage system be established to rid the system of electrons as quickly as they appeared. It was during the "rest period", one which followed each impulse, that the apparatus could discharge its excess electrons into the environment. In this way, a continuous absorption of æther, and elimination of electrons, could be sequentially arranged. In effect, the apparatus was a 2-stroke engine. Æther came in, electrons went out. Tesla did not wish to harvest and use the electrons. Eliminated to the environment in successive pulses, these most certainly produced a distinct species of slow subluminal waves in the ground. Balanced and flowing in æther, the only problem central to the continuous operation of an industrial sized plant would be the safe discharge of excess electrons. He needed some kind of "automatic valve" which could leak the electrons away as quickly as they appeared. The elevated terminal would necessarily now be given a double function. Its large absorption area would appropriate the incoming æther pulses, but a second geometry would work to leak away excess electrons to the air.

Tesla planned a double function in later designs which he patented. In this, dangerous electrons are harmlessly and cyclically "leaked off" into the air through the aerial terminal. A large metal shell with innumerable stipples provided that æther would be absorbed, through the broad surface, while electrons would be dispersed, through the stipples. In the famed embodiment at Wardenclyffe Station, his first industrial Power Broadcaster, the final form of the terminal was to be an edge-rounded hemisphere completely studded with a great quantity of large single terminal vacuum globes. Tesla observed some of these phenomena while yet in his Houston Street Laboratory, and considered several means for eliminating the problem. But here was the very factor which he had so long hoped to find, a means for insuring that Nature could indeed stop the reaction before it grew out of proportion to wreak world havoc.

Engineers who studied his press releases and publications were fixated on the notion hat Tesla was intending to "pump the ground with electricity", an error which has forever clouded the issues germane to comprehending his various World Power Systems. The fact which so few analysts have retained amid their many errors deals with that of "station disengagement from the utilities". Freedom from utilities. Once such an ætheric "channel" had been stimulated through the Transmitter, it would be possible to disengage the apparatus from the electrical power source altogether. The system was made to simply flow in æther current. Once the flowing condition had been sufficiently established, control factors being monitored and adjusted throughout the operation cycle, this system would work on ætheric energy alone. Forever. Such a technological marvel would stimulate a world revolution in power. His Transmitter would effectively become the literal duct or vent wherein such an ætheric channel would actually flow.

The system would be designed to absorb æther pulsations at an accessible natural pulse rate, and then disperse this energy through the medium of the earth at several other pulsation rates. Not only was the system to receive prime æther power, but it would also rebroadcast it through the ground in a host of related pulse rates for utility. Home and industry would receive ætheric current through the ground as planned, none of the pulsation rates interfering with the station operation. The plan was exquisite. The end of fuel. The only electrical application needed was the "initiation train". But this plan required a large installation, one which would not be without its attendant problems.

## AVALANCHE

Tesla chose his site atop a plateau in Colorado Springs, then a virtual pioneer town. At a height of 6000 feet above sea level, the site gave him the required elevation. Here also was sufficient isolation from populations. Placed in solid contact with the plateau tablerock. Tesla chose this geologically deep natural conductor to permit an unhindered downrush of æther, a secret he carried with him. Anticipating the undreamed, he moved all of his more mobile components to this site in May 1899, and began construction. His exertions were astounding. Once the station was complete, several tests would be necessarily conducted to affirm the circuit parameters in the geological site. The station parameters were built on what now appears to be a gigantic scale. The large housing structure was made of wooden beams, of dimensions nearly 100 feet on each side. The roof was nearly as high, reaching 80 feet, having a large sliding section for the elevation of various terminals and capacity surfaces (see figure).

The building was held up with large buttresses. Within this structure were the components of genius. The primary and secondary of the largest Tesla

transformer ever built in history were wound, one above the other, upon an immense cylindrical wall of wooden construction, some 75 feet in diameter and 10 feet in height. An extra coil was poised in the very center of this cylindrical form, elevated on a stand several feet above the flooring. This extra coil had 75 widely spaced wire turns, being wound on a skeletal wooden cylinder. This extra coil was some 10 feet in diameter and 10 feet in height. The elevated capacity terminal, a large wooden ball covered in tinfoil, was connected to this extra coil by a thick cable. Through the roof window, this cable rose to a height of 200 feet, fixed to a tall wooden mast.

Tesla constructed a very ingenious capacitor bank, made of large water bottles. Salt water was poured into each to a fixed height, connector rods fitted into the same. The entire assembly of jars were placed in a large tub of tinfoil, also filled with salt water to a depth of a foot or more. This electrolytic assemblage provided a formidable storage capacity, and was easily modified as well as cost-efficient. Power was provided by a large Westinghouse transformer. This power was used to drive a high voltage dynamo, providing some 50,000 volts DC. The dynamo was connected to a motor driven spark disrupter which provided a preliminary pulsation rate. Through choke coils, this preliminary pulsing current was applied to a large magnetic disrupter. This in turn was applied to the capacitor bank and the large primary coil (see figure).

The first step in his process involved an initiatory "jump-start". When the switch was closed,ætheric shockwave energy passed over the secondary, and flowed up into the elevated terminal. Transformed into the calculated potential of 100,000,000 volts lasting for the calculated (0.0062 milliseconds), æther poured from space into the station during the interval. Each successive impulse was followed by its short but specific rest period, and the process was repeated for as long a time as deemed necessary. Some 150,000 groups of applied impulses and rest periods made up each second's worth of initiation time. In the absence of discernible information from the notes which Tesla left us, this critical "rest period" is difficult to ascertain. Nevertheless it is an important lost piece of information necessary to the reestablishment of any such large-scale station.

The aerial terminal was so designed to absorb æther and discharge electrons in opposed cycles. The incoming æther energy would be handled by the various within the station, side branching circuits made to appropriate the pure pulsing energy, while converting it into various pulse rates for rebroadcast. The initiatory impulse would start the avalanche, the space æther flowing with gradually increasing intensity. Tesla would control and maximize the volumes of incoming æther until the flow became "permanent". At first Tesla had difficulty balancing and establishing proper parameters. Eventually, however, the conditions which originally desired became a routine process. Tesla planned to train his operators in this art, having accepted several personnel to this end. One, Fritz Lowenstein, later was found to be a "spy" for one of his financial enemies. Tesla discovered this when several mysterious "accidents" occurred in the Colorado Springs Station.

During this testing period, Tesla encountered several phenomena for which he was not totally prepared or forearmed. In small preliminary tests, the primary ætheric pulsation produced "stationary waves", fountains of white streamers which appeared instantly and which also grew to large proportions with time all around the activation site. Tesla mentioned the "standing waves" only when referring to the attendant slow electron waves, manufactured through the bombarding action of æther in the earth. The different names of each waveform related different processes, unforeseen phase interferences which Tesla encountered during his tests at the Experimental Station in Colorado.

Problematic to the action of his system, these successive waveforms thus appeared at the station out of phase. Now, both æther waves and electron waves came back to their sourcepoint, the fact that Tesla quizzically mentioned to the press. When stating that "the earth behaves as a conductor of limited extent", he was not referring to the discovery that the earth can store electricity! He already knew this. He was referring to the problem of destructive interference, one of phasing among two contrary and mutually opposed wave species. This behavior of the "earth as a conductor of limited extent" was not a thrilling fact to Tesla. It was an annoying problem. He would have preferred a conductor of infinite extent, one in which all received æther power could be set free, along with the attendant contaminating electrons. Because the earth held onto the electrons so tenaciously, there were literal repercussions at the station which taxed his intellect far too much for his own pleasure.

Here was the situation. Æther waves flowed with superluminal velocity from the station and into the earth proper. These were neutral pressure waves whose instantaneous movement through the ground was slightly slowed by resistance process. A continual lagging backflow of æther "pressure echoes" appeared at the station with unprecedented force. The application of æther to the ground brought a fountain-like condition to the station area. In the absence of appropriate elevated capacity, æther streams stood out of the ground vertically. These were the "stationary waves" of which Tesla so often delighted to speak. These were the powerful ætheric emanations which offered humanity a new means for obtaining limitless power from outer space, and for rebroadcasting the same through the ground to any needed point. Æther waves are neutral pressures of enormous energetic potential. Opposed to the desired neutral æther pressure waves, there were those slow alternating electron waves. Electrons, developed by æther bombardment in the rocky crustal matter at the station, choked the otherwise continuous movement of æther pulses. But the aerial release of these from the system induced slow subluminal electrical waves throughout the earth. The very presence of these completely interfered with the system. Fast downward æther pressure pulses were met by slow rising alternating electrical waves. The opposed pulsation of fast æther and slow alternating electron waves would destructively interfere with one another.

Tesla referred to the ætheric phenomenon as "stationary waves". He referred to the electronic phenomenon as "standing waves". Stationary waves, instantaneous whitefire fountains. Standing waves, slow electron waves. Stationary waves occur in incompressible fluids. Æther is incompressible. Stationary waves are the charge-neutral products of pressured fluids in fixed conductors. Stationary waves pulsate in a unidirectional manner. Standing waves are the result of alternating compressions and rarefactions, characteristic of electron currents in fixed conductors. Tesla knew that these two different waves could react, one upon another, in restricted ways. You will remember that he strove to separate æther streams from electrons. Electrons quenched æther streams by encapsulating and pinching them off. So long as electrons contaminated æther streams, only the gross electrons would dominate. Also, the concentrated ætheric streams actually manufactured electrons. Striking into already manufactured electron streams would simply intensify the condensation process. A veritable electron avalanche would follow, the process so poised as to interfere destructively. Unless a proper relationship could be arranged between the two energy forms, one could not expect a highly efficient acquisition of æther power.

The difference between these two waveforms had been critical for Tesla to comprehend and rearrange. Only a Tesla could have balance the two contrary actions. It was ironically the slower electron waves which determined the tempo at which the system would operate, since these alterations would keep appearing long after the æther flow had begun its resonant rise. Tesla now calculated and readjusted the impulse-rest intervals so that the two opposed wave species would never destructively interfere. Timing was the critical key. Each would glide past the other undisturbed and non-interfering.

The first full-scale tests of this experimental station took place throughout the month of July 1899. Tesla found that each groundward pulsation of the Transmitter brought such a volume of space æther down through the system that it was difficult to control the exchange process. Once the ætheric draft had been successfully induced, charge formation could actually be utilized to slow and moderate the downward growing flood. Tesla always measured increased electron surges in his Transmitters. His aerial terminal bought in an unprecedented electron avalanche, measuring some 1100 amperes of the current. Indirectly this was a measure of æther flow, for it was æther which manufactured the electrons. This current increase demonstrated the continuous formation of charge in the metallic conductors of the Transmitter, the result of ætheric bombardments through the system. It was just as he had foreseen. This central problem which he encountered, and which he finally solved, became the usable solution to his first fears. The formation of electrical charges was being used now to slow the æther flow, which otherwise would continue growing out of control (see figure).

The Transmitter operated as an incredible Magnifier of æther. Tesla noted with fascination the fact that pulsations in the ætheric downpour seemed to formed a zone of ever increasing power. In this zone, successive æther pulses

superimposed in a manner which was not usual. The growth characteristic of these pulsations provided an ever increasing supply, with the local zone surrounding the Transmitter becoming a site of strange effects. He found it indeed possible to disengage the Transmitter from the electrical power source after only a few seconds of application time, the proof encrypted and preserved in his cunningly captioned photographs.

Tesla spoke of two different waveforms, "stationary waves" and "standing waves", when discussing the effects which his Magnifying Transmitter had produced in the earth. The "standing waves" related to the consequences of alternating charge waves stimulated by the successive aerial release of manufactured electrons. The "stationary waves" were wonderful phenomena of ground conducted æther currents. Once the stream began flowing through his system, magnification processes would draw in an ever increasing æther supply. The more "opened" the system became, the more æther would flow. He could moderate this æther avalanche with certain drive coils which slowed the rest intervals during which electrons were released. In this was, the æther would be limited from "going critical".

The avalanche magnification factor would have to be strictly controlled by the station operator. Because æther was rarefied in the space above and around the station, a condition brought about by the downward pumping action, a powerful and dangerous response would result throughout the incoming stream. Working its way back out into space, the pulsations would force the supply streams to flow with greater force into the Transmitter. Because æther responds to simple pressure laws, the Transmitter would ultimately summon responses from its very source. A strange form of communication would this be possible between two very distant points, a communications technique which Tesla mentioned.

The stationary wave was an effect unknown in electrical science. It was unknown because electricity is a bipolar manifestation. Æther, being a neutral Radiant Energy, has more in common with gases. Densified æther streams were more like fluids. Stationary waves were a familiar feature in fluidics, where the application of streams to enclosed containers brought immense fountain-like effects. Tesla played with the science critics when patenting an apparently banal design for a water fountain. In this ovoid shaped system, Tesla encrypted his stationary wave secrets. Years later, Victor Schauberger developed egg-shaped vessels into which streams of water were introduced at high pressure. The result cavitating turbulence produced frothing jets which emerged in pulsations. Stationary waves are produced when force is applied to an incompressible fluid which has been constrained within a fixed volume. The fixed volume of smoothly rounded containers rigidly hold fluidic pressure jets and produced enormous fountains. These fountains appear instantly with the very first application of pressure. The fountains emerge from the entrant orifice, unless otherwise arranged. The effect is illustrated with an ordinary sink which has been filled to a height with water. Drops which have been directed to specific parts of the water surface, at specific velocities, can raise a sudden thin fountain high enough to strike one in the face!

Æther is neutral. Because of its electroneutrality, æther reflections produce no alternations. Æther reflections produce stationary waves, where geometrically fixed zones of streaming æther are observed. Tesla applied æther "blasts" into the ground. These blasts moved the æther reservoir already absorbed within the earth in an instantaneous pulse, resulting in a sudden æther fountain all around his station. The pulse travelled through the ground, unaffected by its encounter with various rock strata. Nevertheless, when this pulse finally reached a sufficient resistance, or change of mass density, the flow was sufficiently refracted to surge back up toward its source. The effect occurs instantaneously because earth absorbed æther is a dense and incompressible fluid. The entire effect thus derives from refraction effects in the variable resistance of earth rock.

The bunching action of æther, both entering the ground from above, and that rising from beneath, produced an overwhelming pressure rise in a fixed location. These waves were, in the Tesla lexicon, truly "stationary". Rising up like a fountain of white light, they remained fixed to the station perimeter and "stationary". In addition, it seems likely that Tesla discovered, natural "vents" where ætheric pressures persistently emerge. Such natural loci evidence strong upwelling gusts of natural æther which may be tapped at for power. These strange natural features explained why certain locations far from his station suddenly erupted with columns of stuttering white light. Indeed, many such locations do exist across the world, places which flow at rare intervals with a white light. This phenomena is due to sudden natural cascades of space æther, an otherwise invisible downpour (see figure).

The "fountain effects" which surrounded his station are not responsible for the ever growing power observed by Tesla. This was the result of an incoming ætheric supply for which his Transmitter gave low-resistant passage. The incoming ætheric flow preferred the transmitter terminal to adjacent, more resistant rock. This gradual flow process soon evidenced itself in magnification effects, ever increasing volumes of flowing æther being measured in his system. Some have argued that Tesla merely stored energy in the earth, extracting it for use later. This is a basic error, the result of imagining the Colorado Springs experiment to be one consisting entirely of electrical effects (Grotz). It is in this light alone that we may comprehend the evident anomalous magnification of ætheric phenomena in his Colorado Springs photographs.

Once æther energy had been obtained from space, it had to be conveyed to consumers. Tesla had arrange for the automatic activation of æther rebroadcast circuits in the station. The downpouring æther were automatically shunted to side circuits through capacitors. In these side branches, æther pulsed through dielectrics and expanded over the surfaces of his smaller coils. Thus stimu-

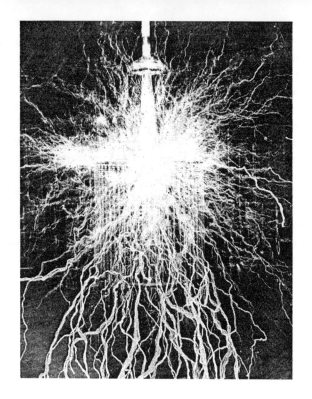

lated to more rapid pulsation rates, they were ready for "rebroadcast". Being rebroadcast away from the station through large vacuum globes, poised on elevated platforms, these were the ætheric pulsations which would be utilized in home and industry. Simple and compact receivers would be established in every home and factory, set to receive ætheric current through the ground. Tests were thrilling. Distant appliances, lamps and motors, responded to the powerful pulsations as if physically connected to the station by wire. A small house-like structure was established some 26 miles away from the station. In it, an ætheric power receiver was tuned to one of the rebroadcast rates. The 200 lamps housed within this structure, each of 50 watts rating, all remained brilliantly illuminated throughout the test runs. This apparently stimulated enough excitement and concern for word of this development to get back east.

Engineers were enraged. Those who had missed his most early shift from alternations to impulses, failed to comprehend the vast distinction between "stationary waves" and "standing waves". The quizzical use of specific terms such as these was a Tesla trademark, one designed to puzzle the minds of those who criticized him the most. With the exception of a very few colleagues who continually made related discoveries in æther physics, most academes had chosen to remain totally ignorant of the new study area. This for example was the case with the Teslian use of the term "frequency" and of "resonance", words which had completely different meanings for Tesla. Teslian "frequency" refers to the repetition of pulses per second. Teslian "resonance" refers to conditions in which æther flows with little or no resistance through systems, whether proximal or widely separated.

Photographs which Tesla sent to his "financiers" were analyzed and reexamined repeatedly from their encrypted meaning. None could decipher the cunning puzzle which Tesla had set before them. Tesla stated that photographs of the ætheric whitefire streamers required several minutes' exposure time before registering the faintest sort of impression. Most of the plates were therefore the result of more than 20 minutes' exposure time. There are a very few plates which, though stated to be the result of "one brief switch closure", are covered with dense, thick white streamers. One fraction of a second closure on the system switch resulted in a twenty minute or more æther avalanche. Magnifying Transformers continued discharging long after the initial impulse had been withdrawn.

## ÆTHER POWER RECEIVERS

Tesla returned to New York exultant. He was about to establish a new world precedent. Venture capitalists were everywhere, looking for their opportunity to enter the "new energy" market. Unknown to Tesla, his station, its tower, the large coils, the capacitors, and all the other marvelous apparatus which demonstrated free ætheric power to the world had been acquired for demolition. Tesla simply went forward, securing new funds from Morgan and others toward the development of a fully functional industry sized station in Long Island. Wardenclyffe Station. Wardenclyffe would be his greatest achievement. Here he would broadcast power to the world, along with a communications network which could span the globe with innumerable available channels. Æther wave communications. Several stations would augment the power of this first station, from which he proposed to rebroadcast 10,000 horsepower. The Station, a wonderful visionary structure which dominated the view of Shoreham, Long Island was not quite complete before it too was seized by court injunctions and torn down (see figure).

Tesla was summoned to appear in court. The amazing transcript of this proceeding has been secured by Mr. Leland Anderson, who has since published a wonderful treatise with this transcript as the centerpiece. Tesla said he wept when he saw the ruined tower in Wardenclyffe. The train ride back from Shoreham was filled with tears and the recounting of every tragedy which marked his life. But the dreams did not die there. In the absence of financial means to construct his gigantic stations, Tesla found ways to build small systems which accomplished the very same objectives. Replacing the large over-

head capacity terminal with material substitutes, radioactive metals in combination with other dense elements, Tesla was able to accrete and focus æther pulsations of super short duration.

Tesla was then plunged into a hellish time, where all but one would neither help or hear him. Dr. John Hammond requested Tesla to be the permanent guest on his family estate. There, amid the family life of Hammond Castle, Tesla shared his dreams and technology. Together, he and Dr. Hammond developed the science of robots and remote guidance. Tesla, impoverished by the inhuman treatment wrought on him by the financial establishment, was nonetheless quite alive and valuable to those having singular ambition to dominate the world radio trade. For a very long time, Nikola Tesla was considered "out of circulation".

But later years turned a kindlier edge toward him. Long after his principle foe had died, others sought him out. Employed by the Rockefellers in their RCA venture, Tesla was given the task of restructuring the now failing Marconi System. David Sarnoff did not permit Tesla the dignity of working under his own name! Nevertheless it was Tesla, not Sarnoff, who redesigned the insufficient RCA radio systems to sufficiently turn a profit for the owners. It is significant that Tesla was not allowed to change the basic design from wave radio to radiant communication. What he achieved required certain strange conversions within the wave radio circuitry, intensifying radiant signals until the operation was much improved, and then converting the amplified signals back to waves once again. All of this was achieved within the chassis, certain of which are now being studied. These Tesla experimental models are typical of the Tesla style, containing no resistors or other such components. These models use simple transmitter tubes and employ a great number of symmetrically disposed conical air coils.

While working for RCA under the name "Terbo", his mother's maiden name, Tesla maintained his two penthouse suites atop the Hotel New Yorker. One penthouse was his living quarters, the other a full scale research laboratory. Tesla designed and built small compact and portable æther energy receivers, a developmental path which he pursued to his passing. Tesla had long investigated the use of pure dielectric field energy, a stream of æther whose individual pulsations were so very ultrashort that science had never found a means to harness the energy impulses. Tesla later held the opinion that dielectric current was composed of radiant particles, ætheric in nature. He therefore sought natural sources in which native dielectric fields could be used as they were, without the need for mammoth voltage "shocks" to stimulate ætheric currents. Tesla knew that if dielectric æther streams could be directly engaged, a true world of the future would be in his grasp. Furthermore, the mass-production of thousands and ten thousands of such power receivers would be an unstoppable army. An army of miniatures which could never be torn down.

The implications were fathomless. Tesla had found a truly new and wonderful approach to an old problem. Once because his technology had not yet grown to the level where this was possible, he had to settle for impressing the naturally prolific æther streams with "extra" pulsations. The Transmitter method was costly, gargantuan, and an easy target for those who hated the notion of future world where dreams rule humanity. Dielectric energy fascinated Tesla. It was everywhere, a natural emanation whose potentials far outproportioned conventional notions of power. Indeed, the early conception of natural radioactivity as an energetic source was nothing in comparison to the potential power inherent in dielectric streams. The new technology would use ultra-short pulsing æther streams, energies which occupied most of his latter press conferences in latter years. Study had convinced Tesla that the apparently smooth and native force characteristic of dielectric field energy was actually a particulate flux, a succession of ultrashort impulses. The derivation of such an impulse train would solve all energy needs for eternity with an elegance far outreaching his own Magnifier Transmitter.

Of a truth, dielectric energy was a native source of incredible proportion and virtually eternal duration. Able to use such a kinetic source, one could dispense entirely with the Power Transmitters necessary in stimulating and impressing "extra pulsations" on the æther flow. Tesla often defined the dielectric field as a natural flow of æther particles, one which seemed impossible to utilize through lack of appropriate resistive materials. In order to obtain momentum from the flowing particles of a dielectric field, one required special matter poised in equally special symmetries. The otherwise continuous flow could be absorbed directly, being exchanged to utilities, appliances, and other applications.

Tesla had already considered the condition of charged particles, each representing a tightly constricted whorl of æther. The force necessarily exerted at close distances by such ætheric constrictions was incalculably large. Ætheric ponderance maintained particulate stability. Crystalline lattices were therefore places within which one could expect to find unexpected voltages. Indeed, the high voltages inherent in certain metallic lattices, intra-atomic field energies, are enormous. The close Coulomb gradient between atomic centers are electrostatic potentials reaching humanly unattainable levels. By comparison, the voltages which Tesla once succeeded in releasing were quite insignificant. In these balanced lattices, Tesla sought the voltages needed to initiate directed ætheric streams in matter. Once such a flow began, one could simply tap the stream for power. In certain materials, these æther streams might automatically produce the contaminating electrons, a source of energy for existing appliances. One could theoretically then "tailor" the materials needed to produce unexpected ætheric power with or without the attendant detrital particles. Tesla did mention the latent ætheric power of charge forces, the explosive potentials of bound æther, and the ætheric power inherent in matter. In these studies, Tesla sought replacement for the 100,000,000 volt initiating pulses which natural law required for the implementation of space æther. Tesla had long been forced to abandon those gigantic means by other, less natural laws.

Thereafter, Tesla shifted his attentions from the appreciation of the gigantic to an appreciation of the miniature. He sought a means for proliferating an immense number of small and compact æther power receivers. With one such device, Tesla succeeded in obtaining power to drive an electric car. But for the exceptional account which follows, we would have little information on this last period in Tesla's productive life, one which very apparently did not cease its prolific streams of creativity to his last breath. The information comes through an unlikely source, one rarely mentioned by Tesla biographers. It chanced that an aeronautical engineer, Derek Ahlers, met with one of Tesla's nephews then living in New York. Theirs was an acquaintance lasting some 10 years, consisting largely of anecdotal commentaries on Dr. Tesla. Mr. Savo provided an enormous fund of knowledge concerning many episodes in Tesla's last years.

Himself an Austrian military man and a trained aviator, Mr. Savo was extremely opened about certain long-cherished incidents in which his uncle's genius was consistently made manifest. Mr. Savo reported that in 1931, he participated in an experiment involving ætheric power. Unexpectedly, almost inappropriately, he was asked to accompany his uncle on a long train ride to Buffalo. A few times in this journey, Mr. Savo asked the nature of their journey. Dr. Tesla remained unwilling to disclose any information, speaking rather directly to this issue. Taken into a small garage, Dr. Tesla walked directly to a Pierce Arrow, opened the hood and began making a few adjustments. In place of the engine, there was an AC motor. This measured a little more than 3 feet long, and a little more than 2 feet in diameter. From it trailed two very thick cables which connected with the dashboard. In addition, there was an ordinary 12 volt storage battery. The motor was rated at 80 horsepower. Maximum rotor speed was stated to be 30 turns per second. A 6 foot antenna rod was fitted into the rear section of the car.

Dr. Tesla stepped into the passenger side and began making adjustments on a "power receiver" which had been built directly into the dashboard. The receiver, no larger than a shortwave radio of the day, used 12 special tubes which Dr. Tesla brought with him in a boxlike case. The device had been pre-fitted into the dashboard, no larger than a shortwave receiver. Mr. Savo told Mr. Ahler that Dr. Tesla built the receiver in his hotel room, a device 2 feet in length, nearly 1 foot wide, a 1/2 foot high. These curiously constructed tubes having been properly installed in their sockets, Dr. Tesla pushed in 2 contact rods and informed Peter that power was now available to drive. Several additional meters read values which Dr. Tesla would not explain. Not sound was heard. Dr. Tesla handed Mr. Savo the ignition key and told him to start the engine, which he promptly did. Yet hearing nothing, the accelerator was applied, and the car instantly moved. Tesla's nephew drove this vehicle without other fuel for an undetermined long interval. Mr. Savo drove a distance of 50 miles through the city and out to the surrounding countryside. The car was tested to speeds of 90 mph, with the speedometer rated to 120.

After a time, and with increasing distance from the city itself, Dr. Tesla felt free enough to speak. Having now become sufficiently impressed with the performance of both his device and the automobile. Dr. Tesla informed his nephew that the device could not only supply the needs of the car forever, but could also supply the needs of a household "with power to spare". When originally asked how the device worked, Tesla was initially adamant and refused to speak. Many who have read this "apocryphal account" have stated it to be the result of an "energy broadcast". This misinterpretation has simply caused further confusions concerning this stage of Tesla's work. He had very obviously succeeded in performing, with this small and compact device, what he had learned in Colorado and Shoreham.

As soon as they were on the country roads, clear of the more congested areas, Tesla began to lecture on the subject. Of the motive source he referred to "a mysterious radiation which comes out of the æther". The small device very obviously and effectively appropriated this energy. Tesla also spoke very glowingly of this providence, saying of the energy itself that "it is available in limitless quantities". Dr. Tesla stated that although "he did not know where it came form, mankind should be very grateful for its presence". The two remained in Buffalo for 8 days, rigorously testing the car in the city and countryside. Dr. Tesla also told Mr. Savo that the device would soon be used to drive boats, planes, trains, and other automobiles. Once, just before leaving the city limits, they stopped at a streetlight and a bystander joyfully commented concerning their lack of exhaust fumes. Mr. Savo spoke up whimsically, saying that they had "no engine". They left Buffalo and travelled to a predetermined location which Dr. Tesla knew, an old farmhouse barn some 20 miles from Buffalo. Dr. Tesla and Mr. Savo left the car in this barn, took the 12 tubes and the ignition key, and departed.

Later on, Mr. Savo heard a rumor that a secretary had spoken candidly about both the receiver and the test run, being promptly fired for the security breach. About a month after the incident, Mr. Savo received a call from a man who identified himself as Lee De Forest, who asked how he enjoyed the car. Mr. Savo expressed his joy over the mysterious affair, and Mr. de Forest declared Tesla the greatest living scientist in the world. Later, Mr. Savo asked his uncle whether or not the power receiver was being used in other applications. He was informed that Dr. Tesla had been negotiating with a major shipbuilding company to build a boat with a similarly outfitted engine. Asked additional questions, Dr. Tesla became annoyed. Highly concerned and personally strained over the security of this design, it seems obvious that Tesla was performing these tests in a desperate degree of secrecy for good reasons. Tesla had already been the victim of several manipulations, deadly actions entirely sourced in a single financial house. For this reason, secrecy and care had become his only recent excess.

## LEGACY

Dr. Nikola Tesla quietly passed away on January 7, 1943. Not many hours after his passing an official operation had been dispatched for the reclamation of all papers by Tesla. To this end, several figures of the National Defense Research Committee along with key members of the Office of Naval Intelligence. Several thousand complete technical transcripts were retrieved, the priceless work of his lifetime. Some 80 to 100 large boxes filled with such completed technical papers were retrieved in this operation. His safe was opened, and the contents removed. Of all the agencies, military or academic, it seemed strange that the Naval Research Laboratory should serve as prime recipient of this literary treasurehouse. It is said that Tesla acted as an unwilling consultant in the infamous Project Rainbow, a reason why perhaps Naval Intelligence would claim this priority.

Official statements concerning these papers essentially proliferate a rumor that these papers contained "nothing of worth". Yet, attempts to retrieve them have been fraught with technical restrictions imposed by an agency which knows their true worth. One fact becomes ever clarified with increasing time. Tesla perfected a science which few yet comprehend or can appreciate. Only when judged against the rigid views held by electrical science, Teslian Technology appears to be an impossibility. In electrical terms, none of the famed Teslian claims can be supported.

Prejudicial in their views of Tesla, chiefly the result of ridicule heaped on him by a few envious members of The Royal Society, Tesla was viewed with increasing concern. Because these individuals did not comprehend the fact that Tesla had indeed abandoned all work on high frequency alternating currents, replacing this with an impulse technology, most continued to deride his work. Then, in order to rationalize what demonstrations they saw Tesla performing, an artificial battery of explanations was concocted from known electrical principles. This is why the contemporary failure to achieve goals Teslian has been so frustrating and enervating to all those who so engage. Such results serve only to frustrate electricians, repel academicians, and tantalize military.

Of these three, the latter knows the truth. The military forms the only core of professionals who know with absolute certainty that Tesla achieved what he claimed. How do they know this? The older remaining officers witnessed Tesla's demonstrations. But this opens a new world of questions. Why had they not appropriated his work while he was available to develop his systems to full perfection? Why had they not given him the much needed laboratory equipment and staffing, in addition to the common courtesies of medical attention and better daily fare, to complete his work? But the truth will out. And only the truth now remains. The rest is silence.

# CHAPTER 2
# Marquese Guglielmo Marconi and Wave Radio

## WIRELESS

Following the work of Nikola Tesla, and by far never able to either duplicate his technology or outdo his demonstrations, came Guglielmo Marconi. In truth, the history of "wireless" begins long before either Tesla or Marconi were born; that term referring to various subaqueous and subterranean communications systems. Dr. C. A. Steinheil (1838) of Munich proved it possible to send telegraphic messages along a single wire when both ends were grounded. He then proved that electrical currents flowed considerable distances away from each end, detecting signals through the ground in complete absence of any metallic connection wires. This was the first recorded instance of wireless electrical signalling. Thereafter, combinations of wires and accidental line breaks showed the possibility that bodies of water, watery grounds, and even special tracts of land could indeed form conductive paths for telegraphic signals. With the development of special break switches and rheostatic tuners, these "conduction wireless" methods gained popularity among telegraph companies. Economical and requiring little maintenance, such natural conductive paths served for years in certain regions, often without need for battery power. As tracts of water and ground grew ever long between telegraph stations, many began exploring other means for establishing signals between stations. These included induction systems which used abrupt shocks applied to aerial metal plates, and large open coils through which to establish magnetoelectric field exchanges (Preece).

Reaching back before the Century's turn, several experimenters demonstrated the exchange of telephonic signals across canals (Morse, 1842), across very wide rivers (Lindsay 1843), and along large lakes and streams (Highton 1852). Antonio Meucci first demonstrated the actual exchange of telephonic signals through large stretches of seawater. He conducted signalling conduction wireless experiments along stretches of beach as well as across harbor areas. Signals were sent in this manner between Staten Island and Manhattan (Meucci, 1852). In addition, Sr. Meucci devised and experimented with aqueous wireless communications systems for divers and ships. His long distance ranging methods were designed to wirelessly guide ships through rocky harbors in fog. Tone signals would be received on board ships from wireless broadcast stations on land. Matched with harbor maps, pilots could easily follow signal tones along clear and safe routed to harbor.

In the aerial realm, D. Mahlon Loomis first demonstrated the exchange of telegraphic signals across 20 miles through kite-lifted copper screen aerials. Thus, without connective wires or battery power, he was first to establish wireless aerial signals (1862). Notable in these developments was the astounding work of Nathan Stubblefield, who exchanged clarified vocal signals through the ground to very great distances without batteries (1872). Dr. Amos Dolbear patented a wonderful wireless telephonic apparatus in 1888. The design evidences knowledge of undulations and ground waves. Dr. Dolbear transmitted and receive vocal signals through the ground, but used a strange system of elevated condensers. This was the world of wireless achievements into which Marconi came.

Marconi displayed the talent which, in adapting widely published experimental apparatus, brought him into a continual series of conflicts with far more original researchers and inventors. A simple addition or combination of already-existing components very often became, for Marconi, an object of original invention. It was in this misused definition of invention, that Marconi was forever to become enslaved. Through his callous and indifferent implementa-

tion of the work of others, an plagiaristic adaptive skill, he consistently made progress. In his early experiments, he made free and unabashed use of Ruhmkorff induction coils, detector circuits of Branly and Hughes (coherer-relays), parabolic reflectors of Heinrich Hertz, the grounded capacity aerials of Tesla, and the several other wireless components which had already formed the common fare of university laboratories.

His youth was an imitative walk through the wonderland which others had discovered. In later years, he simply rebuilt and patented all of these common laboratory components on a gargantuan scale. By implementing a simple telegraphic key among the sparkgap devices of Tesla, Lodge, and Righi, Marconi succeeded in developing weak wireless signalling devices which worked fairly well across rooms. But these experiments were mere reproductions of examples given him in common experimenter's books of the day. In this escapade, Marconi implemented all the known components of the wireless science available to any amateur. These "parlor trick" experiments were applauded by his mother, and reported to his august father. Having proven the practical use of his natural philosophy, the elder Marconi gave financial aid to his son's newfound abilities. The first Marconi experiments simply keyed Lodge sparkgap circuits, by which telegraphic messages could be transmitted across his father's orchards. In this now developing panache, and with financial encouragement from his parents, Marconi developed his systems until several miles could be wirelessly spanned on the family estate. Marconi ignored the fact that others had already done more formidable work in radiosignalling, having reported the fact some twenty years before him.

At a certain point, his experimental results were thought so marvelous that his father encouraged him to seek the commercialization of the small signalling system. For this first step away from the Villa, his mother's affiliations in English Society were enlisted. Guglielmo gained what few outsiders could ever hope to achieve. There was arranged for him a rare audience with English military leaders. The several components which appeared in this demonstration of his "Radio" were noticed by the academicians who invented them. These Royal Society members viewed Marconi and his device with quiet, conservative, and contemplative scorn. His coherer detector had been developed by Eduard Branly. The high frequency discharge oscillator and harmonic tuning circuits were clearly invented by Lodge. Combinations of coils and capacitor plates were derived from circuits invented by Hertz, Edison, Thomson, and Houston. High frequency air-core transformers, capacity aerials, ground connections, and the various tuning components had been invented by Tesla. Beam ultra-shortwave transmitters employed Righi oscillators and the parabolic reflectors of Hertz. British military leaders were interested, and sought acquisition of the system for use in the field.

## PLAGIARIST

In patent after patent, Marconi simply adapted and altered the discoveries and devices made by his former heroes. In several cases, he took the very diagrams which they had previously published with their own classic work on wireless. Marconi simply added some minor component to these systems, calling them his own. Marconi had no shame in this practice. Marconi claimed that such components were like the wheel-and-axle of ancient times, elements which were being developed. He further had the audacity to state that such components, though discovered by others, should be implemented in new ways. He stretched beyond limit the common Victorian laws which governed dignity and decorum. Those who published their discoveries in the traditional style, those who freely shared their inventions before protecting themselves, became favored sources for plagiaristic escapades.

With apparatus, gleaned from the whole world of European invention, Marconi demonstrated his characteristic panache to the hilt. First to admit that he had derived electrical components previously discovered and developed by others, he selectively gave credit to predecessors when it suited his pride to do so. Many of the legends from whom he "adapted components" were still living. By now, his extensive financial base permitted him to cover the numerous suits which were justly levelled against him. But Marconi was ever the victor in court. He now fared with the rich of the earth who gave him strong aid in these bureaucratic matters. J. P. Morgan, no connoisseur of scientific originality, granted Marconi favor for various reasons. We have characterized the relationship between Morgan and Tesla as one of duplicity and excessive animosity. This mutual animosity derived from the fact that Tesla Technology so completely threatened the monopolistic ventures of Morgan. In fact, Tesla developed so many monopoly destabilizing technologies that he was actually targeted on several occasions for death. The commodore needed some individual to "cover" the name, the fame, and the scientific strides of Nikola Tesla. Attending advisors were given this very assignment. The now-public accolades which crowned the young Marconi attracted these attentions.

When questioned by knowledgeable reporters concerning accusations of plagiarism, Marconi was abrupt and diplomatic. He never claimed to have discovered the principles on which Radio was based. He never claimed to have invented Radio either. Marconi claimed that, while experimenters were fascinated by the transmission of electrical power through space, he saw the application of this technique for long-distance signalling. What he claimed was the application of existing components into a radiosignalling system where alternating currents were used to broadcast waves. In essence, Marconi was staking his claim on all wireless components, demanding that none of these inventions alone could be considered a true radio system. Essentially, Marconi expected others to do as he had always done, to view the inventions of his predecessors as "free and public domain". Of course, these demands did not extend to his own patents! When others attempted the use of his own components, he was ruthless.

As his company grew, so also did his plagiaristic method. The "Marconi method" was to patent what he termed "systems". These were always composed of existing apparatus. Connecting them in "new combinations", he then claimed each system as an invention. Thereafter, Marconi engaged in patent "busting", the latter Edisonian method by which previous patents could be changed and slightly redesigned, being licensed as completely new and original inventions. One marvels that, during this period of time, fewer truly original patents appear in the Registry than in the late Nineteenth Century.

After Marconi, the "component derivative method" obtained patents for uninspired inventors who, like himself, made huge commercial profits on their "new and original systems". Though brazenly implementing several of Tesla's patents, Marconi refused to acknowledge Tesla at all. Marconi demonstrated his bureaucratic connections in several court cases. In each court decision, the Marconi claims were persistently upheld. Apparently it was important for certain moguls that Marconi's wireless become the success which history records. Wireless could be used to monitor foreign oil and steel markets with rare swiftness. Unlike Tesla's plan for broadcasting true power along with signals, the Marconi Radio System was a "safe" mode of communications which could not threaten existing fuel dynasties.

Coming mostly from an uneducated populace, the accolades and applause were heaped on Marconi in ignorance of the fact that "his radio" was stolen merchandise. Unfortunately, he had neither the gratitude nor the decency to include those from whom he so liberally and openly stole. In fact, Marconi was a far more successful businessman than an inventor. According to Marconi, while each of these system components stood as original, they did not comprise an invention in combination. In the eyes of those who knew better, Marconi had simply tinkered together an assembly made of parts belonging to others; a system of components which should have delivered royalties to their true inventors. The list would have been staggering. In any other such system, Marconi would have not had enough profits for himself to make the system an international business success.

## ROUTES

Unwilling to accept Teslian æther physics on the basis of pride and the fact that his systems appeared totally ineffective, Marconi restricted his scientific world-view to the existing convention, one which already rejected Tesla's claims. Limited in this myopic viewpoint of natural science, Marconi never strayed far from the academically accepted world of electrical science. He always "played the science game straight", so that ridicule and the possibility of social unpopularity would never come near him. He knew well what happened to Tesla. New and penetrating radio theories would not be heard spouting from his lips. Regardless of the true glory of the legend, Marconi chose to avoid Tesla's legendary route of scientific martyrdom. He insisted that powerful high frequency alternating currents were the only useful means for broadcasting the weak alternating "radio" waves. Though completely inefficient as a message transactive means, Marconi boasted of his ability to make the system a practical utility. Science and finance were each watching, yet remaining uncommitted.

The necessary test of his radiosignalling system, the "acid test" imposed on him now, and annoying necessity. Before seizing the financial profits away from ordinary submarine telegraphic or telephonic exchanges, Marconi had to prove the ability of his weak waves to cross the Atlantic. To this end he was given funds with which to conduct a demonstration of the practical transmission and reception of signals, with clarity. The system had to bring the clarity and speed which submarine telegraphy afforded. High speed telegraphic transmission was the central feature toward which his efforts would be focussed.

The transmission sites were chosen on opposite sides of the North Atlantic: at Glace Bay, Nova Scotia and at Cornwall, England. There, enormous aerial structures were erected. Four huge multi-girdered masts were first erected. Upon these, an immense inverted pyramid of cables were strung. Work on these aerials proceeded slowly, weather conditions prohibiting more rapid deployment of the necessary transmitter components. These sites were chosen because of their obvious close geographic poise, Marconi anticipated that the first signals would be relatively weak and furtive. Until the proper parameters for transmission and reception were chosen, there would be wide room for failure. Transmissions were to proceed from Cornwall, being received at the Nova Scotia side. The famed signal was a simple Morse Code "S"...the three dots. This signal was to be continually broadcast in hopes that the others in Nova Scotia would receive them. Telegraphic affirmations would serve as confirmation of signals received. Marconi swore that soon only waves would be exchanged from coast to coast.

The weather raged against his efforts. The high winds finally destroyed the Nova Scotia reception aerial. With time working against him, Marconi decided to try a simple method for launching an aerial wire to greater altitudes than the original pyramid afforded. Taking a lesson from Mahlon Loomis, Marconi had large kites constructed and outfitted with copper screens. These were sent aloft, using the very winds which destroyed his aerial towers in order to give him aid. Many doubt whether Marconi's signals were ever received, believing that Marconi faked the results in order to stall for time. They assert that his stall technique was based on his confidence that a strong signal could eventually be transferred across the Atlantic, but that the initial attempt had failed. But Marconi's signal, clouded with noise and static, was indeed received across the Atlantic. It was transferred, but not through the power which was provided his transmitter on the western shores of England. Calculations show that the Marconi signal could never have been transferred through the power levels which were employed, the effective output energies of his spark generators being insufficient to produce an intelligible signal through the medium of waves. How then did the signal manage the crossover?

Examination of his methods reveals an astounding fact. Employing large spark gaps, inductors, and capacitors, Marconi's transmitter developed a complex blend of currents. These included high frequency alternations with a strong ætheric component. Calculations have proven that the wave component of this first experiment could never have surpassed the natural transatlantic barrier. The Teslian component however, the ætheric Radiant Energy magnified by highly quenched spark gaps of great power, actually established the signal. It was on the basis of this demonstration success that Marconi received sufficient funds to bridge the Atlantic Ocean.

But Marconi, apparently willing to remain thoroughly ignorant of Tesla's true discoveries and claims, continued to develop only high frequency alternating wave technology. Because he was intent on eliminating every component which was associated with the name of Tesla, Marconi progressively moved away from systems which released radiant ætheric energy, focussing all of his attentions on the development of generators capable of providing a purified high frequency alternating current. Holding to a foolhardy belief that "wave purity" equalled "signal strength", Marconi drove his engineers in the wrong direction. Inefficient on every count, Marconi systems became mammoth reminders of tiny statements made by Tesla throughout the years. Tesla viewed the high frequency alternating currents, his own original developments, as unimaginably inferior to those potent effects produced by unidirectional impulses. The small Radiant Energy transmitters of Nikola Tesla could send strong and clarified signals to great distances with neither the excessive need for power, size, and geological installation of those Marconi Stations which began appearing on every coastland throughout the world. What signalling effects Marconi obtained with his now gigantic stations, Tesla could routinely outdo with a portable field unit. The contrast between the two systems evidenced a fundamental reliance on completely opposed energies.

Realizing only that Tesla's most recent admonitions were potential threats to the World Radio Cartel, Marconi simply derided and excluded Tesla from both his technical conversations and public statements. In this critical time frame, Tesla Power Transmitters and Signalling Systems represented the only real potential threat which Marconi feared, his ambitions to establish a world monopoly in radio communications representing his only recent inventive expression. Marconi excluded Tesla from magazines and texts printed by his now large publication house. The "Marconigraph", the house organ for all things related to the Marconi Radio System, was eagerly bought by enthused amateurs and experimenters the world over. Nowhere therein was the name of Tesla ever found. Marconi deliberately excluded and stonewalled the name of Tesla from his every discussion, lecture, and publication. But the conspicuous absence of Tesla's name in Marconi publications, while evidencing the great exertions spent by Marconi in preserving his own pride, actually stimulated larger questions which Marconi was unwilling to address. The very absence of the Tesla name from radio journals brought shame to Marconi! Marconi was going to crown himself Emperor of Radio!

Despite this disgusting aloofness, the biting arrogance, and the utter conceit, every existing Marconi system was completely plagued with difficulties. Just as Tesla predicted. Inefficient. Waves were viewed by Tesla as the waste heat of electrical alternators. The history of Radiant Energy transmission belongs to Nikola Tesla, a far superior and mysterious technology than the banal wave radio with which we are so familiar. In his own indomitable manner, Marconi gathered engineers to "solve his problems", hoping to slam the Tesla prediction out into oblivion. But no matter. Nothing the engineers could do would solve the inherent problem of signal weakness when utilizing alternating currents. There just was not enough power to "push signal" out into the environment. The absolute need for the stupendous size in both generators, components, aerials, and ground systems, came as a result of using lossy alternating current. Each recalled what Tesla had very early stated, considering carefully their present crisis. Many engineers each gradually realized that Tesla had been right after all. Tesla had already been through each of these steps, years before. Another electrical current had to be found, one whose potential for propagating without significant losses would change the dilemma. They would never dare admit as much, fearing the vengeful and vile wrath of Marconi. Tesla's name was never, ever to be mentioned. Never to be spoken in his presence.

But here they were, well employed by the only wireless company the world had to offer. What the came up with formed the basis of our present commercial radio systems, a commercial divergence from the sure principles enunciated by Tesla. Financial backing simply was heaped upon Marconi, and taken from Tesla. This simple bifurcation, amplified by the countless labor of a great engineering consortium, produced and proliferated Wave Radio. Here indeed, the source of all modern prejudice, ignorance, limitation, restriction, disbelief, derision, error, and frustration. But for this financially empowered deviation from the normal flow of discovery, we would have not questioned discussions on æther and æther physics. Tesla, ignored, ridiculed, and underfunded, had no equivalent offer with which to draw away his own consortium of engineers. Though wishing the pure pursuit of superior Teslian objectives, engineers working for The Marconi Company were held fast by salaries and prestige.

Unchallenged again, Marconi thereafter advanced the Wave Radio scheme. Utilizing ineffective transverse waves to signal across space, long range Marconi communications were made with greatest difficulty. In generating the necessary wave energies required to span thousands of miles, the indomitable Marconi pushed his system into the gargantuan realm. His success was achieved with only the greatest technical effort and financial expenditures. It became obvious to all Tesla aficionada that only the exceptional continued support by Morgan could have graced this failure-bound venture with success.

No such patron ever appeared to freely grant aid to Tesla, whose Ray Transmitters far outstripped Marconi Wave Radio. Tesla threatened Marconi and the Morgan organized General Electric. In its potential for transmitting usable power as well as telephonic communications, Tesla was no longer a welcomed name in financial circles. Content therefore to occupy himself with the inferiority of an electric wave transmission mode, Marconi developed the huge stations by which he was known which required the sizable fortunes of his patron. The Marconi System became the unfortunate radio convention only because it was funded by Morgan, who desired the indirect eradication of anything Teslian.

## POWER

Holding complete sway over his Wave Radio Empire, Marconi was said to have been a thoroughly demanding tyrant. Marconi was far more obsessive and domineering than the numerous emerging characterizations of Tesla. Tesla was disciplined and solitary in his ways. But he could be lighthearted, jovial, even playful at times. It was said that he enjoyed only lighthearted movies, comedies in fact. The real comedy was about to begin, with Marconi in the lead role. Endless confusions plagued Marconi engineers, who were unsure of the differences between "electric waves" and "electric rays". Much of the terminology of that time period show a clear distinction between both, an awareness that there were in fact two very different modes of energetic radiance. One was a penetrating longitudinal ray, the one which Tesla pioneered. The other was wave radiation, the phenomenon which Hertz claimed to have discovered. Knowing the difference and how to release the same would spell either total success or total defeat for the Marconi System.

His engineers began to suspect the real difference, but did not comprehend the initial facts which they considered. Marconi radio is wave technology. Tesla Technology is IMPULSE technology. Waves were weak. Impulses were strong. Only alternating currents will release the weak waves which Marconi insisted on using. Only violent, unidirectional spark discharges will release the mysterious kinds of Radiant Energy effects which Tesla reported. There were those who remembered the European patents in which "shock-excitation" proved to produce a more penetrating and superior kind of wireless signal. Largely pioneered by Germanic wireless developers, these shock-excitation methods were understood to be prolific sources of a different electrical phenomenon altogether. Raymond Heising, Count Georg von Arco, Alexander Meissner, Arno Brasch, Fritz Lange, Max Dahl, Fritz Lowenstein and a host of others recognized that Tesla had indeed found a special and rare kind of electrically stimulated effect.

They had experimental proof that this effect produced a better wireless signal than the high frequency alternating currents could ever be made to yield. Indeed, throughout the years that Dr. Nikola Tesla was treated with such derision and rejection by the local authorities, this Germanic camp came to revere and esteem his work above the others who filled the developing technology. Certain of these staunch and loyal supporters even came to his aid when, years later, his role in the development of wireless arts was held in question. Marconi engineers recognized that a severe and critical divergence was taking place, but they could really do nothing to swerve the progressive dictates of Marconi. He knew enough about their designs and intentions to spot out and eliminate those plans of theirs which even vaguely suggested Teslian methodology. Though the highly damped shock-excited discharges contained something far more potent than the currents produced through high frequency alternators, Marconi would none of it. Thus rejecting a potentially better radio energy "hybrid" on the basis of personal choice, one sourced in jealousy and spite, Marconi plunged into sinusoidal wave radio with a curious and unscientific vengeance. These seemingly "minor details" are critical in comprehending the tremendous consequences which have been passed onto society, the result of his decision.

Marconi was completely disinterested in "theoretical talk" from this time period onward. Business was the movement. Only business, and the establishment of working systems. Yet in disannulling discussions which explored the relative merit of utilizing rays or waves, Marconi had forced a shift in natural development. The rays which Tesla had discovered were so obviously the most powerful expression of natural energies now available. Pride, jealousy, envy, power, rule, domination, self-defined destiny, Marconi would force the world to accept "his radio", even if it meant blinding the world to scientific knowledge. Only his success mattered now.

Marconi, unwilling to be aware of the real differences between waves and rays, chose the weaker mode. By doing this, he forged a path of development on the weakest possible soil. Truly expressing a part of his ego, Marconi began to speak of transmitters and the power required to overcome all natural resistance. He ultimately sought the supreme rule of all wave radio communications systems the world over. And increased transmitter power seemed his only fundamental means for solving the manifold problems posed by the use of alternating currents. Though theoreticians hypothesized that increased power and very low frequencies might help improve the Marconi system, most realized that the real problem lay exactly where Tesla said it would lie: with alternating currents themselves. Power was not the problem. Energetic species were. The current which experimenters used determined the subsequent output. But the resentfully proud Marconi was making all the wrong choices.

Engineers were hired to develop pure sine wave generators, somehow imagining that the smoother the and more harmonic the signal, the better the signals would approach an environment penetrating strength. This was so much nonsense, and most of the engineers knew it. Familiar with the systems which employed abrupt, rapidly quenched spark discharges, their own experiential knowledge taught them that spark-generated signals had a penetrating power not equalled by sinewave currents however powerful or high in frequency. Here was another problem. The higher the frequency, the more efficiently the transmitted wavesignals. Yet, the higher the frequency, the less the signals would traverse the sea. But the spark held the greatest secret. Where harmonic alternating waves lost their power, their "cutting edge", the spark-powered aerials penetrated the natural environment with equally sharp signals. It was the ætheric component, just as Tesla stated, which effected these powerful penetrations. Engineers advised that the first stations should employ spark-generated radio energies. Marconi agreed. The absolute need of the hour was success, not style. Not just yet. Dr. Fessenden, the famed Canadian radio investigator, along with a small group of private experimenters, each independently discovered the first basic radiowave propagation laws. Each found that very low frequency waves, VLF waves, could carry signals to further distances in the natural environment than the medium frequency waves used by many amateur experimenters. The choice of frequency depended solely on finances, a remarkable restriction.

The construction of higher frequency wave radio stations was far less costly and size efficient than undertaking the establishment of a high power VLF station. Therefore, a few fortunate experimenters had designed and built their own VLF stations. Each of these was either independently wealthy, or funded by a substantial financial base. Dr. Fessenden determined that VLF alternating current waves, like low frequency sounds, actually "hugged" the ground and ocean surface as they travelled out from their large transmitters. Launched in specific directions, these VLF waves could maintain their consistency and power for long distances. It was therefor imperative to construct VLF stations at geologically appropriate locations in order to take full advantage of every possible natural enabler. Power would necessarily be extreme, the components huge. Marconi VLF stations were not experimental establishments. They were commercial ventures representing the highest sort of financial "risk" available for the production of large profits. The financial base investing the greatest capital was one for whom failures were not tolerated. The plethora of inventors threatened Marconi. There were many others whose systems performed more adequately and with far less power. They used sharp spark discharges, imitating Tesla to some vague degree.

Inadvertently duplicating work previously completed by Vion, Lemstrom, and Tesla, Marconi began learning about the affects of geomorphology on VLF. Marconi had not yet learned the secret of choosing proper "related" geological points to insure the most powerful signal transactions. It was a fact that certain geological locations exchanged radiowave signals with impossibly great power. Marconi came to rely upon such means in order to boost every fraction of power which his weak wave signalling apparatus could deliver. The goal was simple: drive signals and receive signals across the Atlantic. Using forgotten principles of Antonio Meucci, Marconi frequently employed both conductive geological structures and seawater channels in order to collimate the alternating waves. More like huge natural waveguides or "chutes", as British engineers came to call them, spark-generated waves were directed across the seas through massive aerial structures.

Gone were the large metal plate aerials, those reminders of Tesla and his Wardenclyffe Station. In the absence of creative ability to build the necessary solid plate aerials of this size, articulated aerials began emerging. This development was principally pursued by Marconi for obvious reasons. Furthermore, Marconi found it impossible to develop sufficiently tall aerials having the great capacity needed for achieving a signal transmission "maximum". He therefore developed his own breed of capacity structures in the horizontal mode. The Marconi Bent-L aerial curtain was comprised of several thick braided cables. He and his engineers dissected the otherwise solid geometries of early "capacitor aerials", and produced gigantic cage-like forms. In this direction, Marconi developed "Bent-L" aerials (see figure).

This design was a parallel array of very long terminated powerlines. A great number of cables emerged from their power source, gigantic electrified components housed in an isolated building. Window-sized insulator eyelets directed the thick cables out into the expanding aerial structure. Support towers went straight out into the sea, very often standing in the water. Beneath the entire aerial structure was a buried copper screen, one whose expense was as enormous as its area. The ground screen often went beneath the seawater to several hundreds of yards beyond the aerials. These are yet being discovered off the New Jersey coastline (Dalessio). Many of these mammoth stations went into operation before the first World War. The sheer expense of creating a single VLF station is yet unfathomable for our time, let alone the VLF global "circuit" which the now vaunting Marconi sought to establish. Money and media, the old connection of rulership. Controlling what can be known is always a priority, a method of control.

Forgetfulness is sometimes expensive. There were those who, at the financial base, wished to more than forget Tesla. They wished the eradication of his Technology, and he knew it. This is why Tesla continued arranging his own press interviews. Ever prepared with carefully contrived statements, Tesla designed his interviews to pinpoint specific financiers or monopolies. Provoking his enemies with flawless logic, Tesla made the most of each moment in the spotlight. Meanwhile, Marconi engineers were immersed in problems requiring the help of a Tesla. But no such help would come.

Engineers who knew that wave radio was hopeless advised that a spark generator would be the best radio energy source for his first trans-Atlantic Station. This commercial demonstration was the most important step toward monopolizing Wave Radio. Monies would stop should this plant prove in any way inefficient. Marconi therefore believed that brute force would solve the problem of excessive static and other signal frustrating natural disruptions. It was not therefore curious that Valdemar Poulsen obtained an exclusive contract with Marconi. Poulsen had adopted certain unpatented designs of Nikola Tesla for the production of very high power VLF signals. Tesla designed the arc dischargers to produce impulses. Poulsen adapted this design to the production of VLF waves however, an inferior energetic form. The Poulsen Arc devices began as boiler-sized tanks, capable of safely transforming high voltage direct current into damped radiowaves. As Marconi stations required ever more power, so too did Poulsen develop more gigantic Arc devices. Some of these standard designs were immense house-sized tanks, hydrogen plasma cyclotrons requiring thick-walled shields to block out their dangerous local electrical fields. These mammoth installations generated multimegawatt radio currents as early as 1912. Updated considerably now, they are still in Naval use.

But, Marconi wished to escape every possible inference that Tesla had the superior science, and so the eventual eradication of Poulsen Arc Generators was a consideration of prime importance to Marconi. Marconi directed his engineers to use many common laboratory artifices as models and analogues in this brute force theme. Reconstructed on a gargantuan scale, Marconi obtained coils several stories in height, capacitors which filled warehouses, sparkgaps requiring boiler-sized oil tanks, buried copper screens of an area rivalling a cornfield, and a massive aerial structure several football fields in length and width. Insulators, towers, cable supports, every part of the pre-existing electrical sciences was simply enlarged in the hopes of overpowering natural resistance. Marconi made absolutely sure that each giant version of the classic electrical components were patented as inventive novelties, the basis of size alone. He eagerly sought the development of special radio frequency generators, desiring the complete purge of Tesla-derived components. This was, of course, impossible. Every aspect of radio science had been covered by the now hated genius.

Early high power VLF stations were terminated power stations, launching VLF waves into ocean lanes with special trellis-like arrays. These electrical trellis arrangements grew with the needs of a station, in some cases having been nearly 10 miles or more in length. These trellises went straight out into the seawater, early "directional" aerials. Their equally monstrous ground plane, an immense copper screen which ran the entire length of the aerial trellis, was buried underground. An immense construction operation. Both trellis and ground plane went directly into the seawater, without doubt an invocation of sea conductivity originally devised by Antonio Meucci. Marconi designed his systems to drive signals across the sea by every and any propagation modes possible. In fact, part of these signals were in fact, he result of subaqueous conduction currents.

Hundreds of feet in height, loaded with cables as thick as an arm, the trellis monstrosities seemed to declare a defiance of natural law. They were in fact, just that. Marconi defied the reasonable and more accessible energies which had been revealed to the world through Nikola Tesla solely on the basis of personal dislike. Because of this, he was now compelled to these ridiculous extremes. When these bent-L designs proved to spread out and waste their precious and prodigious supply of high frequency currents, Marconi sought out "antenna experts". Making the most efficient use of the radio power volumes so supplied, Marconi demanded the production of a more directional signal. Designs purloined from Raymond Heising, Alexander Meissner, and Gustav Reuthe proved better able to deliver an adequately "collimated" signal; one whose power retained its "launch shape" despite the hundreds of sea miles between the American east coast and the European west coast. Later, Ernst Alexanderson of GE was called upon to "develop and improve" these designs; his several patents on directional antennas the result.

Brute force was the only means for sending the lossy alternations out across the waves. It s obvious that VLF stations were monstrous affairs, mammoth sites often requiring many hundreds of square acres. The buildings were built on a grand scale, made to rival those which Tesla had long given to the bulldozers of the fearful and the greedy. Marconi wished the complete eradication of Tesla and Tesla technology from both the engineering and the public mind. By building stations to rival the Teslian scale, yet totally ignorant of the true function of stations such as Wardenclyffe, he had hoped to prove himself the more capable inventor. Behind the wild and compulsive ravings, and providing the financial push to establish this condition, sat a pleasantly pleased commodore puffing an imported cigar. The employment of his powerline monopoly became ever the more obvious with each VLF station which went up. VLF stations were monstrous affairs in Marconi's day, There are a great many yet in operation, all part of the Naval Radio Network.

## MONOPOLY

Marconi only sought the complete domination of the radio world. Toward this end he wished the complete eradication of every other radio system and radio inventor. Marconi monopolized every aspect of the now expanding system. The natural growth of scientific thought and experimental curiosity threatened his monopolistic plans. He "solved" this problem by dominating every aspect of wave radio technology with an odious dictatorial attitude. Many young operators simply left the organization and forged their own roads, eagerly in search of Nikola Tesla and Radiant Energy Radio. Where Marconi could not acquire, plagiarize, copy, bust, or by out a component which he required, he would order his engineers to develop a new system. Everything could be bought. To escape the obvious connection of spark generators with things Teslian, Marconi now actively demanded the development of superior harmonic VLF wave generators. Though capable of providing incredibly penetrating power bursts, the huge Poulsen Arc devices were no longer desirable (see figure).

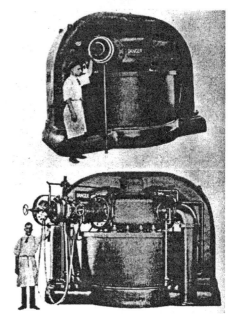

But all of this labor, all this effort proved that he was wrong. The large copies of Tesla rotating machines, high frequency alternators copied by Alexanderson, were wastefully inefficient. Requiring enormous amounts of steam power to drive them at their high rotation speeds, giant cooling systems necessarily kept the coils and other parts from simply melting. Applied to the giant system components, this energy seemed prodigious but was, in actuality, a small fraction of the total applied steam power. For all this input, the Alexanderson alternator did not yield "signal". Fuel was expensive, and Alexanderson Alternators required the burning of huge quantities of coal (see figure).

Despite the use of this wave-generating system, Marconi was never able to broadcast power on any levels but those considered insignificant. Utilizing the lossy wave mode, there were other significant problems which appeared. Mammoth VLF systems produced only frail ghosts of signals, mere wisps whose signal content was so much like gossamer in the wind. Marconi found that his signals, however powerfully impelled, were now also subject to the caprices of Nature. The permeating interference generated by natural phenomena exceeded the ability of his best operators to discern the fractured telegraphic characters, blasted by endless static crashes. Noise, natural interference plagued all of his transmissions. He overcame this natural "offense" in a truly bizarre manner.

Marconi found that trans-Atlantic communications suffered in transit along east-west directions, while north-south trans-Atlantic communications came through with great power. This mystery led him to build a special "radio circuits", signal paths which were rigorously tied to the geophysical environment. Having found such positions, Marconi imagined that he now had dominion over the natural limitations. But poised in sea-bordering valleys and mountain ridges did nothing to compete with natural responses. The violent electrifications which bombarded the geophysical environment from his VLF stations were no match for the effects of auroral and geoelectric disturbances, one of many secrets which Marconi kept close. Additionally, both Marconi and Dr. Fessenden each individually found that daily changes in VLF signal strengths often varied by the minute, a dangerous fact for stockholders to know. VLF signals were found to vary as much as eighty-percent between specific hours of the day. This inefficiency equalled lost revenue, a closely guarded secret. Remedies for these effects were never found. Marconi's method was not to back track his work. A complete revision of Radio would require the change to Teslian radiant energies. While Tesla was patenting his radiant æther systems, designs unfettered by natural electrostatic constraints, Marconi stubbornly continued to demand the improvement of wave technology.

## GLOBAL COMMUNICATION

The history of transoceanic VLF wave radio, an inferior science and technology, thus begins with Guglielmo Marconi. Marconi represents a figure critical to comprehending the relationship of the financial world to technology. Marconi was a not a brilliant financier. Marconi was a brilliantly employed tool for the financial power which supported him. Marconi was effectively used against the normal flow of discovery, of technology, of knowledge, ultimately of civilization itself. Anything and anyone who presumes to force the providential stream pays the heaviest consequence.

Marconi now wished to drive his station building exploitations across the world. The strong lure of fame and fortune had already pulled Guglielmo Marconi into such deep waters that he would later grow to despise his entire achievement. Drawn irresistibly into the world of oaths, promises, contracts, and demands, Marconi found himself no longer in control of "his Radio". Marconi found himself being pressed by investors and patrons. The romantic dream was long gone. The work, no longer a simple parlor trick, became a burden set on him by powerful and demanding investors. Clamoring for the perfection of his promised "global radio circuit", Marconi had to deliver his patrons their due. This meant that he had to conceive and develop original inventions; a task which proved beyond the ability of the experimenter-turned-diplomat.

Ignoring Tesla's established principles of power transmission, Marconi focussed all of his attentions on establishing world wave communications. Developing the lossy systems which Tesla continually upbraided as "inefficient and excessive", a determined and well-financed Marconi established a world-girdling radio communications "circuit". Marconi engaged his financial bases to supply him with necessary capital to establish this global VLF system. Firmly establishing his first reliable TransAtlantic service in 1910, Marconi thereafter strove to establish his planned VLF mammoths on every major coastland of the Atlantic. With later help from General Electric, the Morgan based establishment originally designed to break Teslian patents in Polyphase, Marconi formulated a regime of VLF stations. Marconi established these kinds of "directional beam" VLF stations all along the Atlantic coastlands as early as 1917. Both sides of the Atlantic. Soon, he would be directing the same across the Pacific. It was all so very routine now. While his previous spark generated VLF waves demonstrated ability to penetrate the trans-Atlantic barriers these complex signals, though penetrating, could not support the transmission of vocal signals. Without this new addition, his Radio would be condemned to a telegraphic realm, one which would soon find little utility in a world where telephony was the established standard. Dr. Fessenden was first to broadcast voice transmissions from Brant Rock in Nova Scotia through aerial high frequency waves on Christmas Eve of 1906. Radiotelephony was the new regime, and Marconi hated the notion. This meant new inventions had to be developed and he, plagued with too numerous concerns already, had no creativity left to spare.

Marconi now required continuous wave generators to supply the adequate carrier signal for radiotelephonic signals, a feat which he himself could only direct and manage. This carrier had to be a smooth and consistent harmonic wave alternation of much higher frequency than ordinary VLF, an impossible d requirement. The only such system of which he had knowledge were the designs which were deployed in 1890 by none other than...Nikola Tesla. This would never do. Marconi would never use Tesla's patents. The demand was too pressured however. Develop radiotelephony! General Electric engineers designed these generators, copies of the original Tesla patents. Alexanderson alternators were simply "lifted" Tesla designs on a large scale. The frequency was now somewhat higher than before, but infinitely smoother and more consistent; a condition which Marconi somehow continued to believe would produce more penetrating signals. In light of the actual performances of each such system, we realize the unscientific reasoning, an obvious cover for several other issues. Marconi was compelled to implement the engineering staff of General Electric, In addition, he was required to find market areas for the industrial product lines produced by that Morgan-owned company. Here, industry was now making its dictates to the self-styled and undisputed Ruler of Radio! It was for Marconi an intolerable situation, one from which he would seek escapes.

Stirred in the heart of a greater life, there was an intolerance of another kind altogether. In a truly remarkable and revealing photograph, taken at the dedication of Marconi's New Brunswick Station in New Jersey, a dark faced Nikola Tesla appears. In this revealing portrait, the very soul of Tesla may be seen burning through magnetic eyes. For Tesla, these previously unseen emotions...anger, annoyance, grief, hurt, and sadness...tell us a world of tales. In this photograph, there is only one emotion which pierces time and circumstance, penetrating our present world is his determination. Tesla was determined to proliferate a technology of liberations. He had in fact discovered the technology whose power was so new, so astounding, so completely permeated with unexpected potentials, that humanity would be completely transformed by its use. Tesla had long realized that æther technology was the closest access to the fundamental and truly human agency: consciousness, vision, thought, and sensation. To implement these energies would literally be like turning on a magickal lamp on society. Tesla experimented with hosts of applications, each of which resemble nothing like the world has ever seen. These applications were more like the images evoked by science fiction romance novels where flying platforms serenely sail through luminous pastel skies.

Tesla had a conception of worldwide broadcast which greatly outweighed the mere transaction of words and song, news and weather. Tesla had a conception of a Radio World in which small portable receivers would permit the direct reception of pictures and thought. The medium of words was insufficient to truly change humanity. He had long inferred that pictures could be harmlessly beamed directly into the mind, into neurology. These developments were demonstrated and witnessed, but he kept them close and secret. The world was not yet ready for the release of this information. He is seen among those forces with which he battled all his life: abstraction without experience, and the bureaucratic prostitution of scientific expertise. Tesla appears remarkably youthful, despite the fact that he was already sixty years of age. Thoroughly disgusted with the unnecessary waste of effort, outraged by the display of bureaucratic control, Tesla objected to Marconi himself as well as his inferior system. Yet, we glimpse a rare moment in history (see figure).

Up through this time, Tesla's biography became clouded. This was partly

due to his own growing preference for secrecy and seclusion, so often the victim of hurt and derision. Asked to comment on the new Marconi World System, a vision which he himself had once dreamed to see fulfilled, Tesla made characteristic use of the opportunity. Tesla's mocking indictment of this wasteful broadcast method told why VLF wave communication was prone to interference and natural restrictions. There was a reason why these stations had to be so expensive and mammoth. Tesla published an analysis of the Marconi System in a later mocking indictment, the wasteful broadcast method of waves being explained. In this splendid thesis, entitled "The True Wireless", we are shown that VLF alternating waves resemble the radiation of radio "heat" rather than the more powerful ætheric radiant modes which he himself discovered and developed. The radiation of radio "heat" could not equal or compete with the emission of powerful "electrical rays", which he himself first discovered and developed.

Knowing exactly how to stir Marconi and his financial base directly, he addressed the very heart of the growing communications cartel. Mocking its futile waste of funds, and predicting its eventual failure, Tesla was blunt, derisive, and technical. The latter portion of his statement was directed toward the vast supportive staff of engineers on which Marconi now absolutely relied. This technical swipe had its own determined effect. After the event, after the statements, the press interviews, and the publications, many engineers began to demand an elevated pro-Teslian technology. Having secured sufficient technical information in the older Tesla patents to reconstruct some semblance of the otherwise "lost secrets", there were those who broke all affiliations with Marconi and sought employment in more privatized laboratories. The names of De Moura, Hartmann, Gati, McCullough, Hettinger, Ulivi, Turpain, Reno, Moray, Farnsworth, and others who delved into Teslian technology are not widely known.

We are sure Marconi read all of these publications with exceedingly deep anger. Nevertheless, Marconi was conquering nations now. His empire would not be driven down by this wizard! For the establishment of his Radio Empire, Marconi expected the cooperation of many different nations. This necessarily would be an international network. Nothing would stop his procession of conquest. Toward this end, Marconi first sought the capture of European nobility. Politically and bureaucratically equipped to impress his own system on a worldwide basis, he would sell the idea of a worldwide communications "circuit" first to the aristocracy. The establishment of his huge world-communications "circuit" did not suffer by knowing his mother's family ties in England. Himself a Marchese, this easy access to the major European Houses made his initial foray relatively easy. Perhaps only a Marconi could have suited this role. Stubborn, adamant, glacial in his reserve, the sharp-tongued Marconi managed to insult many a European dignitary with little regard for their dainty feelings. The list included Queen Victoria and Kaiser Wilhelm. In his business affairs, he insisted complete autocratic rule. He envisioned the popular democratic future which his system would unfold with himself as its ruler.

His wireless organization incorporated schools and luxurious hotels for operators. Run as a military organization after the Edison model, Marconi had final and ultimate say over every publication and official release. The deliberation of this action sealed the fate of both the academic and commercial radio world for an entire century. Establishing his Radio System as a monopoly, Marconi could effectively control and regulate all world-financial traffic on behalf of any financial base which bid the highest price. Personal communications with European markets would mean total financial dominion across the world for any individual wishing participation in the new Trans World Radio Circuit. World Wave Communications had arrived. Financiers had their private radio stock-ticker system now.

By far not the first to conceive, investigate, develop, and proliferate radiosignalling apparatus, it remains that Marconi was the first to commercialize wireless communication systems. In this proliferation of wireless communications, he alone remained the paramount business developer. Marconi had the world, and Tesla had his visions. Wave Radio was the inefficient result of a willful ignorance, one which exalted pride above superior discovery. A tragic personal flaw thus became a social contamination. The result has been a world ignorance of the very deepest kind, one which has kept us from having reached the highest quality of life potentially available during this century. This declination from the high mark has touched each one of our lives in more ways than we can possibly know. While capital accretes human talent, labor, and effort to itself, producing profit for those who send it through the social seas, technology fares far better. Technology which reaches the deepest heart of Nature accretes to itself far more than mere capital profit.

Tesla Technology had its powerful potentials aimed at the social eradication of low living standards, disease, isolation, and ignorance. In each of these Tesla, an oftentimes victim of deprivations in America, saw the application of his Radiant Energy Technology to each social problem. While not here able to discuss the psychotronic aspects of Teslian Technology, let it suffice that Tesla had found means for broadcasting vital energies. Tesla Radiant Energy transmitters later evidenced enhanced ability to transmit emotions and even thoughts, a phenomena to which he often referred when speaking of the "Increase of Human Energy".

He had already applied both disease-nullifying and consciousness-elevating broadcasts to himself and his staff. These lingering effects worked, some of which having been later redeveloped by individuals such as Dr. Albert Abrams, Dr. Ruth Drown, Dr. Royal Rife, Antoine Priore, and several others. The social repercussions of such broadcast energies would trigger a world revolution. While financiers doubted the reality behind such reports, deeper consideration proved their fear and hatred of such a possibility. Those whose fortunes were gained as a result of the regulated social ignorance would not tolerate such experimentation. A critical vertex in human history had been reached, and financial clout was again redirecting and distorting the natural flow of human development. Critical knowledge, critical technology, and critical consciousness were each covered and forsaken to the extent that we now even doubt the clarified documentation afforded through patents.

### EMPEROR

There was a final conquest for which Marconi now took the offensive. One last formality was necessary before he could be crowned Emperor of the Radio Empire. He now required the absolute seal of judicial approval, demanding the title "Father of Radio". More than a purely protective act, Marconi simply behaved as a spoiled aristocratic child who believes that money buys entitlement, and legalistic threats honor. Inwardly of course, Marconi himself never truly believed himself worthy of the title. Honor had long flown with his first wind torn kites. Maintaining his sway, one which he could now easily afford, the necessary legislative support came to his aid instantly. His name, his name was enough. The existing media of page and press had long ago obtained his fame. The society which idolized every image forged by the media, had elevated Marconi above all the true originators of radio arts. Society had failed in the pursuit of purity, of revelation, and of vision. His name, a media darling, secured the title long before the court proceeding was actually conferred the title. Financial base weighed and paid the court. The formality would seal the fame.

Marconi was informed that this proceeding would be a routine bureaucratic exercise, a mere flicking of pens in the hands of civil clerks. He was wrong. There now stepped into the spotlight a tall thin smiling man with piercing magnetic eyes. The several caustic public statements concerning Marconi's claim to priority in both the development and deployment of Radiosignalling Systems came from one whose public appearances had, henceforth been rare and furtive. This gentleman made a sudden, unexpected appearance which shook everyone in court. Everyone, including the too poised Marconi; whose nose, for the first time in several years, actually declined a few inches to take note. That person was Nikola Tesla.

Tesla did not care for the title, having patent documentation in proof of his priorities. Tesla came to speak on record. Tesla came to insure that the world would remember its impending decision. If the court was going to declare Marconi the self-proclaimed Emperor of Radio, Tesla was going to make sure that the declaration would not be an easy affair. His appearance insured that the bureaucratic process would find its just resistance. With famed priority in Radio Arts, Tesla had absolute sway in his domain. Tesla reminded the court of his Royal Society Lectures, his lectures in the St. Louis World's Fair, and especially the documentation of his American Patents. Here were solid and admissible evidence that the entire Marconi System had been stolen from him. But why did Tesla come forward, and on whose behalf did he speak? Was it more than the acquisition of priority, or fame, of honors, or fortunes? Tesla knew that there could be no greater priority than the proof of prior years' demonstrations, and legal patent documentation. If these two items failed in court, then there was no real justice in the nation. If priority could be purchased by the highest bidder, then there would be no reason to secure patent privileges at such expense and trouble.

Tesla took time to champion scientific discovery and the superiority of vision above mere technical applications. He explained that the nature of a technology as all-pervasive as Wireless had such powerful effect on society that a mistaken choice, so early in its history, would proliferate a curse rather than a blessing on the entire race. This in fact was what Tesla stated was occurring through the Marconi System. The fact that he had discovered Radiant Energy was not the issue. The fact that Radiant Energy systems offered humanity a far superior potential was the issue. Whenever Tesla spoke, the community listened.

Tesla continued to speak out on behalf of humanity, of civilization. He did so to insure the preservation of every one of his statements, those loaded with data, meaning, inference, and vision. These would be inscribed into the indelible public record. Others would, years later, seek these statement out and study them like a textbook. The visionary Tesla knew this. Encrypting his statements, as only he could, Tesla released sufficient pieces of privileged information to tantalize and draw in the younger engineers for years to come. Vision, was the power. The only power. Tesla knew it. Marconi knew it. Morgan knew it. Invention, embodied vision, was a means by which idea and revelation could be made physical. The archetypal power which carries humanity through its visionary gifts flows into and through visionary invention. Such information, dispersed among society's minds, carry a message of power which is ever new. The message flows out to all who would listen and learn. While these wondrous visions glowed in Tesla's vibrant mind, the predetermined Court awarded Marconi with sole priority of Radio. The decree, the edict was ratified in 1915 with all the pomp and circumstance of a coronation.

## EXILE

The applause and accolades rang on, the crystal tinkling, the wine sparkling ruby red in the raised goblets. Tuxedos and satin, smiles and riches. Somewhere deep within, Marconi looked into a dark corner and saw a young boy tinkering with copper wires in an attic room, and he secretly wept. The crowds left, but a devastating change had come. It was a messenger of life, returning to give testimony to a man whose hardened face and stiff poise could not hide a simple fear. Deep within, Marconi had the soft heart of a sensitive little boy, coddled by his mother and hoping to impress his father. Marconi lost his innocence just before he was able to blossom into true greatness. He knew this far too late. Marconi stopped believing that he was invincible. Very gradually, Marconi learned his true status on the world gameboard. The financiers were now demanding a better system, a more economical system, a more easily deployed system, a system without interference and interruption.

The work, no longer a simple upper room experiment with components belonging to others, became an excessive burden set on him by his principle investor. Constantly clamoring for the perfected systemology of instant world-communications, Marconi had to deliver the patron his due tribute in continual successions. This meant that he had to consistently conceive and develop original inventions; a task which proved beyond the ability of the experimenter-turned-diplomat. Marconi wished to escape all those whose strings pulled him at every turn. He abandoned his VLF stations to technicians and operators in search of his lost dreams. The manifestation of his discontent took itself in a bizarre self-exile which lasted for the remainder of his earthly life. He had lost his first love. He had forfeited his love, the desire to probe the mysteries of Nature. And what had he in exchange for all this? Fame? A title? Too much too soon. Fame at an early age brings rapid rise and rapid demise. The romantic dream was long gone. The upturned nose, so evident in Marconi's earliest portraits was now replaced by a deeply embittered condescension. He had sold his youth away, a prodigal who could not return. Despoiled and jaded, he sought at least some respite from this condition in a new epoch of discovery. He launched out to sea, and never returned again.

Youthful inventors require time during which maturation completes the journey from plagiarism to true originality. Unfortunately the approach of fame and fortune delayed this maturation process. Marconi was never before able to reenter the real world of experimentation without the torment of obligations and scheduled performance. Professional industry had no room for creativity. Every idea which he had developed or even thought to develop had a price tag attached to its ankle. Every single idea. He had so long forbad the creation of anything original, that he realized himself bereft of a single new idea. Lost innocence, lost humility, lost openness, lost willingness to learn. Could these lost treasures return to one who had so offended their presence?

Therefore, Marconi sought refuge in a freedom which he had not long known. The pursuit of his old lost dreams kept him an exile, lost at sea. This self-imposed exile, an absolute necessity for his inner survival, had its terrible price. The price for regaining his lost love and atoning for his years of cruelty to others. Leaving his wife and children behind, he sailed the seas. His wife divorced him, worse than an ultimate insult.

Sailing the world for years in his yacht "Elettra" he finally managed escapes from patrons, media, business, and his own overinflated image. Here there was peace and tranquility, solitude and space out under the night skies. Marconi returned to his boyhood days where, content to read and experiment, he resought his own lost trail. Here, Marconi sought to reconnect with the lost experimenter's theme which form the basis of his young pursuits. The boyish thrill which propelled him too early and too quickly into world prominence would not now defeat his persistent progress toward originality. There at last, away at sea, he could find some truly original thing, perfecting an original design. Giving such a development to humanity without guilt or the entanglements of financiers would fulfill the vacuous space which wealth could not fill. Perhaps he could atone for all the terrible affairs visited by his terrible ambition. He would seek such a wonderful possibility, but not by ambitious efforts. He would wait, wait for the visions to return.

## IONOSPHERE

The sea was now his homeland. Here he could relinquish his titles, his fame, his responsibilities at last as search the world of wonders. The starry night skies drew his gaze, and his heart gradually healed. Enthralled once again with the experimenter's love, he slowly and methodically equipped the central large gallery room of the Elettra with electrical apparatus. Marconi began thinking and researching once again. Soon, he was drawn into a study of the natural electric environment. Exploring the natural phenomena which produced static and noise provided a fascinating study tapestry against his wanderings under the night sky. Process which continued to plague his large VLF stations, the facts which he once strove to secretize, now became a most wonderful new study. It was a liberating experience to study and not be required to report and finalize. Out at sea, there were only secrets, the wonderful secrets of Nature.

Marconi discovered the frailty of wave propagation across the seas. This was a fact reported by Tesla a decade before. He began investigating the electrical layers which he believed were found in some atmospheric layer above the clouds. Mahlon Loomis had suggested this very thing as early as 1864. Marconi reconstructed an apparatus which he had built when yet a boy. It became part of his original demonstration when he transmitted shorter wave signals across Salisbury Plain for the British Military. This shortwave beam signalling device was nothing more than the very oilbath spark generator of Dr. Augusto Righi. Marconi placed the spark gap itself in the bent copper parabolic mirror after the manner of Heinrich Hertz. He then constructed a receiver, similar in construction but differing in function. A variety of sensitive materials and components were used to receive signals. Selenium (Tesla), spiral loops (Tesla), single turn loops (Tesla), nickel powders (Branly), carbon powders (Tommassina), neon bulbs (Vreeland), and several other variations of these. Marconi began performing a series of very interesting transmissions which involved land based receivers and sea-based transmitters. But he did not engage line-of-sight transmissions as he used to do. Now, he aimed the parabolic mirrors toward the sky.

The experiment was performed in hopes that a moderately powered transmitter could reach a distant site by reflection alone. The land based receiver remained fixed, an assistant listening for signals. Marconi took the Elettra straight out to sea, taking a straight route away from the reception site. Aiming the transmitter at the sky, Marconi began tapping out signals. The assistant was to record the time when signals were maximum or minimum. Engaging this procedure several times, Marconi recognized that reflections were indeed taking place. Signals grew to a maximum when he was at a distance from the reception site which formed a nearly perfect forty-five degree angle.

There were diversions from this rule, diversions determined by significant variations in ionospheric height. But these could be virtually predicted by the time of day, another fascinating fact. Publishing these facts, Marconi found that others were drawn to the subject with avid interest. Dr. Fessenden, Kennelly, Austin, Appleton, and many other experimenters investigated the mysterious radio-reflective ionosphere.

The apparatus was relatively easy to make and portable. Tripods were seen in many locations, experimenters aiming their devices toward the sky. The remarkably consistent data, recorded throughout the period following World War I, told a tale of marvel. Here was a means by which shorter wave signals, requiring simple and not very powerful apparatus, could effect communications across great distances. The idea dawned upon Marconi with a flash. Use the sky instead of the ground! Now his path was suddenly clear.

Aimed toward the sky, highly directional shortwave beacons bounced from the ionospheric layers as relatively strong echoes. Thus reflected from the "ionospheric ceiling", signals could be exchanged by anyone from anywhere. The surface of the earth might as well have been the floor of an immense basilica, where the faintest whispers projected from one spot on the floor could be heard in another. Reflection provided another wonderful feature for Marconi. He could use higher frequencies than ever before possible. This meant that his systems could be minuscule, inexpensive, and accessible to others. Popular short-wave radio!

## SHORTWAVE

Marconi eventually explored short and ultra short waves which were best suited for ionospheric bouncing. Bouncing these signals off the ionospheric "ceiling" made long range communication possible. Ever the master of adaptation, Marconi utilized the new and special vacuum electron tubes to both generate and amplify signals. Vacuum triode tubes, the development of Lee De Forest, made shortwave possible, eliminating the need for large systems. In both his shortwave transmitters and receivers, these vacuum tube components produced amazing results. With a vacuum powered transmitter package no larger than a dresser bureau, one could broadcast vocal messages across the sea! Sheer magick. Marconi developed and popularized short alternating waves for public access, opening the wave world of High Frequency, Very High Frequency, and Ultra High Frequency to amateurs. Here was a great idea. But it was not really new. Tesla had spoken of it years before.

Marconi's desire to make transoceanic travel safe and trouble free became a reality. He succeeded in perfecting a number of directional beam transmitters and detectors. With these beacons it was possible to pinpoint a ship on the ocean with great precision. Furthermore, using the sky as a reflective layer, ships could remain in exceedingly long distance communications with relatively compact vacuum tube equipment. The perfection of radiotelephonic transmitters and receivers became routine applications of this new communications art. The rapid deployment of highly commercialized shortwave radios everywhere filled the world with radio enthusiasts. Anyone could now transmit and receive signals, an impossibility with the mammoth VLF systems on which he had too long expended his labors (see figure).

From the very moment in which he began these VHF and UHF experi-

ments, Marconi noticed the powerful effects which the environment exerted on his shortwave signals. Maritime shortwave sets were already becoming the standard navigational tools of every seagoing vessel. With the excessive reliance on these new vacuum tube powered compacts, new phenomena began to be a common feature of radiotelephonic signalling. Operators began recognizing radio "hot spots" and "dead spots" all over the world. Soon thereafter, strange maps of these variable reception zones were made for the wireless operators of seagoing vessels. These revealed travel arcs across the seas, and the expectable signal variables at each point. Other maps were constructed for the express purpose of outlining the various "silent zones" otherwise known as "blindspots". Geologically incapable of finding any discernible pattern in these, the task of mapping such HF and VHF variables was left to empirical discovery (see figure).

This study acquired for itself a vast and fascinating cartography. Locations

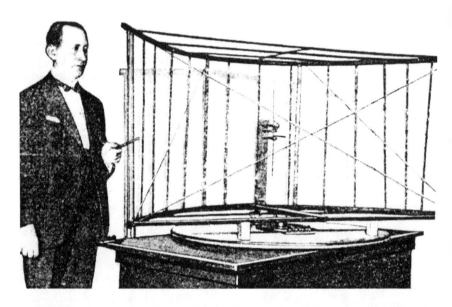

such as the Amazon were noted for their complete fade-out zones, points being reached on the otherwise sea level route where ships in sight of one another were unable to communicate with wireless apparatus. These "screening effects" were also mysteriously found in certain regions out at sea. One famous natural screen was Gibraltar. Not one physicist was able to properly explain these inconsistencies. Each theoretical formulary, each "propagation law" failed at certain locations and with certain frequencies. The problem with theoretical propagation studies was that their perspectives took place in a thought realm and not in the biodynamic continuum, a matrix which thoroughly permeated geological structures adding horizons and topographies all its own. Where this biotopographic landscape met the surface, strange anomalies were observed in ground or aerial linked electrical apparatus.

An incredible new conception in radio broadcasting gradually began taking shape after Dr. Lee De Forest began making daily broadcasts of music, news, weather, time, and anecdotes from his small vacuum tube powered shortwave station KDKA. Soon, the entire nation and finally the world caught onto this broadcasting fad, a commercial deployment on such a far reaching level that even Marconi was surprised. This novelty surpassed his wildest hopes and dreams. Manufacturers now conceived the production of small radiowave receivers for the household, items which sold faster than their suppliers could fill orders.

With his shortwave transmitters and receivers, Marconi successfully saw the popularization of radio, a reality of which he had not previously dreamt. The gigantic bent-L aerials now were miniaturized, so that amateurs the world over could intercommunicate freely. With HF, VHF, and UHF, Marconi escaped his Morgan entanglements. He made more money on shortwave systems than with all of his VLF stations combined. Eventually selling these rights to the Rockefeller owned RCA, Marconi managed to secure the advancement of shortwave to the world. In the inventive sciences, Marconi must remain a minor figure. With shortwave radio, Marconi believed that he had at last undone the monopoly which his principle financier had secured through highly privatized VLF stations. Despite this elevating fact, Marconi had never strayed far from his original wave technology, a tragedy which extended the example of an inferior science and technology to every learning institute vaguely involved in the sciences. Also, the regulatory grip which once latched itself so voraciously onto VLF now appeared in another form. The FCC was developed to monitor, regulate, and otherwise police the new Radio Empire which shortwave opened to the great world public. Through this means, a new democratization process had asserted itself against the privatized VLF radio system.

Shortwave became a worldwide passion. Shortwave groups began appearing everywhere, in every nation. Soon, a vast consortium of wireless operators began bridging gaps between ordinarily impenetrable barriers of ethnicity and nationalism. A working class tide of world citizens began sharing a succinct new consciousness, one which recognized no geopolitical differences. Despite its complete inefficiency, and unfortunate in its newfound popularity as compared to a far better Teslian system, the shortwave revolution did indeed short circuit the firm geopolitical grip which had so isolated and limited working class civilians. Constrained to their work schedule, a population of labor and toils, shortwave pierced the invisible walls on which Oligarchic Houses so depended. People of every land, color, language, and religion found each other once again; an international guild of communicating souls, who shared a common and mysterious consciousness. Stars flickering in a sapphire sky, the ionospheric winds sang their sagas through the earphones of enthralled experimenters, who looked out at their aerials from solitary attic windows.

In the financial application, the commercialization of communications systems, Marconi is the principle showman. Despite the woeful fact that the mere mention of the Marconi name is synonymous with "Radio", "Wireless", and indeed of "Global Communication", history shows that Marconi was a far more successful businessman than an original discoverer of new electrical phenomena. Marconi was only original when he found himself in a position to apply what had been discovered by others. Somehow, he could never comprehend why his first experiments were so successful. Lacking the great power of his VLF mammoths, there was a sense that sparks did hide some unbelievable secret. Marconi's method was not to back track his work as far as Tesla would have insisted, a complete revision of radiant mode. Years later, an aged Nikola Tesla was employed by RCA, the Rockefeller megalith, to make significant corrections on the Marconi Wave Radio System.

It is indeed unfortunate that Guglielmo Marconi was actually prevented from achieving that true originality by which legends are known and remembered. Money and the advantage of noble birth remained his principle obstacles. Because he was financially equipped and socially privileged, he found himself ruling the fate of worlds. Lacking the appropriate knowledge, the position brought forth significant and damaging deviations from the path of natural discovery. In his life, the inner blessing of vision never fully blossomed. He was a tragic figure, a sad statement concerning fame and technology. Marconi was a red rose frozen white in the snow. However Marconi tried to atone for his horrible actions in previous years, he was never able to clearly see the very first mistake which he had made. It began when he sent his first little wireless waves across his attic laboratory. Waves were the problem. Waves are still the problem.

# CHAPTER 3
## *Superior Directives and Privatized Military Research*

### SUPERIOR DIRECTIVES

How do we explain the national and geopolitical tensions so prevalent among social castes and nations, those which demand the continual efforts of a developing military? How will we explain the strivings of military researchers, whose sole function seems to be the development of better offensive and defensive systems? Why is military leadership continually involved in the functions of the bureaucratic machine? To what extent is this involvement necessary or cosmetic? Are the opposed ideologies of opposing nations the fundamental reason for military deployment, or do more permeating directives exist, by which military is empowered to engage the impossible? To whom does military actually respond, the national needs of the governed, or an agenda which is self-serving? Military responds to the several dictates which combine national security, technological competition, and superior directives. But who enunciates the superior directives?

The evidence of history, and the often irrational events with which international history is replete, cannot be the result of chance. More often, at the very highest levels of the social governing structures, we observe the consistent and patterned bureaucratic responses to unnamed authorities. Developing a model based on such observations, one finds sharp correspondence with events historical and actions contemporary which cannot easily be ignored. The consistent patterns strongly suggest the existence of rulership at higher than governmental authority levels. Some accuse that these models are attempts to rationalize the chaos of human affairs and the irrational responses of humanity when placed under duress. Consistent patterns which emerge through bureaucratic networks, whose variables are constantly changing and whose structures are completely variant, are not the result of order from chaos. Such patterns are the result of directed control, descending through the smoke screens of confused bureaucratic labyrinths, and thereafter enunciated and enforced as social policy. An astounding pattern can be traced back through history, a correspondence of our developing models with plausible world reality.

Those who interpret national and international affairs soon discover a consistency which frames specific geopolitical models, that which places aristocratic or Oligarchic Houses both within and over nations. This model provides us with a more clarified and cohesive explanation of tensions social, technological, and military. In this view, the various social tensions within and among nations, of ordinarily unexplained origin, stem from tensions between warring

Houses. The Oligarchic Houses are the "big gears" in the world clock. Oligarchic Houses rule whole sectors of the world, a network of independent rulerships whose history spans the human adventure. Best represented in the ancient totalitarian dynasties of Egypt, one finds all too much evidence that a continuity of Oligarchic rule has indeed conformed and compromised the best geodemocratic ideals. Oligarchic Houses remain mutually independent, the result of ancient growth and conflict. A model which places traditional warring Houses of aristocrats over visible government structures, fares exceedingly well when matched against real world happenings. The patterns of response in government policy follow a path which is not as meandering as most assume. Courses of action follow regular patterns, and are not the combined result of several internal variables. The flash disputes, violent and barbaric confrontations which form among briefly developed nations form an interesting example, the obvious results of external influence for deliberate effect.

Indeed, in all of the international disputes of the Twentieth Century, one perceives and interprets the invisible hand of influence very much at work. More recently, these influences move science and technology into receptive underdeveloped nations, with subsequent deliberations of war. Provisions of arms and munitions daily arriving at the gates, such nations are trained by private militia forces in unmarked uniforms, and raised to fever levels of emotion. Soon thereafter, hostilities break out, and national forces from the Old World or New World appear to "liberate" the oppressed. This model presupposes that complex relationships between warring Houses define the complex international relationships which, on topical inspection, are often imagined to be the result of random social action. Houses each rule whole geopolitical sectors. Each House region is viewed as an occupied territory, one whose ownership flows downward into a pyramidal power structure which it has generated. The obvious pyramidal structure of society is the evidence. Visibility within the pyramid differs for each level, a function of station and knowledge. There are those for whom the upper point of the pyramid will forever remain invisible. Living in the lowest levels of the pyramidal base, we are often able to penetrate the bureaucratic haze upward just enough to glimpse the convergence of power toward a probable point. This point is poised far above mere governmental structure. To those in the working class with eyes to see, the power structure appears truncated. Each House is therefore a virtual pyramid, occupying large portions of geography. A "geopolitical" region. These geopolitical regions of control have changed with time. The shifting of the borders among nations produces effects seen as often unprecedented "national reorganizations".

If social movement depended on the power flow through the pyramid, then only the pyramidal bases would change. The points of power would forever retain their identity. Nevertheless, we live in a biodynamic world, not a world of synthetic rulerships, however traditional. There have been two notable kinds of instances when the points of power have been compelled to move with the base. One is caused by external competition among Houses. The other is caused by "rogue" technological discoveries. The first commands power down through the structure, mobilizing societies to engage the competitor. The second cannot be rationalized or neutralized. Biodynamic technologies conform with naturally enunciated directives. They do not recognize synthetic power structures. Relying on conscious force, they make their unbidden presence felt throughout the entire pyramid, demanding change. Ideas penetrate the structures of power, shaking the seemingly rigid gantry asunder. The true and enslaving nature of power becomes evident during those instances, for not only are those who serve enslaved to the ruling power, but those who rule are compelled to follow the movements of their property. This property, whether geographic or social, becomes a cohesive structure which binds and restricts all freedoms, both for those at the bottom as well as those at the top.

Modern geopolitical regions are Oligarchies, House possessed world regions. Western Europe (WEO), Central Asian (CAO), South East Asian (SEAO), and the several isolated groups in India (IO), China (CO), and Japan (JO). From our accessible ground view, these territories are not connected by national or ethnic unities as much as they are by economic unities (Napolitano). The discovery and acquisition of the New World afforded new territories for certain Houses. Warring House are in sometimes vicious competition with one another. Their sometimes hostile relationship is entirely predicated on the personal ambitions and desires of the oligarch in question. Because the geopolitical regions of each House support the pyramidal point, the actual seat of power, ambitious or warring Houses may attempt hostile takeovers at a great number of levels. One may subvert economical levels, wasting potential capital from a House. One may subvert bureaucracy with "foreign" ideologies. One may actually attempt a forced geographic takeover, otherwise known as a "war. The needs of the House power structure therefore "become" the needs of those who are kept under its thralldom. If wars are waged against the local House, citizens will fight that war. Therefore the military has its prepared intentions; personal survival needs enunciated by the presence of superior command.

Wars find their rational explanations in the manipulations and machinations of warring Geopolitical Houses. If we assume that divisions and separations exist between Geopolitical Houses, cracks as it were in the ceiling structure of society, we find the real origin points of invisible instabilities through which international disputes are most likely generated. This model serves us well in comprehending the operation of nations under superior directives. Perceiving and observing this implicate structure teaches us the real flow of power within the nation, permitting us now to best comprehend the role of military as enforcement agency. Today, oligarchies require a complex labyrinth of mirrorworks by which to divert the gaze of a working class public. Therefore various Intelligence branches are sequestered and used to prepare "operations" well in advance of acquisitions. Military Operations are convenient "excuses" for imperialistic acquisitions, excuses for the eyes of a now-watching world.

Since there are rarely any viable reasons for armed conflicts or escalations leading to land invasions of foreign territories, we are led to consider the possibilities toward which the aforementioned geopolitical model invariably leads. One does not imagine that mildly frictive relationships between neighboring nations can realistically mount from violent acts to declarations of war without the stimulations of a catalytic agency. Geopolitical Houses, their nations, and their military aggregates explain the movements of military might in prearranged seasons. Warring Geopolitical Houses prompt their military aggregates to develop superior weaponry in the event that external hostilities bring land assaults to the borders of their authority. On their behalf, and by their explicit permission, military is to develop weapons, but never to become a private power unto themselves. Only those who dictate move power. Those who obey receive permissions. But now, do the words of rule always carry the greater force? Are there natural emerging phenomena whose unexpected manifestation reveals the limits of oligarchy and rule?

Because of the potentials afforded through new ventures, and the limited world extent of powerful exercise, Houses are never in mutually benign relationship. Since so much of the world is owned, the acquisitions of one House are necessarily the loss of another. The fundamental rules of supply and demand are thus apparently quite intact at even these high extra-social levels. It is only at successively lower social levels that manipulations can be so direct and complete. Oligarchs arrange economic depressions and recessions at their own convenience and in fulfillment of their own desires for their regions. But these actions among geopolitical power centers, among pyramidal structures, are more slowly applicable. As each geopolitical House strives against the others, there is a slow and creeping forward of progress attempting its exertions toward total world rule. When those exertions become necessarily quickened by internal circumstance, of which we may only guess, wars result.

Geopolitical Houses war over the control of geopolitical regions, the boundaries of which have been clearly delineated by traditional conflicts and subsequent diplomatic persuasions among the same. In this model, the continual exertions of military force and international manifestations of violence is explained by opposing Houses whose violent relationships are founded in centuries' old conflict. Warring Geopolitical Houses produce the defined geopolitical splits, both historical and contemporary, which appear across the world. The nature of oligarchic rule and the permeating power locally exerted by that superior command become the personal need and liability of the entire society. Gathered by each House, the complex collection of governments, bureaucracies, and citizen-workers all became liabilities in a world of sometimes hostile Houses. Because of these sometimes warring Houses, oligarchs are each necessarily driven to defend their societies and lands through varieties of means. Military means represent the very last line of defense in the conflict. First are those channels through which Houses "communicate"; those economic "messages" which are wordlessly sent throughout the world of pyramids. The Geopolitical Houses each use those nations in which they have based their operations. The working class population labors on their behalf, serving the principle supportive function of profit generation. Geopolitical Houses each require and accrete a corps-cooperatif, a host on which to subsist. Drawing life and blood from the labors of their base nations is an occupation of generations. The dreams of the few became the loss of the many.

## DIRECTIONS

Tesla and Marconi. The two principle figures in wireless communication have never stood shoulder to shoulder as equals. Misunderstanding kept Marconi from ever comprehending the superior discovery which Tesla had indeed made. It is not believed that he ever recognized the difference between electric RAYS and WAVES. How the relative worth of each seems to loom over the other in importance is as intriguing as he manner in which each was treated by the world. Closest to the source of the divergence, we find that Tesla and Marconi were viewed as complete opposites. In addition, different levels of honor were ascribed to each, with Tesla receiving honors befitting an original discoverer, and Marconi as a blatant plagiarist. Strangely however, this view completely reversed its polarity. The mystery of that shift in esteem from Tesla to Marconi has formed a most startling study in human behavior, for it is believed the two had become separate foci for two very opposed kinds of social forces. Knowing these differences is important to our discussion, since it serves to clarify the reasons for our modern dilemma. Perhaps we may find all of our answers in a particular era when all these issues were being designed. Only an examination of the historical trends which so rigidified the hierarchy of superior command, a hierarchy which does not have its origins within any agency, division, or branch of the government, will provide us with clarified answers. There was time when military interest in matters technological took a decisive turn in the wrong direction.

Tesla appeared on the scientific and social scene long before Marconi. We recall that most common people did not even know the name of Tesla. For most of society's working class, Tesla did not exist. The only persons who apprehended his work and his worth were, for two different reasons, found in the upper class. One group formed the educated elite. The others formed the business community. The first group was attracted to Tesla after the second group had found his inventive skills all too capable for rendering them the service of profit. In short, as long as Tesla was able to make money for the various financial bases in New York and Europe, he was applauded and "loved". It is also for this reason that Tesla grew into extravagant tastes in his youth. Mingling with the upper social classes in New York had its definite advantages. Increased contact also stimulated increased interest.

Tesla was indeed an original discoverer of natural electrical phenomena, a research experimenter of the very highest quality. Tesla was already a scholar in his own right, a visionary who coupled revelations with rare inventive skills. Speaking several languages fluently, and having the bearing and poise of a prince in his own right, Tesla was suddenly seized upon by the New York upper class. Had Tesla been anyone else, he would never have travelled as far in these circles. The class distinctions were rigidly held

by most of these families throughout the time that Tesla was moving among them. What affiliations Tesla made in these circles was the result of his genius and suave princely manners. His was indeed one whose charms were difficult, if not impossible, to ignore. Wealth and fame brought him this mystique for a time. Socialites pushed their daughters upon him, but his was not a long lived favor. Viewed from a distance, Tesla was certainly not a long lived star in their space. As soon as the time of his favor had passed, most forgot Tesla and shifted their eyes to some other trifle.

These effects spread from the social centers of wealth outward in larger circles. Those members of the New York Academy of Science, and of the London Royal Society, who once idolized Tesla, those who indeed watched him demonstrate the impossible before their very eyes, were later found wholly given to a strange repudiation of the man and his work. The contradictory focussing and refocusing of attention on each of the two different men is not difficult for us to understand when taking note of the social caste which was directing the attention and deliberating their relative value.

## DEVIATIONS

Tesla was not from the upper class. Tesla therefore did not understand the real nature of his rejection by either The London Royal Society, the New York Academy of Sciences, or The United States Military. Despite his astounding demonstrations, patents, and superior technological achievements, Tesla seemed never able to attract that kind of serious interest which would have secured him a firm place in the convention. Their rejection was not based on an inability to apprehend the truth, but on a boredom with "the show". The fickle attentions of this community were so obviously unwilling to delve into Teslian discoveries that The very criticisms of his work reveal a singular vacuousness, one not based in scientific reasoning whatsoever. The inability to reproduce his clearly defined parameters, those which would release for them the power of Radiant Energy and all of its wondrous potentials, was actually an unwillingness to apply their hands to work. Only two individuals out of the entire British consortium reported their experiments in this regards.

Sir William Crookes and Sir Oliver Lodge tried the Tesla experiments. Though neither was able to achieve the same results, only Sir William corresponded with Tesla to determine the curious cause of his own failure. Sir Oliver Lodge, very apparently, did not understand at all what Tesla had defined as the only means for obtaining Radiant Energy effects. Lodge had previously developed high frequency alternating circuits which used sparkgaps. These were similar only in their appearance with some of Tesla's apparatus. Lodge somehow completely reinterpreted or misinterpreted Tesla's lecture to match his own priority in the subject area, a remarkable phenomenon of misunderstanding. On wonders "where" Sir Oliver was wandering during the famed Tesla Lectures, which provoked a long standing ovation from the London Society. The very same effect was observed in the New York Academy, where Michael Pupin claimed inability to reproduce Teslian effects, and later claimed that Tesla was a charlatan. Indeed in certain last New York public lectures, Tesla endured loud verbal abuse from Pupin and others during his talk.

It was precisely about this time that Guglielmo Marconi appeared on the scene. While the Royal Society originally condemned Marconi as a first-rate plagiarist and thief, they later grew to adore him. This sort of reversal further baffled the innocent Nikola Tesla. Directed into the idolization of Guglielmo Marconi for reasons only having to do with his class and his wealth, Marconi continued being favored. Marconi was both a Marchese, extremely wealthy by birth, and his mother was a member of the honored English Aristocracy: attributes which endeared him to the Royal Society despite an initial contemptuousness. It is patently obvious that the rejection of Tesla was not therefore based on scientific reasoning at all. Indeed, the acceptance of Marconi was not based on scientific reasoning at all. Each response manifested the overwhelming affectations of an erudite class, a response having everything to do with position, wealth, and political connection. Fame followed wealth, as Marconi entered center stage and Tesla was asked to leave. Tesla was eliminated from these upper class deliberations with the same aloof command given to a dispatched servant. Tesla was on his own again, relying on his own wealth to carry his dreams. But certain others spied this out, and destroyed the bulk of his wealth in the fire which almost also cost him his very life.

The two different and opposed personalities of Nikola Tesla and Guglielmo Marconi received their respective treatments amid an elite and upperclass academic consortium. The preference for caste and wealth apparently yet remains the fundamental "scientific" consideration. Deviations induced by caste affiliations expanded the persona of Marconi beyond his due, propelling him and his inferior technology out into a world now prepared to idolize him.

Thereafter, the wealth which attached itself to his fame permitted the further expansion of the inferior wave technology which has overwhelmed society. Over commercialized in the consumer marketplaces, Marconi wave radio flooded the world. This flood proliferated not only inferior communications modes but also an inferior engineering science, one which now denies the very existence of Teslian Radiant Stream Energy. Nevertheless, The weak radiative wave energy of Marconi could never and will never compete with the Radiant Stream Energy which Tesla championed.

The favors, lavished upon a supposed scientific member of the European high caste, has resulted in a deviation from the intended path which has lasted for nearly a century. Because of the weight placed on Marconi, a superior Teslian technology was ignored. The repercussions of this completely irrational maneuver have condemned the world to a continued reliance on inferior technologies and, in a more ultimate sense, on an obsolescent utilization of fuel products. This impossibly dense situation has proven far too resistive for even those best equipped and motivated to undertake the reproduction of Teslian technology. Military personnel who have long had a similar fickle relationship with things Teslian began their search only after the inventor himself had passed away. But the history of their involvement with the new technological forays marking the last century's turn is just as fascinating as he manner in which academia treated the sciences of waves and rays.

## CORPS ELITE

Eighteenth Century Military leadership became a rigidified elite group, a foppish reversal of their onetime low social caste as blood-encrusted servant-warriors. Their newfound poise as decorated officers and gentlemen compelled an innate abhorrence of scientific accoutrements, contraptions considered "frivolous" and "undignified". The overestimation of blackstrap leather, square jawed grit, and sheer strength of numbers versus "applications intellectual" took a violent turn two minutes into the first battle of World War I, where Nineteenth Century military brawn was introduced to Twentieth Century scientific warfare. Empowered by years of prior research and development, the new battlefront of steel helmets, tight-fitting canvas uniforms, deadly gas, gas masks, tanks, hand grenades, field radio communications, and superior artillery wiped away those first feather-festooned officers in satin who rose over the hill on horseback. Later developments introduced the world of armies to a new battlefield in the skies. Dirigibles, airplanes, airgunners, airbombers, and all the subsequent tactical developments accompanying the acquisition of new materiel for war, suddenly and unexpectedly made their unwelcome appearance. Now, even in the absence of "battle-ready" proof, the military simply began entertaining every sort of potential weapon system. Not one such technological possibility was to be rejected.

Science had become the tool of power on all fronts. With or without military approvals, science had become the eyes and ears of all world power. Hard scientific prowess, not military format, did more than turn any geopolitical conflict. Scientific equipment always enunciated the outcome. Military were traditionally too proud to admit this fact. Scientists, not well groomed officers, provided the modern route toward battle victory. Military leaders found themselves training with their men in the use of all these new scientific tactical advantages. The employment of experimenters and researchers began the long tradition of liaisons between the creative community and the commanding community. The initially rude and brusque encounter between military leadership and pedestrian experimenters grew into a flame of wonders, a flame from which projected so many new and diverse sparklets. These sparklets flooded the decade between World Wars, the last decade where strange and anomalous natural discoveries arrived in a mysterious and thrilling starfall. Military leaders appropriated weapons-potential hardware as soon as it appeared. A new thought regime began connecting the two diverse weapons regimes together in a truly bizarre manner, an equally bizarre concept emerging. Once the absolute bastion of all that was practical and reasonable, the military research teams began entertaining more of the exotic and the outlandish in scientific possibility. This method, the "way of dreamers", had proven itself to be an inestimable advantage, now even a necessity.

How were the superior rayic technologies of Nikola Tesla overshadowed by the inferior wave radio applications of Guglielmo Marconi? What kind of strange legerdemain had Marconi so successfully employed that he could so completely dominate the industry of communications that his name alone is equated with radio? In order to comprehend the nature of this ludicrous opinion, so fervently maintained by the turn of the century academicians and military, we must examine the atmosphere acquired by Marconi through all of his public relations support structures. Military, a traditionally elitist organization, at once grasped the tremendous potential of radio communications in the worldwide theatre which they embraced. Military prized the potentials of every technological breakthrough. Naval authority especially sought the new development of Radio for its obvious utility in defense.

While appreciation of the potential "science advantage" had sometimes reached the attentions of military groups at the turn of the Century, the strong reliance on systems scientific had not yet completely come of age. Examination of patents, just before the onset of World War I, reflect the excessive deliberations of inventors and researchers who found a sure market in developing military equipment. Bidding for the attention of military leaders in this time period was never easy. One had to overcome the hardened elitism which characterized the archetypal officer, the pure soldier. Marconi had done just this in England, but only through auspices secured by his English mother, of aristocratic birth. Marconi was able to sell to the British military a system which their own scientists had already devised. But for his bravado and aristocratic connection, he would have been rebuked for the insolence. Through this incursion, as it were, wave radio made its contaminating appearance first in the British military, and then in the world at large.

Arranging demonstrations with these men was never an opportunity to be trifled with, evidence of an aristocratic carry-over which, though thoroughly undemocratic and contradictory, was indeed revealing. The military tradition, one whose themes run prior to the advent of national government, had long elevated themselves to elite levels rivalling those born of royal blood. Great ceremony accompanied the early turn of the Century encounters between inventors and military leaders; events which often proved or disproved the worth of featured hardware in a single shot. Heated debates among various division leaders often argued the relative practical worth of technical systems, usually viewed in a dubious military eye. Military leaders of different service branches were in constant competition to prove their non-reliance on scientific hardware, as if this was but another measure of strength and pride. Army, Navy, and a young developing Air Force now were in fierce personal competition.

Elite military leaders, themselves from the upper caste, were most interested in obtaining stations for their own purposes. The innermost predispositions of major historical figures is revealed in their actions. History records the military willingness to first seek out Marconi rather than Dr. Tesla. This preference was predicated on all the reasons which have previously been outlined: class elitism and the self-attractions of that self-centered clique. But this list of influences was balanced against the one item which sealed the destiny of Marconi. His perceived superiority was based entirely on his financial resource. Unlike the process which used Tesla in order to assess his potential achievements, with subsequent removal of funding at critical moments in his final moments of preparation, the continued funding to Marconi insured his success on many fronts. Highly prestigious authorities perceived Marconi as the only source from which to learn and acquire the secrets of Radio. The growth process which eventually produced a privatized military Signal Corps was the result of the manner in which wave radio technology began emerging as the "only possible wireless communications system".

Radio offered military a manifold battle presence. Not only for its tactical advantages on the global scene, but also because hostile others were engaged in like research, different branches of the military now actively arranged liaison with The Marconi Company. Contrary to the prestige and perception of Marconi, other researchers were already experimenting in wave radio. Some had successfully duplicated and surpassed the Marconi System in Europe, a secret which Marconi continually managed to enforce. Those whose experimental work encompassed these topics knew that several key figures had long delved into the wireless arts. With the first appearance of Marconi, several adventurous experimenters, Count Georg von Arco, Fr. Joseph Murgas, Sigmund Musits, Harry Shoemaker, Dr. Fessenden, Lt. Com. William Hogg, Alexander Meissner, and a long list of others who had already perfected variant radio systems. Each of these wave radio systems operated with great power and clarity in a wide range of higher than VLF frequencies.

Demanding entry into the new radiotelegraphy field was not easy however. Sheer indomitable willpower however was not enough in this battlefront. At the time, a formidable Emperor had to be carefully approached and appeased. Elitist met with elitist, the one now subservient to the other. In this case, it was a surprising obeisance, where the American military was required to kneel before a single individual. The pressures which forced Military into the initially subservient relationship with Marconi came from already mentioned prejudices, and the growing threat of a world poised on the brink of European War. Military requested assistance in developing their own transoceanic communications systems against that eventuality. The Marconi Company became the original contractor for these first military radio projects.

What had Marconi represented to the military? How was he perceived? Marconi was indeed a source of radio technology for which military recognized obvious advantages and potentials. But, despite all of the mentioned attribute given him through advantage and prestige, Marconi was a civilian. This status permitted a strong and advantageous separation through which a convenient ultimate divorce would be arranged. Military did not wish subservience to one who owed allegiance to neither national fronts, defense initiatives, or historical loyalties. Marconi was a monopolist, a business privateer, a foreigner. Marconi willingly supplied military with systems of their own.

Believing the extensive lie that wave radio was indeed "the only radio", they were forced to come to Marconi. He supposedly had the secrets. His very fame seemed to be a declaration of dependable expertise. The military was always fixated on that term, "dependable". Close after this word, the terms "reliable" and "practical" follow. In this evidence of rigid fixations, military authorities are not always correct in their assessments and trusts. The Marconi organization offered some kind of proof of control. The propaganda taught that Marconi was in absolute of the wave world. He was the one to see.

Before the military could launch their own radio waves out across the seas, before structuring and controlling their own wave world, they had to acquire both these secrets and this experience. Marconi's initial contracts had been signed with the British military, a contract which became valuable to both parties. Having forced British military into a position of subservience, Marconi exacted an excessive tribute. Marconi, heir apparent of the "wave secrets", used his position and their admiration to draw out every possible pound sterling while he could. American military had already observed these maneuvers. Yet, Marconi wanted a contract with them. His desire allowed them to shape their end of the bargain, one in which they planned an ultimate and complete break. Military in America had no desire to perpetuate a relationship with a civilian who swaggered with the false air of a tyrant.

Their approach was simple, it having already been strategically planned that their young officers in training absorb as much learning as possible from the Marconi Institutes. The entire affair in no way differed from an espionage operation. Thereafter, certain military corpsmen were to concentrate on the examination of his VLF installations. Others were to gain operating experience. Yet others were to become proficient in engineering aspects of his technology. Once a thorough saturation of this knowledge and experience had been acquired, the corpsmen were to leave the Marconi System altogether. Thereafter, military engineering corps could design and develop their own systems. Privatized systems.

### DIVORCE

Ultimately, the establishment of a Signal Corps of highly trained engineers emerged from an intensive period of involvement with the Marconi Global Communication Systems. Having now obtained a vast experiential fund of wireless science, the were in a possession to develop superior forms of the same systems for their own purposes, an eventuality which Marconi anticipated. As the split between himself and military was occurring, Marconi tried suing the military. Military claimed independence, and developed Marconi technology into a power technology which he would never duplicate for sheer size. Once thus established in the attendant expertise of such technology, military personnel soon divorced themselves from commercial contractors. Marconi, one who was used to "getting his way" in court proceedings, could not win a battle with such forces.

The precedent having been set, military radio technology began a separate developmental agenda. In this clean break with Marconi, military established an historical precedent in which they now hold complete and unobstructed authority in projects over which they retain high priority classifications. In this precedent, military rulership of certain technologies exceeds certain Executive access privileges. By World War I, privatized military VLF stations rivalled those of Marconi for sheer size and power output. Subterranean and subaqueous radio was developed into a powerful tool, the technology of Murgas and Rogers having been periodically classified and unavailable to researchers. Naval authorities began researching deep VLF and ELF frequencies without supervision or assistance from civilian sectors just after World War I. These systems were better equipped, larger installations. Fitted into natural geotopography with engineering precision, the powerful waves from these surprisingly powerful multimegawatt power stations were pumped into the seas through deep submarine valleys and natural channels.

Radio wave systems which were developed by James H. Rogers stimulated interest in deep-sea communications. His wave radio systems made direct communications with deeply submerged vessels possible, designs which employed buried antennas. Rogers began conducted tests with a great number of such systems before the first World War, continuing his developments with various buried and submerged antennas throughout the 1920's. Naval authorities approached Rogers during the War, classifying and implementing his numerous patents.

These submergible antenna systems had no precedent in the wave radio arts, representing an anomalous and unexpected variant of the Marconi powerline aerial. The performance of these systems, in both transmission and reception, proved quite remarkable. Static and interference were virtually eliminated by the buried lines, filtered as it were by direct contact with a the solid medium of the earth. Because of the obvious implications of such wave propagation, Rogers contacted Dr. Tesla. The two corresponded quite often in a friendly and filial scientific relationship lasting several years until the death of Rogers. In the strangely empowered operation of these wave radio antenna systems, Rogers indeed glimpsed something of the æther theories put forth by Dr. Tesla. Required in maintaining worldwide deep-sea communications with submarines, the NRL quickly implemented experimental findings in these directions throughout the period leading to and following World War II. Dr. Thomas Hieronymus, a significant early researcher in radionic science reported the impossibility of obtaining Rogers antenna patents during such times of national emergency. These designs later became components in the Naval ELF wave radio system known as SANGUINE and SEAFARER.

Military engineers experimented in worldwide communications, encryption, jamming techniques, and hybrid combinations of radio systems yet largely unrecognized. In this latter aspect, were those systems which employed luminal carriers for radio frequency pulsations, beacons and beams closely patterned after Teslian descriptions. Despite these extensive experiments, military engineers found Teslian Technology mysteriously impossible to reach, a token which some considered as proof that Tesla was exaggerating his claims. Nevertheless, and most importantly, military researchers became fixated on themes which Tesla was enunciating. Though viewing his claims as the exaggerated ravings of a dreamer without substance, they thought to implement his inspiration, interpreting his visions to achieve his objectives. They were wrong. Using the lessons learned through their contaminating tutelage at Marconi's feet, military found themselves forever being eluded by Teslian technology, the demonstrations which some experts had indeed witnessed.

The bitter lesson, learned in the World War I conflict with the Kaiser's scientifically equipped Army, would not be forgotten. Empowered with the cruelties of chemical warfare, large tanks, and aerial bombers, this rolling force was virtually unstoppable until met by equivalent and superior "scientific" opposition. Science became more than the communications wave medium. Science was the war wave of the future. A new corps-elite which appreciated the power of science to deliver new kinds of weaponry was now actively supported and applauded. Science gave the winning edge. Science determined the wins and losses, turned the battle, ended the war. Science was the victory wreath. So complete was this conversion from the former martial attitude, which relied on infantry muscle and brilliant field campaigns to win conflicts, that one cannot now think of the military without its sizable investment in every conceivable new technology. Martial technology rivals the research volumes of industry as a matter of necessity. Maintaining the upper hand on any possible state of art weaponry is now an absolute and continuous pursuit. One could not tell when an opposing force might develop some new and threatening weapon capable of breaching the national borders. It was especially after the First World War, a horror from which many have said the Century never recovered, that science became the prime military source for the development of new war tools. And then an amazing phenomenon swept the world.

Experimenters throughout the world had begun observing strange radiant phenomena in their course of research, phenomena which closely resembled effects claimed by Nikola Tesla. Implementing the same in equally bizarre apparatus, these inventors began assailing patent offices the world over. This new flood of developments from the amateurs deeply intrigued the military in every nation. Pandora's Box had been opened, and the horrors had been unleashed. Many of these applications were very obvious weapons-potential systems. Because of this unexpected tide of such inventions from amateurs and privateers, military now entertained the possibility that radio wave technology might be transformed into a new a frightful kind of weaponry or communications technology. It was long before World War I that certain researchers, notably Turpain (1894), MacFarland-Moore (1898), and Ulivi (1914) had each reported phenomena closely shadowing those effects reported by Tesla. This pattern of close Teslian approximations continued to flood the scientific journals between the World Wars; a legacy of vision, a natural phenomenon of the most significant order. Such inventors were very quickly contacted by specific military agencies for classified funding, research, and development of their however meritorious systems.

The proliferation of this visionary trend continued throughout the period between and after the Second World War, one which we will closely examine in the next few chapters. Here was evidence of an unsuspected visionary resource in the civilian population, one long championed by Nikola Tesla. Dreams and their technologies were truly unstoppable. The conduction raybeam devices of H. Grindell-Matthews (1917), J. Hettinger (1919), F. McCullough (1922), and C. Reno (1924), became mere shadows of weaponry developed and demonstrated by Tesla. These were systems tested and classified during World

War II, systems which will shortly be described. The trend had not ceased by the mid-1940's, new beamray systems having been developed and reported by Riley, Gosztonyi, Pribil, Mohr, Salisbury, Chapman, Claudel, May, Longoria, and hosts of others. The list has never any end of names. It continues to this very day.

Throughout the time when Tesla openly offered his beamray systems to the United States, military remained aloof. Were they truly ignorant of his successes? Were they prevented from knowing of his achievements? Were they commanded never to deal with him? Was their aloofness a sign of ignorance or of unwillingness to move on his behalf? What superior command held the military so enthralled that they were incapable of appropriating the wonders which came from the fertile mind of Tesla while he was available? What, if any, alternative technology kept them so disinterested in Tesla that they failed so miserably and completely at the supreme opportunity of a lifetime? Either these personnel have no insight whatsoever, a highly unlikely possibility, or they have been constrained by private agencies of superior command. Made all the more clear through their very sudden Cold War interest in Teslian technology, one wonders whether they "just woke up". Tragically, typically, military experts appeared suddenly and completely enraptured by Teslian æther technology after his death in 1943. But what could have so reversed their decision to alternately ignore, and then adore the work of Nikola Tesla? What has so completely overcome reason among military leadership, that complete and absolute rejection has now become adoration? To whom is the military held completely captive?

POWERFLOW

How curious that the flow of power through bureaucratic structures so closely mimics the natural flow of current in the ground, the currents whose power is to enliven and sustain. Unlike those biovital currents which so many inventors studied, the flow of power from the Geopolitical Houses is not intended to enliven. Moving forcefully through all the governmental bureaucracies, through the military, and into the population, this enslaving power does not normally reverse its directions. Government bureaucracy evidences arbitrations on behalf of citizens at the very lowest levels. Above these, citizens are effectively divorced and alienated from all other bureaucratic portions. When anger and hostility is expressed from the citizenry, the sometimes violent interchange is effectively blocked from ever reaching higher government levels by police force at the lowest levels. In this manner, the oligarchy maintains absolute separation between its own "free enterprise" and the citizen. The bureaucratic distance between oligarch and citizen is a labyrinthine maze of blind alleys and circular force-loops which blocks those who would see "further up" from those who "see down". According to the model, there is a directed flow to the power which proceeds down from any one Oligarchic House. The Intelligence Networks, whose presence permeates each subordinate nation, is first to receive that superior command. Next in the division of authority is the bureaucracy of government, which processes each command directive down, delegating the further subdivision of tasks to each governmental compartment. Power finally stops flowing, just before the masses of governed citizens are reached.

# CHAPTER 4
# Nuclear Weaponry and Nuclear Hybrids

## TABLEAU

Discussions concerning geopolitical models have been a most necessary part of our thesis. One cannot conceive of the forces and directives capable of stimulating all of the technology which has been developed since the military divorcement. From the days when military engaged Marconi and his Global Communications Company until today, we are witnessing an astounding proliferation of scientifically empowered thrusts whose whole aim and purpose it is to develop superior weaponry. The geopolitical arena into which these military and conventional systems have been deployed is the most critical part of our thesis, forming the tableau against which technology has defined impact. The technological impact on the various oligarchic rulerships, the Houses which possess multinational clusters, cannot be properly appreciated. The technological revolution was one whose power is yet distrusted and hated among the oligarchs.

Why this attitude has suffused the rulership with definitive and malicious antitechnological policies has everything to do with the interference which technology introduces in the otherwise smooth exercise of oligarchic power. Technology introduces unexpected and destabilizing variables into the geopolitical theatrum. Technology is a hurricane force of unstoppable potentials, forcing the hand of power to bend and sway uncontrollable vectors. World order, however Old or New, is the unwitting slave of Technology. Once a technological manifestation appears, particularly if it is vision laden, the entire world is polarized. But technology is but the mere embodiment of a far more demonstrative power, one for which there can be no defense. The rulership too late realized this, when the sheer force of a new consciousness powerful pounced upon their otherwise isolated thresholds and brought them to their knees. How this revolutionary storm has thoroughly infused the working class is a study all its own, a first step toward comprehending the full weight of the Atomic Age.

This is a chapter which deals with Power and concentrations of Power in the world of actions. The development of the nuclear industry, and its subsequent perversion into weaponry, has provoked far more devastations throughout the world order than normally imagined. These devastations exist in realms of emotion, consciousness, perception, as well as in the various military-industrial arenas of the world. The release of nuclear energy was a demonstration of superior power on many different levels. Nuclear energy represented far more than a new energy potential. Indeed, the release of this energy has had defined impact on realms both scientific and social. Because of the unexpected emergence of this seemingly ultimate earthly force, we will see that the power of rulership was shifted back and forth between the very highest and the very lowest levels of earthly authority; this the result of technological developments alone. This chapter also introduces the several directions into which military technology moved from the Second World War, through the Cold War period, and into our present time frame. This chapter therefore introduces the divisions in technology which lead directly to HAARP and beyond.

## INFINITESIMALS

Through a most mysterious and permeating influence, one which came like the roaring wind, working class consciousness was all too rapidly expanding into scientific directions. At about the middle of the Nineteenth Century, this far superior phenomenon of power manifested itself throughout the clustered nations of the Northern Hemisphere. Oligarchic rule could neither repel or resist its movements. It was a fiery baptism whose permeating blasts have long lingered among the impassioned working class. Futuristic dreams and visions flooded into their minds with such force that many did not sleep for days on end. When under the supernatural influence of these visitations, many could not or would not sleep until they had completed their designs.

The consciousness, so powerfully shared by the working masses, was one which first amplified consciousness. The thirst for knowledge and the subsequent creativity which emerged in new and revolutionary directions began impacting the traditional order with deadly force. Social movements of this revolutionary character, movements in mind, suddenly struck the stability of House Order and rocked its foundations across the world. Researching, building, devising, machining, the inventive thrust swept the nations with a lion-like ferocity. Here was an ordained directive whose power was indeed far superior to all others. Here was a directive to create, one whose social implications yet remain unfathomable. With sudden and uncalculated social leverages, the Sciences and Technologies very quickly destroyed the aristocratic mould whose deliberate and cruel tradition was never otherwise to change or move.

Diligent comparisons made between this period and all those previous in national archives reveal the extent of this social explosion. With its principle actors solely among the working class, the astounding and unforeseen emergence of a higher conscious state cultivated a new thematic thrust. Examination of the scholarly Periodicals and Patent Record proves that a remarkable social phenomenon took place shortly before 1850; where the volume of scientific research and inventions suddenly became magnified beyond all bounds. Working class inventors were in shops everywhere, responding to a flood of visionary energy so powerful that those who moved with its powerful surges could scarcely believe the achievements which so liberally poured out of their workshops. Here was a far superior consciousness on the loose, released in a social group which was never valued as other than a servant class.

The separations existing between caste levels, a fixture established by tradition, actually afforded the insulation necessary for the new consciousness to be cultivated and appreciated. Here also, and most curiously, was a permeating power which was not shared by the aristocrats. They seemed incapable of appropriating the new consciousness, however schooled or familiar they or their children became with scientific topic areas. Though available to all, Science and Technology had forever become a segregated gift, an implacable dividing line through which only certain sensitive working class individuals could move.

Science and Technology, the onetime trifling amusement of mercantile aristocrats, was never anticipated by the oligarchy as a potential threat to either their continued security or their power to rule absolutely. But inexplicably, certainly not by their decree, this new flood of consciousness and vision had been unleashed among the social masses. All too suddenly, new and significant tides breaking down the whole rigidified order and structure of the traditional rulership. So complete was this social reorganization that by the end of the last century, a working class revolution in science and technology permeated and dominated the traditional world order without mercy. The mind revolution raised diligent scholars like Michael Faraday and William Crookes from their working class homes into the halls of legend. Recall also that Tesla was working class.

Though Tesla managed to become fabulously wealthy before the age of thirty, and despite his suave and gentlemanly European manner, he was not heir to those same old family privileges as one Marchese Guglielmo Marconi. Despite receptions among the upper class, receptions in which Tesla had unknowingly been cast as intriguing entertainment, he was not as truly welcomed by those seeking bizarre and furtive amusements. In comparison, we consider the aristocrat Guglielmo Marconi, member of a family whose matriarch was English aristocracy. It was perhaps on this basis alone that the elitists "forgave" his Italian aristocratic lineage. Is it more clear why these upperclass receptions responded so favorably and persistently to Marconi and not to Tesla?

Technology enters a pre-existent world where various powers have produced their stagnant structure, one designed to promote their rulership and continual supply of wealth. While rising above the populations they use, such powers repress, redirect, and divest the dreams of humanity. No greater earthly power could ever have dissuaded the invisible hands of oligarchic control, until the unforeseen change forever established its presence. The sudden appearance of this irresistible antagonist was one whose permeating presence could not be quantified in coin or person. Incapable of being caught and executed, this foe was free to spread its message of liberty to those sensitive enough to receive it. This was an organized anarchy, a disciplined and deliberate movement toward visionary objectives, whose inspiring leader could neither be located or eradicated. Obviously ordained by far superior authority, this was a thematic social movement whose power was successfully codified into a new ethos and mythos. Moreover, it was a consciousness uniquely framed for the working classes. It was in their life-style of urgencies, passions, necessities, devotions, and personal sacrifices that this consciousness best blossomed. Those higher castes who attempted its importation were shocked to find themselves incapable of keeping and cultivated its favors. In later times, oligarchs were forced to have their bureaucracies hire working class minds as advisers.

Whereas aristocratic natural philosophers once toyed with the forces of Nature, and spent their days toying with their thoughts on the same, the new revolution produced definitive hardware. Equipped with this new consciousness, and coupled with the inheritance of Old World trade skills, of which they were the devoted custodians, the servant class inventive revolution went forward with no opposition. The ghost walked in its machines. As the New Century came, the new and powerful consciousness swept their world with an indifferent superiority all its own. Here was a victorious conqueror whose spirit remained more unseen than even oligarchs themselves. Power was rapidly refocussing in deeper levels than even the bureaucratic structures made to maintain social rigidity.

A dynamic and thrilling power was suddenly released in and among the working class with no possibility of flow back up into the oligarchic structures. This was a spontaneous generation of power, an undefinable phenomenon to all who could only watch its unhindered progress. This revolution was one whose power was not obtained by usurping the traditional sources. Here was a power derived from a new consciousness alone. In the flood of such new awakenings, new demands were enunciated by the working class. But these demands included neither bureaucracy nor oligarchy at all. Many whose awareness level saw the comparison between former repressive times and their present liberation took the matter further, by annihilating the bureaucracy and ferreting out the oligarchy toward the same ends.

## ATOMIC FUEL

Throughout the years preceding World War II, a small group of widely separated researchers successfully demonstrated the possibility of deriving energy from the atomic lattices of various materials. This development was the result of methodic investigations in photoelectric and photonuclear processes, conducted by Dr. Gustav Le Bon in Belgium (1897). The next appearance of this thought regime came when Dr. Andre Helbronner in France (1920), and

Dr. Fritz Paneth and Dr. Kurt Peters in Germany (1926) each independently began studying electrical discharge processes in pure hydrogen gas, a dangerous experimental line to pursue even in university laboratories. Each researcher discovered that "extra energy", in exceedingly great supplies, could be obtained for hours from their experimental apparatus. Long after an initial high voltage electrical discharge had been made to pass across tungsten or palladium arc electrodes, and then withdrawn, their strange and continued red glowing heat was observed. Here was the clearest suggestion that an unknown energy process had been accidentally tapped.

In varieties of these experiments, the properties of uranium and other heavy isotopes were found to release similar, though limited energetic streams. Some utilized uranium, radium, and thorium electrodes in other gaseous atmospheres, obtaining electrical outputs as well as heat. Tubes in this regard were built and used by Ainsworth (1915), Winkelmann (1923), Metzger (1925), McElrath (1936), The use of purified uranium in small laboratory experiments by Fermi proved to be the more inferior of all the methods, ultimately requiring highly privatized and expensive systems for the production of "fuel". Here was a new technology which could be made inaccessible to civilian privateers by virtue of its excessive industrial support structures. The purification of uranium required gigantic facilities requiring great financial expenditures. Here was the perfect opportunity to institute a new monopoly at the ground floor!

But this experimental pursuit, while remaining a laboratory secret, also had its malignant side. Besides being a deadly radioactive poison, uranium had another potential utility. These researches released one of the most terrifying secrets in all of Nature. Both regulators, their servant minions, and the rest of society came face to face with the dread power of the insignificant. What was once perceived as weak, became the horrid strength. And not one of the controlling factions could have foreseen the nightmare which was released. And then, just as sudden, the regulatory commissions found themselves staring into an abyss of horror in which every Old World method had found its new world end.

Warring Houses stimulate international wars for the acquisition of land, resource, and populations. Warring Houses therefore depend on the superiority of their military forces to turn the tide of victory in their favor. Science, that infant-terrible from the lower classes, proved to have merit in military applications. So long as military force was controllable, limited, regulated, even wars could be tolerated among Houses. Blasting, destroying, devastating, and killing were all part of he strivings of power. Wars were very controlled events. But, as scientific research was making its progress into the very wheelworks of Nature, an unexpected developed emerged. The science and technology, whose ghost could not be contained, spawned a conundrum. Science found itself beholding, in deep recesses of matter, a natural power capable of annihilating all earthly power. And very suddenly, all natural and social powers bent down toward the infinitesimal, toward the atom and its hideous energies.

In the conflict of World War II, threats that the Nazi regime had developed an atomic weapon were more than conceivable. Lingering rumours teach that Nazi physicists had already tested small atomic weapons. Having found the repercussions of these weapons inefficient from the conqueror's standpoint, their later development of neutron-emitting weapons has been more than a matter of speculation. Wrenched toward the headlong development of an atomic arsenal, the real power once again refocused without permission or delegation. Predicated on the inescapable demands of war, oligarchs were again force to watch the power leave their centers of control, as power was being spontaneously generated in working class laboratories. Moreover, the threat was such that the rulership had to expend capital in order to insure that they would first acquire their version of the "Atomic Bomb". In this incredible turn, atomic energy research neutralized the repressive tide of decrees with which rulership had punished the working class. But those of the working class who labored on the new "device" were not prepared for the path into which they would soon find themselves walking. It was at this very point in history that the initial and wonderful visionary potential of atomic energy was to be twisted into a thing completely devastating for humanity.

The result of decades' dreaming and experimental research produced, not the intended glory of an endless and safe energy source, but an absolute livid horror. The envisioned goal was never to use the heavy metals at all, but to employ light metals, and the solar energies of which Tesla and Le Bon spoke. The real atomic energy was a natural release of energetic streams, a direct process of conversion which produced pure electrical currents, not radioactive debris. But with the hot body-permeating green-white flash of the Alamogordo experiment, all those dreams were exploded away in a thousand thunders. Indeed those once confident regulators, who so pushed for the "bigger Bomb" were scrambling for assistance and explanation. Here was an unreckoned force, an unknown whose repercussions were far more horrific than the thunderous blast which reminded many of eternal judgement.

Atomic weaponry best expressed the power of consciousness and its embodiment in technology. For those whose policies sought the eradication of visionary science, here was a true horror. The Atomic Bomb was a destroying power unlike all others, released through a simple application of theoretical analysis. A simple mental application by a working class consortium. Here was the earthly equalizer. The untamed and irrepressible world annihilator. The Bomb was impersonal, ultimate, and unregulated. Fear was the force inherent in this natural energy. Fear and respect for those who wielded The Weapon.

The oligarchy viewed Atomic Bombs as destroying weapons from whose aftermath there could be no hope of resource acquisition. These were absolute weapons of threat, weapons used to do permanent and final damage to hostile Houses. Such damage could be inflicted, so it was commonly thought, with absolute impunity. No repercussions. To destroy an opposing House with finality would be the threat which balanced the often expressed ambitions. Houses would be forced to speak one with the other through diplomatic channels at the very highest intelligence levels. These weapons could effect the total destruction of an enemy House region and its territories, a subsequent total takeover being then possible. Many controlling agencies in the bureaucracy comforted themselves in this notion, somehow imagining that the atomic weapon under construction was but a larger version of any conventional chemical explosive. Most thought the Atomic Bomb to be a larger blockbuster type bomb, with no major difference but blast size. Typical was the self-indulgent response of the rulership, which anticipated no real distinction between chemical and atomic weaponry.

The race to produce a working atomic prototype is a tale told in madness, a device the result of madness. Forged in the fear that hostile others would, at some indistinct future produce just such a terror weapon, NAO research teams were literally pushed against all reason into the atomic fires. The totality of an American working force misapplied its intellect and labors, permanently stained by the mere touch of their new and pernicious acquaintance, Uranium. Ironically, uranium was discovered by Martin Klaproth, a German apothecary. During this time, uranium found use only as a ceramic glaze, producing yellow, orange, brown, and black enamels, and in glass. Used to make in vacuum capacitors, uranium glass gave a pearly yellow color with a strange green fluorescence. These radioactive components produced an extraordinarily stable high capacitance per unit volume, and were used in highpower Naval UHF and RADAR transmitters. The Westinghouse Lamp Division briefly experimented with uranium-doped tungsten filaments, a means by which indefinite lamp life had been demonstrated.

Experimenters and researchers, once fascinated with the phenomenon of radioactivity, turned their minds only on deriving benefit from the strange natural variety of radioactive minerals. Not one of the early experimenters required the purification of uranium for the powerful effects which they had discovered. Indeed, it had been found that natural uranium ores were sufficient for the production of electrical currents and other such exoenergetic effects (Le Bon, Tesla, Moray, Ainsworth, Winkelmann, Metzger, Moray, McElrath). The mad rush toward the development of atomic weaponry provoked an unmetered lunge into an oblivion, one in which the wonderful dreams were for a time forgotten. The atomic threat was a hideous and macabre shadow, standing at the very edge of awareness. Fear of this figure momentarily covered all of the dreams which the previous Century had succeeded in delivering to humanity. Atomic fear was a vacuum, drawing out the life of dreamers and other children. But for the old patents of radioactive tubes, special medical beam energies, and other such devices, the old knowledge comprising the mysterious atomic dream was nearly lost.

Careful study of the radioactive attributes of uranium convinced Leo Szilard that highly purified uranium isotopes could function in a chain reaction of unmentionable power. Neutrons, the primary particulate radiation of the metal, and the neutron-absorptive resonant qualities of the heavy uranium nucleus, would combine to produce explosive chain reactions. Uranium was the element of choice. Toward these ends, uranium was sought in huge quantities now, an unnatural condition. Nature did not concentrate uranium in such vast quantities. Researchers were now prepared to defy Nature and all natural law. Pushing the limits of blind scientific will, science committees now demanded uranium supplies. In June 1940, 1200 tons of high-grade uranium ore was shipped to New York Harbor, and stored in an isolate warehouse on Staten Island. While 20 other such shipments made their way to Tennessee and Washington State, this first shipment was "forgotten".

Sitting in the warehouse for two full years, the Staten Island northshore site became fully contaminated. The uranium cache was finally sold by Belgian importer Edgar Sengiere, to Colonel Kenneth Nichols of the US Army for $1.35 per pound (September 1942). This uranium ore was reduced to solid metal in Bloomfield, New Jersey; a process which exposed uranyl nitrate to sunlight in opened rooftop evaporating tanks. Metallic uranium powder was obtained by electrolyzing the resulting green salts. Pressed into briquettes and melted in vacuum into 1 inch-diameter wafers, the discs were priced at $2000 each. The factory produced a little more than 1 pound uranium metal per month. In upscaled production, the sunlight process produced 65 tons of uranium metal at the original New Jersey site.

On Boston's northshore, industrial chemists melted a mixture of uranium ore with calcium compounds. Hundreds of pounds uranium powder were produced by this method. The highly reactive metal powder, capable of bursting into flames in air, was packed around with crushed dry ice. These were each shipped in one gallon dry ice covered containers to MIT for vacuum melting. This method was much improved by the mixing of uranium tetrafluoride salt with pure calcium. The resultant product produced 6 parts pure uranium metal for every 10 parts tetrafluoride salt. Vacuum melted, these castings measured 2 inches in diameter and 5 inches long. Each casting weighed 11 pounds. Later magnesium was mixed with uranium tetrafluoride and melted, a process which produced 100 pounds pure uranium metal weekly. Mallinckrodt, in St. Louis, developed an ether purification process which produced one daily ton of uranium metal. Every vessel, every accoutrement, every bit of ground, or laboratory table, shipping room floor, or workmen's aprons...everything was contaminated with the radioactive poison. The dust lingered for years in locations which merely shipped the dust. Hapless machinists, mere cogs in the radioactive machine, were later given highly purified uranium castings for tooling. The flakes which fell from lathes, yet hopelessly contaminated with the poisoning, exploded into smoky flames. Now what of those innocent souls who held castings and tools together, breathing radioactive smoke, and who stooped to pick up each burning flake?

The developmental problem was not now one which lacked for high grade uranium metal, but for high grade fissile uranium. Now the problem was to obtain the highly purified U-235 isotope, a natural rarity, and produce it in large quantities. Only the nuclei of neutron-emitting U-235 atoms could be made to ring like a bell and split into neat fragments. This was "bomb material". This would only happen when the nuclei were made to absorb more neutrons. But U-235 percentages in metallic uranium were low, a weak 0.7 percent of the supply. Furthermore, the separation of fissile U-235 from natural U-238 was problematic on several engineering levels. The other possible material was plutonium, another fissile element altogether. Theory taught that smaller amounts of plutonium would produce more violent fissile energies than the now-precious uranium-235.

Thermal diffusion, directed by Philip Abelson at the NRL, was pioneered in Nazi Germany. Thermal diffusion separated isotopes by placing thermal gradients across isotope rich solutions, mass differences separating the isotopes. A thermal diffusion pilot plant was managed by Naval Authority in Philadelphia. Gaseous diffusion, directed by John Dunning of Columbia University, required greatest care, an engineering nightmare. Heated until it became a caustic radioactive gas, uranium isotopic mixtures were pressured through an extensive baffle of filters. Diffusion separated the relatively light U-238 nuclei from those slightly heavier U-235 nuclei. Both of these processes were time consuming and dangerous, a chemical engineering nightmare. The gaseous diffusion method was the most hazardous method, provoking a great deal of concern. There would be no permissible accidental oversights. The nature of these unnaturally concentrated elements was found not to be a forgiving one. Enrico Fermi successfully designed a workable atomic "reactor" (December 2, 1942). Chain reactor conversion, pioneered by Dr. Fermi, irradiated uranium slugs with neutrons, gradually building plutonium over a period of months. Magnetic separation, a method proposed by Nobel Laureate, Dr. Ernest Lawrence, seemed to be the quickest means for separating uranium isotopes. His miniature models at Berkeley successfully produced milligrams of 30 percent pure U-235. Larger systems would separate and purify isotopes with speed and in quantity.

Government authority stepped into highest gear now, allocating funds and lands which dwarfed all the previous expenditures. Two work sites were chosen, each for their remoteness and proximity to hydroelectric energy sources. One site was constructed in Hanford, Washington. Hanford was built around three Chain Reactors, B, D, and F, for the production of plutonium, and a large adjacent separation plant. The other site, in Clinton, Tennessee, became popularly known as Oakridge. This was the site of several different isotope separation systems. The 2 Megawatt Chain Reactor (X-10), gaseous diffusion plant (the "gasworks", Project K-25), thermal diffusion plant (the "fox farm", Project S-50), and the magnetic separator (the "racetrack", Project Y-12). It is quite obvious that government bureaucracy was given full authority to engage all possible means for producing fissile materials at any cost. So great was the fear that hostile others would appropriate the knowledge and loose the terror first. Save in the D-Day Invasive Force, where lives and machines flooded the seas, never before in history had such unlimited funding been expended.

The first plant to begin production was the Y-12 of Dr. Lawrence. The device required to rapidly manufacture this material had to be many times more powerful than any cyclotron in existence. Calculated at 12,000 times the combined acceleration and volume transport of any existing cyclotron, twelve of these huge magnetic separation systems (CALUTRONS) were constructed. Each such system required tons of iron core material and equivalent tonnages of silver magnet wire. Nearly 400 million dollars worth of pure silver was convoyed from West Point to Bayway, New Jersey, where it was formed by Phelps Dodge. This wire was then trucked in convoy to Milwaukee, where the thick silver ribbon was wrapped around massive iron cores. These gigantic magnet sections were shipped to Clinton on opened flatbed trucks, a total of 14 thousand tons of silver ribbon (see figure).

The Y-12 system utilized 9 oval (YA-12), and three linear (YB-12) shaped hard vacuum "race tracks". The CALUTRON System combined an accelerative potential with enormous transportative volume, an incredible isotopic nucleonic flux. Highly charged input nucleons were fired into the systems. Each CALUTRON was equipped with 96 separate "receivers", targets into which the light U-235 nuclei were absorbed. Dr. Lawrence and his team studied 71 input systems and 115 receivers. Each of the racetracks could be set into operation independent of the others. These "batch operations" could be set into action around the clock. Enriched material from any one CALUTRON could be fed back into any other, further enrichment thus being achieved. Not only capable of isotopic mass separation, redesigned forms could produce new fissile elements from existing ones. The Y-12 System could operate as an enormously powerful transmuter of elements. One could bombard target receivers with literally any kind of nucleons. Y-12 produced the fissile uranium for the Hiroshima Bomb.

By February 1945, Hanford had produced plutonium. The gold covered slugs were literally "hot" to the touch with radiative emanations. This fissile

material was sent under radio contact convoy to Alamogordo to make the "test Bomb". Now theoreticians faced an essential problem in approach. Theory was always derived from some previous knowledge. Theories were perfected "a posteriori", after sufficient knowledge had been gathered. Theories relied on such funds of gradually acquired knowledge, from which to make statements and compose descriptions. But now there were no guidelines, no pathways. Bringing together sufficient quantities of fissile matter could be disastrous. Even manufacturing it could have had disastrous effects. Were the critical mass ever reached in one of the Y-12 units, the reaction would have destroyed the entire site in one brief flash. But how much?

Determining the "critical mass" of U-235 could not be an empirical process. An accident would wreak havoc with those whose wished use of the phenomenon on their enemies. There were those experiments, frightening accounts known as "Tickling the Dragon's Tail". In these extremely hazardous experiments, fissile matter was arranged in various symmetries and briefly brought together. Whether tapped together with a long screwdriver, rolled on ramps, or allowed to fall through tubes past static fissile matter, this empirical process represented the first attempt at gauging relative critical mass values for A-Bomb production. These empirical experiments were required for each of the fissile elements, U-235 and Plutonium. After countless castings and recastings, after many strangely shaped geometries of the fissile matter, the hideous device was complete. Technicians and engineers assembled and hoisted "the device".

## ATOMIC FIRE

The oligarchy under whose sponsorship this new weapon was developed now sat in the world supreme, quite unaware of all that was to follow. For them, they owned the "Big Bomb", terror weapon for those other Houses who may have now thought several times about either threatening them with hostility or resisting them in their imperialistic ventures. For the oligarchy, whatever nuclear side-effects there were had been ameliorated by a policy now using expendable troops and occupied populations. To fulfill the ambitions of this North American Oligarchy (NAO), all would be conscripted to service. The first test had marked the time in world history when nuclear weaponry would become the new defining power. Conventional encounters had actually become the bane of nuclear reliant superpowers. The thought of physical close encounters on the battleground were seemingly a thing of the past, a lost cause in a world where nuclear answers to international threats promised solution to the problem of hand-to-hand combat. The horrors of the previous war would be wiped away in a green-white, conscience-searing flash. Horror had been unleashed. Horror. Yet, the comforting thoughts came forth, answers to a new regime of fear. No young soldiers would have to die in a foreign conflict designed to acquire wealth for the wealthy.

Other than its larger and more effective blast size, this bomb was viewed as just another tool for war. The oligarchy now sought the use of this bomb to end the aggression which had been stimulated in the Pacific theatre. Orders which dispatched the use of this terror weapon went forth without delay. A public demonstration in the war theatre was greatly desired. No other publicity need have promoted the power of the North American Oligarchy (NAO). Japanese military was adamant. Only the suicide of their entire race would suffice in convincing the older European Powers of their resolute stand. Nothing less than this would satisfy the indomitable pride which imperialistically vaunted itself into the Pacific Theatre. The light industrial city of Hiroshima was the first directed nuclear casualty, the date was August 6, 1945. The presidential admonition that "they may expect a rain of ruin from the air" yet remained unheeded. Western minds found it inconceivable that this single Bomb could not provoke an immediate surrender from Japan. Instead, Japanese military ignored the destruction of Hiroshima.

*Hiroshima Aerial photo*

But those who had long observed this stoic apathy, the arrogance unto death, had already made their voices best heard in circles of authority. Their voice had almost come too late in the inevitable process which led to Hiroshima. Timing in the application of force was the essential. Deploy, then wait. Deploy again, then wait again. Few believed that the Japanese military would play their arrogant pride, not a virtue, to the hilt. Perhaps they did not "hear properly" the first time? It was not an unexpected response. A few voices had earlier expressed concern that even an Atomic Bomb might not convince the Japanese Military of impending ruin. This possibility, more a probability to some military analysts, that the first Bomb drop might neither be heeded or addressed by Japanese military, that more fissile material was demanded. All of the available fissile material had been primarily directed to the Alamogordo test and the manufacture of the Hiroshima Bomb. Plutonium production was stepped up just before preparation of the "Little Boy" Bomb for many reasons. Time being of the essence, far less plutonium than U-235 would be needed to prepare a second or even a third Bomb package. But neither thermal diffusion, reactor production, nor gaseous diffusion could produce the required material on such "sudden" notice.

The rapid production of more fissile material required the Y-12 method. To meet this deadline, fissile material was manufactured artificially by a transmutation process in the linear CALUTRONS. Input systems had been rearranged to produce intense volumes of neutron beams. These were directed into uranium-238 receivers. The process would rapidly produce very high grade plutonium. The process required two weeks of continual high speed neutron bombardment. The continual charging and discharging of powerful capacitor banks fired alpha particles into beryllium targets to produce beams of volumetrically large neutron populations at high energy. The input was discharged some 1400 times per 24 hour period, a total of nearly 20,000 successive bombardments. Sufficient material had now been transmuted to manufacture several plutonium bombs. Once the proper amount of fissile material had been manufactured with these ends in mind, several laboring personnel were required to actually enter the CALUTRON room, which had now become dangerously radioactive. It is said that this accelerator could not be approached for months. The subsequent status of these workers, for very obvious reasons remains unknown.

Some have noticed that the Nagasaki explosion (August 9) was visibly different from the Hiroshima weapon, these differences the result of two different fissile materials. The more vicious detonation obviously having been produced through the plutonium weapon, all subsequent atomic bombs would use plutonium. The terror of these two civilian encounters with atomic fire proved greater for those who wielded the power. Even after this second Bomb, the Japanese bureaucracy required 5 full days to reach a decision of surrender. This was formally related to the appropriate authorities on August 14. It is apparent that Japanese military may never have been moved with pity for their own people, even after the promised "rain of ruin". But the halt to this deployment was necessary on many counts. Both of the Atomic Bombs had produced far more than the fire bomb effects observed in Dresden, where rapidly ascending whirlwind flames sucked the breath out of civilians. These early firebombs, which later became the Napalm bombs and other chemical approximations of small yield nuclear weapons, did not produce the unique and deadly fire stimulated by nuclear reactions. Nuclear fire reached deep into the inertial side of matter, releasing its deadly debris into a world which had never known its likes. Here was fire from such deep energetic states that exposed materials were reduced to atomic vapor. The atomic bomb was a true terror weapon, and the whole world stood back in awe.

## NUCLEAR PRIDE

Oligarchs were secure. They had their terror weapon. Nuclear weaponry and everything having to do with uranium production had been transformed into a very obvious product of terror. This bomb, the result of working class labors and minds, was now the very embodiment of technological revolution. The Bomb reaffirmed a new definition of power for this social class. The Bomb was a reminder of ultimate power, of supreme power. There would be no control of the military privatization of this weapon. Here was a dynamic tension never before encountered. These were weapons which could destroy the planet. Moreover, the Bomb had not simply refocused power among mere researchers, those who first secured proof of its potentials. Now, power had been permanently concentrated in the military. It was at this point in time that rulership realized the impossibility of regulating or containing The Weapon. Once in military hands, there the weapon would remain. Though the weapon was no ordinary explosive, the military attitude concerning secrecy and national security remained the same. None could bind the consciousness which had both produced The Weapon and the new attitude which surrounded its development. Here was property of a complex ownership. Having materials, the result of oligarchic patronage, the secrets were now the permanent property of bureaucracy! Power remained in the military. The rulership would do its all to seize the whole nuclear technology package.

The concept of nuclear regulation signalled the soft first reassertions of demands from the oligarchy. The ultimate aim of these overtures was to "secure the property". The rulership promoted the case that the nuclear processing systems were nothing more than new industry, and definitely their property. Here at least they were on the begging end. The Atomic Energy Commission was the attempt, at a higher than martial bureaucratic level, to take the quantifiable accoutrements of the Nuclear Age: uranium, nuclear bombs, processing plants, assembly facilities, researchers, academic advisers, finished weapons, and military leadership. Now military and academic personnel, along with the purification plants, the uranium mines, in short every piece of the Nuclear Industry which was not classified, became tagged property. But there was a catch.

Were they to exercise the full weight of their means in obtaining the materials of nuclear industry, the highly classified secrets would yet remain unobtainable by Federal Law. Completely separate from the civilian population, the severity of military position in the hierarchy provided a powerful deadlock between those who claimed the nuclear secrets as "their property" and those who claimed trusteeship of the national defense. The military would divulge none of the information. The only way an information "leak" could be arranged would be through bureaucratic agencies of command, none of which would dare interfere. Military correctly resisted even executive pressures to release the secrets to the United States Government, citing the imposture of exposing such highly classified and potentially deadly secrets to any potential security risk. By exerting the full measure of their privileges in this respect, they effectively isolated themselves from every other level of the executive bureaucracy. In short, the military seized the secrets of the nuclear weapons, and by so doing, became now the principle owner of that property. No private militia group could be mounted to seize the power back. Who would mount an armed assault on the United States military?

A nuclear power struggle had begun, one which moved within the offices of bureaucracy in deep tides. Agencies, divisions, and branches of military jurisdiction maintained silence. The frightful power of this martial consortium was one whose newly privatized power would not easily bow to or conform with superior command at any level. This is why President Eisenhower, years after the incident, spoke out against the new consolidation. Publicly indicted by his statements, the phrase "military-industrial complex" was first heard in a new light. His forceful statements were the result of experience with the inner machinations of a short-lived military rule, in which the very Commander-in-Chief had been restricted from exercising his full authority.

The nuclear secrets! They held the power in this new nuclear arena now. The balance of powers-bureaucratic were now feeling the effects of nuclear power. Nuclear power had modified and redefined every familiar governmental relationship in which politicians and bureaucrats once freely moved under superior command. Now there would be an end to these slippages hither and thither. Impervious security would now limit and restrict aristocratic demands on every bureaucratic level. Transforming and isolating the bureaucratic relationships as well as every legislated limit of these authorities, a nuclear-empowered military began exercising their newfound strength in the political arenas. Here was an intriguing standoff, one which had been awaited for a long, long time.

Nuclear weaponry marked a new definition in military power. Military concentrated this power to itself. After World War II, military hierarchy began recognizing that technology alone could be the answer to a new warfare. During this time period strange and bold related projects began emerging from research laboratories across the nation. The fear gave way to a hubris of power. To wield the nuclear weapon was a matter of choice now. To use it, to imply its use in mildly threatening gestures, was a liberating pride which went deep into the military heart. With military in control of the weaponry, regulation was a mere clattering of words. Because of the Bomb, military ceased considering small theatres of conflict, and suddenly thought of war in global terms only. The vast arsenal used in the former war was now forgotten. The Bomb now literally exploded every possible battle theatre, every wartime scenario out into a huge scale, the scale of a nuclear blast. Here was indeed the power to destroy whole nations in a few strikes. The Bomb marked a sharp division between everything past and all things future. The dividing line was not vague, it was drawn by a nuclear blast in New Mexico. The Nuclear Age.

For military, there was no past. Everything was future. The white blast and the thunderous unhinging of things terrestrial seemed to wipe away all of the past, all of the wars, all of the errors. Now and henceforth, all weaponry had to be nuclear. Discussion of nuclear weaponry was now a routine function of military conversation. New applications of the hideous energy were required. What else could the Bomb do in warfare? Could nuclear weapons be made to any specification? To any size? How big? How small? Could one "shape" and direct the charge? Could other nuclear applications be devised besides those which used fission reactions? Military demands now directed the engineers, who conferred with physicists on a regular basis. Military, academia, and industry worked together.

Up to this time, nuclear weaponry was deployed by Air Force superfortresses. Differing branches of the military began struggling over the weaponry, and then began struggling one against the another. The Army demanded its due, its own nuclear applications. In response, military engineers now began developing a new breed of nuclear weapons systems, tailor made to each of the military branches. At the time, these were simple nuclear analogues of the past arsenals and weaponry: nuclear shells, nuclear cannons, nuclear mines, nuclear torpedoes. Testing in the field began anew. Small or large, few of these were announced. Expansions of nuclear pride followed each upward radioactive plume, as nuclear blasts became a routine experience for local residents upon whom deadly isotopic dust settled with the winds and rains. The military wished the extension of its elite new nuclear force into the international scene. Such extreme power and an extreme sense of postwar victory became a fearful combination for NATO allies who now had no command of the situation. The American Military had no inclination to share its secrets either.

President Truman made it clear that the nuclear secret would remain safely in American hands. US Military was therefore free to unsheathe the flaming sword at any time, letting slip the sheath before allies and enemies alike as often as it wished. There was no argument. NATO tried using diplomacy, the magick of words, to twist a pathway into the secret. All to no avail. The problem of nuclear proliferation, at this early phase of the age, was not an American dilemma. The Bomb modified military thought completely. Many military leaders were no longer able to foresee the possibility of small local conflicts, the more conventional and traditional encounters, without invoking "the Bomb". Battle strategies were each gauged against the diameter of a nuclear bomb. The pride of nuclear weaponry pressured an over inflated philosophy of war, one which eventually proved unrealistic. The meetings were filled with a euphoric laughter, there seeming to be virtually no reason to engage battle studies any longer. The Bomb solved all the problems of war.

The Bomb seemed to provide a neutralization of fear among military leaders. Having the Bomb was imagined to be a magick bullet for all and any world-be enemy assaults. With the threat of war no longer being considered, the nation could sleep without fear. The only lingering fear was fear of the weaponry itself and distrust of those who held it in their possession. With the advent of the Bomb Foreign obstructions against a nation with ultimate earthly power would now be laughable and humorous. Diplomatic interactions would no longer be strenuous and laborious. With the nuclear bomb backing one's words, international discussions could be terminated whenever desired. Nuclear weaponry replaced every conventional weapon, a new arsenal being required by an ever more powerful military. The military had become an independent agency, distanced so far from every earthly power by virtue of its newfound fearless handling of the ultimate fire.

The enlarging effect on the military mind, brought about by the possession of this single weaponry, absolutely shocked every superior command. The shock threaded its twisting pathway back through the bureaucracy, through the Congress, through the Commander in Chief, and straight through every part of the caste labyrinth leading directly into the aristocratic centers of national control. In the heat of this time period, General MacArthur was publicly brought down for planning the routine tactical use of such weaponry in an impending Asian crisis. This public rebuke, delivered to one so highly esteemed, marked a critical event in our national history. It signals the reemergence of control in an arena where, otherwise, there are no control factors.

## NUCLEAR LEAK

In the eyes of those who developed the nuclear industry, the dilemma was severe. Though this direct confrontation between working class science and rulership was final, it had fallen into martial context. Limited by the demands of that consortium, the further development of the nuclear power potential beyond weaponry would be frozen. From the military perspective, the situation called for diplomatic prudence. The strong hand was on their side of the table. Nuclear power had become a token of the struggle between two castes, and it was not one which was likely to be undone by ordinary measures. Control was out of the question now. Those who had the secrets, all the secrets, were not going to share them. Thought to be the exclusive property of a singular House military agency, those who held the secrets forgot the larger perspectives of international espionage. The soft military coups-d'etat prevailed until an unexpected occurrence reestablished balance in the world equation.

Secrets, however tightly bound in walls and prisons of steel, will out. In an incident which, in this light remains suspicious, a nuclear technician passed the secrets of nuclear power to Communist agents. In a short time, through the auspices of one, Klaus Fuchs, the Soviet Union developed its own nuclear arsenal. In this seemingly inexplicable manner, the deadlock had been broken from the outside world. Fuchs worked in at the University of Birmingham on the gaseous diffusion. He and three other technicians, each working under the British aegis, passed critical information. It is most curious that the paradoxical Armand Hamer, an industrialist who made his home in Communist Russia, so freely travelled between Europe and Moscow without any security requirements. Hamer seemed to be the principle financier of the Bolshevik Revolution. Creating and maintaining the Soviet Union as a business enterprise, one in which he alone held the title deed, forms the basis of suspicions surrounding the theft of nuclear secrets.

It was well known that Hamer's movements in the Soviet Union were so highly respected that Soviet Premiers would personally await his arrivals. Debarking from his private jet, a Soviet military escort brought him to the gates of his large private mansion. Even in his absence, servants worked around the clock, and throughout the year; an aristocratic throne in a communist nation. Before engaging any kind of international action, Soviet Premiers went to Hamer for permissions and advisements. Thus poised against all flags, Hamer seemed to be much more than his popular image portrays. More than an unusual Old World privateer. The facts made sense only if Hamer was indeed an Oligarch. Perhaps then, an Oligarch of pernicious and world dominating ambitions? If so, then he was the prime opposition of oligarchs which exercise their power throughout North America, the prime enemy of the North American Oligarchy (the NAO). The surreptitious acquisition of nuclear secrets from the outside effectively broke the world exclusive power which United States military so prized.

Were Fuchs a product of the unexpected, a wildcard, his was an unusual and suspect background. Not randomly selected from the deck of intellectuals, Fuchs was as rigorously searched as was Dr. J. Robert Oppenheimer. Fuchs was not, however, harassed over his affiliations with members of the communist party as was Dr. Oppenheimer. Mysteriously, neither the character of Fuchs nor the sincerity of his national loyalties were ever brought into question, as was Dr. Oppenheimer. Was Fuchs a possible "plant", deliberately infiltrating the Los Alamos site with a predetermined agenda to leak atomic secrets to the Soviet Union. This action was highly organized and arranged, one which probably occurred in 1946. Fuchs emigrated back to England, where he continued working in the Atomic Research Station in Harwell. On his incarceration, Fuchs seemed resigned to his fate, confessing to treason on January 27, 1950. Fuchs was not executed, the usual punishment for such an offense. In an otherwise most curious affair, Fuchs was released after a decade in prison and sent to Eastern Germany.

Was he an agent working for the oligarch Armand Hamer? If breaking the deadlock on nuclear weapons was the goal of this individual, then Fuchs achieved for him the unimaginable. The result of this leak, and the subsequent development of nuclear weaponry in the Soviet Union, did more to destabilize the traditional form of world rulership than all the centuries of struggle preceding the incident. Considering the veracity of other oligarchies, both West and East, here now was a duality of power between which balanced the fate of the whole world. Having no world-priority on nuclear secrets now, the martial power in North America had been brought down. The coups was over. The situation did not require the actual possession of the secrets.

Klaus Fuchs

They were virtually unimportant when considering the larger scope of tensions developed by the leak. The new twist on the nuclear age prompted a rapid development and deployment of battle-ready nuclear weapons systems. Military perceived the threat of hostile nuclear action as a new and terrifying war potential. Power was again refocussing in higher levels, where rule sought new protections. Greatly concerned over these mutually destructive potentials, directives were now issued to pursue development of fail-safe defensive and offensive systems. Nuclear arsenals would necessarily be proliferated, with an emphasis on blast yield.

It was during this time period that several divergent projects began, the real basis for all of our forthcoming discussions. The divergence of these projects encompassed a broad spectrum of technical potentials, each having their origins in phenomena produced by the release of nuclear energy. Here then is where our discussion finds its modern impetus, a consideration of the various technical products and applications of the nuclear military industry. Money was lavished on the military now, an incredible sponsorship having a seeming limitless supply. The thrust of all these sponsorships from the oligarchy was the protection of all regions, territories, and future potentials. Fear was the ruling stimulus, the foreign existence of nuclear arsenals being now the single greatest source of that fear. It was indeed known what nuclear actions would do. The thought that radioactive laden lands would be the inheritance of oligarchic dynasties was worse than abhorrent. The extremity of their nuclear fear gripped the entire nation. This new attitude marked a defined break from Old World policies. This was a Nuclear Age in more ways that only a precursory examination of the phrase could suggest.

For the first time since oligarchies had been established, these individuals pulled closer to the nucleus of social action. Science and technology, industry and military were suddenly seen as potential protectors of the oligarchy. In this needy state there would be concessions of a more liberal trend until power had been reconsolidated. Then, perhaps the former state of isolation and alienating policies would be reasserted. Until that time, the chief emphasis would be cooperative. Oligarchy knew that the absence of usable land, inhabitable land, would spell the end of all rule. No world, no rulership. But the news became increasingly worse. The returns were coming in, From Hiroshima. From Nagasaki.

The horrid reports produced a trail of never ending fatalities. From the conqueror's point of view, all reconstruction attempts were cosmetic. Both Hiroshima and Nagasaki were cities shunned as "unclean" cities. Allied occupation troops realized the extent of the permanent damage when dangerously high radioactivity levels were measured in every corner of the cities and their outlying districts. Oligarchies were only concerned with the expenditure of reconstruction. This final phase of atomic warfare, the necessary reconstruction of a potential target city, proved an impossibly complex and dangerous operation. Of teams assigned to the task, every exposed personnel member was ultimately added to the fatality lists. Thereafter, and even under military duress, troops refused to enter the area. Ultimately, the labor of reconstruction was bureaucratically delivered into Japanese hands. This rendered more cost effective, the policy for reclamation of acquired lands would be delivered to those who had been conquered.

The dirty aftermath was viewed with dispassion. Aftermaths, however dirty and contaminated, would be cleanup operations capable of generating capital. Regardless, The Bomb now remained the prime weapon of threat, the prime weapon of choice for oligarchic extensions of power. The atomic bomb was then viewed as a new means for the acquisition of foreign ground. What needed now to be tested was the potential threat of bomb blasts on troops who would necessarily be deployed to occupy blasted ground. While wielding the atomic threat over the world with a confident air, the most highly classified secret was not the design of the Bomb itself. The most highly classified secret was the universal fear which had gripped the hearts of the supposed fearless. Fear of the atomic force ran deep in the hearts of even military officers who heard the expectable outcome of each new test blast. What the bomb blasts did to their troops was worse. Regulators simply turned the task of bomb development to the military. Clearly, the military was given the dirty work, to deliver an answer to frightened aristocrats who hid themselves in dark mahogany-lined rooms.

Now the power returned to the military, themselves fearing what they had released. The aftereffects of these nuclear "tools for peace" left their killing mark in the air, in the ground, in the bodies of those who entered the areas where blasts had been directed. Suddenly, all too suddenly, all of the parties in the power chain recognized the threat which had been unleashed. Not the simple "push the button and forget" motto now. Once released, this Bomb would return with a thousand radioactive winds to destroy one's own House and holdings. Fallout was the poison in the rain. In the years following the conclusion of the Second World War, each test blast seemed to spell the murder of the whole race. Fear of the Bomb entered the very heart of society. There was now a very clear radioactive stain which would never wash from the hands of those who commanded, and the hands of those who obeyed. Worse. There were radioactive stains which would not wash from the seared bodies exposed in a decade of atomic tests in which both civilian and troop test participants were employed. The hideous Nazi-like medical tests used young infantrymen of the lowest rank. These mere uniformed children were made to walk through the stinging white dust which had been propelled into their faces, clothing, and lungs by the rising plasma columns, which had only seconds before been detonated.

Youthful pilots were made to fly through the very clouds raised by the explosion plasma. Pilots told that they could see the blast through the metal floors of their planes. Some said that they saw their own skeletons through tightly closed eyes. Data was methodically and routinely collected in an emotionless manner. Assessments were made. Yes, a land invasion could be commandeered to occupy areas which had been the scene of atomic devastation. None of these troops lived long enough to protest, the expendable supply produced by working class families. Moloch, the eater of children. The cruel wickedness of Nazi atrocities had apparently found a new home base. When questioned by a growing civilian concern, military authorities "could not be contacted" for commentary.

Each successive Bomb test would bring poison rain to the whole world. In the winds, in the blowing winds. The whole world would soon be covered in the poison dust. Strontium-90 in dairy milk, children's milk. These and a hundred other radioactive contaminants were the glowing flowers which nuclear weaponry had planted. Hoping perhaps to ameliorate their own horror with familiarity and experience of the new weaponry, perhaps believing that repetition would desensitize them form the nightmare vision of that first atomic sun, American Military teams continually unleashed the atomic terror. In a series of tests which rained deadly white dust all across the national southwest, military first tested the various tactical applications of the atomic bomb. New detonators, new fissile materials, new hybrid weapons packages, new weapons emplacements, new yield variations. But no amount of technical jargon, no excessive number of tests could remove the memory and inescapable thought which escaped with each rumbling eruption. The ultimate radioactive stain was fear. And the dust, the dust which returned with every breath of wind.

Those working class minds who pursued the goal of nuclear weaponry now looked back in surprise at what they had been compelled to achieve. The first dream of atomic energy was a quest for endless light, a means to liberate humanity with free and limitless energy. Energy to light cities, to raise aircraft, to power ocean liners, to travel into space, to pursue all the dreams of humanity. But now, what had they actually achieved, and for whom? Murderers, continually returning to a killing floor, the tests were repeated and repeated. But neither the hellish scene which was continually reproduced before their unbelieving eyes, nor the resulting illnesses of young troops would depart from their conscience.

The searing white heat, vaporized metals, the unearthly light which permeated stone, the sand melted into basins of green glass, the bodies quivering with radiation fevers, the troops who grew weak with anemia and died. Each hot blast burned its signature of a death spectre through the very soul of each watcher. Atomic. The very word was equated with death. Bureaucrats replaced it with a subliminal, designed to evoke feelings of newness and clarity. NUCLEAR energy was a word having no connection with Hiroshima, with Nagasaki, with endless series of merciless troop tests, with civilian studies where fallout plumes covered neighboring towns. Fallout. The word burned itself into the world mind, from the oligarchs down to the laborer. Fallout was the return, the reaction, the blood of another House on one's hands. Fallout would return to speak for those who had been burned, the haunting which crept into the window of their children's playrooms, however isolated from all of society. After the winds would strew its killing poison across the world, with traces on the grass, fallout would not be stopped. Burying itself in a thousand different ways, fallout would sprout again in flowers, in corn, in cattle, in the oceans, for a thousand generations. The poison would not cease in any future. After the blast, long after the thunder, fallout would remain. Fallout would burn the earth.

## NUCLEAR FACTORY

Oligarchs and civilians alike now came to grips with the facts. Nuclear weapons were not simple devices capable of insuring world peace. They were weapons soaked in a consciousness of fear. Those who held them as tools of threat held only their own destruction. The weapons themselves were anomalies, things that should not exist. The Bomb was no blessing. Oligarchs came to appreciate the implication of total devastation. Not just the blast, but the aftermath; the hideous dust-filled aftermath where food could not be eaten for fear of the poison it contained. Oligarchs dreaded the thought of such an hideous Armageddon. Nuclear weapons would be the very last tool of a future conflict.

No one could turn the clock back. No one can. Power cannot, superior command cannot. Were it possible to turn the clock, the effort would have focussed on the microsecond before the triggering mechanism snapped into placed over Alamogordo, that instant when Dr. Oppenheimer spoke the verses of horror at what had been achieved. Nothing would ever be the same again, a world where the Golem had been unleashed. Faceless, vague, lumbering in the streets, the avenger. The nuclear prize had literally turned in radioactive ash in the hands of those whose pride it once filled. The surprise was complete, and terrifying. The dust, the ash, became the very symbol of this fear. No long concerned only about nuclear fire. In the end, the fear of fire acquired a companion. Fear of the dust. To breath it brought death.

But there were other complexities now. Others in the equation. Enemies. Enemies with nuclear horrors in their hands. Perhaps these enemies would not appreciate the true nature of what they had stolen and made. Perhaps they did not comprehend the terrifying aftermaths of Hiroshima, of Nagasaki. Of dust, of poison in their children's milk. Perhaps they did not cling so much to life as to refrain from using their nuclear stores in a vengeful madness. The world had become convoluted. It turned in on itself now. Here was a weapon which threatened terror, but which could never be used. And worse, it could not be returned to its source. The manifestation which had embodied itself in this terror weapon was a message for those who resist the deep.

The reversal in thought was striking. How to prevent one's enemy from using the Bomb which one used to threaten that enemy? Clarity was gone. Ambiguity was the gameboard. Sanity was gone. Only intensely convoluted thought, its twisting plots, and its distorted vision remained. Amid the surreal developments, one now had to somehow undo that which was done; a task too unwieldy for human beings to engage without serious personal and social risks. Now there had to be a way to stop the proliferation of nuclear weapons. To place a freeze on nuclear fire and its poison dust. Until these weapons could be replaced by another, there would be only the tensions of a world on the brink of doom. To live in such an atmosphere of fear, of terror, of threat provoked social revolutions on such a vast scale that the world has been changed and demoralized. The diplomatic games necessary would provoke panic and anxiety until the task of undoing the nuclear knot was accomplished.

The steps toward achieving these objectives therefore took a turn toward madness, and for a time it seemed as though the world had been turned over to madmen in uniforms. Indeed, it had been. Before other nations developed nuclear arsenals of their own, neither military nor military engineers never considered the need for developing nuclear countermeasures. The Bomb was thought to be the only weapon of importance. But now the tables were reversed. The avowed enemy had this Bomb. The balance was frustrating. What could be done to suitably impress the Soviet Union, whose successive nuclear detonations were being monitored throughout the seismographic stations of a worldwide surveillance cooperative? In what must remain, perhaps the most singularly aristocratic solution to the problem, a command directive was given to develop a "bigger Bomb", one which the Soviets supposedly could never steal. The opinion of them was that these thieves of the Atomic Bomb were barely able to thresh their own wheat on time, let alone develop a thermonuclear weapon. A bigger Bomb might shake the pride of that nation down. Complete idiocy, the conclusions of those who never walked on city streets.

Based on theoretical work completed by Hans Bethe, who proposed that greater energy could be derived from the fusion of lighter nuclei than the fission of heavy ones, a new nuclear weapon was quickly transformed from contemplation to design. The working model for the new Hydrogen Bomb was developed by Edward Teller, who used a small yield plutonium bomb as the trigger for a fixed volume deuterium reaction. This project was referred to as the GREENHOUSE experiment. The first such thermonuclear weapon, was demonstrated in the Pacific in 1951, a public spectacle of purposeful intent. The Soviets, who measured the blast on a hundred different meters across their vast territory, were now greatly concerned over this weapon; whose yield per weapon, according to the claims, was apparently unlimited. Lifting from the horizon as a veritable dome of sun-like brilliance, replete with incandescent amoeba-like plasmoids, the Hydrogen Bomb became a new and true terror to other nations. Madness. Surrealism. And then the Soviets developed their own version and shocked those weak minded aristocrats who hoped to so shock them.

The fear, the cold fear of nuclear fire. Now there would be only a careful bureaucratic withdrawal of boldness, of pride, of public demonstrations of force. Now there would be UN test ban treaties, UN restrictions, UN inspections. The international forum would be the stage where the best and the worst of diplomatic assertions would be viewed by the world. The poised Adlai Stevenson, reading from prepared notes. The raucous Nikita Khrushchev, pounding tables with his shoes. The contemplative and tragic Dag Hammerskjold. The world held its breath and prayed that every meeting would bring about the erasure of the nuclear terror. But it would not disappear. It was a reminder of doom, one whose spectre hung over the head with every breath. One awoke each morning with the fear of it. The poison had to be daily buried by its priests.

National policy on the international scene ridiculed reason. While protesting those additional nations who sought the development of their own nuclear arsenals, military built up an arsenal which defied logic. More bombs, bigger bombs, silos, Trident missiles, SAC headquarters, a proliferation on the one side of the mouth, while demanding peace from the other. Indeed, handling radioactive materials had become as routine as making automobiles. The bombs came in different polished colors. Polished and sleek, like cars coming off the assembly line. Some yellow, others red, yet others black. The mass production techniques were exactly the same, adaptations of industry to nuclear war. Whether or not they recognized it, the working class had been tied to the task

of working for a nuclear factory. A nuclear war had indeed already occurred in the mind of the world at large. In the future, the social stresses would prove too much to bear.

The society began to fracture and liquefy. Out from this amalgam of despair and fear came mutations on a grand social scale. Nuclear stimulated mutations. The White House was draped in black. The music grew loud, the hair fell long, the clothes of the peaceful resistance were surplus military, and the winters were white. All the while, the military laboratories built up an arsenal which was measured in terms of how many times over the world could be destroyed. The Soviets did the same. Now the world could be destroyed so many times over, times two. Adding up the combined nuclear arsenals of the other members in the "Nuclear Club", it might have become times three. So, the world powers knew that the whole global expense could be blasted beyond memory...a hundred times...times three.

The intellectual factions in society observed this ineffectual and idiotic thought mold, recognizing the aristocratic hand in all the nuclear proliferations. That dispassionate and shallow inability to create anything original, or to solve any problem in a new way, was showing through all the teleprompted media readers who droned on and on. The nuclear circus was a show which the intellectual turned off. When the youth severed their relationship with the national program, the police were called out. But when the working class elders severed their relationship and participation in the bureaucratic dictates, the oligarchy was taken aback. Here was a revolution which swept the entire pyramidal base, shaking the power at its point to and fro. Deep in the center of all these pyramidal happenings, military branches each came to grips with the fact that nuclear weaponry, in its then present form, could never be used in war scenarios. To do so would spell the ruin of all futures. No one would stop making the weapons, but recognized that they could not be used. Methodically stockpiled on the one side, military strove to develop the antidote on the other. Nuclear induced madness. Humankind seemed lost in a labyrinth of uranium, a maze from which there seemed no escape.

NUCLEAR LIGHTNING

Effort was continually applied toward discovering antidotes to the poison of nuclear weaponry, a poison which had spilled everywhere. The antidotes would necessarily have to be as frightening as the nuclear threat itself, but with none of the hazards involved in purifying, shipping, handling, assembling, storing, and actually using the weapons. Military wanted weapons they could use. If potentials for the development of such weapons existed, they would be found. Projects were initiated in every academic institute, the development of new weaponry and weapon systems being the sole effort of the day. In accord with these developments, science was applying itself to the sundry problems of nuclear age espionage. Information itself was a weapon. Acquiring information, clear photographic information of every Soviet weapons complex was another aim, a research avenue ultimately leading to space technologies. Knowing the potentials of one's avowed enemies was of prime importance in possible future confrontations. Paths spread out in a thousand different directions, the researchers leaving nothing to chance.

Now there were more stringent demands placed on military laboratories and technology-related industry. One could not simply investigate the endless inventions and hardware of the creative working class experimenters, whose work was once distorted ever so slightly to produce "safe" weapons. In a world where any such weapons potentials might appear again in a future conflict, military was compelled to thoroughly examine and develop far more than the chance invention or hardware having weapons potential. Now, every systems-potential phenomenon had to be examined. Soviet scientists were searching through the same natural world for secrets, secrets to use in war.

One could never leave any stone unturned. One had to be alert, contemporary, almost futuristic. Cold War researchers had to see through every natural display which might be an advantage against the "other side". Both sides however played this game, constantly imagining what the other had or had not researched. Military used the very best minds which money could buy in order to assess and determine the relative worth of natural anomalies which began appearing during their own research progress. No phenomenon, no special effect, however minor, could be overlooked now. Any one of these strange and vague phenomena might provide the answer to their search for an escape from the present nuclear dilemma. A nuclear escape. Small research teams, having as their goal the thorough examination of academic and even of private experimental findings has been a constant and routine feature of military bureaucracy since this time period.

Surveillance, communications, delivery, and weapons. These four were the chief headings under which military applied its combined strengths to produce the new and hopefully saving technologies designed to end what had been initiated. Filled with the sense that they were indeed planning the future of the world, these researchers excused their consciences and went on with their new occupations. Information was coming in from everywhere. Analysts were everywhere. The first line of research necessarily engaged the nuclear weapons "problem" directly. The first problem dealt with the possibility of a first strike from the perceived enemy. What could one expect? After all, the Allies were not under the bombs used in Japan. The most dreadful experience to which they were exposed took them through the streets of the devastated cities, those deemed unclean by their own people. And this phase, the aftermath was horrifying. What measures would be required for a military core group to maintain command perspective during a possible nuclear assault. The problem was a necessary horror to face. Therefore data of the first several tests would necessarily have to be scrutinized.

Whenever explosive releases of nuclear energy are engaged, a host of strange and unforeseen geophysical effects follow. These suites of effects, the consequences of unknown energetic correspondences and modulations, provoked a great deal of intrigue among the many gathered scientific researchers. The several test detonations of both nuclear fission and nuclear fusion devices were followed by a host of unexpected natural phenomena, which trained observers were quick to recognize. Of greatest note were the more direct impacts on both personnel and measuring equipment. Nuclear testing produced ancillary phenomena, unexpected occurrences, providing certain new weapons development possibilities. One such phenomenon provoked a line of research which led directly to the development of modern beamray weapons. Comprehending the geophysical nature of nuclear detonations was a gradual realization having several immediate consequences. Nuclear explosions impacted both the magnetic and dielectric fields of the whole planet in ways which suggested new weapons themes.

The first few research tests of relatively low yield nuclear weapons burned out sensitive instrument packages which had been placed at a safe distance from the blast effects. This could not be explained. When heavy shielding failed to block the burn phenomenon, engineers became suspicious that another effect had been stimulated. Furthermore, when local power systems experienced complete "burnout", an effect which occurred at the very instant in which the nuclear test charge had been detonated, there was no doubt as to the cause. Here was an electrical impulse effect which, in this instance, could not truly be explained. How was the sudden and tremendous volume of current generated by a nuclear blast? Close study of the blast dynamic itself produced no real answer.

There was a sequence to the progress of a nuclear blast, details which unfolded themselves within microseconds. Analysis of the total energetic output of a nuclear fission explosion reveals the continuous spectrum of energetic forms. Every octave in the electromagnetic spectrum is thoroughly covered in such a blast. The initial radiation of a nuclear blast, consisting of intense infrared, ultraviolet, X-Rays, and Gamma Rays, expands outward to a diameter exceeding one mile. Absorbed by the atmosphere, this deadly radiation shockwave heats the very air to incandescence. This radiation shockwave is lost to the distant surroundings in a few microseconds. With this radiation shock, a powerful neutron flux showers the surrounding area to within one mile from the blast epicenter. As the fireball rises, the incandescent air itself radiates hard infrared, ultraviolet, and X-Rays in a continuous and bright display. This plasma radiant irradiation of the surroundings continues even as the blast ring is escaping into the upper atmosphere. These rays, a wide and combined spectrum of deadly content, thoroughly roast the surroundings. Because of the complete electromagnetic coverage by the fireball. This is the source of that "second" and prolonged heat which nuclear observers have so often reported. The effects had devastating import for military scientists, effects which they had never anticipated.

Once the initial radiative components of the blast were dispersed to the surroundings, the heated ball of plasma impacted the surrounding air. Shaped by temperature differentials and the continuous supply of inrushing air, this plasma ball became a plasma ring. Rotating "from the inside out", the plasma vortex rose as a deadly conflagration. But the rising plasma ring began manifesting other macroscopic features which could not be simply derived from analysis of the aerodynamic differentials alone. How was the coherent emergence of an electrical current, to be explained. In such a hot plasma, one whose convolutions are massive and chaotic, there can be no development of microscopic order unless some formative agency induces that order...from the outside. To explain the "mechanism" by which electrons are apparently driven around the rising plasma ring, one must seriously bend the laws of electrodynamics. But many began appreciating the fact that this powerful electrical nature, this manifestation of internal order in chaos, could only be derived from the available formative forces in the environment. Indeed, without a consideration of coupling effects more "geophysical" in nature, there was no logical explanation for the electrical organization.

It became obvious that the plasma ring interacted in strange ways with the dielectric field of the earth itself, drawing the vertical field lines into itself. The

mere presence of the highly energetic plasma represented a dynamic and electro-permeable volume having fluidic attributes. The plasma ring was the focal point of a process in which all of the dielectric field energy surrounding the blast site were forcibly pulled into the fireball. The rising plasma ring effectively became the plate of an immense capacitor, gathering charge and mounting in saturate density. This gave rise to the lightning discharges often seen associated with test shots in an ordinarily blue sky environment. This increased dielectric permeability required special locations for the maximum nuclear effect, a fact not widely considered. The notion of nuclear detonations as geoelectric or even as geomagnetic modulators began to occupy the minds of researchers now.

The electrical nature of rising plasma ring, concentrated enough electrical charge to effectively destroy electronics packages with a regularity which became routine for the test engineers. First attempts at shielding equipment from these electrical effects proved impossible. The effect reached such a nuisance level that a deliberated investigation of this feature alone was demanded. Tests measured the ground rising currents responsible for this "burnout" effect, current densities often exceeding several thousand amperes. These currents did not flow in the brief instant of a lightning bolt. They were maintained for a sustained time interval. The nanosecond release of intense fission reactions evoked the upward current flow, a vertical avalanche predicated on the enormous concentration of the terrestrial dielectric field. This new awareness of geophysical coupling effects suddenly became the new research objective of this study group.

The nuclear blast produced a penetrating electrical phenomenon, similar to an effect which had been observed before in connection with sudden electrical discharges. RADAR researchers had long observed the impulse phenomenon which burned out nearby receivers and instrument packages. While those effects were usually directed phenomena, directed through RADAR beams of manageable output, these nuclear related were completely unprecedented. Indeed, they were virtually unmeasurable. Even military command centres which were distant from any blast epicenter would be completely vulnerable to the nuclear communications "burnout" effect. Every piece of electronics equipment would be totally and hopelessly incinerated in the upward current rush. Worse than that, if deeply buried and highly protected command centers managed to somehow escape that initial EMP, the residual effects on both the atmosphere and ionosphere would present a second and equally formidable security breach.

Protecting against Nuclear EMP potential was the first goal, if indeed this possibility existed. What kind of shielding could block a sustained lightning discharge? Had anyone in scientific history dealt with sustained discharges of this voltage and volume? Only one. That person was Nikola Tesla, who in 1899 perfected apparatus capable of handling such energetic volumes. Therefore, Tesla patents became a study area of necessity once again. Developing large metallic shields for buried command centers required knowledge of Tesla methods.

Consideration of these catastrophic electric effects against military command centers was of first level importance. Military forces, against whom such weapons were used, would be the helpless victims of a complete and prolonged communications burnout. But if they managed to safely endure the blast scenario, the resultant radiowave "blackout" would bring their best communications efforts to an abrupt and disappointing end. Worse than disappointing, the blackout period could spell total annihilation. After a nuclear blast of sufficient magntude and aerial placement, the blackout effect could last for days. This ionospheric blackout phenomenon, revealed that communications channels could be destroyed across an incredible range of electrical frequencies. This range was found to begin in the ELF bands, the operating frequencies of electrical power generators, and indeed surpass the centimeter waves of superhigh frequency RADAR.

After the initial blast and fireball sequence, only the optical and radiative channels would remain clear of the "blackout" effect; a fact having defined consequence in the future of military communications technology. The extended blackout, forced upon the victims of such an event, would prolong a critical time period during which no possibility of an organized military action could be coordinated. No information could be exchanged except through rapidly deployed line-of-sight systems. Therefore, much beyond considerations of the blast shock hazard itself, both the burnout and blackout phenomena were themselves tactical weapons in their own right. Here were nuclear weapons effects which had to be breached.

RADAR engineers had observed these effects during the Second World War, when extremely brief highpower pulsed RADAR bursts were beamed toward communications and other electronics equipment. Proper shielding was able to block the penetrating power of those pulsed RADAR bursts. But without special shielding, electronics packages were incinerated as if exposed to explosive fire. These RADAR effects were reminiscent of reports given by Dr. Tesla, when discussing his Radiant Energy technology. The superficial effects proved to have succinct causes which, on deeper evaluation, proved the difference in power between true impulse singularities and wave bursts. The Teslian phenomenon was the result of succinct electroshocks, unidirectional blasts of singular, well spaced impulses. RADAR wave impact was effective only in that initial wave crest. The sudden rise in electric potential from zero was the active agent in burning and bursting materials. Each subsequent wave alternation added no more energy to the effect. Since only the leading wave crest was the effective energetic portion, the rest was "lost" as heat. Thus only "the lead edge" of each long burst was useful in producing EMP effects.

Dr. Tesla taught that effective conservation of the effect relied on conservation of the impulse energy. The impulse singularity was only part of his process however, the separation of charge carriers from ætheric components being the critical factor. For Tesla, the "shock excitation" provided a means for heating the currents to sufficient chaotic levels for their separation in magnetic disrupters. Nevertheless, succinct electric impulses were the only means by which these effects could be most powerfully initiated. While RADAR burst or "EMP" effects were powerful, Nuclear EMP were overwhelming. Nuclear EMP burned electrically conductive systems. Grounded systems were especially vulnerable, but aerial systems packages could be destroyed as well. Dielectric field energy simply focussed into any conductive medium, stimulated sudden high voltage surges, and quickly heated metals. Much of the metal vaporizing power of a nuclear blast was contained in the NUCLEAR EMP phenomenon. If the metal materials were articulate and frail, such as those in any radio apparatus, that system would be burned to a cinder. It was enough for engineers to know that Nuclear EMP rendered radio systems useless. The miliary believed it had in its sights a new means for destroying all enemy communications systems.

## NUCLEAR PULSE

Nuclear EMP can do more than destroy electrical systems. Nuclear EMP can kill people. The instantaneous release of penetrating electrical currents was capable of raising deadly geoelectrical discharges in any grounded object. This included infantrymen and civilians. By scaling the size of a nuclear blast, perhaps modifying the characteristics of the blast itself, one could maximize the desired Nuclear EMP effects. Hotter, more concentrated, and faster fissile reactions would produce fireball plasma of a requisite structure to concentrate dielectric field energy. EMP from such weapons, however small the actual blast size, would produce tremendous electrically stimulated damage. Military experts hoped to design tiny nuclear weapons packages capable of releasing such maximal Nuclear EMP effects. They perceived that this research avenue represented a new approach toward the final nuclear antidote.

Throughout the remainder of this chapter we will routinely discuss the most singularly horrifying and unsettling weapons which, in the ordinary comfort of our lives, will come to us as a deep shock. This indeed has been my own experience throughout this research. Yet, the process of learning requires constant exposure to knowledge which will produce its disturbing responses in us. The degree to which we are yet able to sense such pain and distaste is a measure of our humanity. It is a reminder that war represents the wicked side of human nature, made all the more wicked by the fact that we are too often compelled to serve in foreign military operations which have nothing at all to do with real issues of liberty or humanity. While not taking delight in the constant discovery and recovery of these weapons, we are compelled to expose the artifacts of death by dragging them into the light.

A fearful, nightmarish atmosphere is provoked by reading weapons patents, whose banal presentations speak of deadly devices without feeling or concern for the potential victims. Such desensitization is perhaps more frightening than the devices which arrange the eradication of one's enemies by frightening energies. To know is better than not to know. Knowledge and exposure to these matters may for a time bring sadness and heartache. Yet, I have found that the wisdom which subsequently develops within the bruised heart becomes a relentless will, without which no seekers of truth will make progress. It is in the development of this indomitable and undissuaded pursuit of truth that a newer consciousness is developed among a small consortium. The resultant concentration of such consciousness releases visionary power. Visionary power produces the new technologies whose congruence with biodynamic energies prove to be far superior to the cruel might of nuclear weaponry.

The first military considerations of nuclear weapons had considered only blast potentials and blast radii. The larger the devastation, the better the bomb. The vaporization and desertification of a blasted area was judged by the degree of buildings left standing. Used in this primitive manner, nuclear weapons were mere pressure bombs, whose outward energetic release produced immeasurable atmospheric shockwave effects. But the continual testing of these weapons came new offensive and defensive weapons potentials: the Nuclear EMP effect. The incredibly powerful manifestation of Nuclear EMP phenomenon was an unprecedented discovery. Nuclear EMP was an unstoppable force. It burned cables, destroyed all grounded systems, and penetrated the heaviest shielding. Strategists suggested that the effects of an EMP strike alone could be more decisive than an outright nuclear assault. Tests affirmed that the size of the blast was not critical. Plasma shock was the effective agency in releasing Nuclear EMP, new and special detonators being devised and implemented to develop more rapid fission reactions. Well-engineered "filtered" nuclear blasts produced immeasurably powerful Nuclear EMP effects. Military tests obtained data on Nuclear EMP phenomena with great rapidity. Tests conducted with these objectives in mind continued even after the above ground test ban treaties were signed.

Local small nuclear weapons, of yield far less than a kiloton, were specifically designed to produce local Nuclear EMP effects. These tests repeatedly burned out local power grids in Nevada. Developers realized that directing the Nuclear EMP against any foe would produce incapacitating physiological effects which reached killing potentials if properly delivered into an enemy offensive. Ground lighting would simply rise into any grounded object, the probable origin of those parallel ribbon discharges early observed in desert nuclear tests. Killing potentials, power grid blackouts in cities, as well as military electronics burnouts, could now be engineered by deliberate design. At this time in the weapons program, electrical blackout was now viewed as the most decisive and therefore desirable effects of nuclear detonations. During such blackout periods, offensive military units could sweep through a sector and bring any offensive assault to a swift finale. EMP maximized nuclear warheads would effect conquest with as little physical damage as possible. Here was a new concept in nuclear weapons applications, where nuclear blasts were valued, not for their airshock potentials, but for their radiant outputs. Certain research divisions set to work immediately on the task of developing non-damaging nuclear weapons, once thought a contradiction in definitions. New engineering views would consider the maximization of radiant, electromagnetic, and particulate emissions of nuclear blasts for use in battle scenarios.

The tactical application of Nuclear EMP effects would require pulse-impervious technical support systems. An EMP strike would insure the total destruction of all electronics packages in among enemy forces. Any military offensive which relied on nuclear-triggered EMP would also of necessity require its own EMP safe communications systems. In this, the concept of new non-electronic communications systems was born. Optical communications links were reexamined and developed, one of the early origins of optical fibre technology. Components which employed optical energy and not electron currents, would be completely EMP immune. Some researchers recognized that nuclear detonations were not the sole agencies capable of releasing EMP effects. Strong electrical discharges produced EMP effects, although the shockwaves of some chemical explosions could be harnessed toward their production. The whole secret was in the production of a highly electropermeable volume of hot gas: plasma. Any means for producing such a volume would absorb sufficient dielectric field energy to become a local EMP source.

Indeed, several non-nuclear techniques for releasing powerful EMP effects took the form of highly salted explosives and resonant cannon barrels. Aimed toward an enemy installation, the intense plasma burst of these cannons produced a directed EMP of penetrating strength, the local dielectric field flowing through the target launched plasma fireball. These results encouraged the development of yet other EMP productive systems. RADAR seemed to be a very accessible means for producing EMP effects in a highly directed manner. The RADAR pulse provided the plasma formation power on a focussed point, the terrestrial dielectric field would perform the work. Such a concept seemed to be a most remarkable means by which the use of nuclear weapons might be discouraged. If electrical weaponry ever became the world military trend, then nuclear weaponry would become an obsolescent technology.

## NUCLEAR SPACE

The postwar military thought only in terms of mass-devastation. The eradication of hostile ideologies through nuclear means. Military viewed large blast craters and the complete annihilation of enemy cities and territories as the single goal of nuclear weaponry. Now however, the global view of nuclear weaponry in the theatre of war had been greatly modified. Precision and definition was the theme now. How to use the nuclear release of energy to best tactical advantage in using nuclear weapons to best advantage was the new thrust, the only reason for such intensive and extensive research. Once the Nuclear EMP method was discerned to be a new and novel tool in warfare, certain advisers began extending their vision of its use to a much larger theatre. Large-scale Nuclear EMP blackouts could be an effective means of blanketing a continent-sized region in critical times. For an EMP to have decisive effect during this time, it had to effectively blackout the whole Eastern Hemisphere! US military engineers began examining the possibility that aerial nuclear blasts might provide such a large-scale effect. Military attentions shifted away from nuclear ground blasts and EMP effects, out into space. Testing nuclear weapons in space was the next challenge, the next high frontier.

Because of these new potentials, the sponsorship continued its supplies of capital. This movement of power toward the development of practical safe-nuclear systems betrayed a singular desperation, descried by a few astute observers. Who greatly desired these new developments, and why? The supporting concept providing power to this thrust was simple. It was understood that only the continual pursuit and development of nonnuclear weaponry would ultimately reach such a degree of refinement that a new hightech standard would, in time be reached. A nonnuclear standard. This would effectively demand the dismantling of nuclear weapons, the proliferation and reliance on more decisive nonnuclear systems being the result. At such a point in time and technological development, power could be withdrawn back into the control center. Military would be kept "on hold", using its weapons potentials only when called upon the achieve new foreign acquisitions. Nevertheless, oligarchs failed to recognize that their acquisition of such foreign lands was always predicated on the demands of new technology. The reason why so many foreign operations had taken ground in Africa was precisely for the uranium resources contained therein. Technology was still enunciating the movements of rulership toward the acquisition of power-amplifying wealth. This is where we are now met in time, a most critical period in geopolitical history which seems to be filled with "peace". The public dismantling of warheads is but a sign that more pernicious weapons are actually the resource on which military will now depend.

The new Cold War notion of nuclear victory enunciated a theme of nonnuclear warfare. Unlike former military commanders who imagined the routine use of nuclear weaponry in the war theatre, the new emphasis was to refrain from nuclear weaponry at all costs. Backing the force of this restraint was the continual development, sometimes public testing, and industrial proliferation of whole new weapons suites. One new research pursuit which captured the greatest military attention came again as a result of geophysical coupling effects between nuclear detonations and the planet.

The International Geophysical Year (IGY) was an attempt to cool the Cold War among political superpowers. The international cooperative succeeded in producing several astounding discoveries. After examining radiation counts from the Explorer I satellite, Dr. James Van Allen determined the existence of two vast toroidal shells above the earth. Dr. Van Allen described these "radiation belts", were found surrounding the earth in 1958. They were appropriately named the "Van Allen" Belts. All but those who remembered the words of Nikola Tesla were shocked by the implications of this discovery. Dr. Tesla lectured on his concept of the turbulent vacuum-filling æther, the gaseous atmosphere which constantly bombarded the planet in a dense and continual groundward flood.

According to Dr. Tesla, the bombardments of ultimate particles produced aerial free charges. Tesla predicted that these aerial charges, his "secondary radiations" would be found in specific layers surrounding the earth. Every major newspaper in the nation showed maps of the Belts and school children wrote reports on their dangerous characteristics. The Van Allen Belts were equated with the radiation produced in large particle accelerators. Exposure to the accelerated plasma flux would spell death for any would-be space traveller, a fact well noted by those having such high altitude aspirations. Future space travel would avoid these zones with care. But there were other concerns in connection with this notable rediscovery, and they were military concerns. Particle accelerators bombarded neutral metals with the same kinds of currents as were theoretically found in the Belts. Ordinary metals were converted into radioactive materials by such exposures. Radioactive materials were also dangerously modified by such exposures. Plutonium could be altered in such a way as to produce premature detonations. It was also postulated that the unpredictable nature of solar flares could actually neutralize high-soaring nuclear weapons packages. But why was military so concerned about accelerated charge processes occurring in space at all?

A new breed of payload delivery systems was appearing. ICBM's would be launched into suborbital or even orbital arcs. This would bring their nuclear payloads into the Van Allen Belts. What indeed would these relativistic particle currents do to plutonium warheads? Would Plutonium retain its fissile character? Would warheads lose their radioactive stability, being self-triggered in some unpredictable manner? Would plutonium become transmuted into a new and unknown element? Neutrons were known to decay in 12 minutes when not bombarded by permeative particles. Would exposure to the Belt currents effect some strange modification? If an accidental nuclear blast occurred in the Van Allen Belts, what would be the geophysical result? Could a nuclear explosion trigger a chain reaction in these Belts, one which would effectively burn them away in a single blast? Only a test could prove the truth or falsehood of these endless concerns.

Two tests preceded the orbital detonation of three separate warheads. The TEAK experiment was detonated at a height of 45 miles directly over Johnston Island in the Mid-Pacific. Auroral skies dominated the hemisphere. Electromagnetic disturbances become total in the shortwave spectra for hours afterward. Encouraged by this test, the second experiment, code-name ORANGE, was rapidly formalized to study effects closer to the ground. This warhead was detonated at a height of only 25 miles directly over the same islands. New auroras developed, but had far less intensity than TEAK, an obvious weak geophysical coupling effect. Project ARGUS was formalized in 1958, an experiment designed to test the effects of detonating nuclear warheads in orbit. The test itself constituted a potential international dilemma, the test objective clearly being for wartime application. Theoretical predictions remained uncertain. The effects of an aerial nuclear blast over a hemisphere was no small consideration.

Those participating in Project ARGUS did not suppose that the ignition of the weapon at such an altitude could wreak such sustained havoc with every shortwave communications system on earth. Theoreticians expected that Nuclear EMP effects would burn away receiving systems directly below the blast. The orbital height at which each test warhead was ignited would therefore be critical to civilian and commercial safety. The only expected geophysical effects would be an augmentation of the various ionospheric strata underlying the Belts directly below the blast point. Layers D, E, F, an G would be completely deranged for a time. Extra free charges would be released into these layers, synthetic auroras being the expected visual outcome of the blast. It was thought that a partial shortwave communications blackout might occur for several hours at most. Airlines and ocean going vessels had to be warned to clear the entire region below the blast site, as the United States imposed their test on the whole world.

ARGUS I was launched from the South Atlantic on 29 August 1958 and was detonated at a height of 12,900 miles. This placed the blast well within the newly discovered Van Allen Belts. Mimicking the disruptive force of a solar flare, the artificial irradiation of the Van Allen Belts did more than destroy electronic receivers beneath the blast site. The resultant Nuclear EMP completely destroyed powergrid integrity in several cities, an unexpected side effect. No one had believed this stupendous demonstration could occur from such an elevation. The high aerial plasma had sufficiently concentrated enough dielectric energy to bring these effects up into ground surface locations directly beneath the blast. The other unexpected effect had tremendous significance, as an impervious curtain of radio static and UHF distortion completely destroyed the integrity of all but certain high powered VLF channels. The effects lasted on certain channels for days. Here was a new weapons potential, one which could neutralize any offensive force without destroying cities or territories. First the EMP, then the blackout; a twofold "punch".

Here was the deliberate manufacture of sustained communications blackouts on a world wide scale. Its effect greatly cushioned by magnetic pressures, the power of this single Nuclear EMP was spread across the Inner Belt. Colorful auroras flooded the entire hemisphere, conjugately following the magnetic lines to the North Atlantic. This expansion across the Belt wiped out all normal radio communications for more than a day, an effect which greatly disturbed military around the world. Instruments indicated the formation of an artificial shell of ions, an additional zone created within the natural Van Allen Belts.

ARGUS II (30 August) and ARGUS III (6 September) followed in relatively quick succession. A total of three nuclear blasts, and Project ARGUS was terminated. What the military had ascertained did not concern itself only with the behavior of nuclear weapons in suborbital transit. Whatever effects they observed has remained classified, facts which do not concern our discussion. While the weapons packages were not to our knowledge substantially altered, damaged, or transmuted by passage through the Van Allen Belts, other important data now emerged. This data suggested that other methods might produce the desired communications blackout effect without a nuclear evoked EMP. The synthetic auroral effect which used nuclear warheads could not pinpoint any single target for the blackout phenomenon. No specified city or territorial locus could be precisely affected without wreaking havoc across the entire hemisphere. Lacking such precision however, did not eliminate the technique as a potential nonnuclear application.

Nuclear EMP could not be relied upon in conventional conflicts, but a few geophysicists understood how this blackout condition might be engineered from the ground. This triggered a new research direction which eventually produced "ionospheric heaters". Project STARFISH (1962) placed a thermonuclear warhead in the Belts at 27,000 miles near the North Magnetic Pole. This experiment was designed to produce an artificial ionization layer. Part of its several goals was the development of persistent ionization layers at specified extreme altitudes. The use of such a persistent ionization layer, one capable of reflecting RADAR beacons over the horizon, represented an attempt at rapid "over the horizon" identification of warheads transiting the north polar route. This blast produced an immense Nuclear EMP shockwave which deformed magnetic and terrestrial dielectric fields southward across North America. EMP strikes occurred everywhere, accompanied by worldwide communications blackouts. In certain cities, regional powergrids overloaded and failed. A technique for the purposeful disruption of enemy communications on a worldwide front had now been secured. An indirect means for interrupting electromagnetic systems across the world had been demonstrated, the remarkable result of nuclear-induced geoelectric modulation.

Despite all of these tests, true geophysical hazards, one fact remained clear.

Target precision did not yet exist in the Nuclear EMP method. Moreover, it became clear that the United States was not alone in the new capability. Later in the same year, the Soviets tested their space weapons potential at 16,000 miles, producing a synthetic ionization zone which corroborated the US findings. Projects ARGUS (1958) and STARFISH (1962) taught United States Military how to best use space detonated nuclear weapons to produce EMP and other plasma effects both in the ionosphere and on the ground. These effects were not restricted to the region directly below the blast area. Sourcetexts indicate the effective destruction of several large powergrids in the Pacific area, positioned several hundred miles over the horizon from actual blast effects. In these demonstrations were realized the modulation of geomagnetic and geoelectric energies by nuclear detonations.

The effect was especially potent when used at the poles. The radial nature of geomagnetic lines at polar positions could literally guide the blast products all along a conjugate "route". Terrestrial geoelectric concentrations would magnify the effect, by using the plasma ball as a permeable focus. A blast focus placed to one side or the other of a geomagnetic pole could produce literally explosive Nuclear EMP effects all along a specific geomagnetic sector. One could, by appropriate adjustments of altitude also specify the effective width of Nuclear EMP effects along that route, the "skewing" of Nuclear EMP effects being controlled by proximity from ground. These geophysical modulations produced effects far in excess of those attained by the blast focus alone. Here, military might was obtaining new potentials for destruction by direct coupling with geophysical potentials. But even now, with better and more refined data, the technique could not be truly referred to as "failproof". The use of nuclear detonations, while potent and instantaneous, was far too precarious a tool to employ. How would one isolate a target zone and localize the EMP effects in wartime?

Those who had observed the effects of the nuclear stimulated EMP effects recognized that the essential part of the dynamic involved the sudden placement of a rapidly expanding population of extra charged particles injected directly into geomagnetic field. This densified population of extra charges represented an intense pressure focus which, in the near vacuum of the space into which they been introduced, literally exploded in all directions. The kinetic energy of this dense charge population, representing the explosive potential of a nuclear detonation, pressed outward in all directions. But it was the containing thrust exerted by the geomagnetic field which constrained all the particles from escaping altogether. After the nuclear blast had radiated all of the optical and photonic energies away, energies which are not influenced by the geomagnetic field, the particles followed. The nuclear fireball was constrained from literally spreading out at right angles to the field lines. Particles moving directly away from the earth were thrust sideways into a wide plume. Their outward escape slowed by the continual magnetic sidethrust, negative beta particles moved eastward, while positive alpha particles moved toward the west.

But the greatest mobility of particles moved along the geomagnetic lines, where very little side thrusting resisted their movement. Those particles which had slight angular movement with respect to the field simply spiralled in long helical paths. Depending upon their placement with respect to the field, the fireball was thus spread out into a wide pole-to-pole plume. Researchers who continued investigating the "radio blackout" technique realized that other means had become available to them for the possible simulation of the nuclear triggered effect. Those who published works on the EMP techniques had concluded that nuclear stimulated blackouts, while effective for certain attack scenarios, remained completely impractical. In a world filled with allies and neutral nations, one could never use such a "brute force" method. Blanketing the whole hemisphere with such a communications disruption would be an act of war. Research was conducted on several related fronts.

One could not very well risk offending one's allies, and single miss could create just such an international incident. It was here that the EMP technique took a decided turn away from nuclear detonations and toward pure electromagnetic stimulations, the central lead theme of our next chapter. In one departure from the nuclear detonation method, military developers produced small cannons whose high velocity charges were designed to fire intensely ionized shockwaves with high directional accuracy. Such shells could destroy the electronics systems of opponents in a succession of highly directed blasts. Triggered EMP effects on land without nuclear detonations were a most "convenient" means. A few hundred of these resonant cannons could replace the dangerously radioactive nuclear warheads which would otherwise produce deadly conditions for occupation troops. The plasma shocks, emerging as miniature vortices from these cannons, were empowered by terrestrial dielectricity; a limitless power supply.

## NEUTRON BOMBS

Perceiving nuclear weapons as powerful, instantaneous potentials capable of driving various earth processes was a new concept having radical impact on military weapons developments. Such geophysically coupled weapons systems brought researchers into a consideration of nonnuclear means for achieving the very same objectives. Despite the domination of bomb development by nuclear physicists, chemists had not ceased developing higher yield chemical explosives. It was during this time frame that chemical aerosol bombs, having high kiloton yield, were tested. Such weapons were recognized for their tactical advantage and ease of handling. There were those early nuclear hybrids termed "dirty bombs" whose intended use was the complete poisoning of an enemy territory with long-lived radioactive fallout products. Encasing a nuclear warhead in uranium-238 produced a truly "filthy" explosion. But this was not the new research avenue, where clean precision in killing was desired.

Nuclear detonations are prolific producers of a broadband of energetic spectra. These reach from very lowest electrical signals, below ULF as DC, and range well above hard gamma rays. Energetic outputs of fissile materials, and admixtures of these materials, each contained very specific orders of electric, radiant, and particulate products. It was found that appropriately prepared weapons geometries could be made to reduce blast size, while maximizing specific portions of those products. The development of nuclear hybrid systems began after sufficient data had been gathered concerning such nuclear outputs. The increased efficiency in producing very specific nuclear outputs came as a result of studies which explored basic beam-target phenomena. Applied to weapons, these otherwise profound nuclear phenomena became the knowledge on which true horror was proliferated.

So successful were each of these methods that a new regime of nuclear hybrid devices, hideously efficient killing weapons, was stimulated into production. Thus, developers founds ways to maximize the particulate or radiant outputs with precision. Weapons engineers investigated the possibility that small high-radiation emitting nuclear detonations could be far more devastating than those which simply added higher kiloton and megaton blast potentials. The first new application of these concepts successfully produced high flux neutron-emitting bombs, where blast size was minimized and particle radiation, maximized.

Why these effects were at all intriguing derives from the peaceful applications which experimenters such as Dr. Gustav Le Bon and Dr. Thomas Moray each independently pursued, applications which successfully produced selective streams of particles or radiant energies for energy and medical purposes. Dr. Le Bon produced reactions in which light metals were converted directly into particulate emissions and ætheric streams. Dr. Moray produced high energy gamma rays whose mysterious therapeutic potentials were used by him in the curing of several supposed incurable illnesses. Dr. Moray also applied his selective stream emissions to force the crystallization of gold crystals from mining refuse. Specific applications of high energy particle combinations were found able to measurably raise the gold content of these refuse soils. Mining assays confirmed and documented these findings. There were other, more wonderful applications of these mysterious energies.

But military planners who needed to cover their hideous research with similar kinds of peaceful applications were not as sincere, and never as convincing. Project PLOWSHARE had been initiated under President Eisenhower to explore the peacetime uses of nuclear energy. But this investigation, a publicity relations effort to "clean up" the otherwise "dirty" atom, succeeded only in blasting large caverns in the desert and irradiating corn seeds with gamma rays. While these highly visible projects were daily reported in major newspapers and school weekly readers, the weapons devisers were deeply entrenched in the exploration of new horrors. The first neutron weapon was reported in 1961, it having been claimed that tests had been successful in these directions. Soviet sources protested the hideousness of such weaponry. It was odd that twenty years later, the very same announcement was reported under President Carter. The concept that a small yield nuclear detonator could "spare the cities and kill the enemy" was appealing to those in position to use the weaponry. Magnified neutron blasts did not produce a truly "clean" weapon. Neutron fluxes were so high from these truly small blast sites, usually a city block square, that every piece of surrounding matter became hopelessly radioactive. Neutron irradiation produced a "trace" whose signature was so deadly that the weapon, though approaching the "ideal" nuclear application, was yet not a perfect weapon for tactical occupation. Several neutron bomb explosions, and the population would indeed be destroyed; but the buildings which were left standing would be uninhabitable for centuries.

But in these weapons, scholars perceived a new kind of secretized knowledge; knowledge kept from the technical universities and libraries. What these weapons signalled was a new and highly privatized knowledge of nuclear energy, the surprising development of very small yield nuclear detonations having been secured. It has often been thought that nuclear weapons are necessarily high yield packages, this the result of fixed critical mass requirements. This restrictive view is obviously incorrect, as recovered patents on special optoexplosive systems teach. These hybrid nuclear weapons systems are also referred to as explosive light generating systems (ELGS). Depending on the explosion employed, physicists knew that highly penetrating radiations and particulate emissions would be accordingly produced. A very bizarre tellurian system arranged the reflection and redirection of radiation products from small yield nuclear explosives. Buried beneath the desert floor in heavily lined concrete conduits or in granitic strata, both nuclear explosives (NX) or chemical explosives (CX) were used to produce unimaginable beams of Clear Atomic Light (CAL). Producing curious cruciform beams of unprecedented brilliance, radiant energies were directed toward special targets for the production of otherwise unattainable high intensity particle beams.

These buried tellurian systems had very obvious applications in other nuclear applications. With simple conversions, these systems could be inverted and placed in orbit. Arranged in various large volume baffle-shaped conduits, systems are described as requiring surprisingly small yield nuclear blasts. These included nuclear explosives of yield as small as 1 or 2 Tons. Specially doped with light metals, the emerging radiant beams were directed by large mirrors to strike targets. In the literature, these experiments were referred to as "High Parameter Energy-Matter Interactions". Blast and shock formation was minimized by using complex cross-tunnels; N-shaped, Z-shaped, and triangle-shaped tunnels. These baffles were arranged with proper lengths and widths to isolate debris products from the emerging light pulse. With a great deal of help from data gained through Project PLOWSHARE, a great deal of research went into the construction of these thick-walled tellurian chambers (OPERATION DISTANT PLAIN).

Thus free of explosion debris, beams of nuclear brilliance levels were obtained just before the units self-destructed. The large reflector surfaces employed in such systems were consumed with each test run. Reflectors were often simple plastic sheets, or polished metals, and were therefore inexpensive arrangements. The production of reflectable X-Ray, ultraviolet, infrared, or trans-infrared, was thus secured. These clean atomic light beams (CAL) could be shaped be appropriate optical means, producing shaped atomic light (SAL). The optoexplosive technology found new applications, a long series of test allocation granting an array of available nuclear explosives to assess the other weapons potentials of the system. Light pulses from these tests proved conclusively that the emissions were sinusoidal in character, an amazing fact which reveals something of the nuclear blast nature. Close examination of high speed nuclear blast movies reveals a curious darkening effect just preceding the sudden explosive emission of light energies, evidence of a collapsing energy field just prior to explosion. These sudden first darkening effects are not the result of intense brilliance and film burns.

Patent texts teach that the optoexplosive weaponry worked best in greatly lowered atmospheric pressures, producing transcending X-Ray yields. In analogous design tests, obviously conducted in high altitude settings, trials describe concern for atmospheric clarity; a specific space-prone intention. In addition to these nuclear explosives, a series of tests were conducted using high-speed chemical explosives of various compositions, PETN explosives representing the highest speed detonations (8.3 kilometer/sec burn rate). These were doped with a great variety of metallic elements (Ti, Zr, Th, U) to obtain very special radiant characteristics. In addition, a large arsenal of small yield electroexplosives were employed in calibration tests. Abandoned railroad tunnels, missile silos, mine shafts, and artificially scoured tunnels were used as test sites. Tests were conducted from September 1957, both in Montana and Nebraska. The HARDTACK series lists five NX shots during October 1958. Each experiment used nuclear explosives of various small yields and burial depths. TAMALPAIS 72 Ton NX, EVANS 55 Ton NX, NEPTUNE 90 Ton NX, RAINIER 1.7 Kiloton NX, LOGAN 5 Kiloton NX, and BLANCA 19 Kiloton NX. Burial depths ranged from 330 feet to 840 feet. The GNOME NX shot in December 1961 used a 3.5 Kiloton warhead at. HARDHAT shot in 1962 used 5 Kiloton NX at 939 feet below sea level.

Fifty percent of NX radiation energy was confined to infrared spectra, ten percent to Ultraviolet, and forty percent to the visible. The thermal X-Ray pulse was absorbed within 10 feet of the blast site, contributing chiefly to plasma fireball expansion. NX shots at 50 miles above sea level altered all of these photon yields, X-Ray pulses being measured out to 10 miles. Metal doping powders could modify all of the resultant spectra. Dopant-enhancement employed foil coatings and particulates (Ag, Cd, Zn, Au, Pb, W, Nb, Ta, Si, B, Li, Be, Ce). Chemical salt dopants were used (chlorides and halides of Sn, Si, Ge) to coat the large plastic reflector diaphragms. Each obtained very specific radiation energy yields. The incredible photon yields from these blasts were used to pump and produce frightfully powerful laser beams, a brilliance comprising a 10 Terrawatt per square meter beam of deadly light energy. While the researchers spent an extensive amount of time studying a wide range of related natural phenomena and effects, these experiments had their deadly directives.

## GAMMA RAY BOMBS

A very strange phenomenon involving the gamma ray emissions of specific radioactive transition metal isotopes and rare earth isotopes was observed by Rudolph L. Mossbauer, then a graduate student at Caltech. Gamma ray emissions from these specific elements occur with the emission of phonons, acoustic waves of atomic wavelength. Each gamma ray emitted from the crystalline lattice of one of these elements is accompanied by a constant production of superhigh frequency sound. The phenomenon was considered to be an amazing natural behavior, the consequence of recoil in a crystalline structure. Each gamma ray emitted, results in an equal and opposite phonon emission in the lattice. Here for the first time, scientists were observing the details of radioactive decay, noting that photons, an energy phenomenon, were always accompanied by phonons, a material phenomenon.

Further study of this effect was fruitful on many fronts. The condition was found capable of being modified, modulated by an external application of sound energy. It was found that additions of sound energy to small wire samples of these elements, later known as "Mossbauer Isotopes", produced very sharp gamma ray emissions. The sharpness defined a condition in which gamma ray emissions were obviously being produced in the lattice with specific energy. The energetic release was coherent in terms of the energy states of each gamma ray in the emission, energy states which were identical. This was the equivalent of phenomena in which excited materials release monochromatic light energy, that produced for example in sodium vapor lamps. Released gamma rays from these isotopes were "monochromatic".

The effect was studied closely through very simple acoustic means, applying soundwaves directly to Mossbauer Isotope samples. It was found that gamma ray emissions from these peculiar isotopes could be phase modulated, a process involving gamma ray absorption in adjacent Mossbauer materials. By vibrating these materials across a gap at certain acoustic rates, one could literally force the rays to be released in surges. The intensity of these surges was a function of acoustic frequency, proximity, isotopic material, material volume, and test geometry. Sound energy was thus found able to modify the production of "monochromatic" gamma rays, effectively forcing their emission from the samples through sound application. One could theoretically "pump" such isotopes until all their radioactive emissions had been wasted to the surrounding space. Here, the mutability of radioactive half-life was demonstrated, where the entire sum of gamma ray emissions could be theoretically released in a single massive pulse.

Examination of these effects progressed into the dangerous study of shockwave phenomena applied to Mossbauer Isotopes. In highly shielded experimental facilities, the sudden acoustic energy represented by powerful shockwave applications to these materials resulted in massive and penetrating releases of very sharp gamma ray spectra. The danger level was reached when sharp shockwave applications effectively coupled with crystalline lattice structures in a real mass-related resonance, one in which a massive gamma ray emission incinerated the entire apparatus in a single blinding high density flash of deadliest radiation. The hideous spinoffs from research on filtered nuclear effects succeeded in producing pure radiant emitters. Gamma Ray Bombs. Such weaponry realizes the initial and perverse "dream" of those in authority who wished the complete obsolescence of heavy metal nuclear applications. In the emergence of superior and "clean" nuclear weapons, the obsolescence of the older weapons would permit a relaxation of fears that the territories of the world would be obliterated by explosive fury. In the emergence of such weaponry, deemed "clean", one could make a public showing of good will. One could dismantle all nuclear warheads in methodical process, taken by the deluded eyes of the world as a manifest token of the peaceful intention of any such nation. One does not publicly "disarm" unless far better tactical weapons exist.

Now, military held a device which could be detonated with virtually no blast potential, no explosive effect at all. A single small flash, like that of a white flare, would be the only sign that a weapon had been deployed at all. The entire energetic emission being a radiant one, an entire city of people could be thus carbonized in the gamma pulse. The implications of such weaponry is truly hideous, the detonation of a small Gamma Ray Bomb would effectively carbonize every living thing within a specified "kill" radius. Only the land, resources, cities, and their buildings would remain completely intact. Not one long lingering radioactive residue would remain after the detonation. Occupation troops could move in without any of the just concern expressed during the cleanup operations in Hiroshima and Nagasaki. The "perfection" of nuclear weaponry did not cease with the production and proliferation of these weapons.

These explosive radiation weapons (ERW) demanded none of the high restriction handling requirements of heavy metal nuclear warheads. Troops could deploy them, a mere exercise in artillery fire. In fact, similar such designs have been deployed, the tactical nuclear weapons which have been used in battle. In their smallest embodiments, cannon fired armor-piercing darts, tank personnel have been "carbonized". Tank bodies were recently welded shut by an intense thermal energy far beyond the capability of ordinary chemical explosives. The APDS (Armor Piercing Discarding Sabot) is a small "penetrator rod", manufactured from depleted uranium fuel rods. The central dart is encased in a light aluminum casing, the primary round of the MIAI Abrams 120 millimetre Gun. Fired, the impact sheds the aluminum casing. The uranium rod, no larger than a pencil, impacts the tank casing. These darts, ignited by PIEZONUCLEAR stimulation, melt their way into the central tank cavity. The sharp impact of such isotopic darts into armor plating stimulates the Mossbauer effect. Directed radiation "flares" move through the plating without effort, the results being decisive and terminal. But these scenarios of death, the perversion of an original great and visionary discovery, have their overwhelming reply in a much forgotten episode involving the neutralization of radioactive sources.

## NUCLEAR NEUTRALIZATION

One notices the strange appearance of numerous parallel electrical striations during certain of the nuclear detonations. These parallel ribbon varieties, all nearly vertical, are electrical discharges often accompanied by smoky precipitations. These phenomena are easily discerned in the documentary stock footage from the era. Most did not recognize these forced geoelectric discharges with any concern. But some researchers of the qualitative sciences, those never considered as part of the conventional consortium, were sure they knew why these vertical striations were appearing.

Greatly concerned with the entire nuclear proliferation for reasons unappreciated by the academic world of researchers, these scientific investigators perceived that these electrical discharges were environmental "responses" to the application of nuclear "irritants", the back-response of mysterious earth energies to the geophysical application of nuclear irritations. These mysterious vertical striations were but one of the electrical aspects, instantaneous "shrieks" provoked by nuclear detonations in the environment.

No one comprehended or appreciated the meaning of these responses more than a consortium of scientific researchers, who relied entirely on special physiological, biological, and organic instrumentation. Relying entirely such sensors to evaluate the energetic conditions of isolated material samples, human subjects, and the geophysical environment, such biosensitive instrumentation revealed an alarming decrease in the energetic response of plant tissue samples with each nuclear test. These well corroborated energy decreases evidenced biointerference on such a wide scale as to be unimaginable. The over-the-horizon neutralization effects absolutely ruined the normal high sensitivity of radionic instruments the world over. This gradual realization gave rise to the notion of a "biodynamic environment", in which vital energies actually surged and fluctuated in continual pulsating process.

These researchers had long measured the responses of their biosensors to environmental changes stimulated by thunderstorms, earthquakes, eclipses, solar flares, and auroras. These effects on the biodynamic environment were temporary, a manifestation of natural process. But whenever nuclear weaponry was being tested, and those tests went on with regularity throughout the postwar period, the radionic responses of their biosensors simply "went dead". The biological responses of sensors remained "dead" for hours, and in some locations, for days after each nuclear "shot". In addition after these bomb tests, certain researchers noticed that the crystallization of certain organic substances became deranged and, in some cases, completely altered. The derangement of molecular and even of atomic process in normal crystallizing solutions was also observed at great distances from the bomb test epicenters. Derangement on such atomic and molecular levels evidenced a desperate condition which was now proliferating itself across the world without constraint. It was obvious that the biodynamic environment had been disturbed to a frightening and permeating degree. Reports of these findings were not appreciated by military researchers, who could not register any of the effects with their instruments. These effects did not register on either electrical or magnetic instrumentation, the standard battery of "inertial force" instruments.

Incapable of detecting the articulate and prolific detail of such an effect, the protests of this consortium were rejected and then officially denied. But the long distance "deadening effects" did not cease with these laboratory biosensor measurements. The lassitude which many sensitive individuals reported after such tests was taken to be a product of hysteria and suggestibility. Quoting the erudite opinions that such visceral responses could be nothing more than the "placebo effect" on a grand social scale did not help those who, hundreds of miles away from the tests, began reporting the same debilitating effects. The sudden wave of nausea, the sharp and complete loss of balance, the sense that "the floor has given way" represent effects in the autonomic nervous system, a demonstration of bio-geodynamic modulation. Only Radionic Science could account for the effects, which were instantaneous and biological in their impact. Others who began studying these effects decided that they could only be the result of geoelectric or geomagnetic modulations, a vast study on the phenomenon being conducted by the NRL and the Air Force operated Phillips Corporation (Puthoff, Persinger).

One researcher was not surprised by the official response, a characteristic "biopathic response" in his revolutionary terminology. A colleague of Sigmund Freud, Dr. Wilhelm Reich, was all too familiar with these "dead responses" among the academic convention whenever confronted by these kinds of biosensitive phenomena. Conventional science remained both unable and unwilling to consider the possibility that environmental responses, viewed in mechanistic terms as inert force exchanges, might actually be macroscopic bioresponses. Organization on such a grand scale intimated that the environment could act as a whole aggregate, rather than as an inert and interrelated collection of forces and masses. Dr. Reich voiced the opinion, as so many had, that the biodynamic environment was behaving as...a living being.

Dr. Reich had long considered the absolute reality of the Freudian libido concept. Taken by most as a mere metaphor, Dr. Reich believed that the libido was a very real and unexplored energy; one which could be isolated and studied. Toward these ends he employed numerous biosensors and human subjects. Observing the enormous muscle contractions and dilations of "pleasure-pain" responses, he measured bioelectric currents. Attempts at reproducing the same muscle effects with applications of equivalent electric currents failed. With this demonstration, Dr. Reich quickly determined that an unaccounted energy was producing the powerful responses. Evidence that the new energy was distinct from all of the other natural forces became evident in a great number of now-classic qualitative experiments. Dr. Reich found it possible to greatly amplify muscular bioresponse with special large multi-plate capacitors of his own design. Though muscles so exposed produced more powerful and "complete" contractions, Dr. Reich found that the bioelectric values remained absolutely unchanged. It was obvious that the sensitive galvanometers, inert instrumentation, could not measure the unknown force. He believed that he had isolated the libidinous energy, which he termed ORGONE.

Conventional instrumentation had not been able to reveal this energy. Inert meters could not measure the force, because they could not respond with the force. Orgone was a force requiring response, biological response. Only biosensors could therefore reveal its presence. This explained the inability of researchers to measure Orgone. But the unwillingness of researchers, despite numerous demonstrations of his findings, prompted Dr. Reich toward a new psycho-evaluation of the academic world. Academes who did not want to find evidence of "life force" were everywhere to be found now. They had produced nuclear weaponry, evidence that a specific mindstate permeated the pursuit of this science. Was it any wonder then that the effects of this avenue of nuclear research could never produce any life-positive effects? Dr. Reich published his analysis of the "biopathic condition", a powerful and accurate thesis which explains both the fixation on death-oriented technology and the unwillingness of certain scientists to open themselves to biodynamic realities.

It was known that intense gamma ray bombardment of fissile materials could literally reduce and even remove the radioactive characteristics of those materials. This process had been developed, the accidental discovery of several researchers, who found it possible to so "treat" and neutralize spent reactor fuel rods and other hazardously radioactive waste products. Indeed, these discoveries derive from the work of Dr. Gustav Le Bon who found it possible to reduce and even remove the "radioactive character" of radium both by heating and exposing it to "neutral" radiations. Dr. Le Bon found it also possible to manufacture radioactive materials by exposing them to concentrated streams of sunlight. Experiments in which tin and magnesium were so exposed, produced such a radioactive effluence that Dr. Le Bon could not distinguish, save in the volume of material equivalences, between the intensities of these radioactive metals and radium itself. In one natural instance of this natural transmutation, from neutral to radioactive, it was known that sunlight exposure could modify roof copper sheeting to a very radioactive state.

But what was Orgone itself? It was sensibly "breezy", a dense and flowing stream which was far more than a particulate emanation. Best secured as a powerful stream, when his capacitor-accumulators were thoroughly grounded, or connected by flexible metal hosing to running water sources, Dr. Reich explored the possible ætheric nature of these natural manifestations. He also explored the environment with a host of special telescopic aids and sensors, finding that this "orgone energy" was everywhere in the environment...especially in sunlight. Building on his discovery of the vitalizing energy, Dr. Reich discovered that his capacitor, which he called an "Orgone Accumulator", evidenced very strange visceral, thermal, and visual phenomena. In absolute darkness, he and others reported the visual manifestation of foggy blue-grey light all around the Accumulator.

After years of fascinating study and discovery, a most enlightening bibliography, Dr. Reich began experimenting with the strange biological energy and its relationships with magnetic, electric, and nuclear energy. Each of the inert energies were found to be in antagonistic relationship with biological energy, each provoking degrees of measurable biological devitalizations. These devitalizations were each in proportion with the species of energy used, previously an unrecognized fact. Subjects exposed to magnetic fields evidenced visceral symptoms of depression which were far weaker than those hyperactive conditions stimulated by weak electric fields. These effects have been reproduced by military and private experimenters.

In this spectrum of devitalizing reactions, none proved as deadly as the effects of nuclear energy. Dr. Reich placed a small radium needle in a large Orgone Accumulator to test the antagonism between biological energy and radioactive matter. In a short while however, a wave of nausea spread among all of the personnel in the large research facility. This initial nausea soon became a proliferation of critically dangerous symptoms. This effect spread throughout and beyond the entire grounds of his facility with deadly force. Personnel had to be removed from the area. Their symptoms included nausea, imbalance, fatigue, heart palpitations, asthmatic constrictions, fevers, and nervous hyperactivity. Placed thus in the large Accumulator, Dr. Reich had inadvertently provoked an antagonistic reaction between biological energy and nuclear irritants which, because of the grounded Accumulator had somehow stimulated a reaction of geophysical proportions.

The condition lasted for months, an unfamiliar demonstration of biodynamic "catabolism". Here, the natural environment was very evidently digesting the powerful irritations of radiation; and would not cease until all of the irritant had been consumed. With biodynamic energy so powerfully focussed on the radium needle, its ordinary functions in supporting surrounding life, indeed of the enlivening the environment itself, was withdrawn. Constricting into the radium needle, and thus away from all surroundings immediate to the laboratory, the region grew dark and deathly. Dr. Reich hypothesized this to be the mechanism by which natural energy digested bioirritants, a "bombarding" means also by which matter might be transformed into new states. The disastrous condition, a "death phase" of enormous power, gave rise to a new dawn. A little more than a year after this hideous event, and after untold physical maladies had gradually disappeared, Dr. Reich made an earth shattering discovery. Reexamination of the original radium needle, that which provoked the reaction, proved that its radioactivity had been removed. During the deadly days of this unexpected reaction, Dr. Reich and a close colleague, Dr. Robert McCullough, had buried all of the laboratory radioactive sources in a thick lead container several miles from the laboratory. Now, they went back to the burial site and dug up the container. Strangely, miraculously, each of these materials had been neutralized. It was impossible to measure any radioactive levels in these normally lethal sources. Indeed, the strange facts taught that exposures to special energetic streams could methodically neutralize radioactivity in Radium and Cobalt-60.

The deadly large scale reaction was the result of an unmoderated exposure of radioactive material to the biological energy stream. What would a moderated treatment of the same materials produce? Dr. Reich discovered that directed biological energy streams, when properly moderated and controlled, produced measurable and continual decreases in new radioactive samples. Through the use of special beam-type projectors, Dr. Reich demonstrated how these effects could be produced at great distances, hypothesizing that nuclear weapons could be deactivated. The use of special energy streams such as these could be employed. His notion was part of a defense proposal, the goal being to produce a nuclear warhead "deactivator". Securing a highly concentrated stream of biological energy could so significantly reduce the radioactivity of fissile mater that the weaponry would be rendered useless. By his method, enemy weaponry could be neutralized on its way toward national targets. This statement provoked an official response of the very highest biopathic variety. On trumped up charges of "malpractice", Dr. Reich was sentenced under

Federal law. He thereafter died in Federal Prison.

In truth, the ability to neutralize a power is far greater evidence of supremacy than the exercises which implement that power. That vacant "power" which only appropriates the inherent strength in Technology, that which moves through the halls of earthly rule, has little of which to boast when measured against the real world-foundations. How is it that the world-foundational biodynamic energies stand in such sharp and antagonistic contrast to that vacuous force? The "biodynamic atomic energy" of Le Bon, Tesla, Paneth, Moray, Reich, Pons, Fleischmann, Mills, Patterson, and others represents a natural expression of deep consequence. Biodynamic continua, a marvelous stratification, exerts powerful destabilizing thrusts against the geopolitical rule by decrees which represent authority of the most extraordinary fundamental kind. The natural order subverts geopolitical rule simply because geopolitics are synthetic, artificial; themselves arbitrary and easily substituted. Anarchy exists in the natural order, breaking down these rulerships at every moment in ways not adequately appreciated, not immediately obvious, and not possibly eradicated. The antiprogressive stagnancy which has been proliferated by oligarchic rulership has so resisted and antagonized the biodynamic continuum that natural repercussions must be shortly expected.

Thoughts of this kind impact military agencies, shocking every station in a chain reaction of fear which leads straight through every part of the caste labyrinth, and directly into the oligarchic control centers. The thought that any nuclear neutralizing force could be found was actually more of a threat to military weapons capability than the fear of total planetary obliteration. Clearly, someone wanted those warheads to work. But fear is evidence of possible loss, and loss is not an aspect of the most fundamental world energy. True power comes from far deeper reserves in the natural creation. Therefore is it not curious that the deeper energies, so manifest throughout the deepest conscious levels of creation, have their devastating effect on world rulership? Alienated from this conscious substratum, earthly rule cannot stand in its presence, and so rejects every manifestation of vital energy, that to merely infer its technical applications is to infer total eradication of rulership. What a strange tautology. The biopathic reaction. These two antagonists then, power versus dream, each determine world directions. Of the two, the dreamers are more completely in communion with the natural conscious foundations which generate and define world directions.

Regardless of the futile struggle, the streams of vitalizing energy, the biodynamic energy so prevalent in Nature, are those potent currents which neutralize and reverse all subordinate manifestations. Here then is an exercise of curious faith, a tender feeling in the dark after the Divine. The vital energies reveal a spectrum of strata, one each deeper than the other. The sooner humanity will relinquish its pedantic examination of Nature as a collection of inert forces, the sooner it may allow itself to rediscover and "permit" the very obvious bioorganismic attribute of the world at large. Once this macroorganization has been realized, its overwhelming proofs will drive away the mechanistic paradigm which has so thoroughly contaminated the intellectual community for three centuries. These realities are discovered through personal experiment, wherein one learns that language which draws humanity; the metaphoric themes running through the natural tapestry. When the world as a whole will begin again to comprehend the endless glories which persons, derisively termed "dreamers", have always enjoyed, then vision will guide and preserve the true power. In truth, those whose devoted desire is to seek out and find the biodynamic generators of Nature hold the only true power on earth.

# CHAPTER 5
## Radar EMP and Ionoscatter Technology

### REPERCUSSIONS

When Guglielmo Marconi advanced the weak and failure-prone wave radio, he passed on a legacy of technological inferiority to the world. First to seize the method, without any objections or comparative standards, was the military. Military privatization of radio technology represents an event of major importance. This act of secretization permanently sealed the eyes and ears of engineers who would seek military employ as consultants and developers in the well funded laboratories. Money poured in from the ruling structure in an unremitting flood, as military agencies were permitted to engage industry with a free hand. So long as Intelligence overseers were permitted access to the laboratories and factories at any moment's notice, military became for a while the "heir apparent" of the ruling structure, the favored child in bureaucratic halls.

Military were of course completely cooperative, exercising their ambitions with relatively no other constraints; a demonstration of the refocusing of power at a lower level than the oligarchic throne. This state of affairs, this internal warfare with a lower class consortium was to be a temporary concession. It was one predicated on the existence of hideous weaponry, on the existence of enemies who also possessed nuclear capabilities, and on a world revolution in working class consciousness over which rulership had absolutely no power. But the fixations of power, at lower than rulership stations, were not the only stubborn facts which this new technological world had to offer.

There were fixations of mind which, for working class intellect, formed a resolute and impervious wall of restraint. There were technologies which had been removed from the seas of social exchange which needed to be returned to their rightful owners before true and protective custody of the local geopolitical territories and regions could be secured. There were those technological means which Dr. Nikola Tesla had long championed, those systems which would have actually prevented the nuclear horror. Were they allowed their free and unrestricted flow among the working class devotees, nuclear weaponry would never have become the pressured raced which events had succeeded in producing; the now weaponry of military choice throughout the world. Geopolitical structures had become complex, claustrophobic, and fraught with the potential for complete and utter obliteration. The mere presence of nuclear awareness had been enough of a stimulant to drive the world beyond the once potent dictates of the rulership itself. This was a condition, unstable and precarious, not well favored.

Therefore monies would flow, power would flow, and all attentions would flow in directions downward. Waterfalls of power would continue flowing down into the social cataracts of the working class until a balancing solution had been found. Found by those whose meddling pursuits had succeed in rending power into their own hands. When once again the balance had been reached, a task which they would fulfill on behalf of threatened rule, then a new status quo would be enforced. Once the solution to nuclear horror had been secured and proliferated among those who shared its horrors, a world of unchanging perfection would once again be attained; one where rulership would again withdraw and withhold all power. A golden "new age" of isolation and social stagnation was anticipated before the new millennium, where perfect and utter control would at last be the reestablished and ruthless world norm. But this was not such an easy task, especially because the means for achieving those enunciated ends had already been shared with rulership well over a previous century.

The individual who had presented his technologies and unfettered wonders had been rejected. His work suppressed, he himself now deceased, there were few modern alternatives to the dilemma at hand. But now, rulership was constrained forever to consider these unworthy and power removing considerations. The revolution in consciousness had already revealed its permanent effect on rule by its very presence, one which would never be removed from the theatrum of rule again. The imbalancing element was not found in the technological accoutrements. These were but the solidified expressions of its energetic exercises. The imbalancing element was a thought frame, an active awareness, a conscious sea whose waves could not be controlled. And the removal of knowledge, another of its expressions, had resulted in a far greater tide of fright than even those which Tesla had enunciated. For it was obvious that the repression of Tesla and his Technology, now viewed as a blessing, was the direct cause of the inferior route through which a tsunami of nuclear weaponry had been generated. One could not rule the waves of this vast sea.

The Teslian secrets which could have prevented nuclear horror, the potential world annihilation, were not comprehended by the majority of those consumed with the consciousness of technology. Since before World War I, Marconi Wave Radio became the only available technology which military was willing to consider or pursue. We have already discussed the many convoluted prejudices which held Tesla and his technology in an antagonism of disfavor. We have seen how the extensive social favors, lavished on Marconi by the elite, found equal favor by the elitist military of the time period. Military came to devalue the findings of Tesla, while highly valuing Marconi. Aristocratic in its early expression, military cadets were the chosen of the most chosen families. Their predilections for aristocratic favor and pride would not prove to work in their best favor, nor in the interest of the world into which their children would come.

Their tutorial favor under Marconi, though couched as sincere surrender to his dictatorial sway, was actually a ploy to steal his secrets and form a military radio corps in which they were to be given first rank. When the smoke had cleared however, the well poised and smooth faced cadets, pedigrees of mercantile society, were neither equipped nor creative enough to produce a military radio corps of their own. The cadets had inherited one skill however, the knowledge of management. They therefore spent the next 25 years, well into the vestibules of a Second World War, before substantial and reliable military radiowave systems had been developed. It had been commandeered by cadets, now grey and stooped. But it had been engineered by working class minds, eyes, hearts, and hands.

The unfortunate and foolish adoption of wave radio, both by industry and by military, was not therefore the result of superior engineering directives which Tesla had enunciated. The systems which had been favored by the managerial cadets yet insisted on the weak and ineffectual systems which Marconi had actually purloined from a host of European sources. Those European academes had not themselves been able to obtain better than frail results from their apparatus. When Tesla announced his new and revolutionary findings in America, they so challenged the existing mindset that neither aristocratic academes nor pedigreed military could or would receive what appeared to be the dissent of a foreigner. The hostile and fiery reception which became his familiar experience in America was a complex blend of prejudices and rejections, later to return on those who rendered him such disfavor as a white flash in the desert. Here were repercussions which few properly assessed, and which fewer observed. Yet the rejection of Dr. Tesla and the emergence of nuclear weaponry are two separate events connected by a single line. The one produced the other.

## SEARCHLIGHT

We have shown how the extensive experiments with short radiowaves had been conducted for years by Marconi at sea. Hoping to turn the tide of his former life, hoping to throw off the yoke of his enslavements to a ruthless financial mogul, and hoping to return to the world some measure of the good which he felt he had taken, Marconi introduced his shortwave systems openly to the public. Neither for gain nor for fame, this new beginning literally signalled his own attempt to regain the lost flower of his youth, a route which he, very tragically, had not enough time to retrace. Had he the time however, Marconi would have eventually realized what Tesla had been insisting all along. The reasons for his rejection of Marconi wave technology had nothing at all to do with personal disfavor. The rebuttals which Tesla repeatedly made of Marconi wave radio were based on a discovery of more wonderful natural phenomena than Marconi had ever known. I am sure that, had the inquisitive young Marconi been given those Teslian secrets from the start, he would have been its most prolific protagonist.

In the absence of these awarenesses however, Marconi pursued what he thought far outweighed his VLF mammoths; the global radio circuits for which he had expended his energies, his fortunes, his innocence, and his love. During the time of his self-exile, Marconi discovered how readily the small and compact short radiowave systems could propagate signals to great distances with clarity. Shortwave was portable and required far less power to go an equivalent distance as VLF waves, apparently relying on the skies for their great distance-reaching capabilities. To him, short radiowaves represented a wonderful new potential, by which small stations could communicate freely and without extensive expenditures of finance and technical dimension. Shortwave represented a new social revolution in world communications which could not be owned by monopolists, nor truly regulated by bureaucracies. This was Marconi's way of casting fire among his bridges.

Study of the period journals reveals that military radio science seemed completely captivated by the advancements which Marconi introduced after his abandonment of VLF systems. It seemed as though, dominated by his early training of military cadets, military radio corpsmen were largely uncreative. Both periodicals and patent records actually support this outlandish claim. Military radio engineers did not begin experimenting and innovating until long into the 1930's, and that the result of "imported creativity". Marconi's introduction of shortwave systems, triggered an enormous new impetus to the communications arts. The minuscule shortwave radio transmitters were, by comparison with his gigantic VLF wave stations, a new revolution in communications. It was through shortwave that radio actually became a social force. Civilians were thus given a rare access to the world. No earthly point was inaccessible.

Marconi, Fessenden, and others reported the reflection of short radiowave signals from various high altitude layers. Beginning with high altitude clouds in the Tropopause, and reaching up into space, the reflection of shortwaves became more than a fascinating natural study. In certain conditions, it was found possible to "skip" signals across incredible, normally impossibly great distances. The conditions of these reflective "skips" varied with weather, season, time of day, with lunar phase, and even with planetary configurations (Austin, Appleton, Nelson). Though few comprehended the reasoning behind these strange phenomena, none argued with the empirical observations that they contributed to very long range, shortwave transmissions. It was then that military researchers began funding scientific researchers to study these natural variables for them. Developing a solid communications link among military branches and their divisions everywhere remained a command base priority. They themselves were unfortunately far too sleek to be creative in their own right. Increased civilian experimentation with shortwave radio brought new discoveries to the scientific bibliography, and this formed the core of every avenue which military would pursue. In the absence of Marconi, there would be ample resource on which to draw.

Here was a prolific period of design and development, amateurs everywhere becoming the inventors of completely new radio components and refinements. These individuals, highly experienced in both transmitting and "pulling signal" from the skies, formed the very heart of a new radio consortium which military came to respect and eventually employ. Several previous experimenters had performed demonstrations of highly directional ultrahigh and superhigh frequency electrical alternating waves long before Marconi. David Hughes, Heinrich Hertz, Augusto Righi, Sir Oliver Lodge, Daniel MacFarland-Moore, Christian Hulsmeyer, and others discovered means for beaming extremely high frequency waves in beams to great distances. Early experiments proved that strong sparkgap oscillators, when enclosed in copper pipes of various dimensions, projected highly directional radio beacons. With the improvement of oil-quenched sparkgaps, electrical discharges became greatly intensified, and powerful beams could be made to carry telegraphic information. The sparkgap beam projectors of most experimenters were designed to carry communications signals. A few others however used these beams for distance-ranging. One of these early systems belong to Christian Hulsmeyer, whose "radio searchlight" was an early SHF wave system (1904).

Projected and reflected from metallic objects, the basic principles which later led to a host of radio sciences were briefly examined. These primitive UHF and microwave apparatus formed the basis of modern communications systems. Some experimenters discovered that these energies could produce heating effects at a distance. Others retrieved usable electrical energy by rectifying these otherwise high frequency alternating wave beams. Experimenters began investigating the possibility that these extremely high frequency radiowaves might provide better transmission properties with low power application. It was anticipated that increased frequency would yield increased communications "reach". These researches began with transmitters which could beam vocal signals across a meadow. They were, in fact, barely improved versions of those used by Augusto Righi and Oliver Lodge. In time, a new application of vacuum tubes began developing and extending the available radio range to unheard frequencies. "Superhigh" radiowave frequencies, though invisible, had concentrated power approaching that of arc light beacons.

The decade between 1920 and 1930 proved to be a most remarkable demonstration of the inventive resource represented by an international consortium of radio experimenters. New super high frequency generators appeared everywhere, patents abounding. Vacuum tubes of a great variety began coming into vogue, as amateur experimenters investigated the mysteries of SHF radiowave transmission. Invented by a great population of enthused amateur experimenters, the flood of superhigh frequency vacuum tube generators represented a trend which, in the minds of those who so invented, desperately hoped to imitate Tesla and his distinctive systems. Inadvertently, a few young inventors actually did succeed in rediscovering somewhat of his technology; but these were weak and undeveloped embodiments of systems which Tesla himself had already greatly surpassed. The inventors who brought their Tesla-like systems forward were not disfavored, but were not encouraged to pursue their revolutionary trends. Therefore, these inventions came as "one hit wonders", there usually being nothing more from the names which so fervently produced them. Nevertheless, there are those few patents which represent this accidental replication of Teslian findings in impulse technology. Impulse transmitters of Roberto de Mouro, Bela Gati, Frederick S. McCullough, Conrad Reno, and others are true wonders; representatives of that phenomena in which repressed discoveries continually reemerge.

## SUPERHIGH FREQUENCY WAVES

The first major development of Super High Frequency tubes came with the needs of World War II England. The heavy bombing raids on English soil, the early attempt by the Luftwaffe of Adolf Hitler to crush that nation, was resisted through an initially meagre scientific resource. Only the indomitable fortitude of brave souls fighting impossible odds proved the turning of a tide, in both revolutionary science and in the eradication of tyranny. The two seemed closely associated in that the rise of science spelled defeat for fascism. The only available technology for the "early warning" of Nazi air raids were acoustic listening systems, technology adapted from the scientific amusement pages of Victorian Epoch periodicals. Though developed into a wonderful state of perfection, these large multiple concave cup systems mounted on swivels, could not provide the fast warning capabilities so desperately sought. The only other tools for early warning were the and fog penetrating arclamps, yet another science which had been perfected before the prior Century's turn. The challenge stood before those whose tasks were now doubled, fighting the foe while simultaneously producing new technology.

Those who at last had begun enjoying peace were not concerned with the outlandish threat of a Second World War. Nevertheless as guided missiles became the vengeful expressions of lunacy, the absolute need for readiness, for new technology to defeat and utterly obliterate the Nazi foe, commenced. An enemy unseen is a frightful prospect to defeat. An enemy seen is not threatening. Soaring at supersonic speeds across the English Channel, V-1 "buzz bombs", and later V-2 missiles, required an alert ready system. Having an ability to reach targets miles out over the sea, long before they reached the coast. A new radiobeam technology was desperately sought. Those who recalled the UHF "radio searchlight" of Christian Hulsmeyer attempted duplication and adaptation of the same for their more contemporary and immediate needs. Science again was coming to the needs of an assailed people.

By August 1938, North Sea and Channel coastlines were watched by a chain of "metric" (UHF) radar stations. After observing the initial experimental results and military effectiveness of the first simple "longwave" RADAR systems, engineers were encouraged to pursue their objectives with neither delay nor diminished effort. What began with UHF beams soon shifted the emphasis toward the development of a SHF beam system for long distance ranging and detection. The essential problem facing these engineers was that of power. The effectiveness of the system depended upon the intensity of reflected energies. The extensive sea-searching beams now required both higher resolution as well as extremely high power.

SHF beams were relatively more "optical" than the UHF metric waves, being required precisely because of their high resolving properties. Bounced from metal surfaces, these echoes contained inherent detail which could be discriminated by appropriate scanning detectors, at first a simple oscilloscope. The engineering problems demanded the generation of these super high frequencies. Additionally, these SHF signals had to be enormous in strength. The extensive sea-searching beacons, required by a coastal watch along both the North Sea and the Channel, demanded power levels of a megawatt per system. But those UHF and SHF vacuum tubes of the 1920's, considered novelties of the electronic tube trade, were not made to produce powerful signals at these frequency levels. Electron currents had to release enormous amounts of SHF energies, and supply this amount of power in a continuous reserve. The operation characteristics of any potential RADAR power source were already theoretically severe.

Superhigh frequency vacuum tubes of this era may be classified into three succinct categories. Notable in this first expansion of frequencies upward were the early "lighthouse" and "acorn" tubes, which attempted the generation of SHF across the smallest possible vacuum gaps. These simple and straightforward designs, named for their actual appearance, were analogues of triodes. These tiny embodiments sought the achievement of UHF and SHF energies in an analogous manner as triodes, which used resonant circuits to build up powerful self-regenerating alternations. The chief importance of these early tubes was that they permitted the study of UHF and SHF energies, radio frequencies so very high that they could only be measured in terms of wavelength! The problem with SHF alternations was their small resonant product values. There were geometric reasons why certain radio frequencies became the most powerful expressions of the art, reasons which successfully produced the most powerful communication embodiments. These tubes could employ neither the large capacitor surfaces nor inductors which, in triodes, produced the most powerful high frequency alternations.

Lighthouse and Acorn tubes suffered greatly from extreme frequency drift. As continued use heated their metal parts, the rigidly fixed grids and plates moved to the point where their operating characteristics were significantly changed. Furthermore, not much SHF power could be derived from these tubes, whose size was the limiting factor. While representing the very first vacuum tubes capable of generating the SHF energies, neither Lighthouse nor Acorn tubes could carry sufficient energy for the needs of an efficient RADAR system. These little tubes were excellent in experimental demonstration of UHF and SHF energies, and retained their use in low power transmitters. The UHF and SHF tubes of Russel Ohl (1928) are still used in radiosondes and other such small SHF communications applications. Capable of transmitting low power superhigh frequency radiowaves, many of these little tubes combine tube and transmitter in one piece.

Some of these tubes were fitted with an extension lead or pointed metallic caps, SHF energy being removed through the little wire antennae. Placed in copper pipe or at the focus of polished metal concaves, these first SHF transmitters proved to give surprising line-of-sight signalling capabilities. Mounted on tripods, these simple first transmitters bore remarkable resemblance to modern microwave comlink systems. But another means for generating SHF energy had to be found which employed some new and more potent alternation phenomenon. These means were sought in the development of Klystron tubes and Magnetrons, the two other SHF classes which were developed during the preceding decade. When developed, none of these tubes were intended for wartime use. They were therefore not powerful embodiments, and the war demands for superhigh radio frequency power demanded substantial new upgrades which could not yet have been anticipated by engineers of the day. Klystron tubes took their name from a Greek term which means "clustre" or "bunch", the electronic action on which their operation depended.

The first Klystron tubes were relatively short affairs, not unlike Lighthouse tubes. Electrons were directed through two annular rings, each externally connected through a resonant circuit made to alternate with fixed superhigh frequency. Streams of thermionic electrons approached the first ring and, while passing through it, induced an electrical wave pulse in the external circuit. This pulse sped through the external circuit to the opposed ring. Electrons which reached the ring before this pulse were pushed into the anode. But those electrons caught between the rings were "bunched" or "clustred" back into a fixed volume. The coordinated alternations provided by the external circuit induced bunching throughout the normally steady electron streams. Each clustre arrived in the ring spaces at just the right time to induce very powerful SHF alternations.

As successful as this simple American made device became, it yet could not provide the sheer power required by the British engineers. Even after Klystron tube improvements had lengthened the electron path, while also internalizing and replacing the resonant circuit with a resonant copper cylinder, these tubes could not provide explosive SHF power. The chief advantage of Klystrons was and is their continuous operating characteristics which, provided moderately high power in continuous supply. Klystron tube improvement has now permitted the use of geometrically large tube geometries. Klystron tubes are miniature linear accelerators, often standing several feet in height. They are the transmitting tubes of choice in microwave arts today, using phase velocity bunching to produce successive electron pulses of great power. High current super short period successions are induced in their electron streams. Stable coordination between the alternations and the clustering effect occurs, the result being a steady pulsations of very powerful fixed SHF output.

Farnsworth "Multipactor" tubes were super powerful embodiments of UHF tubes, a rarity even in their time (1937). Invented by Dr. Philo Farnsworth to serve the transmission needs of his original and first television system, Multipactor Tube operation, depended on the photoelectric effect. All the more curious because they were electrical oscillators, the cold cathode tubes relied on the cascade release of photoelectrons produced by bombardment. Two large surface concave electrodes, coated with radioactive combinations of caesium, thorium, or even radium, produced incredible amounts of UHF power per unit volume tube space. Indeed, these devices steadily increased their efficiencies with continued use, becoming problematic to radio engineers who could never account for their virtually lossless conversion efficiencies. Multipactors used magnetic fields to restrained photoelectrons within the action space, one through which photoelectrons grew in density, while drifting through several successive cylindrical geometries. Strong UHF and SHF oscillations naturally began appearing when the external leads of these cylinders were connected with various lumped resonance circuits.

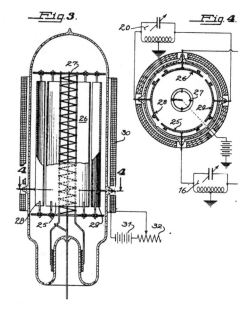

*Multipactor Oscillator and Amplifier*

## MAGNETRON RADAR

These yet unusual and highly efficient electron tubes could easily have been adapted to the production of SHF radio beacons, but remained unnoticed and unrecognized. The least likely tube for British consideration was the lowly "Magnetron" tubes, simple constructions which utilized axially applied magnetic fields in conjunction with a cylindrical anode (Hull, Hennelly 1921). The use of magnetic fields was predicated on an observation made when developing discharge switching tubes early in the century. It had been observed that magnetic fields frustrated and actually inhibited the approach of electrons to target anodes. By using a tangentially applied magnetic field, it was possible to actually "load" the space between cathode and anode with ever concentrated thermionic electrons. Electrons experienced side-thrusting because of the strong magnetic field applied along the tube axis. A simple adjustment in the voltage bias between cathode and anode balanced the forces on electrons in their space. Electrons then orbited the cylindrical anode but could be made never to reach the anode. The combinations of magnetic side thrust and the forward kinetic energy of electrons could produce such a high density "space charge" that the tubes began acting as capacitors.

In their initial embodiments, these tubes were useful as switching devices. They also found use as amplifiers for a variety of radio applications. Alexanderson of General Electric purloined the design for use in shortwave applications. Magnetron tubes were yet little more than curiosities, a means for providing high current alternations at shortwave broadcasting frequencies. With the experimental innovation of a split anode cylinder, new and wonderful phenomena were observed. Split along its axis, the normally solid cylindrical anode became the unexpected site where powerful SHF alternations were suddenly being generated. When pulsed with a powerful and sudden voltage application, their SHF output was significant. Furthermore such tubes proved stable over continued periods of time. The Magnetron Tube, once a mere curiosity of electrical science, suddenly revealed itself as the probable solution to the RADAR problem. Sidestepping the Farnsworth Multipactor, the Magnetron suddenly became the prime device on which British engineers focussed all of their attentions. Magnetron development was taken into the halls of Birmingham University, a top secret project headed by Robert Watson-Watt.

Arranging several magnetrons in tandem proved impractical and difficult. The resultant output of these combinations was greatly enhanced by the apparent coordination of alternations set up in each single tube. This was especially evident when connective circuits were properly adjusted. The concept of joining all of the tube elements in a single vacuum envelope became a developmental path which eventually led to the great success of the RADAR project, a "multicavity" magnetron being secretly developed. A honeycomb geometry, where six adjacent cores were drilled through a thick copper disc, formed the "multicavity" space. Directly through the center of this honeycomb was drilled a central chamber, the location of an axial cathode. The entire disc was sealed, highly evacuated, and placed between the poles of a powerful permanent "horn" magnet. The cathode, curiously coated with thorium and caesium, formed the axis from which powerful pulses of thermal electrons were projected toward the inner cavity walls. Constrained by this magnetic field, space charge gathered between cathode and anode with the very first application of power. These "space charge" electrons became a veritable electron cloud, rotating around its emitter cathode.

As this rotating space charge passed each face plate of the separate semicylindrical cavities, powerful clustering action occurred. This immediately set up coordinated resonations throughout the copper disc housing. Reacting back on the dense space charge, electrons began automatically clustering and cooperating with the cavity-induced oscillations. This effectively caused electron clustres to move with a specific orbit velocity around the central cathode, the "cyclotron" frequency. Cyclotron frequency and cavity oscillation were coordinated by external calibration, and SHF currents were drawn out of the device through a single wire probe. Energies of these frequencies required conductive hollow piping rather than wire lines. Waveguiding used copper piping of rectangular cross-section. Multicavity Magnetrons were powered by special highpower pulsing circuits, combinations of capacitance and inductance capable of sustaining several thousand volts of significant amperages. When so operated, SHF energy effects were deadly.

This energy, pulsed through concentrating reflectors produced megawatt SHF beacons. Such beacons produced such prodigious echoes from even the smallest metallic object, that receiving circuits could mark the relative distance of any such object with greatest accuracy. First RADAR installations used Doppler effects to compare each initial transmission pulse with subsequent echoes. The difference between these two positions on a luminous display scope could accurately range small objects though yet miles away. First tests with these revolutionary High Pulse Magnetron Systems were indeed impressive. The top secret RADAR project received the strongest encouragement and recommendation from no other than Sir Winston Churchill himself. His comment that "I have just witnessed the weapon which will win the War" stimulated the necessary inspiration which drove the small group of engineers toward the unstoppable conclusion of total success.

After that approval monies and manpower appeared, and RADAR became a matter of factory line production. The RDF (Radio Direction Finding) systems were deployed everywhere along the coastlands by 1940. Regardless of time and weather, British RAF and Naval forces were on first alert. Nazi Luftwaffe and U-Boats personnel were continually shocked to discover that, despite their stealth and strategic maneuvers, their British antagonists were perpetually prepared well in advance. In the war to end Hitler and Nazism, RADAR won the war. As far as Allied military was concerned, RADAR was now the wave tool of choice.

As improved Magnetron Tubes made their appearance, RADAR became a powerful standard tool for Allied aerial and maritime forces alike. Magnetron systems became compact miniatures, and highly portable. Attack planes all carried their RADAR packages. Military flights and seagoing missions could now take place at night with absolute safety, a surprising precision in shellfire being the principal repellant for enemy forces on all fronts of the War. As with every aspect of the developing radio technology, RADAR had now become permanent military hardware. Surprise attacks could never occur as long as RADAR was sweeping the air and sea. The infamous Pearl Harbor was actually the result of distrust or permission. The RADAR operator, whose screen literally ignited with the glowing evidence of an unprecedented incoming air assault, was repeatedly stalled while reporting his observation. Informed that his gear was probably out of order, he was ordered to recalibrate each component, until it was too late. Such questionable incidents find their solution in simple geopolitical models and answers. It is rather obvious that oligarchic forces in North America, the NAO (North American Oligarchy), wished the acquisition of resource and territory in the South Pacific; a condition which, contrary to much public opinion today, has actually been achieved. The highly industrialized and over esteemed island empire is nothing more than an offshore manufacturing facility for nationally based financiers.

## RADAR EMP

Radio engineers had long known that strong and distant electrical discharges could burn out any resonantly tuned receiver. This rare occurrence was early noted when the harmonic content of certain lightning bursts were coincidentally received by shortwave systems. A station did not have to be "struck by lightning" in order to obtain the very same burn out effects! Even commercial power stations and their substations were often rendered useless when distant lightning stimulated certain impulse absorptions, explosively blasting components to pieces as if from an unknown source. Feeding enough electromotive force into any harmonically receptive system would suffice in destroying that system. Shortwave communications could be very easily "jammed" by loading the local continuum with static. It is curious again that these static techniques, Tesla techniques, used the explosive non-alternating impulses produced by powerful spark systems.

These systems, connected to the ground or to large overheard capacitances, absolutely overloaded all enemy transmission whenever desired. These jamming systems used both DC pulsed trains, as well as HF alternations. Sparks contained an enormous volume of harmonics. They were thus infinitely more capable of jamming every communications channel which surrounded their fundamental frequency. Jamming devices were designed to provide as broad band of disturbing static as possible. During the instances when these methods were used, Allied Forces employed the optical infrared or ultraviolet photophonic methods of Zinckler, Hartmann, Stevens, Larigaldie, Case, and Coblentz. In equally safe-security communications links, military often employed subterranean communications methods; radiosignalling methods which use conduction effects in the ground or water. In this avenue of research, VLF and ELF systems were eventually developed, supposed unreachable and unjammable radiowave channels.

In none of the developments associated with RADAR science had engineers realized those achievement of Dr. Nikola Tesla, whose pulsed Radiant Energy streams were neither electromagnetic waves, particles, nor commonly understood rays. In only one instance of the RADAR system development did engineers glimpse the truth of which Tesla spoke. The development of pulse systems required the production of abrupt, explosive electrical reports of short duration. Toward this goal, engineers instinctively ran to the old wireless literature and scoured the patents for a simple means to effect the needed pulsations. The decision to produce a pulse system required special new components, upgraded versions of those much older sparkgap systems so prevalent in the early days of wireless. Charged by a DC high voltage source, the energy stored in specially made oil-filled capacitors was discharged in a variety of ways.

How curious that the demanded requirements of RADAR were compelled to follow the lead already completed and advanced by Tesla. This path of redevelopment was one of necessity, Tesla having obeyed natural laws in his first electroimpulse investigations. In each component, the methods of Tesla had been closely, and inadvertently followed. The oil-filled capacitors were one of his early patents in impulse technology. In one system, engineers used the rotating sparkgap method to obtain a rapid series of brief high power pulses. These motor-rotated discharges, applied directly to the magnetron, proved unsuitable. The sharpness, or abruptness of motor-driven discharges produced "blurry" currents; slow on the leading crest, and slower on the trailing crest. Seeking for a means to produce sharp and definitive impulses, the British engineers decided to redevelop certain of the fixed-gap shock excitation methods which were so prevalent throughout the early Century. They knew that there was an essential mystery to the high power developed in these early methods.

One favored experimental arrangement utilized an enclosed gap method, once described by Tesla. When atmospheric "quenching gaps" proved too noisy and unstable, they attempted sealing the sparkgap into specially made discharge tubes. Sealed glass discharge tubes were filled with pure hydrogen gas at low atmosphere pressure. Igniter electrodes were sealed into both tube ends. These, coated with a mixture of radioactive materials, fired only when critical thresholds were reached. These Thyratron Tubes, highly radioactive, could be clamped in series to form several highly resistant barriers. Across this long and highly resistant gap, capacitor charge could reach extremely high values until discharge. When they fired, the discharges were sharp and explosive.

These effects reminded the older engineers of rumours concerning unexplained munitions explosions near old wireless transmitters. In particular, there were several instances where these effects could be repeated, indeed implemented as weaponry. The strange UHF hybrid of Dr. Turpain, a French scientist, accidentally triggered munitions explosions in a nearby weapons cache. The vacuum tube spark relays of Daniel MacFarland-Moore were said to produce munitions explosions at great distances. This vacuum relay tube, patented in 1898, was reinvestigated with every succeeding war. The power released through sharp electroimpulse, the methods of Tesla, exceeded every radiowave method conceived as weaponry.

With each step in the development of rapid pulse, highpower RADAR, engineers realized their own proximity with the very effects which Tesla had so advocated as the only worthy electrical manifestation worth exploring. As these pulse methods were reaching their state of refinement, engineers found it possible to produce single DC impulses of extraordinary power. Components often ruptured when these explosive electrical applications were employed. Wires exploded. Gaskets and sealed electrodes ruptured. Magnetron tubes, high vacuum vessels, literally exploded. Here was that phenomenon of which Tesla spoke so highly. Here was the force which he so greatly esteemed. These explosive effects were the bizarre results of microsecond power pulses applied to magnetron tubes. The output of these tubes was therefore a train of successive RADAR wave alternations, nearly a thousand alternations per train. If it were possible to concentrate all this applied energy to a single, non-alternating RADAR burst, one would nearly approximate some of the effects of which Tesla later spoke. Attempts made to stimulate single pulse RADAR bursts require switching systems capable of firing prodigious power in equivalent to RADAR half-wave periods, a formidable task.

But there was now no time to stop and study these remarkable effects. The War had its demands. And so the dream, the imagination, the wonder, all were put aside as production went on. The few who took notice, and vowed to pursue the phenomenon which they had observed, very unfortunately became the leaders of a new field of weapons research. Tesla, who was first to advance the discovery of electroimpulse effects, was only devoted to the development of humanly elevating and beneficial applications. Tesla spoke of weaponry only with the emergence of each new war. The several conflicts which provoked his passive discussion of these matters through the Twentieth Century were forever mocked by the press, rejected by the academes, and studied by the military. There were those who observed his use of such beam instruments, notably those assistants who witnessed these powerful beamray tests in Colorado and in Wardenclyffe.

The sizable nuclear weapons bibliography which had been amassed, provided enough data for planners to recognize the new research avenues required by their laboratories. In order to "keep ahead of the competition", in both Allied forces and hostile nations, military gradually recognized that a multiple approach to modern warfare was now necessary. The nuclear hubris burned itself away, but left a yet needy oligarchy securing favors from the military. These favors requested the development of nonnuclear means of warfare. Military found new opportunity now. RADAR EMP phenomena might provide such means, and could be privatized, developed, and deployed without the jurisdiction of overseers and other taskmasters. An army equipped with RADAR EMP systems could move forward into enemy camps through the haze of destroyed communications equipment and, in the extreme use of the art, over the felled bodies of infantrymen burned by the encounter.

In the existing state of nuclear art, all military activities had been turned over to air squadrons. They were the messengers who would carry the nuclear arsenals into "enemy House" territories. But an EMP assault would return the art of battle to a more controllable and conventional status, a condition now highly desired by ground oriented branches of the military. There were permissions and finances now flowing like wine over every military project. There could be no failure, no impossibilities, no resistance. Former years had not been as kind to the military. Budget allocations were meagre. Military authorities were supposed to plan and provide for the common defense in order to promote the general welfare. These post-War years were different, predicated on nuclear themes of fear and greatest concern for world security. Research on developing both weapons potentials and defense systems could proceed along simultaneous and parallel fronts. A great number of projects could now be developed. The world had grown complex, and military was supplying the most immediate kinds of security now. Moreover the oligarchy was supplying the funds.

With the development of very large Multi-Gigawatt Magnetron Systems, devices some six feet in diameter, new power thresholds were available for a variety of possible uses. With the new high-pulse RADAR systems came new methods which exceeded every shortwave jamming technique, but not because they produced disturbing static. Powerful pulsed RADAR beams could literally burn receiving circuitry into a useless hash. In some cases, and depending on the brevity of the applied power, high-pulse RADAR was actually able to burst radio receivers. Highly directed high-pulse RADAR energy were also found able to explode electronic systems at great distance. Reaching into enemy strongholds with all the stealth of an invisible plague, sudden highpower RADAR pulses could effectively destroy all communications equipment in a single burst. This was but one of the instances in which military personnel had observed "Electric Burst", "Electro Magnetic Pulse", or "EMP" effects. Tesla, whose work was completely based on this electroshock phenomenon, forever mentioned the EMP effect. He cited it as the main source of a new and unrecognized natural force. Having developed means for generating, controlling, and directing the effect, Tesla utilized radiations from the EMP to drive all of his apparatus. Electric impulse was the essential feature of all Tesla devices.

RADAR technology once again became the subject of intense research, the impetus to advance the art finding ample cause in the now ongoing Cold War. Laboratory consultants were acquired from a great number of universities and industries, as military assumed a new managerial poise. High power pulsed designs were methodically produced by various laboratories who worked under military auspices. Designing powerfully efficient pulse systems required the expertise of those who studied the Tesla patents. These new systems were capacitor dischargers utilizing equally special cold cathode sparkgaps, and produced extremely powerful non-alternating discharges. In its more benign applications, RADAR provided the possibility of multichannelled military communications links across the world. But other potentials had then occurred to engineers who perceived that the power delivered through the RADAR beams were not responsible for most of the effects. With more "geophysical" perspectives, it was gradually understood that RADAR generated conditions became the site where terrestrial energies were focussing, a RADAR pulse, if sufficiently potent to ionize an aerial path, would focus enough dielectric energy to constitute an ultimately powerful EMP ray.

In repeated tests, highly shielded radio equipment was completely burned by these sudden RADAR pulses. No amount of shielding could stop these explosive blasts. During wartime, such "electromotive shrapnel" could insure victory. Totally dependent on electronic communications, no enemy could withstand a multiple headed EMP assault. Those who wielded communications disruption techniques would win any future war. Indeed, those air squadrons which first move into battle theatres are the very ones equipped to jam and burn out enemy electronics systems. Fitted with large aerodynamic pods under their wings, the combined highpower RADAR pulses which they project are sufficiently powerful as to permanently destroy all radiowave communications systems.

## IONOSCATTER

The Second World War had gained for the radio sciences a prodigious volume of information. The rapid deployment of virtually every kind of radio system during the War provided a test field of incredible and prolific extent, one whose resulting acquisition of data required extensive study. Phenomena in which radiowaves behaved strangely in varieties of circumstances, whether man-made or natural, formed the resource from which surprising new radio systems were subsequently devised. Just before the advent of very large RADAR installations across the polar reaches of North America, military briefly employed tremendous arrays which were made to support the requirements of VHF and UHF transmitters.

The use of higher frequencies taught the existence of several natural reflective layers in the atmosphere. The older HF relays were plagued with all kinds of inconsistencies and interference phenomena, but the implementation of higher frequencies in VHF bands gave greater reach and better signal clarity. It was known that VHF signals could be literally guided along the upper boundary layer of the tropopause, using water vapor for the scattering layer. UHF beacons reached into the ionosphere, providing greatly increased efficiencies of the same. From the end of the Second World War, and well into the several decades of Cold War, the United States established a great number of "ionospheric backscatter" systems. These, placed all along specific defensive lines, incorporated sufficient VHF and UHF power to beam very long range communications signals through equally enormous distances.

Very high carrier frequencies were used to reach across the long distances represented by the required line of defense. The Air Force directed the construction of a huge combination VHF-UHF Ionospheric "backscatter" telemetry system across the Pacific just after World War II. The Pacific Scatter System, consisted of eight radio relay links, connecting Hawaii, Midway, Wake, Ponape, Guam, Palau, the Phillipines, and Okinawa. This system was built to operate at 800 Megacycles. This operating frequency nearly matched those first experimental longwave RADAR frequencies of early World War II. Made specifically to implement the ionospheric scatter technique, the system was virtually as large as an early Marconi aerial array. The scatter technique itself required the employment of very powerful beacon energies, usually provided by large Klystron beam tubes. The Pacific Backscatter System used several VHF and UHF sources amounting to some 40 Kilowatt.

In the method employed, two separate antenna bays were rigidly fixed to a vast YAGI structure. The fixed geometry directed either VHF or UHF beacon energies at a fixed specified angle from zenith. UHF permitted greater access to atmospheric and high atmospheric ionization layers. Power was directed into either the tropopause (VHF array) or the ionosphere (UHF array), where signal beams were literally bent, in some cases literally "guided" along portions of the layers, and then reflected down at a specific "scatter angle". At the general skip distance which had been prearranged, another station could receive the incoming communications, amplify and clean the signal, and then rebeam the messages to the next skip station. Engineers estimated the efficiencies of these stations, relying entirely upon weather and ionospheric conditions for the performance of this relay system. Signals initiated at one end of the relay were automatically dispatched across the system with little delay. These were the days before communications satellites, when ground relays were the only way for sending messages across great distances.

Scattered from such high altitude regions, an incredible signal reach was achieved with UHF. Relay transmitters such as these were all necessarily large structures, requiring equally large support facilities for their operation and maintenance. Riggers were constantly braving the winds to climb onto these multiwired structures and effect repairs. In each of these large and bombastic systems, the ineffective methods of Marconi were fully realized. The vast and inefficient power requirements of these monstrosities, coupled with the unwieldy size of the UHF arrays, evidenced yet more reason that Tesla had been absolutely correct in his predictions concerning wave radio and its final consequences as a tool for serving humanity. Despite his many simple and well-experienced admonitions. Military insisted on using the lossy wave energies, spending billions to defy the natural odds and, if it were possible, force nature

to work by their demands.

The Pacific Scatter System joined stations along a 7400 mile route. Itself barely practical for use in the Pacific, such extensive stations would be completely unfeasible in the Arctic; where a new defense line was necessitated against Stalinist Russia. But experiments with UHF scatter techniques were brief, the military preference moving directly into RADAR applications. After the Second World War the development of better and more powerful RADAR technology became a singular priority. Now applications technology was being harnessed to serve the military, and power refocused away from the general populace. As military took power from the oligarchy, it selectively privatized technology. In doing this, military removed power from the society from whom the technology came, and for whom the technology was originally planned. Knowledge, tools, access, and systems consolidated military power. Society waited for the "spin-offs", a polite term for "the crumbs". But defense was the alert requirement of the day, and military took the lead. This eventually would lead to conditions in the society which did not look upon military with favor, rather looking upon it with clear vision and recognizing an extension of the rulership, now in uniform.

On one research front, the establishment of a RADAR alert system, a veritable line of RADAR beacons, was first on the list. Because of the hardened dictatorial poise of Stalin and his predecessors, American military fully anticipated missile assaults across the polar route from the Soviet heartland. Every possible means of reconnaissance was investigated toward these objectives. This would ultimately lead to the development of novel aeronautic and space technologies. Forming the prime national defensive technology, and stretching across the North American continent in Arctic latitudes, RADAR was the best existing means for early missile warning. SHF waves were reflected from deep portions of ionospheric layers normally not accessed with ordinary shortwave or VHF systems. They therefore provide defense corps with multiple communications and early-warning surveillance capabilities.

The systems required to scan the skies for aerial nuclear assaults were quickly assembled, being large versions of Second World War RADAR technologies. Upgraded by a vast electronics consortium, installations were amassed all along the north polar borders of North America. Anticipating and alerting aerial attacks of various kinds from the Soviet Union was the arduous responsibility of a new military corps. These necessities provoked an enormous assortment of theories and systems hardware in both weaponry and communications technologies. Several such technological avenues of note are represented by various systems used in RADAR surveillance, ionospheric jamming technology, super pulse RADAR weaponry, VLF and ELF communications, EMP weaponry, special radiation bombs, hybrid nuclear beam weaponry, space reconnaissance, space communications, radiation communication links, stimulated radiation beam weaponry, and a host of yet undisclosed hardware developed for military functions.

## IONOSPHERIC EMP

Those who studied both Nuclear EMP and RADAR EMP recognized the inherent differences between the two techniques. In nuclear stimulated EMP, the power was enormous, and highly concentrated. But nuclear weapons were the very thing which researchers were attempting to eradicate, devices not permissible for use. The central causative agency in both was plasma formation. Plasma represented a conductive agency which had superior characteristics, almost superconductive attributes. Terrestrial dielectricity seemed to accrete into volumes of highly concentrated plasma with greater affinity than it did for metals. Nuclear EMP had the power and brevity of energy release to produce that kind of dense plasma fireball to stimulate terrestrial dielectric focussing. The earth dielectric field, vertically disposed, from ground to space, was pulled into the nuclear fireball with incredible fury. Part of the blackening of a nuclear blast area was a direct result of this dielectric focussing effect. Some believed this effect to be a film artifact, the result of burning.

The RADAR induced EMP method had inherent limitations, limitations imposed by the natural behavior of RADAR beams in atmospheric immersion. The air did not normally absorb RADAR energies enough to produce this kind of high density plasma near the ground. In order for this condition to be established, RADAR energies had to be focussed and potent. RADAR installations of this kind were large and not portable. They would have limited effectiveness in direct conflict. Ground battle would be out of the question. So a ground directed EMP effect, while possible, would not be available in battle theatres unless mounted on large seagoing vessels. But another though occurred to the designers. Were it possible to direct a RADAR beam of sufficient power to a point in the sky, producing a plasma volume in a lower atmospheric pressure, then it might be possible to direct either EMP effects or blackout effects from a fixed station. The concept of producing high altitude plasma bursts derived from several factors. First, lower air pressure meant faster plasma formation under focussed RADAR energy. Second, higher aerial placement of the plasma would permit RADAR direction of the effect, far from the transmit site. Were this method perfected, one would literally have a directable EMP source.

Researchers considered the atmospheric layers available for this kind of treatment, selecting first the D-Layer which is just above the Stratosphere. Some experimenters, largely geophysicists working under government sponsorship, believed they could create special precursory EMP conditions at these lower-than-ionospheric levels with pulsed RADAR beams alone. Once it could be demonstrated that a higher than normal RADAR reflective layer could be produced in th D-Layer, these systems would be given a far greater "reach". Angular direction of the RADAR beam would send the focussed plasma over any coastal or border threat. The high altitude aerial plasma would follow the beam focus, dragging the EMP effect along any determined route.

The problem of producing such a powerful pulse was solved by the design and construction of very large Multigigawatt Magnetrons and new power pulse thyratrons. Closely modelled after Poulsen Arc switches, and forming the heart of many superhigh power RADAR systems, Gammatrons and other such high power thyratron tubes flood the literature. Having greater effectiveness and further effective range, these highpower rapid pulse RADAR beams were given a greater than line-of-sight reach to a potential target zone. The concept of producing active ionizing paths in the atmosphere had become more than a working hypothesis. The conditions had been achieved early in the Century by several individuals. In each of these early demonstrations, methods perfected before 195, a conductive path was produced in the air by intensely collimated beams of hard ultraviolet light. Producing a preliminary ionized path in the atmosphere, enormous bursts of high voltage current were then applied directly into this conductive path. Only capable of projecting several hundred feet from the power source, these systems scarcely delivered sufficient penetrating energy to achieve their claimed objectives: the destruction of airplane engines, explosion of aerial bombs, and the shearing open of airships. These effects were subject to atmospheric variables and other hazardous problems associated with deadly arc effects.

H. Grindell-Matthews (1917) used combination of intense UV and X-ray beams to establish a conductive aerial path, a weakly ionized path in the air. His device interfered with airplane engines, causing furtive piston misfire, and munitions eruptions. J. Hettinger used the intense UV from tightly focussed carbon arcs to produce a transmission system for borough wide power distribution. Hettinger also utilized these conductive UV beacons and high voltage pulsations to create nonmaterial aerials of great vertical extent. Made of ionized air, he synthetically produced "ionized atmospheric aerials". The total length of the conductive channel permitted signalling capabilities, intensified and stabilized by focussed light and applied electrical alternations. Both individuals patented their designs, although those of Grindell-Matthews remain curiously classified until today.

Later, university researchers succeeded in producing small snapping plasma "points" in across-the-room laboratory demonstrations; the application of focussed RADAR pulses being coupled with focussed ultraviolet light beams. Though achieved with difficulty, the demonstration proved feasible the central notion. An artificially aerial plasma discharge would resist the RADAR source beacon enough to absorb energy from it. Once substantially absorptive, the plasma would focus dielectric lines. Ultraviolet light was available in great quantities in high altitudes. This energetic presence would add to the plasma formative process. The concept that EMP productive RADAR could be reflected from the sky to a distant point began to gather much support. The RADAR application of troposcatter and ionoscatter techniques seemed a simple conclusion. EMP effects would literally be drawn over intended target areas, wreaking havoc with both electrical and electronic systems. These would necessarily be target zones limited by the line-of sight. Though limited in this parameter, these systems could serve in guarding borders and coastlands. Clearly, the reach of any RADAR beam system becomes its chief advantage in such an application. Any means found to effectively increase this range, beyond the line-of-sight limits, would effectively release the system to work its application beyond the "horizon limit". Recalling the fact that Projects ARGUS and STARFISH demonstrated just this very phenomenon, liberated research from its limited consideration, to a major military focus of interest. Ionospheric EMP would require a detailed knowledge of both  geoelectric and geomagnetic field natures. It was the combine fields which seemed to glide EMP effects in ARGUS along geomagnetic lines, throughout given world sectors. One could strike terror into distant enemy forces from a local ground station.

Rapidly pulsed RADAR beams of sufficient strength could be aimed into a specific ionospheric layer, producing an instantaneous plasma burst which would glide of its own accord along the geomagnetic sector. This would not secure pinpoint accuracy, but would effect EMP all along any given sector. Terrestrial dielectricity would provide the power. One could theoretically "guide and glide" disruptive EMP energies toward any ground point from a high density plasma layer. The efficiency of each RADAR burst would be determined by charge density and stability. Using the thrust of the natural geomagnetic field, one could theoretically extend the "reach" of EMP effects over the literal horizon. With this capability, the controlled, nonnuclear EMP method might find its liberation from the normally fixed sweep perimeter. The development of super powerful RADAR systems commenced. With such powerful beams, pointed directly into the zenith, highly localized ionization states should be produced. RADAR engineers were now directed to develop a means for beaming RADAR energy bursts of very great intensity directly into the ionosphere.

The possibilities of "zone limited" battles greatly appealed to military hierarchy. This regime of research attracted a tremendous military response, the obvious employment of the method would represent controllable EMP and communications blackout techniques. Controlled EMP conditions could be assigned to any quadrant or sector of the geomagnetic field. Placed near the poles, and with properly directed RADAR beams, one could sweep across the polar sky, the controlled EMP effects being assigned on a worldwide basis if needed. One could literally spray the ionosphere with RADAR energy, predetermining the length of time for the EMP. Small additional impulses could prolong the effects for as long a time as desired. Control was therefore acquired over potential EMP and communications blackout effects.

## CLOUDS

Precise ionosphere-destabilizing methods, by which the simple flick of a switch could effectively disrupt radio communications with great accuracy, demanded testing. Experimental tests to determine the relative worth of these schemes commenced in 1963. Controlled from ground-based stations, beam projectors attempted the modulation of ionospheric states through the application of momentary and sustained blasts of RADAR energy. These initial tests were performed at various launch angles, producing EMP phenomena beneath the aerial plasma focus. The more prominent effects were the radio blackouts. Energies of specific frequency were found especially effective in targeting specific ionospheric layers. The EMP effect were made to spread along the geomagnetic meridians north and south along the field, but needed great power to do so. Beamed electrical inductions wee best applied to the ionosphere when aligned with the geomagnetic field. In this manner the superhigh frequency alternations, beamed from the ground base, would form successive "clustres" in the plasma. These progressive pulsation propagated as a communications disturbance which flowed effortlessly along the geomagnetic lines. Control of the projected beam aperture could effect a weak degree of precision in the subsequent meridian path and width of the EMP. The natural sidethrusts, the result of gradually divergent geomagnetic field lines, tended to "smear" the effect out into an ever widening arc. Unless the applied power was excessive therefore, only a blackout effect would be launched.

First experiments with RADAR EMP revealed that plasma density and concentration were necessary for the production of strong EMP effects. Who could have supposed that it would be possible to simulate what Nature was forever doing to shortwave transmissions? Those who were familiar with the problems of such wave radio systems and the devious distortions played on them by ionospheric winds, were called into the study program. The use of existing RADAR power alone proved incapable of effecting the highly deranged, high density conditions required before EMP effects made their appearance. But now, how to synthetically create such ionization states? In attempts to assist the process, several different schemes were tested. These tests were very much in the public eye, being the subject of intense popular attentions and discussions. PROJECT WESTFORD (1962) employed a payload of some 350,000 short copper wires. Once in orbit, the payload was designed to burst and spill out the wire cargo. Distributed in orbit, the wires were to form a metallic veil. This veil could be used as a resonant target for ground based pulsed RADAR beams. The idea was to limit the required amount of beam wattage and increase the attainable ionization states. Loudly proclaimed by Network Media as a means for establishing television communications across the ocean. In order to justify and rationalize this ridiculous cover story, military personnel had MIT bounce a television signal off the layer. The horribly distorted images appeared in every major newspaper the very next day. This supposed precursor to orbital communications satellites was nothing of the kind. In fact, the test was a dismal and much derided failure. The wires clumped together and never dispersed as intended. PROJECT WESTFORD did establish a precedent along a specific trend of thought which the military did not abandon.

A new regime of methods was developed to produce high plasma conductivity and density before application of the RADAR pulse. Aerobee rockets with chemical payloads were launched into the ionosphere. The concentrated solutions were exploded at specific aerial sites, where they dispersed. School children were directed by Media to watch the night skies for the pretty glowing color blooms. These colorful clouds of barium, strontium, lithium, and caesium salts behaved as absorptive RADAR focal points. Such chemical clouds proved stable, the dynamic ionosphere rapidly dispersing the initial cloud concentrations along the assigned geomagnetic route in a steady stream. Despite these cloud-assisted effects, the more prominent phenomena concentrated themselves as communications blackouts.

Thus, the success of the super highpower RADAR wave tests remained in demonstrating that a potent and long lasting communications "blackout" period could be arranged when needed. In this deft exercise of electronic warfare, one could at least waste an enemy's reliance on the natural continuum for communications. And here is precisely where the excessive research attentions refocused. Every available geophysicist and RADAR engineer was called in to develop this new breed of jamming technology. And in this new awareness came a sudden liberation in thought process, one which began to show a bit more promise in the quest to create a new and nonnuclear weaponry. It was here that military vision began to appreciate the possibility that an entirely new regime of electronic weapons might be the key to their quest. The military directed its efforts to this singular tactical advantage, perfecting the skill. Though

RADAR induced EMP did not produce the degree and intensity of effects achieved through NUCLEAR EMP, it nonetheless demonstrated a theoretical departure from the cage into which geopolitical power had maneuvered itself.

## FIXATIONS

But the new and radical thought departure, while enlightening and motivating the engineering and military mindset in every way, was not a complete liberation from the real crux of their problem. The radiowave systems which Marconi developed, and passed onto the world at large, produced a legacy of such disappointments and frustrations. Convinced that only higher frequency alternations could actually "radiate" into space, engineers were continually finding themselves unable to "decipher" the Tesla puzzle. But the potent and penetrating Radiant Energy beams of Tesla were derived from a natural force which could never be suspected; a fact which characterizes the very greatest and most fundamentally revolutionary discoveries. Inherently inferior in comparison to the Radiant Energy systems of Tesla, the science of Maxwell, Hertz, and Marconi influenced academic thought and engineering research along a constrained horizon. It was this binding influence, this constraint on the once free and imaginative process of Victorian scientific inquiry, which has been lost as a direct result. Incapable of recognizing or even postulating the existence of another energy continuum besides those enunciated by the Marconi-compromised convention, not one major finding managed to break away from the little, tightly fixated orbit of wave radio. The waves, however short, however potent, remained waves. Inferior technology.

It was said by those who witnessed his demonstrations that Tesla beamray systems were able to project their sometimes visible white streams directly through the ionosphere without resistance. How did he achieve this condition? RADAR wave energies were only superhigh frequency alternations. They succeed only in agitating the ionospheric plasma. But Tesla was operating in another realm altogether, one which plumbed the æther and not the upper ionized atmosphere. Ultimately, the requirements for achieving RADAR EMP required excessive power volumes, those which were well beyond the capabilities of even the most potent MultiGigawatt Magnetron RADAR wave systems available. The problem was one so fundamental that highly trained engineers, ever so schooled in the conventional paradigms of Maxwell, found themselves trapped in a maze of constraints.

# CHAPTER 6
# Military VLF and ELF Technology

### INTERFERENCE

The development of Ionospheric EMP techniques, and the threat of nuclear assault from hostile Houses yet very much a possibility, Military leadership imposed a first class research priority toward developing the "unjammable" communications system. The use of EMP as a tactical "first-strike" represented new weaponry requiring the development of new secure-communications systems. Geophysicists and radio communications engineers knew that sufficiently empowered EMP weaponry would be ruinous for a wide range of communications channels. Completely dependent upon the ionospheric media, certain channels would be totally eradicated, a condition which could be prolonged indefinitely. Military deep-space test shots in Project ARGUS and STARFISH proved that a succession of small, well-placed nuclear blasts could maintain his curtain of silence for months. RADAR EMP could also maintain these states without the implementation of nuclear shots. Since the common feature in all of these disturbances was the Ionosphere itself, the key to the development of an unjammable radiowave system would be one whose dependence on ionospheric states was minimal. An "invincible" radio communications system.

VLF wave stations, exact duplicates of Marconi VLF systems, had progressed in their improvements through some 40 years of military engineering. Redesigned primarily by the Naval Research Laboratory to serve the very diverse needs of submerged and seagoing fleets, these systems grew into the highly efficient radiowave mammoths known today. Close examination of these stations reveals the severity of military entrapment in the Marconi wave radio paradigm, a reliance on alternating radio currents which effectively limited both the operational effectiveness of these technologies and the mindset of military planners. The huge powerplants, the grand radio frequency generators, enormous capacitor-inductor rooms, the geologically coupled aerials, and the extensive ground planes; all these found their origin with Guglielmo Marconi, father of inefficient wave radio.

When one considers the sheer size and extreme power requirements for the successful operation of systems such as these, one can well appreciate the absolute disgust with which Tesla viewed their ambitious, though futile construction. Having already estimated the effective rage and limits of wave radio technologies on every frequency band, Tesla continually commented on the available Radiant Energy spectra which he alone seemed able to engage. The history of VLF does not begin with LORAN VLF or ELF projects such as SANGUINE. It begins with Marconi and those who were attracted and enthralled with his modest and thoroughly plagiarized achievements.

Despite the fact that Marconi stations utilized VLF alternations of excessive power, these stations were incapable of driving their slow telegraphic signals across the sea. Unlike the aerial paths which early UHF type sparkgap beams, those of Hertz, Righi, and Lodge, the VLF wave signal was largely propagated directly through the ground. It was discovered that VLF wave signals would be most powerfully launched across the oceans only when geophysically coupled to "highly conductive" geological formations. More like huge guides or "chutes", as referred to by early British wireless designers, VLF waves were directed across the seas through massive aerial structures built directly into the ground. There were consequences to these applications of VLF radiowave energies directly into the geophysical environment however, consequences which became his worst nightmare. Ultimately, Marconi would abandon the VLF endeavor to his engineers, while he sailed out to sea in search of lost dreams and shortwaves.

In the coupling of his VLF stations to the ground, certain sea-connecting valleys were found to be the very best sites, but not all. Certain "highly conductive" bedrocks and soils were very good sites, but not all. And certain geological features were extremely good sites, but not all. And this inconsistency in discerning the best station sites represented both an essential mystery and impediment to the radio station engineers of the Marconi Company. Familiar with the vagaries of early earth and aqueous conduction radio, many experimenters believed that both subterranean and suboceanic geology were entirely responsible for these effects. But despite both these theoretical views, and their best efforts, no consistency in actual test transmissions could ever be obtained.

The mystery represented by this phenomenon, where certain topographies seemed to best launch VLF waves as opposed to identically composed or oriented others, was by then beyond the deciphering ability of the Marconi Radio engineering community. Able to discern the best VLF station locations, they remained unable to use geological considerations alone in planning VLF wave launch sites. Neither geological strata, nor geosynclines, nor faultlines could be equated with the very best station sites. It was clear that some mysterious "parageological structure" was exercising its powerful and elusive influence on VLF signals. Those who glimpsed the reality of anomalous subterranean superventions were never quite able to discover the consistent geological patterns with which these were associated. This influence was not variable. It maintained its character over time, and thus represented a solid structural reality, a topography whose exact nature could somehow never quite be determined by quantitative measurements alone.

Marconi engineers recognized that VLF signals tunneled into mysterious natural "channels" the structure of which was not apparent to instrumental measurement at all. Launched across the seas, there were specific which seemed capable of transmitting VLF with seemingly incredible magnifications in power; routes where the weakest signal often arrived in Europe with uncommon strength. Yet other routes were found to offer impossibly resistance to the most powerful energetic applications; routes which quenched VLF signals much more rapidly than theory predicted as possible. In the stubborn insistence of some engineers, those who demanded that these effects were entirely due to "inaccessible" geological features alone, we see evidence of the fundamental difference between view quantitative and view qualitative. Geological guidance, those superficial considerations incapable of providing consistent engineering guidance, never provided the accuracy of a much more archane geomantic science upon which early ground conduction experimenters based their successes.

No differences in geological structure, conductivity, or mineral predominance were ever determined in this study. VLF seemed to obey the strict dictates of strata which had no discernible geophysical boundaries. VLF ground pathways depended upon the existence of a deeper than geological structure, one which could be "felt" and "sensed", but never measured. This permeating "biodynamic structure", which could not be measured with inert and unresponsive instruments, absolutely constrained the proper construction of VLF stations; a secret which most VLF engineers did not openly admit. Dubious to some, the experimental achievements of these early investigators proved the biodynamic theory. The observed results of these legendary accounts remain impossible to obtain otherwise. Ground propagation signalling formed the historical heart of experimental radio systems. Ground conduction radio signals were strong only when specific "conduction lanes" were located, the proper location of these ground conduction lanes requiring careful old prospecting methods. Noticing the "energetic flowlines" in a district is yet not considered scientific. Nevertheless, these geomantic methods proved their effectiveness in establishing the very best telegraphic and telephonic routes in the years just preceding the ground radio experiments. Those who early discovered that telegraphic and vocal signals could be transmitted from point to point through the ground were, in most instances, thoroughly familiar with these methods.

Indeed, there were those whose sensitivities alone could discern the invisible "structure", that geology-surpassing structure which remained rigid and invariant with time. These natural sensitives could sense those geographic locations which could never receive radiowave signals of any kind. Such "blind spots" could never be rationalized through the models afforded by electrical science. How curious it is that quantitative science, claiming to be completely objective in its assessments of natural phenomena, relies on human assessments to establish its dogmas. The rules by which quantitative science constrains reliance on human senses are proposed by those who use those senses to make their assertions! In truth, the implementation of biological and organic sensors has exonerated the ultimate sensitive value of the human sensorium above all inertial measuring instruments. Therefore, those who demonstrated excessive sensitivity in discerning the best location for ground conduction and VLF signal stations were to be commended and not rather derided. Implementing these sensitive means, the geomantic art, their subsequent stationing of groundlink relays produced operative results which are yet considered anomalous. In this unique technology the exchange of telephonic signals had been established, in many instances, entirely without the need for external battery power. The ground telephonic exchange systems of Nathan Stubblefield (1872) were known for their extreme power, rich tone, and vocal clarity. His system operated 24 hours a day without need for battery replacement or excessive maintenance.

Experimenters, including Marconi, now began observing and collating these transmission anomalies. While the collations of experimenters were based entirely on the need to know, those of Marconi were based entirely on the need to succeed. Business was his goal. The improper positioning of a VLF wave launch cite would be financially ruinous. Not one such failure could be allowed, therefore his methods required empirical testing. In this empirical testing, those ordinarily experiential discernments were completely endorsed. This is why empirical experimentation far surpasses thought experimentation, producing results which intertwine with yet unknown natural realities, those which surpass theoretical perspectives. From the very moment in which his first VLF mammoth was keyed, Marconi recognized the insidious influences of this strange and parageological subterranean structure; an influence which prevented VLF signalling with certain European stations, while opening strangely powerful links with others.

Marconi found that TransAtlantic communications suffered greatly in transit along strict east-west directions, Further complicating this observation, were those north-south communications paths which produced uncommonly great signal power. This mystery further constrained his selection of VLF station sites. Because of his reliance on wave radio methods, his creation of special world-wide "radio circuits" was thoroughly plagued with natural resistances and impediments. VLF signal paths were obviously and rigorously tied to parageological features, and required his engineers to find those limited sites where the "mystery structure" merged on sea level coastlines. Marconi found these constraints especially frustrating when attempting the construction of his world wide VLF "circuit". Besides these rigorous constraints, imposed on him by mysterious natural principles, the actual construction of his large installations posed a seemingly insurmountable engineering problem. Fitting the giant structures into the superficial geology was an engineering task requiring new techniques, skills, maneuvers, and components. Large aerial supporting pylons, continuing in orderly rows for one mile into the sea, may yet be found offshore on both coasts of North America. Receiving sections were necessarily placed several miles adjacent to the transmitter site, for fear that the delicate apparatus would simply be incinerated by the transmitter output; an early observation of the "jamming" effect. Military signal corps maintained these formats, observing similar geomantic principles for deciding the placement of their VLF wave stations.

## RESPONSES

Because of this exceptional "geophysical access" to the environment, Marconi was able to discover several natural phenomena which influenced both his VLF transmissions and signal receptions. These influences seemed especially powerful during certain times of the day, a feature which Marconi secretized. Signal anomalies commenced almost immediately with the first application of current in each Marconi VLF Station. Transmission intensities were found to vary forty times within a single minute of signalling. Marconi had also long observed the "distortion" of TransAtlantic signals, a phenomenon which shifted the frequency of signals transmitted and received. This was yet another secret which remained "Company business". These were, in his thought agenda, likened to industrial secrets. He did not permit his operators to share these "operating secrets of the art" with the outside. Marconi kept these phenomena secret, sharing them only among his operators, out of fear. The fear was that his wealthy patronage, for whom the wireless financial reports rendered service, would drop his systems in favor of the much older established wired telegraph lines.

At the time, Marconi did not really offer a competitive advantage against those TransAtlantic telegraph cable companies. His construction and maintenance costs were far less lucrative than he would ever admit, a fact which was never mentioned when Tesla was upbraided for the cost of the Wardenclyffe Power Broadcasting Station. Furthermore, for all their size, excessive power requirements, and costs, Marconi VLF stations were useful only in telegraphic communications. They were slow, capable of transmitting a few words at most per minute. Telegraph operators required a very "steady hand" when sending signals through these gigantic systems. The entire aerial system glowed and buzzed with a deadly violet corona with each dot or dash. The entire structure sizzled and actually rang with each signal. Anyone who knew the code could hear whatever was being transmitted merely by listening and watching. Those who wished to "steal" insider financial reports would simply need a good telescope.

VLF wave signals arrived in European stations with greatest difficulty at certain hours of the day. These signals were often totally distorted by unknown cause, the result of wave transmission modes on which Marconi insisted. Stubbornly ignoring he "fundamental obvious", Marconi looked everywhere for answers to these perplexing natural interferences. Tesla had already foreseen these foibles, constantly deriding Marconi in his very technical and pointed public statements. Where publishers would permit him a platform to express these views, Tesla made the best use of his moment. Tesla already knew that Marconi was unable to exchange signals at certain hours of the day. He also peered into the Marconi "secrets" and exposed the probable fact that certain VLF frequencies would most likely give the Marconi Company a most difficult time because of natural static and other prevalent interference. Marconi hated these technical truths, unerringly accurate in their assessments of his best efforts. Indeed though coastland weather on either sides of the Atlantic might be clear, storms prevalent in the intervening seas could introduce "natural noise". Signals, though sent out with greatest available power, would become a crashing incoherence once passing through a midoceanic storm.

VLF signal propagation was completely at the mercy of natural influences which indeed varied in complex ways throughout the year. Weather patterns modified the signals beyond recognition at times, and thunderstorms prohibited signalling for fear of lightning strikes. Lightning, the bane of telegraph operators, often killed men at the keys instantly without warning. The Marconi aerials were so large that dielectric field stresses produced deadly voltages which, if merely brushed against, would kill. Storms were not the only natural static generators which produced interference. There were indeed others which, while introducing so much static that they eradicated the clearest and most critical financial reports, could never be explained by conventional science. Implacable in his attitude, Marconi continued withholding "his big secret". Foreseeing the exposure of this very apparent frailty, Marconi attempted the premature introduction of his "world wide radio circuit".

Reginald Fessenden, the famed Canadian radio investigator, was more the pure experimenter than Marconi. Equipped with independent means, and thoroughly impassioned in his devotion to wireless science, Dr. Fessenden decided to announce his findings on VLF interference. He published a rare report exposing the fact that his TransAtlantic signals often varied with each minute of transmission time! According to Fessenden, these mysterious signal annulments came through misunderstood high atmospheric conductivity effects. Voicing the opinion that an ionospheric layer was responsible for the fluctuations, research commenced at once on the task of determining ionospheric pulsations. Reliance on the reflectivity and conductivity of the ionosphere proved to be the Achilles heel of shortwave radio, even as Tesla had stated years earlier. Regardless of frequency or power, wave radio relied on the vagaries of ionospheric conditions which were beyond the control of the operators, a singular fact that was known by Marconi even in his early shortwave experiments.

Linking the VLF signal variables directly with both the daily or seasonal spatial and solar variables seemed far too unscientific and metaphysical for many academes. Nevertheless, these facts were empirical and consistent. When stating these views, each honest researcher was simply echoing the very words which Nikola Tesla had mentioned throughout the years. His statements, also based on astute empirical observation, were unerring in their accuracy. Tesla also had mentioned more esoteric phenomena which none were yet able or willing to accept. He spoke of cosmic radiations and their causative effects on ionospheric pulsations. Tesla also spoke of these cosmic radiations and their relationship with planetary and lunar influences, not a popular topic for academes to entertain. Nevertheless, the unwanted Fessenden report seemed to spell disaster for the early Marconi Company, an exposure of inherent frailties in VLF wireless; a fact which Marconi wished had never been told. Nevertheless, the report which Dr. Fessenden published provoked commentary by the silent Marconi; who very promptly published his statement, insisting now that he had been "first to observe" these effects. Thereafter, research commenced among the small consortium of VLF wireless experimenters, with the expressed purpose of determining the variables of VLF propagation.

Stockholders were outraged. The proud Marconi maintained his glacier-like effrontery, and declared that a only worldwide circuit of wireless stations would absolutely solve the problem. They believed him. With increasing finances, Marconi was able to begin construction on every world coastland. This included the vast Pacific Basin, a task which seemed unconquerable. Marconi knew that TransAtlantic signals did not easily "flow" along east-west lines, but later found that Transpacific signals exhibited the same weakening effect along north-south lines. There was indeed also evidence that a natural predisposition for the efficacy of certain frequencies would place other ruling restrictions on wave radio, the very fact which Tesla tacitly mentioned.

With increasing experience came increasing observations. The manner in which the natural environment "treated" the VLF wave launches showed an uncanny behavior, a response attribute not normally ascribed to inert forces. Were these natural distortions and interference patterns to be interpreted metaphorically, one might be compelled to declare them as evidencing "geobiological" responses to the electrical irritant. Indeed, Nature seemed to actively "digest" and "catabolize" the signals. Launched signals did not take straight paths. This became obvious in the Pacific, where relay stations often had great difficulty intercepted VLF signals which "should have been" found along a very straight line path. Engineering adjustments in relay aerial directions showed that these signal paths not only curved, but meandered all along the propagation path: natural radiowave alleys. VLF propagation was not found to occur in a "smooth" glide function across geological and oceanic surfaces, the result of simple conductivity variables. Contrary to theoretical papers and analysis in later years (Austin, Appleton), theoretical reductions which seemed "simple and reasonable", the propagation of VLF waveforms engaged suboceanic influences more in the manner of response. In all of these VLF deformations, operators observed evidence of a biodynamic structure having total influence on every irritating VLF application to the environment.

## LIAISONS

Under the demanding dictates of their tutorial head, military radio corpsmen had already absorbed their fill of Marconi, his Technology, and his tyrannical sway. They had in fact, thought themselves adequately schooled in every aspect of his burgeoning art to now divorce themselves from his Company, their original intent, and privatize their own radio systemologies. Now the "M" on the flag of their loyalties would no longer stand for "Marconi", but for "Military". Therefore the divorce was engaged, not without some difficulties from the legal-minded Marconi, but nonetheless successful and complete. This split, no doubt the result of bureaucratic maneuvers at higher levels, was viewed as the first step toward achieving a Military Radio Network

capable of serving the bureaucratic needs of military forces, wherever in the world, and receiving a steady flow of superior directives from the geopolitical House command central. Military personnel desired complete separations between themselves and the Industrial enterprises. They valued and intensified this separation with time, as military radio secrets remained the exclusive property of military engineers. It was thus that military radio projects began their long covert history.

It was because of this secrecy and the privatization process which so characterized the military, that a command directive placed Intelligence Officers everywhere within military bureaucracy. Intelligence reports represented the presence of rulership within the secretive halls of military deliberations for a reason. Thus it was that Intelligence Agencies and Military began their tense relationship, one intended to insure that the commands of rulership would indeed be obeyed and enforced. Ultimately, Intelligence themselves would seek private communications systems which would be completely secretized, divorced from the military from whom they would now learn the secret art.

The years following military departures from Marconi Company were not creative ones. For all their time under the coy Marconi, handpicked cadet trainees were found incapable of developing any original and new themes by which to advance the radio art. This critical time period provoked an uncommon response from leadership, one which we have already mentioned as an unwilling concession to civilian hirelings. But the circumstance and the pressing needs which the world had imposed upon them would now press their unwillingness into a tense dialogue. This dialogue, this deadlock, between experimenters and military leadership, formed the traditional confrontation of powers which has forever defined their sometimes rocky relationship. The experimenters themselves contained and consolidated the creative power. The ability to invent. And the military knew it. The employment of private experimenters and systems designers began.

Experimenters who neither wished to engage, nor be engaged by the military elite, would not be dissuaded from their own secure positions. For these services, the military were required to pressure their demands further in a great number of ways, the misuse of exceptionally personal information notwithstanding. Experimenters who offered their too independent attitude, an independence of action which irked military superiors, were often dealt with in a less "kind" manner. Soon, special liaison personnel, often out of uniform, encouraged talented academes and privateers to work on their behalf. These small bureaucratic concessions preserved both the aristocratic poise of senior officers and the sometimes flamboyant independence of the researchers. It was this very independence however, through which the superior and manifest creativity had flourished. Of this there could be no doubt, the working class mind held he secret to systems In this somber awakening it was inwardly acknowledged that the consortium of working class experimenters sustained a commodity which the highly groomed military elite could never produce.

Eventually, the awkward and threatening gestures between military and researcher grew into a working relationship whose rewards were shared by those engaged in the various projects for which they were hired. The employment of working class experimenters was indeed, not disappointing at all. In fact, these experimenters built the military systems on which leadership so relies. A steady line of military-tailored radio systems were developed between the early World Wars of the Twentieth Century, a proliferation of wave radio systems predicated on an unfortunate first step into error. The consequences of this first step into inferiority would require decades before the error could even be recognized.

During the years following World War I, there were several critical Military Radio developments which completely distanced them from their former Marconi affiliation. First, a commission was established by the Federal Bureau of Standards to learn all about radio signal propagation across both the Atlantic and Pacific. The thoroughly academic study engaged propagation characteristics covering a broad radio frequency spectrum, one which began with tests in the deep VLF and proceeded up into the available UHF band. These tests provoked the design and redesign of numerous antennas, transmitters, vacuum tubes, receiving sets, and an unbelievable flood of highly improved radio components. Indeed, it was during the wondrous years before the Second World War that a great military indulgence of civilian research schemes was given funding on the chance that, all possibilities being equal, some great new development could make its unexpected appearance. New affiliations and industries were spawned and proliferated in this beneficial interchange, a thoroughly productive and zealously patriotic time period. Indeed, the military now found their research atmosphere so admired by the experimenter-privateer, that they themselves could begin enunciating the terms of their relationship with far greater command once again.

## NAVAL VLF

Each of the military branches benefited enormously by the interchange between military supervision and civilian researchers. Naval authorities benefited the most from these findings. VLF wave aerials were redesigned by Naval employed engineers, reliable frequencies were discovered, and suitable power sources were established. The enormously potent Poulsen Arc dischargers continued being used by the most powerful Naval Radio Stations. Being the only available means for maintaining continuous wireless communications, VLF wave Radio became an exclusive Naval possession. Even when shortwave became the vogue, the Navy did not abandon its VLF stations. Navy authorities managed the investigation and development of shortwave systems for their own special needs. Nonetheless, Naval authorities would not disallow the VLF stations simply because they were so reliable. Reliable and virtually unstoppable. Especially in the very deep VLF range. Only the deep VLF wave stations were thoroughly reliable. Those systems used by Marconi were susceptible to interference because of their relatively "high" frequency! Realize

that the distance between successive wave alternations in a typical Marconi VLF station measured at roughly 10 kilometers. Navy began experimenting with longer waves, very much longer than 20 or 30 kilometers. They also began increasing power levels in these systems, often reaching output levels of a searing 2 Megawatts. Near these aerials, sparks literally jump from the ground whenever systems are "keyed". Automobile parking lots on their grounds require thick copper bus-bars against which to be grounded. Indeed, touching any ungrounded volumes of metal nearby is lethal (Lehr).

But for the several operating frequencies which engaged geoelectrical effects and bringing signal attenuations, each successive increase in wavelength obtained very strong and lossless signals. The drive to bring frequency down came as the remarkable result of several experiments with subsurface radio. Notable in this regard are the ground conduction radio systems of Nathan Stubblefield, John Trowbridge, Sir William Preece, Fr. Joseph Murgas, James Harris Rogers, Ferdinand Braun, Georg von Arco, Sigmund Musits, G. W. Pickard, and a host of many others. Each developed various kinds of subterranean and subaqueous aerials. Those of James Harris Rogers were especially attractive to Naval authorities, since his designs provided a remarkable and clarified communications continuity with submarines. Largely derived from several unpatented Tesla designs, these were simple buried dipoles. Two well insulated cables, were stretched out and buried to a depth of 1 or more feet. Their center wires were then connected to any receiver. Radio reception through these buried cables provided an astounding static-free signal between any points on the earth, regardless of distance.

Their simple and cost-effective nature made them perfect candidates for use in Naval deep VLF stations. The high insulation requirement was not an excessive problem in the upscaled versions. These simple buried dipoles also served in transmitting deep VLF to any point on earth, or under earth. The Rogers antennas found their most amazing use in maintaining undersea communications. Signals injected into the earth in this manner was able to permeate seawater to great depth. Also, wireless signals transmitted out from submerged vessels were detectable at great distances by the buried Rogers dipole. To the Navy, the system represented a true marvel. Rogers patents have been alternately classified and declassified over the years. They amount to a wonderful patent file, a veritable study collection in the art of deep earth signalling.

Having become intimately familiar with each of these systems, radio engineers began designing systems to meet the peculiar requirements of the military. The capabilities of various style Military VLF wave radio, both elevated trellis and buried aerial forms, soon rivalled those of the original Marconi Company. Naval radio engineers reporting and registered every minor experience with VLF variables until a thorough empirical familiarity with the related geoprocesses had been amassed. It was discovered that minor environmental variations increasingly insignificant distortions to VLF the lower the frequency.

At these deep VLF frequencies, significant departures from the theoretical propagation laws began working on their behalf, strange and misunderstood geoprocesses actually seemed to empower propagation without the predicted attenuations. What this represented was a new means for establishing and maintaining a noise free, interference-proof radiosignalling system, whose terrestrial reach seemed to be virtually unlimited. Naval operators observed the solar driven geoprocesses which very slightly distorted their deep VLF signals, but did not dampen their resilience or strength. The only times in which deep VLF broadcasts experienced distortions and interferences was during certain extreme solar conditions. To this day, a military bureau studies, monitors, and reports solar flare conditions to the national communications community.

Communications is the absolute foundation for all Naval operations. Without unbroken secure-communications channels, naval operations are impossible. Naval radio Networks grew around deep VLF, often using valley-coupled catenary suspension aerials which resembled suspension bridges for size. Operating as low as 12 Kilocycles, these signals went out through both ground an sea, an unjammable, unstoppable signal capable of reaching submerged submarines. Only deep VLF could reach across the world without apparent loss, interconnecting both deep-sea and distant ocean going vessels with unstoppable efficiency. Naval deep VLF stations have remained the most dependable radiowave communications system for maintaining continuous telegraphic communications between fleet and command central. Naval deep VLF stations are huge and powerful, rivaling those which Marconi taught. Several of these systems employed very large Alexanderson rotating radio frequency alternators. Others have maintained their use of surprisingly large Poulsen Arcs, these magnetron-like components often measuring in excess of ten feet per side in their larger embodiments. Most of he Naval deep VLF stations are yet in operation, a continuity which seems to speaks well of both their reliability and their status.

Deep VLF was restricted to the old radiotelegraphic mode, slow and laborious, Nevertheless, deep VLF was penetrating and powerful, capable of communicating through astounding distances of land and sea without interference of any kind. After the establishment of these very large geophysically coupled stations, new radiotelephonic methods made themselves available for ordinary non-classified Naval communications. While reliance on deep VLF wave transmitters remained the backbone of Naval reliance, reserved for secret coded communications and other command priorities, Naval engineers sought the advancement of the newer radiotelephonic shortwave systems. These systems, rapidly becoming available after World War I, were made possible by the advent of vacuum tubes. The subsequent applications of these revolutionary components to compact and powerful shortwave radio became a matter of Naval R & D priority. The NRL Radio Division engaged every possible new kind of electronics component and system in a rigorous and methodic search toward development of the very best equipment.

Naval undertook the development and proliferation of "darklight" communications systems, those optical communications systems which grew out of research on crystals, crystal sensitivities, and optical energy research. Notable in these regards were the systems of Dr. William Coblentz, the first infrared radiophones. Using molybdenite, a mineral crystal extremely sensitive to infrared light fluctuations, Dr. Coblentz developed an invisible ship-to-ship and ship-to-shore signalling system which was indispensable throughout World War II. This prolific time of technical development in the radio arts began between the World Wars. Therefore Naval radio systems developed into more diversities than practically all the other military branches, a veritable research assault along many streams of thought. It was the Navy which first succeeded in reaching their own hightech state of electronics technology. It remains in their hands to this day.

## PANGLOSS

By the end of World War II, Naval authorities had already begun drawing up their research agendas. It was they who, through oceanic testing of nuclear warheads, were some of the very first military groups to observe and recognize the implications in the EMP effects. Appreciating the need for maintaining secure-communications of an unjammable kind, Naval authority was quick to recognize that VLF, however deep, might not thoroughly serve the new world situation. The nuclear weaponry, whose unexpected appearance rocked the entire military community, exerted its lasting demands on their research expertise. This technology-demanding shockwave lasted long after the nuclear shots had long dissipated.

NRL directed a wide variety of experimental tests on much deeper VLF than had ever been conducted on such a grand scale. They already knew that the deeper the VLF signal frequency, the less ruffled signal continuity would be. Indeed, it was found that deeper than VLF waves could sustain EMP phenomena with no blackout vulnerability whatsoever. In this light, the numerous drawbacks of deepest VLF was not now objectionable. If radiowave systems were going to be relied upon at all, then these were the very epitome of reliance. Moving to even lower frequencies was going to place heavier requirements on the engineers, to build the monstrous stations, and on operators, who would now have to slow down their signalling to inhuman tempi. Indeed, automatic digital systems would be required to tap out the encrypted messages which had been loaded into their new electronic memory banks. Deepest VLF would indeed be very slow, a laborious means for exchanging large volumes of critical information. Nevertheless, here was the only alternative then available to the military community. In truth, during territorial emergency, only deepest VLF would maintain secure-communications continuity.

Some objected that such signal energy demonstrated an alarming ability to permeate even "enemy" ground. Once launched from their geological "chutes", deepest VLF signals spread out rapidly across the surface of the earth. Entering its meandering routes, such VLF signals could easily be intercepted anywhere, by anyone. While this fact was not problematic during the early years of ground conduction VLF systems before World War I, strict techniques for the preservation of military secrecy would now be an absolute. Furthermore, such energies could not be served by the military encryption systems which served radiotelephonic channels. New digital code encryption techniques would now be developed and implemented. Deepest VLF wave transmission was the available reliable communications channel.

An objection to the establishment of these stations considered the that these easily discerned structures would be among the very first target-strike zones. The large fixed VLF installations were captives of their own monstrous size. RCA directed the construction of the 10 Megawatt Jim Creek Station, call letters NLK, in Oso, Washington. The Naval VLF station NAA is a 2 Megawatt station which operates at 14.8 Kilocycles. Comprising 26 towers, each an average of 900 feet height, NAA occupies a peninsula of 300 acres in Cutler, Maine. Military planners did not appreciate the fact that VLF stations such as this represented such easy wartime targets. VLF wave stations could be destroyed in a single blast. For this reason, the military devised an elaborate ground-based scheme to incorporate a great number of simultaneous triggered stations, a VLF Network. Operating in synchronous intermittent blasts, the VLF stations would be switched on and off by a central command control system. The possible destruction of any one such site would in no way damage the integrity of the whole Network. No one site would carry all the information of a single transmission. In addition, VLF is virtually impossible to triangulate. The nature of the deep ground-hugging signal precludes any ordinary radio scanning means by which to ascertain the exact target location of any one such station. Therefore, unless espionage had provided very exact coordinates on these systems, there would be no possibility of their immediate destruction. In addition, these sites would be the most highly defended national zones in such an emergency.

A small amount of deep VLF energy was found to have an effective and remarkable long distance range. Ionospheric ceilings did not drastically distort deep VLF wave signals. Both NUCLEAR and RADAR EMP methods could scramble all electromagnetic wave channels for dangerously long time periods by disturbing the ionosphere directly, artificial chaotic conditions. All channels which relied on excessive skywave components were thus rendered useless by the method, a new breed of electronic push-button weaponry. But deep VLF wave channels were not nearly affected at all. This proved to be especially true with decreasing VLF frequency, an inference that at lowest frequencies, one might find a zero disturbance condition. Such a frequency band would then offer secure-communications continuity despite the disturbing detonation of hundreds of nuclear warheads. This observation prompted several new projects, the first practical necessity being to establish more resilient deep VLF wave stations.

The NRL began working closely with VLF experts to produce an ELF communications system which, relying on ground wave conduction, could not be disrupted by high altitude EMP's. Several preliminary tests were conducted with LORAN-C broadcasts to assess the power efficiencies of such a scheme. Naval VLF stations joined in several cooperatives, broadcasting and monitoring signals along specific pathways. Terrestrial magnetic variables were extremely responsive to EMP currents. Deep VLF wave correlated studies followed nearly perfect compass headings. Such channels were not completely impervious to space EMP effects. The last two nuclear space blasts of Project ARGUS proved the availability of ELF channels in catastrophic EMP. The direction was clear, the new quest was to devise an ELF communications system.

There was another purpose in these directions. The newly established nuclear submarine fleet had new and demanding requirements. The obvious need for complete secrecy in deep submarine communications brought about an amplified interest in ELF systems. Fleet ballistic missile submarines (POLARIS) necessarily remained submerged at very great depths for long time periods. Traditional surface communications modes were abandoned by these submarine nuclear armories, where such vulnerability would be negated by a new mode. It was well established that radiowaves were attenuated by seawater inversely as the frequency decreased. ELF ground conduction waves were found capable of reaching any required depth. Continually transmitting and receiving command base messages while completely submerged, POLARIS submarines could then engage enemy forces with previously unheard tactical efficiency. In addition to these low propagation losses, ELF signals demonstrated a remarkable resistance to natural and EMP disturbances. A project was initiated for the explicit construction of an EMP safe radiowave communications system in the Extra Low Frequency band of the wave radio spectrum.

## ELF TECHNOLOGY

Not surprisingly, RCA initiated experiments on the first new Naval ELF technologies. Their project was originally called PANGLOSS (1959), a reference to panglobal submarine systems. The ominous project title was changed to SANGUINE (1962). RCA supplied over 100 senior engineers and science advisers to this task by 1963. In the interest of averting engagements with a growing public awareness, the name SEAFARER as finally chosen (1973).

This latter less threatening name referred analysts to communications aspects of the project. The Project had several problems to solve. The first was the establishment of landbased ELF antennas. The second was the deployment of systems made for submerged craft. ELF brought with it an encumbrance to submarines, the required antennas being extreme in length. Submarines would be equipped with a highly insulated trailing antenna of a kilometer or more length. Antennas used in the SEAFARER project would necessarily be deployed during communications, and reeled back into the craft during battle.

Rogers VLF wave antennas formed the original group of patents serving submarines. Naval high classification status was periodically granted and revoked on these antenna systems throughout the years between the World Wars. These patents formed the core of renewed interest in ELF communications, the conductivity and propagation attributes of seawater being critical to the success of the venture. The World War I Rogers designs were restudied. Rogers employed VLF dipoles which spanned the submarines of that time. Because of the frequencies employed, submarines would necessarily rise close to the surface when communicating with their command base. If these methods were scarcely acceptable during World War II, they were now certainly out of the question. POLARIS bearing submarines would have to remain completely submerged at all times, and only ELF could completely penetrate seawater to their extreme depths. Engineering contracts were issued to several research groups in order to learn more about this mysterious extra low frequency region. The hope was that ELF would provide military with an "invincible" communications system.

Radio energies in the ELF and ULF spectra were each reexamined as means for establishing powerful new communications throughout the world. Headed primarily by Galejs, Watt, and Christofilos, ELF radiowave systems found their strongest supporters in the academic circles. A tremendous amount of preliminary study and experimental work preceded the actual construction of SANGUINE. The Naval VLF station at Jim Creek was driven down to an operating frequency of 4000 cycles per second in a test which spanned the continent. Successive testing brought this operating frequency further down, to 100 cycles per second. Tests, conducted on the propagation of yet lower harmonics across the continent and planet itself, came through and among Naval VLF stations. Toward the development of a true and operable ELF transmitter, military engineers attacked each problematic facet of the ELF art. ELF radio transmitters had far more stringent requirements than VLF stations, and would be enormous in actual size. The radiating structure was the main problem. How would a system of this size manage its electrical supply? Maintaining a consistent ELF current throughout a huge aerial array would require the antenna to adopt new geometrical dispositions. For the design of these new structures, a methodic study of older ground conduction systems was engaged. Of particular note were the articulate buried well terminals of Fr. Joseph Murgas. Murgas antennas (1906) were more like terminals than wave antennas. Since traditionally accepted antenna lengths did not limit Murgas antennas, they were studied with great interest by those planning the SEAFARER system.

The Murgas system employed vertical ground rods. In early systems, Fr. Murgas simply drove very long rods into the ground with hammers. Later designs were far more visionary in aspect. Wells were sunk to very great depths for their original purpose of achieving transcontinental or transoceanic communications. In some of the Murgas designs energetic transfer was achieved by direct conduction with the rock walls. In variations, an insulative seal was maintained with surrounding rock strata, Fr. Murgas often implementing water or oil filled wells. Finding these designs capable of powerfully transmitting ELF signals, Murgas antennas were employed in propagation experiments all along the eastern coast of North America (1964). Tests were conducted at 50 kilocycles, using 300 meter deep wells.

Variations of the Murgas method proved that rock conductivity does indeed provide an important subterranean communications channel, the variations of rock strata and rock attributes being critical. The efficiency of these transmissions were found to vary with rock conductivity. Specific stations would therefore be established toward achieving these increased efficiencies. Murgas antennas did not have to be as long as the waves by which they were energized, their operation depending on largely unstudied phenomena. When proper geological strata were found, horizons of conductive and insulative rock, transmissions produced anomalous efficiencies. The Murgas system provided vocal communication to unheard distances. When driven at Extra Low frequencies, these deepwell conduction antennas transmitted great power.

Other experiments employed natural structures as ground antennas of huge extent. Coastal geological formations of iron clays between strata of highly insulative sandstones represented an engineering dream. Requiring no construction work other than the drilling of power injection wells, these geological antennas could be established wherever similar conductive-insulative conditions were present. Applications of ELF directly into these geological strata produced interesting and classified results which served Naval experiments in deep subsurface communications. There were those RCA engineers who, for purely commercial reasons, insisted that true "wave type" antennas would produce better results. They were wrong. Rogers type antennas were buried at some slight depth or simply laid along the ground surface, being energized at 70 Kilocycles. Rogers antennas suffered from certain reflective distortions, increasing in efficiency with increased frequency.

## SANGUINE

Before building the SEAFARER system, military engineers examined all the previous work in VLF and ELF transmission. Several specialists began examining all propagation aspects of the new deep-sea communications frontier, the greatest concern being the security of signals so employed. Command base transmitters would be monstrous in size, definitely located in the American heartland. ELF communications would employ specially designed AC generators, identical to conventional power machines. If traditional wave antennas were to be used, then the efficient transfer of these currents to the earth itself required radiating structures of extreme dimensions. In fact, these ELF aerials would dwarf those VLF structures used in the first Marconi Stations. The theoretical halfwave dipolar aerial for a 100 cycle generator required 1400 kilometers of cable! It was obvious that other modes of energetic transfer would be crucial to the success of the proposed system. There were those whose early research produced subterranean radio systems. Murgas and Rogers were able to transmit and receive radio signals through the ground. Using both monopolar and dipolar aerials, each system represented a possible answer to the military dilemma.

Conductivity radio was a study area largely ignored and forgotten. Air Force experimenters reinvoked the forgotten technologies. Murgas antennas were more like terminals than wave antennas. Since traditionally accepted antenna lengths did not limit Murgas antennas, they were studied with great interest by those planning the SEAFARER system. The Murgas system employed vertical ground rods sunk to great depths. Finding these capable of powerfully transmitting ELF signals, Murgas antennas were employed in propagation experiments all along the eastern coast of North America. Tests were conducted at 50 kilocycles, using 300 meter deep wells. Variations of the Murgas method proved that rock conductivity does indeed provide an important subterranean communications channel. The efficiency of these transmissions were found to vary with rock conductivity. Specific stations would therefore be established toward achieving these increased efficiencies. Murgas antennas did not have to be as long as the waves by which they were energized, their operation depending on largely unstudied phenomena. These deepwell conduction antennas transmitted great power at extra low frequency.

Variations of these experiments employed natural structures as huge ground antennas. Coastal geological formations of iron clays between strata of highly insulative sandstones represented an engineering dream. Requiring no construction work other than the drilling of power injection wells, these geological antennas could be established wherever similar conductive-insulative conditions were present. Applications of ELF directly into these geological strata produced interesting and classified results which served Naval experiments in deep subsurface communications.

There were those RCA engineers who, for purely commercial reasons, insisted that true wave type antennas would produce better results. Rogers type antennas, buried at some slight depth or simply laid along the ground surface, suffered from reflective distortions. Energized at 70 kilocycles, Rogers antennas increased broadcast efficiency with increased frequency. To satisfy contractual obligations, some combination of both designs was sought. Spanning great area, the SEAFARER ELF signalling system is a matrix of small power transformers, raised lines, and ground plates. SEAFARER went operational in 1989 broadcasting coded messages on an assigned carrier frequency of 76 cycles per second.

In sites which have been loudly announced by government publications, the SEAFARER system pumps the earth with ELF power of closely monitored intensities in both Michigan and Wisconsin. SEAFARER uses the multiple ground system, the entire array behaving as a conduction strip of great extent. ELF aerials may be rectilinear or circular. Properly phased ground currents are driven back and forth along the miles-long strip of chosen geology. The weak alternating disturbance spreads outward for thousands of miles. The Wisconsin aerial consists of two lines, each 14 miles long. The Michigan aerial consists of 3 lines: two of 14 miles length and one of 28 miles length. Both systems are phase coordinated. Both aerials must work in tandem, each broadcasting a piece of the total communications intended at any instant. Phase coordination permits ELF radiation without the need for an excessive physical structure by creating coordinated electromotive tensions. Each link in the ELF antenna pulses any singular signal along.

The SEAFARER system is a poor solution to an otherwise impossible requirement. Phased wave integrity between the two sites is exact. With coordinated electromotive tensions existing between the two sites, the ELF signal conductively spreads through the long groundpath. Unfortunately there is destructive interference of a degree which seriously limits the total amount of dipole radiated ELF. Ground currents neutralize at each successive ground plate in the phase sequence. Consequently, not much ELF actually disperses to greater distances. This is why the excessive generators are required. Ever more obvious with time, radiowave communications become less preferred communications channels. While SEAFARER was being completed, another communications development was already making ELF obsolescent. The deployment of high orbital geostationary satellites, coupled with the development of highpower multispectrum lasers, gave military hierarchy a superior communications system which already exceeds the capabilities of radio.

## ELF JAMMING

Throughout this intense research period, experimenters assumed that ELF radio modes represented a "unjammable" communications core. Whether through natural or human agency, it was believed that SEAFARER would remain immune to any means of disruptive interference. When tested against the electromagnetic ravages of certain natural sources, ELF systems performed with remarkable consistency. Producing only extremely insignificant depressions, even solar flares did not effect diminished signal strength or signal integrity for certain ELF signals. While experts were amazed at ELF resilience to natural impacts, only a few realized that ELF was not invincible to human interruptions.

Several American experimenters found out just how efficient and invincible SEAFARER is. When their use of ground injected audio signals brought government officials to their door, the real truth was out. The introduction of a few audio frequency watts into the earth can sufficiently disrupt the supposed invincible SEAFARER System! It is obvious that ELF can be jammed. Any RF signal can be jammed. So many engineers published on this fact, yet were not included in the main thrust in Project analysis. Project contractors published a great deal on coding-decoding schemes for averting several different kinds of jamming methods. Other researchers remained entirely unconvinced.

Soviet ELF systems concentrated on designs perfected by Nikola Tesla in 1899. Low frequency alternating interpretations of Tesla designs, Soviet systems are ELF monopoles. Theirs is a brilliantly simple and effective means for "pumping the ground" with ELF. The system has demonstrated great power in a relatively compact size. The ELF spreads as circular waves of electromotive tension from the monopolar ground site. Requiring only that appropriate absorptive capacity structures be built, several of these structures were supposedly built throughout the last twenty years. There were those who believed these to be part of an ELF jamming system, their most notable encrypted broadcast being referred to as the "Russian Woodpecker". In light of these new facts, many began to openly question the operation of SEAFARER and other ELF projects. If SEAFARER was not the "invincible" radio system which billions of tax dollars proclaimed, then exactly what was its purpose? Both seasoned analysts and conspiratists alike seized upon this theme with an unprecedented tenacity during the late 1980's. These writers began to see an insidious weapon in the ELF potential of SEAFARER and other such military sponsored ELF systems. In an unprecedented openness, military reports were released in which ELF safety margins were clearly outlined. SEAFARER engineers and advocates loudly proclaimed the harmlessness of their new communications system, one which they insisted was built solely for submarine communications.

Meanwhile, other researchers began recognizing the biologically related hazards of ELF. Numerous university researchers discovered the effects of ELF electrostatic and ELF magnetic potentials on test subjects. Potent emotional and mental derangements were observed when the EM vectors were slightly modified (Hunt). Numerous individuals began "hearing" a strange and penetrating "hum" which could not be recorded acoustically. Besides the sentiments against AC power industries and the growing number of high voltage lines, civilian anger over earth applied ELF potentials was especially aimed at military research groups. It was during this time that numerous highly qualified analysts misunderstood the true potential of the SEAFARER system. They claimed it to be an ELF radiator whose peak pulsed applications could kill. It was claimed that the SEAFARER system could reach peak potentials of nearly one megawatt. In their opinion, the SEAFARER system was much more than a communications device. The conspiratorial scenario was fever pitched. Pulsed at its supposed peak potential, a sudden electromagnetic fluctuation would pass through every grounded object. Any population exposed to the inductive effects of such a burst would suffer terrible consequences. Conspiracy writers considered the biological potency of ELF signals, insisting that SEAFARER could be used in "genocidal" operations.

Legitimate research studies were used to prove these assertions, pointing out that heart attacks could be induced by even mild ELF inductive effects. These effects, they believed, could be broadcast to any region with push-button speed. The frightening results of ULF energy and the neurological entrainment of test subjects was then employed to prove the sinister and covert purpose of SEAFARER, military sponsored ELF studies being quoted in these regards (Grissett, deLorge, Wever). SEAFARER was viewed as a means for regulating the chaos of society with deliberate neurological entrainments. This trend focussed on the possible use of ELF to warp human perceptions on a mass scale. Specific ELF frequencies of very low intensity could induce passivity, sleep, coma, seizures, insomnia, hallucinations, hysteria, insanity, violence, and more. Broadcast into any target population, ELF systems would effect malevolent designs on the unsuspecting.

Scrutinizing all ELF projects from this paranoid perspective, "population control" became the topic of conspiracy writers. Radio talk shows, journals, lectures, tapes and videos. The message went out. Certain writers began citing the use of ELF entrainment to suppress social chaos. Electrical nerve gas. Scenarios of famine and deprivation were assessed by conspiracy writers as requiring metropolitan riot control systems. Violent inner city riots would be quelled, managed, or eradicated at will by ELF weapons. Underground bunkers, hooded ELF corpsmen, triangulations, electrical fireballs, target populations, black helicopters. Others described means by which ELF inductions could be sent to specific regions through methods of "triangulation", a blatant impossibility (Bearden). So much conspiratorial interference demands complete clarification. Facts must precede evaluations. First critical fact: ELF is not effectively broadcast through space by aerials. ELF is primarily ground conduction communications. ELF signal consistency varies with ground conductivity, this is why the original SANGUINE engineers devoted an entire study toward geologically optimizing station sites. ELF propagation is completely dependent on ground surface electron currents. Though the immense aerial structures in Michigan and Wisconsin use phased ground conduction effects, the resultant signal is weak. Regardless of aerial dimensions, ELF signal transfer is weak. This is why they require extremely powerful alternating drivers.

Second fact: ELF alternating currents cannot be directed to any specific earth point. ELF spreads out across broad surfaces of ground. ELF completely disperses in transit from its broadcast source. ELF is inherently incapable of being focussed. There are those who describe ELF operation by which nodes and antinodes may be concentrated at specific earth points. In order to effect such a condition, each station in the SEAFARER network would add its small increment of power toward a distant target. ELF surface standing waves must first pass through the broadcasting station before being established.

At the SEAFARER operating frequency of 76 cycles, the wavelength is 2447.37 miles. Taking half the earth circumference as 12444.5 miles, there would be approximately 5.035 standing wave zones formed on the surface of the earth. Because of inconsistencies in both tuning and earth surface features, the ELF nodes would slowly drift along the ground. Sweeping the entire surface of the earth, the condition would kill the station operators and everyone else in the expanding wave path. If this wavetrain could be intensified above its present inefficiencies, worldwide genocide would occur in a few seconds.

Claims concerning the "triangulation" of ELF is the result of writers who do not make distinctions between the energetic species and mode employed by Tesla and those used by the Military. Tesla used penetrating electrical rays. The Military uses electromagnetic waves. Tesla effects greatly exceeded the realm of electromagnetic waves. Rays can be triangulated to specific points. While the Russians employed the structures and symmetries of the Tesla method, they did not utilize the arc impulses of Tesla. Thus however large the power supply of these ELF engines, they do not operate in the true Tesla mode. The supposed means for directing enormous ELF wave energies to distant sites do not exist.

Third fact: There is no immunity from ELF transmissions of this magnitude. Ground applied ELF potentials stimulate alternating ground currents. All grounded objects would be electrified at these potentials by conduction. Insulated objects would be bathed in an overwhelming fluctuating induction field. If such a genocidal operation was actually conducted, nothing and no one could escape the permeating ELF energies. Were such an operative activated, everyone would suffer and die. Everyone. This includes the personnel who supposedly operate the system. No ELF transmission site remains immune from its own pulsed outputs. Were such an absurdity performed, all personnel conducting the operation would become affected by the transmission with the first switch closure. Each operating crew would suffer the effects of its own signal transmission. A death transmission would kill every national SEAFARER station crew. Transmitting behavior modifying waves would likewise affect and damage each SEAFARER crew. In truth, only Tesla was able to achieve these objectives, using DC impulses in his systems.

Fourth fact: ELF cannot produce the neurological effects of ULF at 7, 8, 9 or 10 cycles per second. SEAFARER is limited to an operating frequency of 76 cycles per second. SEAFARER cannot operate at the ultralow frequencies demanded by those who accused that military neuro-entrainment capacities were being worked into SEAFARER. We see therefore that such objectionable uses of SEAFARER cannot hold under real examination. But here we have a genuine mystery. If SEAFARER is so weak that amateurs can interfere with its operation, what is its possible worth?

# CHAPTER 7
## Auroral Energy Research and Project HAARP

### PATTERNS

The summary of military radio projects, a succession which spans a century, has been a lengthy yet necessary recapitulation. Reaching satisfactory prooftexts for our central thesis, which truly does not end with the IRI, can be achieved in no other manner. Having read through the history of Radio Science and Technology now, we have unwittingly passed through developmental successions which voracious military projects have pursued with an unmistakable tenacity. Each major military project, since the horror of the Nuclear Age was fully recognized, is a stepwise walk through a defined series. It is this series, one so accurate, so methodic, so completely obvious in its character, which has revealed the greatest principle for ascertaining without fail the reality behind so-called covert military projects.

Military projects which have been outlined in this lay text offer but the major and superficial steps in an otherwise long military line. If you really read through the lines, you saw the defined and unmistakable pattern; one which was very evident throughout the previous chapters. Consider them and see that pattern. What have the military been attempting to duplicate? In every single Post War step by which the military has aggressively pursued revolutionary technology we see the unmistakable traces of one who is now a haunting spectre. This one, whose work is so compelling, represents the highest frontier to which military aspires. In truth, they have not attained it. The altogether excessive expenditures which waste oligarchic capital, so freely poured out on military, has proven unsuccessful in duplicating the so greatly desired mystery Technology. It is intriguing that this figure, whose work was initially derided and then eliminated from all serious consideration, found such favor all so quickly among those who helped eradicate him. The unexpected emergence of the nuclear horror suddenly found an all too fickle favor. The ways of the elite who pick and choose their pleasures.

Count the steps and see. Radio communication, Global communication, RADAR beams, RADAR EMP, Nuclear Energy, Deep VLF, ELF Technology, Radiation Weaponry, Radiation Communications...each is a very obvious and frail attempt at duplicating each item of Tesla Radiant Energy Technology. The demand to find antidotes for the nuclear nightmare, the Bomb which so completely horrified oligarchs who finally understood its horrid longterm effects, provoked a superior directive toward the military, It was their task to find those "antidotes for the nuclear poison". Military of course, has not historically been the most creative group of personnel in the bureaucracy. We recounted the historical record which shows why their leadership was compelled to hire working class experimenters, inventors, and other scholars just at the onset, and after World War I. Despite the excessive training of their cadet corps under Marconi, the entire company, save one or two, remained essentially uninspired and thoroughly unable to create anything of worth. Examination of the patents proves that military instances of radio innovation were always plagiaristic versions of components which Marconi plagiarized!

The initial unwilling poise with which privateer-experimenters were received

by elitist military leadership prior to World War I changed its tune with the Second World War; a war between warring Geopolitical Houses which proved at every turn that scientific advantage could turn the battle tide. But the nuclear weapon, so ambitiously developed as a "bigger bomb", turned into a Gorgon so horrifying that even the thought of it turned the human heart to stone. Working class society feared it. Mercantile aristocrats feared it. Bureaucrats feared it. Oligarchs feared it. The Bomb demanded an antidote for which military had no creative response. They had not invented the Bomb. Military leadership could not rest the stiff upperstick elitism which blocked their creative passions from flowing forth in innovative new solutions. When their shallow assessments were given vent, they succeeded only in developing a "bigger bomb"; thermonuclear weapons whose world devastating potentials were unlimited.

So much for the ineffectual leadership which merely manages and imports minds and creativity. In the pressure of having to produce original antidotes for the nuclear horror, military took up the Tesla Biography, and outlined a simple and thematic course for success. The steps seemed simple enough to follow. The radiowave systems which Marconi developed, and passed onto the world at large, produced a legacy of disappointments. Inherently inferior, in comparison to the Radiant Energy systems of Tesla, futile wave radio concepts influenced academic thought, experimental research, and engineering designs along a tightly constrained military horizon. Incapable of recognizing or even postulating the existence of another energy continuum, not one major research group managed to break away from the tightly fixated orbits of Wave Radio. So permeative are these wave radio conceptions that they have leaked their influence into those studies which treat of quanta and photons, a thoroughly contaminated and fixating mindset. So complete is this fixation, that contemporary academes ridicule and reject every claim for another energy continuum. Besides the electromagnetic spectrum theoretically outlined by Maxwell, investigated by Hertz, and commercialized by Marconi, for the academic world there exist no other possible energetic expressions in Nature.

It was thus that military became entrapped in a helpless tautology. Empowered only with Marconi wave radio, they were enamored with Tesla technology. Unable to achieve Tesla objectives, they have consistently been attempting the reproduction of his every demonstration; a succession which evidences their possessions of secretized assurances concerning the reality of his claims. These facts have not stopped military researchers from using the Tesla name in every project proposal of which this discussion has been primarily engaged. Neither has this inconsistent record prevented the droves of conspiratist writers from squeaking the Tesla name out with every mere mention of the terms "resonance", "ELF", "ray weapons", each complete impostures based on incomplete knowledge. Nonetheless, this simple maxim sums up the quest of military engineers and researchers: Tesla is the rule. Tesla is the pattern. Well armed with this "Tesla Rule", we can easily unravel and accurately assess each new and controversial military project which manages to reach the social eye. If we wish to know what the military is pursuing, we have only to compare their projects with the Tesla Biography. The rest is a pedantic process in identification.

Finally, knowing the facts is neither concession nor willingness to accept HAARP technology. Of this, make no mistake. We do not endorse, approve, or applaud this infernal deployment. Knowing the facts is not affirming the right of military engineers to continue deploying such projects. But knowing the facts empowers our confidence in relinquishing concern over a technology which, it will be learned, cannot wreak the environmental destructions which certain publishing houses are using to best lucrative advantage. Do not allow yourself to be used by conspiracy writers. They rely on your hysterical response for their success. You need facts. And only historical facts will clear the issues.

Finally, concern is tempered by knowledge. Knowledge is an item which does not easily sway in the winds of hysteria. Only the loss of discipline in scholarly research causes us to slip into hysteria. Statements made in ignorance cannot be accepted with the gravity and concern so vehemently projected by the hysterical conspiratists. There is nothing covert in HAARP which cannot be clearly affirmed through careful and meticulous study of the available patents, patents which greatly exceed those recently claimed to envelop the Project. The historical bibliography provides every clear developmental path which led to these present designs. It remains treasurehouse filled with innumerable gem-studded ravines. We find their repetitive patterns crossing and recrossing in continual affirmations. These kinds of illuminated studies alone reveal the truth behind the fears. In this chapter we will see how the Industry-directed radio project known as HAARP seeks the evocation of forces which Tesla successfully secured one hundred years ago. Incidentally, they will never reach their goal, and this can be adduced by examining the techniques which have been claimed for the process.

Apart from these historical fascinations, the pleasurable and elevating examine of deep forgotten bibliographic treasuries, there remain those inscrutable considerations which HAARP has so provoked. Technological considerations. Of course, there are those aspects of HAARP which seem too thoroughly intertwined in social energy, a manifestation that consciousness has somehow been aggravated and irritated by the mere building of the IRI. It is therefore that all who undertake a serious study of the HAARP Project encounter an unbelievable maze of conundrums; a maze which oscillates in its path among considerations technological, considerations geopolitical, considerations bureaucratic, and considerations social. In truth, the HAARP Project raises questions having a most perplexing and contradictory assortment of answers.

The realization of this shifting and mirage-like nature, which suffuses the HAARP Project, is the very first clue that there is more to HAARP than commonly known. Examining the nature of these "blinding diversions", these mazeworks and deceptions, can be best addressed by examining the assortment of jigsaw pieces before our eyes. Yes, we have all the pieces, not one is missing. Those which we do not hold in our hands, are clarified and revealed by solid templates and models. Inferences can be considered, especially when observing the concerns and movement os power so clearly evidenced in the Industrial and military treatments of HAARP. If indeed the "Tesla Rule" gives us the pattern, the analytical guideline by which covert projects can be unraveled and understood, then we can easily penetrate the HAARP mystery without concern. It is against this historical backdrop that we are in a position to now qualify the HAARP Project. Indeed, before we can know what HAARP is, we must know what it is NOT. So, what is HAARP not?

The intense military involvement surrounding HAARP is always equated with weapons research. Indeed, many inexperienced analysts conclude that HAARP is a weapons project on this basis alone. But it is no such thing. One must examine the scenario in question before jumping to such prejudicial conclusions. Those who read the military involvement in HAARP as proof of a secret weapons program have not logged in the adequate research time. Had they done so, they would never have arrived at these pedantic and embarrassing conclusions. Let us begin our discussion here by stating that the modern presence of military in any project is insufficient proof that project is a weapon. In order to understand this seemingly contradictory statement, we must comprehend the changes which have been taking place in our world right from the beginning of SDI. There has been a change in the power allocation which once placed military ahead of Industry. This positional empowerment was necessitated for the various reasons which have been already shared. The original refocussing of power took place when nuclear secrets were leaked to the Soviets, proliferating a horror of potential world devastations. Because of this emergency world condition, military was empowered to solve the problem. If not for the nuclear secrets leak to the Soviets, military would not have received the subsequent allotment of authority and unlimited capital required to undo that fiasco.

Anticipating only devastations, superior command directed military to achieve every necessary solution to the nuclear dilemma. In the rare incident which precipitated the uncontrollable international proliferation of nuclear weaponry, military was supplied with endless funds to labor over the problem of neutralizing the threat. With those funds, military hired sufficient talent and creativity towards the realization of those Cold War objectives. With its supply of unlimited funds and enormous academic resources, military achieved the objectives for which it originally received empowerment. Let it be stated here that the complete obsolescence of fissile and fusile nuclear weaponry has been achieved. In our later chapters we will study the several patents by which we recognize how these goals have indeed been fulfilled. These are systems which have not been openly discussed in public forum. And it is necessary that these items be mentioned in public forum, since it was working class labor which ultimately supplied both the energy, the ideas, the designs, the material, the sheer labor, and all of the capital increases. Therefore it is fitting that we should so share a new awareness.

All Geopolitical Houses came to recognize the suicidal nature of nuclear weaponry. They each now know that the use of but one such weapon on another House will return with thousandfold vengeance on their territories and children's children. Therefore, each has resorted to another weapon systemology in order to reinvigorate the power game. The entire concession has been the result of knowledge concerning the Bomb. Infused as it is with fear and the consciousness of imminent annihilation, it has become a symbol of contradiction. It is the weapon which none dare use. This of course does not mean that those who lack sufficient consciousness will not use nuclear weapons, a high probability in a world of underdeveloped nations which act entirely without awareness. But this is precisely why world Intelligence Agencies are constantly surveying every possible nuclear leak, an oligarchic police force.

The new weapons status was not reached and enriched during the SDI years. The SDI years marked the public unveiling of projects which had already reached their objective conclusions several years before. Presidential and military media releases of the time period evidenced a curious enthused relief. The bureaucratic agencies seemingly shared some secret knowledge, for which claim was made to change the "world order". The SDI years, where nuclear weaponry was actually made obsolescent by more frightful and controllable designs, has indeed brought about a defined world change. But it is not a New world change, certainly not a "New World Order" at all. We are living in the post SDI years, the years where oligarchs are resuming their Old World Order. The order which was interrupted by nuclear fear.

In this present time period, we have been witness to severe structural reorganizations within various bureaucratic levels. These changes signal a reversal of policies which held their sway throughout the Cold War Years. Because of the present condition of nuclear disarmament, one based solely on the proliferation of newer weaponry, the phase relationship of power has shifted circumstance. The military rule of Industry has been terminated. The Industrial command of military has commenced. Industries have been given unlimited power and resource now to achieve new world dominations in wealth and power. Superior directives have stimulated Industry with both authoritative empowerment and adequate funds to reengage the capital-building regime, that world order which had been breached through the international proliferation of nuclear weapons.

Oligarchy, Intelligence, Military, Industry, Academician. This was the directed Cold War alignment within the bureaucracy. This order has changed. In the renewed Old World Order, the Oligarchy has begun again to delegate power to specifically selected Industrial Bases for the designed purpose of wealth multiplication. What has so changed the structure of these liaisons? Nuclear proliferation. The subsequent development of highly controllable weapons of far greater potential has erased the threat. The resumption of Old World conditions in a new status quo has resumed.

Industries, specific Industries, have thus become the powerful new focal points of highly delegated wealth and authority. Absolutely replacing the military in this new elevated role, the power has forcibly been shifted. The once servile Industry has become the new overseer of Military process. Projects such as HAARP become the focus of several different groups: Intelligence,

Industry, Academicians, and Military. This, for the conspiratists, represents a seemingly meaningful amalgam. They do not see as they should. Military no longer initiates. The one time it did, was its last time. Thus we learn the simple promotions and demotions which are dispersed with the vagrant needs of the Oligarchy. Oligarchy initiates. Military obeys. Oligarchy dictates. Military executes. Industrial Objectives enunciate military involvement now. Oligarchy, Intelligence, Industry, Military, Academician. The qualifications of academicians were once scrutinized by military consortium. Industry waited on military authority in the Cold War Era.

The presence of academicians in projects such as HAARP is predicated on the needs of Industry now, the years of the Renewed Old World Order. The select Industries, who have been empowered with vast wealth, once offered to the military, are now those actively engaged in recruiting academicians sufficient to achieve their secretive objectives. The only covert operations now are covert Industrial operations. Oligarchic control has now shifted its emphasis away from the once necessary eradication of the nuclear threat to a resumed posture of wealth multiplications, territorial acquisitions, and the withdrawal of delegated power from lower bureaucratic levels. Military involvement is a servile role now. When Industry seeks academes suited to the achievements of its endeavors, military bureaucracy is summoned along to function as organizer. It is therefore in this limited role that military now has been made to serve the various delegated aspects of Industrial deliberation. Central Intelligence monitors and reports the progressive development of military research groups directly to the Oligarchy.

Military leadership now serves to bureaucratically oversee every aspect of mandated Industrial directives. It is a fact that military agency has been called to organize the Industrially owned project known as HAARP. Other than this, the military has no ownership in HAARP. Industry owns HAARP. And Industry is enunciating directives to military. Military is simply overseeing the HAARP Project. It is neither devising the necessary components, nor investing in its ultimate goals. Military is managing HAARP for a more powerful Industrial objective. Why is the military overseeing a commercial venture? On whose behalf are such strict research directives being enforced?

## INTENT

Why indeed was the IRI developed? For whom are its effects prepared? The imaginary applications which hysteria composes from a few dissociated facts cannot be achieved in HAARP technology. There are several convoluted themes through which we can pick our way in order to penetrate the fog which has been deliberately cast around HAARP. One examines the numerous wild claims which have been spawned in this ignorance. The Ionospheric Research

Instrument (IRI) is a device whose construction and operation is obviously being directed by the military. What is furthermore perplexing in most topical examinations of HAARP is the obvious puzzle of discovering why HAARP was founded on land owned by the Department of Defense. Examining both the original reasons for Defense ownership of those regions, and the powerful Industry which has now acquired rights to that land, will give obvious answer to this pointed question. The Department of Defense acquired those lands during the years when ground-based Early Warning RADOMES were established across the northern lands bordering the Arctic Circle. Government and Military Bureaucracies have been directed into a joint and subordinate involvement in the project; one which is completely owned and funded by a megalithic Industry.

In the military weapons theme, some imagine the IRI to be a sophisticated ionospheric "backscatter" communications system, patterned after those trans-Pacific systems developed during the Cold War years. This simplistic notion is eliminated by the very existence of satellite technology, a deployment which renders all such radio technology obsolescent. Furthermore, if the IRI is just such a backscatter transmitter, then where are its receivers? If its directed beam is manufacturing ionospheric plasmas for the express purpose of launching and storing radio signals into long world-girdling routes, those responsible for anomalous hours-long signal delays, then where are its HF ground stations? More recently, certain writers have mentioned HAARP as a highly directional communications "blackout" system. Coupled with the fact that the HF beacon of the IRI can be skewed from its vertical launch path toward the zenith, some have imagined HAARP to be a directional EMP weapon. The radial magnetic symmetry available to the IRI, so near the North Geomagnetic Pole, would seem to afford a convenient means for launching sudden plasma concentrations along any radial route.

To effect this weapons potential, the IRI beacon is not in perfect position to both "touch" various geomagnetic radii and launch disruptive plasma clouds toward the south. To do this, the IRI would necessary have to be directly adjacent to geomagnetic north. There, where the field lines are emerging from the bedrock, such an operation could conceivably be attempted. But the latitude of Gakona, Alaska is insufficiently polar to achieve these perspectives. There are those who cite the fact that the IRI can be skewed from vertical, through a wide angular degree of freedom. It is inferred by this comment that the IRI beacon could be skewed into pole-emerging geomagnetic lines.

Even if this High Frequency wave radio beam could be skewed to the very horizon, such a process could never export the beacon into those very distant locations. Poised where it is, the IRI beam would only succeed in producing a plasma cloud, whose particles would fan out at right angles to the geomagnetic field. Such a cloud would describe an auroral arc rapidly travelling along an east-west orbital path. The local geomagnetic field, parallel with respect to ground and perpendicular with respect to the IRI propagation path, would effectively constrain and contain the plasma cloud within the aforementioned widening arc. Continued application beam energies would increase both the size and concentration of this plasma arc, until the arc at last passed over both horizons. Skewed IRI beams would produce ever widening plasma arcs whose drift would take them south, providing perhaps a momentary ripple in shortwave communications at southern locations. As a potential means for effecting auroral storms, the IRI is an unlikely candidate for a functioning weapons system of any dependability. The IRI cannot effect controlled conjugate auroral storms along longitude lines. Even the claimed immensity of the upscaled IRI output is yet insufficient for even radiowave communications blackouts. Daily solar eruptions, imminently incalculable in power in terrestrial impact, do not produce total communications blackouts.

In a more practical perspective, the enormous size of systems such as HAARP and SEAFARER preclude them from being weapons. The very activation of such a blackout system, unless precise, decisive, and devastating to any Geopolitical House, would stimulate vengeful repercussions. A worthless initiation. It would the have been better to withdraw its very construction. First strike activity would deal with the IRI long before such an activation potential was reached. In this use, the IRI would have served as a very expensive "one-shot" weapon. Military would have preferred aerial nuclear detonations, the only terrestrial means by which significant EMP effects are achieved.

Other misguided thought has imagined the IRI as a "directional ELF system", a thoroughly convoluted and ludicrous notion. In this scheme, the IRI projects a concentrated beam toward the zenith, a beam which renders the very air conductive. It is upon this supposed thoroughly conductive aerial beam "carrier line" that Extra Low Frequency alternations are then impressed. Systems independently developed by H. Grindell-Matthews (1917) and J. Hettinger (1919) utilized deep ultraviolet generated ionization paths to provide a pathway for applied high voltage DC pulses and radio frequency currents. These systems did not produce powerful effects beyond a given reach. Indeed, such beacons do not provide the capability of carrying alternating currents to any sufficient distance without severe ground arcs. The impossibility of attempting the actual insulation of such a conductive beacon would defy natural tendencies of electric charge. Others have believed it possible to "impress ELF signals" on shortwave carriers in order to resonate some ionospheric portion at Extra Low Frequency. Shortwave energies can be modulated with ELF energies, but the resultant waveforms produce only a slowly modulated train of high frequency waves. This is equivalent to scrambling the ionosphere in slow pulses. No electrical signal in the ELF band can be projected to the zenith through such an uninformed scheme. Indeed, HF wave energies are completely incapable of effecting the coherent ELF pulsations made possible by large generators such as SEAFARER, and cannot conceivably be employed to use the ionosphere as an immense ELF aerial.

Certain writers have viewed both Project SEAFARER and Project HAARP as psychotronic applications, capable of transmitting deadly ELF throughout the civilian population. Supposedly designed to modulate and entrain both circadian cycles and thought process, these systems are made for controlling and maintaining the local population. Simple thought of these matters should inform the woeful that such an operation would effectively wipe out both operators and their target populations. Furthermore, one cannot target any site with ELF, neither can one remain insulated from their effect while supposedly "exporting" a distant damage. The most casual knowledge of both radio theory and military deployments rules out each such possibility. ELF energy cannot be directed. ELF spreads out across space and ground, saturating geology in ever-expanding propagation paths from its source. ELF continuously affects all who lie in the transmission path. This begins from the very source site, and would either kill or modify the minds of those involved in transmitting the signals.

Furthermore, there is a group who believe that several distantly poised ELF generators can be phase modulated to "triangulate" specific targets. In this complete misunderstanding of ELF alternations, it is believed that ELF "standing waves" would direct deadly effects to specific points on the planet, while shielding all others. These effects, the supposed result of interference effects, would be the rationale behind ELF deployments. First, ELF energy is alternating wave energy. Standing waves alternate, passing from maxima to minima over a wave period. Despite triangulations, there is no "safe zone", no "target zone" anywhere. ELF energy lends itself neither to triangulation methods, or to "safe-zone" isolations. ELF energies are insidious, their sources cannot easily be located with precision for this reason. Because of these principles, one cannot "focus" ELF energy on any single geographic point. Several widely separated stations, operating in synchronous phase, would not succeed in isolating a tight active zone of ELF alternations.

Considering the IRI to be a beam weapons system is part of the repertoire of paranoia, an anachronistic and foolhardy evaluation. Why would the military spend billions on so large and unwieldy a target as the IRI if it were a weapon? The IRI cannot achieve weapons objectives. Neither can it launch clustered particle beams along the geomagnetic field lines to specific targets. In a more benign function, some writers have mentioned the IRI in conjunction with surveillance technology. But the IRI is no mere military listening post. The overwhelming number of military satellites can do far better in the surveillance arena. Furthermore those who make the ridiculous claim that "deep earth tomography" is a possible application of the IRI have much to learn in basic physics. Recall that ELF wavelengths literally span continents. How are such waves to be employed in a technique which would seek out the detail of "subterranean tunnels"? Such tomography requires the projection of waves more minute than those of the infrared band.

Those who cite ELF methods in this respect simply do not understand the nature of ELF and its inability to reveal such detail. Waves this large can define nothing smaller than their own dimensions. How then can they resolve small subterranean tunnels beneath an equally small geographic section? Conclusions such as these are evidence of unfortunate misdirected and unschooled zeal among those who are easily dissuaded from observing the obvious. Deep earth tomography can be accomplished by orbital means with far greater definition and access. All surface, submerged, or entrenched installations require the penetrating gaze of more powerful emissions. But the well documented and patented techniques of X-Ray and Gamma Ray technology will elsewhere be discussed.

There are those who have suggested that the IRI is a missile tracking system, one whose sophistication utilizes a supposedly new "bent beam" plasma phenomenon. In this view, the IRI skewing potential bends a focussed HF beacon into the ionospheric layers, and allows a signal-modulated plasma to bend out and around the earth along geomagnetic great circle loops. When writers describe this scheme, one is asked to believe that such a plasma-bending method will allow stationary observation of distant aerial movements, notably the signature discernment of hostile missiles. But this is so much fantasy! In no means can the IRI so skew its signals as to propel such a plasma great circle route to a directed location. Once the beam has produced any plasmic streaming, that streaming is at the mercy of natural forces for which there can be no directing influence.

The double dipole system is supposedly a "transmit-read" couple, one bay blasting space with modulated plasma generating streams, the other bay receiving and reading "back signals". If such a technique were indeed possible, there is no means to receive the sign that some mere speck of metal has flown into that beacon, for a missile at these distances would be no more than a metallic dust speck. Also the consideration of the possible signal-to-noise ratio involved in discerning any such "mobile signature" is impossible to rationalize, no such clarity being recognized through such an auroral hash of natural noise. But the exact conductive means through which a continual stream of "return signals" is to be engaged seems to escape genre writers. In truth, such a signature recognition route, a ground based conductive reading system which brings information back to base, is not provided in the Gakona site.

## OBJECTIONS

In brief, genre writers and supposed scholars on the topic of HAARP have continually betrayed an alarming ignorance concerning both system feasibility and radio behavior. But more so, they have demonstrated a complete miscomprehension of technological state-of-art, and a fundamental inability to recognize what space technology has achieved for military. In the plethora of orbital stations which have consistently been deployed through the decades, one would wonder why military would desire a ground based system of such enormous expense, high visibility, and by now antiquated technology. Furthermore, the Raytheon Company, whose unquestioned expertise is established in a host of highly classified communications related projects, would not expend such time and labor on a ground based system when orbital space technology is available. Space reconnaissance and weapons capabilities far exceed the bombastic and now obsolescent VLF and ELF capabilities. Clearly then, another experimental series is being carefully monitored; one whose nature seems now evident from the balance of our deductions. Every possible interpretation of HAARP has been eliminated save one. The most obvious one. But his most obvious possibility requires familiarity with the prior years of radio phenomena and geophysical explorations of auroral process.

One asks why megalithic Industry would actually resort to building a radio ionospheric backscatter technology, one which was already abandoned by the time satellite communications relay satellites had become the routine channels. If for mere study purposes, then there were already stations in existence for this application. Military had sufficient remnant stations of this kind throughout the decades to satisfy the academic curiosities of several university generations. Not a backscatter system, not a HF research tool, not an ELF tomography system, not an ELF impressment system, not a means for changing weather, not a way to bend sunlight, not a means for peering over the horizon and locating missile launches, not a means for directing radio energy to incinerate distant incoming missiles, not just another system for exploring auroral process. Indeed, since 1958, satellite technology has been rapidly replacing every landbased radio technology. Indeed, the old Naval VLF stations are gradually and methodically being dismantled; a fact which few seem to be recognizing. The military shift of technology for reconnaissance, communications, and weaponry has been moving out toward space in methodic and routine steps since the CORONA PROJECT.

Pointing out the fact that those who both own the land, the IRI, and all of the pertinent patents to the study field are heavily committed to fossil fuels, there are those who find evidence that the IRI is a beam-energy transmitter for the deliberate transformation of natural gas into microwave beacons. There are those who contend that HAARP is a project which Atlantic Richfield organized for the purpose of exporting the otherwise unusable gas reserves of the North Slope. Directed to a space poised reflector, this microwave energy is supposedly beamed back to base receivers and there converted into usable 60-cycle current. Distributed throughout the local power grids. Well and good, except for the fact that nowhere in the IRI do we see any evidence of a microwave transmitting system. And no space platform can capture or reflect an HF field, regardless of the claimed IRI super potential.

The bibliography dealing with radio technology is replete with examples of projects of which HAARP is supposedly the most recent and sophisticated example. One would question the expertise of those who insist that HAARP is both a new style communications relay and a tracking system. Most of these gigantic systems were developed prior to World War II. Projects exactly like those claimed for HAARP have already been established and discarded before 1930! Indeed, texts and periodicals on VLF, ionoscatter, RADAR EMP, and ELF, flood the technical shelves. The information, opened and declassified, is waiting to be read. Source critical in comprehending the function or purpose of HAARP does not require examination of the Eastlund patents. That often quoted patent "base" on which Project HAARP was supposedly framed has little to do with the actual device in Gakona. The Eastlund patents present a confusing assortment of components and proposals, all the more dubious because of its claims. The device demands several completely contradictory applications. One reads that the fully operational system will "modify weather patterns...derange incoming missiles...focus sunlight on distant areas...lift enormous sections of atmosphere to unprecedented heights...create strong updrafts...evacuate atmospheric regions...target specific locales to produce drought...stimulate ELF signals in the Schumann natural waveguide...a duplication of Tesla techniques".

The Eastlund patent collection certainly does not represent a system capable of achieving any of its proposed applications. Previous geophysics research teams achieved each of the claims in some measure. Surely Industry did not wish to simply reproduce the list of previous geophysical achievements! But perhaps Industry was interested in buying out all the relevant Eastlund-like patents simply because it had already ventured into a new and revolutionary technology designed to produce billion of dollars in yearly revenues. In such a case, we would then assume that Industrial act of purchasing the complete Eastlund patent series of was an unintentional disclosure of in-

tent! We would therefore never expect the Eastlund patent to appear at all in the Industry HAARP project. In fact, photographic evidence proves this assertion to be correct. Neither diagrammatically nor descriptively, it is clear that the IRI has nothing at all in common with the Eastlund disclosures.

Finally, and unequivocally, HAARP is wave radio technology. HAARP has nothing at all to do with Tesla Impulse Technology. HAARP employs technology which Tesla continually berated! HAARP is the very antithesis of systems developed by Tesla, and only uses the Tesla name as a very effective publicity buzzword. As with so many other designs, Industry acquired the rights to the Eastlund patents for a singular developmental purpose. The Eastlund patent group was certainly not the only collective representation which Raytheon acquired when it "swept the patent floor"; a self-protective act. "Patent sweeping" is common practice in business ventures when one wishes to eradicate potentially threatening technologies. The concomitant fact that Industry directed the actual building of HAARP has eliminated that scenario. Why then did Industry buy up all of these patents on ionospheric heaters? Because it wishes to deploy a weapon? How ridiculous. Weapons are deployed with no permissions or requests. Infringement suits do not occur when military directed projects are concerned. But why did Industry acquire such patents at all? Furthermore, why did Industry form separate management groups for the development of its HAARP Project?

## SNOW

We are sufficiently familiar with the several claims made for HAARP by genre writers, and are not sufficiently satisfied that any have really examined the IRI itself with any clarity of understanding. Project HAARP is not a weapons program. There are unlearned and paranoid speculators who have surrounded HAARP with a ragged entourage of supposed weapons applications which, from every military and engineering viewpoint, can never possibly be fulfilled. Even after the substantial modifications which have been both planned and openly announced, HAARP will never be exercised in these speculated functions. The complete engineering details concerning the IRI are buried under the cold white snow of a corporate megalith which, thus far, has maintained its frigid silence.

Weapons programs absorb and confiscate patents without permission. This is how security is maintained. Industry has absorbed every patent related to the HAARP effort. Were HAARP a weapon, no such affirmation would have been permitted. One does not purchase and collect such volumes of related patents except when preparing for some future venture. When one is developing a revolutionary technology, having potential entanglements and infringements from commercial and private sectors, one sweeps the patent floor. Were

Industry operating on behalf of a military weapons project, they would never have called attention to themselves in purchasing these rights. Therefore, Industry's involvement in HAARP can only be a commercial venture. The seemingly sizeable payments paid out when acquiring potential contestants is infinitesimal when compared with the projected profits of a revolutionary new commercial technology. Raytheon is thus compelled to protect itself against potential future infringement suits only if HAARP is indeed a business venture. This is precisely what the Industry has been doing all along.

The actual number of HAARP related patents acquired by the Raytheon Company greatly exceed those which other journalists have been able to ascertain or report. Furthermore, the often cited Eastlund Patent group was but one minor acquisition among the innumerable others which Raytheon absorbed in its preparatory tour-de-force. The IRI has been well camouflaged by the astounding variety of contradictory rumours. The mere absence of competitors indicates the degree of empowerment which Industry has been given. But for what purpose is such overwhelming authority and priority so directed?

If there were astute competitors, the IRI seems to be a new and unfamiliar technology which cannot adequately be assessed. Because it remains unfamiliar and unexpected, few view it as a financial threat. For this and other reasons, none think of questioning IRI development. Though few suspect the IRI as a new card in the hand, there is a single potential which the IRI serves. Every new announcement compounds the indication that the IRI will serve a singular function whose venture potential can literally change the world of energy commodities and utilities. To a very few who know the history of such devices, the IRI has a very obvious purpose. Besides opening a great many debates on the obsolescence of every residual radiowave technology, we are left with a clear path through which to understand HAARP; a design which is by no means the ultimate representation of its class. Two separate ionospheric heating facilities have tested in North America. The Arecibo facility in Puerto Rico is geophysically coupled to a natural mountain basin, some 1000 feet in diameter. The HIPAS facility near Fairbanks, Alaska was designed to focus radio energy on the ionosphere at one-quarter the rated output of HAARP, a value of some 250 Megawatts. Besides being a very poorly designed example of a large-scale influence-type transmitter, a technology which needs serious examination, the IRI does not yet exist! Its weak developmental prototype (the DP) is what has been so much discussed.

## IONOSPHERIC RESEARCH INSTRUMENT

The time for extensive expenditures on new weapons projects commenced with SDI in 1983 and was discontinued by the end of the same decade. While the IRI is intended to be an expensive experimental station, whose data can be used toward the development of several distinct systems in the future, it is clearly an attempt in a singular scientific direction. The IRI has been recently hailed as a "diagnostic tool" which will soon have multiple experimental applications. But what will the chief application of the IRI be? What do our evaluations finally conclude? The one military release which attracts my attention is the least mentioned throughout the literature of hysteria. It is the one description which accurately matches the existing structure in Gakona that I am surprised so few of the more prolific researchers have focussed their more scholarly attentions thereto.

HAARP is a project whose Staff and advisement council having been determined by Phillips Laboratories (Air Force) and the NRL directly. The "Ionospheric Research Instrument" (IRI) itself has not yet been built on the Alaskan North Slope near Gakona. Its developmental prototype, the DP has been built first. The DP is what the photographs reveal. The DP, as presently established, consists of a primary HF transmitter field, an assemblage of HF antennas, and a host of sophisticated diagnostic equipment. The DP itself was constructed by Power Technologies Incorporated (APTI), managed through E-Systems, and is owned by Raytheon. It is probable that Raytheon has either leased or purchased the land on which the DP now sits. This is their business, not ours. Examination of the photographic evidence is thoroughly disappointing, truly disappointing. The HAARP site is not the monstrous multigabled structure befitting the hysterical claims. It is pitiful assemblage of frail uprights and cross wires, the whole system duplicating obsolescent Marconi HF and VHF arrays.

The first impression reminds the trained eye of a powergrid. A total of 48 towers comprise the DP. Each tower stands 72 feet high. Although the lot on which this fastidious assembly stands covers a 33 acre field, the actual DP site measures some 500 by 800 feet; very roughly 12 acres in area. It is important

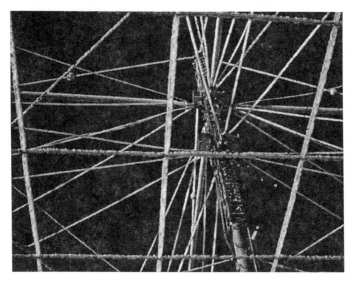

for us to understand that of the 48 towers now standing, only 18 are ever actually energized. Each tower is founded on a 12 by 15 foot rectangular base. These are each spaced 80 feet apart. So much for the physical dimensions. Tesla achieved much more with less space. No part of the otherwise standard equipment appears novel or inspired, save in the vastness and geometrically positioning of the intended IRI collection. Each of the towers support a double crossed dipole. Upper dipole sets operate from 2.8 to 7 Megacycles, lower sets operate from 7 to 10 Megacycles.

Beneath the existing vertical array is a 12 acre copper screen. This singularly curious structure, supposedly a reflective screen, is poised on insulators 15 feet above the ground. The distance of the copper screen "reflector" to the ground permits vehicle access to and from the various shelters of the facility. Prime electric power for the DP is provided by 3 diesel driven generators, each providing 300 Kilowatts. Radio energy for the huge assembly is derived from transmitters housed in separate shelters which have been spread across the 12 acre plot. Only 3 such generating shelters now exist, each shelter containing 6 pairs of 10 Kilowatt transmitters; the total output being 360 Kilowatts HF energy.

Bombastic and ineffectual, it is stated that vertical wave radiation from this array will be phased controlled to produce net circular polarizations at the ionospheric point of contact. Contrary to the many overstatements, neither the DP nor the IRI can focus radiative energy to a tight point in various selected ionospheric strata. The point of focus realistically claimed for the IRI is a "region" which may vary from 18 kilometers to 80 kilometers in diameter. This is hardly a focal "point" at all! Concentrated radio energy from the DP is frequency directed into specified ionospheric strata. There the energy is absorbed in a layer a few hundred meters thick, a process which requires deeper examination. But more fundamental and immediate questions need be asked here. The vertical beam can be skewed and therefore aimed toward various compass headings, a process which diminishes the effective energetic cross-section at the aerial target site.

### THE RING

Why have global cartels actively poured monies into Project HAARP? Why are these financial activities being masked by Industrial, Governmental, and Military bureaucracies? What covert business arrangement guides the efforts in Gakona? How has the stalemate in OPEC Policies and Petroleum Resources compelled the powerful "outsider cartels" toward new destabilizing ventures on the world stage? What is the "merchandise" which HAARP promises to yield? How have auroral anomalies provided certain cartels with a new power alternative? It is obvious that the DP has been deployed in the northlands to achieve a very specific objective. If it were not so, then the present design which we see would never have been given funding.

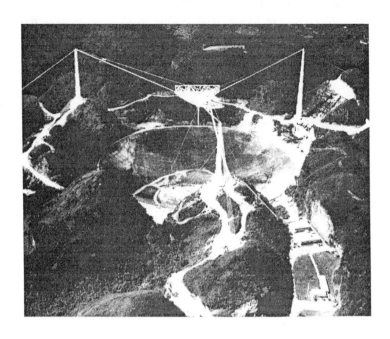

The Arecibo facility in Puerto Rico, a geophysically coupled RADAR telescope, could certainly have been outfitted with more powerful radar transmitters than those of which the DP presently boasts. In such a case, Arecibo would have greatly outperformed the intended IRI on several counts. Operating in the superhigh frequency range, the total amount of deliverable energy to the ionosphere would be immense in comparison with the HF energy of even the planned IRI. The enormous parabolic RADAR mirror at Arecibo, built into a natural basin by the Air Force for Cornell University, could most certainly have focussed more heat on the ionosphere than the IRI can ever hope to produce. The Arecibo facility is an 18 acre reflector already in existence. The planned IRI will cover a 33 acre reflective field. But the waves projected by the IRI will be 30 meters, while those at Arecibo are as small as 0.03 meters. The IRI has to be 1000 times the size of Arecibo in order to equate with its effective EM output! Indeed, if we shrank the intended IRI to an equivalent energy-acreage with Arecibo, the IRI would actually measure one six-hundredth the actual size of Arecibo. This is precisely why the IRI requires the intended 1 Gigawatt of HF energy. Balanced out, this energy performs the same ionospheric work as 1.6 Megawatts RADAR frequency energy. So why the expense and the labor?

There is an all important and revealing difference between the two sites, one which leads directly to our conclusion concerning the HAARP Project. Though intensely more powerful than the IRI will ever be, Arecibo does not have the northern access for which the Gakona site has been specifically based. Why north? Why so lose to the geomagnetic pole? Well, what is the stated value of the Project? In the words of the military releases, the DP "stimulates and controls plasma processes" in the northern auroral zone. This is the most clarified comment made by the military press releases, the very one least favored and most understood by the many popular writers on the subject. Examine the evidence. Why is the DP so close to magnetic north? This is the very heart of the HAARP Project, the High Frequency "Active Auroral" Research Program. Why "active auroral"?

Why build so vast a station beneath the auroral ring current? What does Industry want with the Aurora Borealis? Look at the sheer size of the DP. Why the enormous surface area? What has Industry already proven, and what are they hoping to perfect? The history and development of "aerial batteries", indeed of "earth batteries" as well, is a fascinating and unexpected study. The very first technique used to obtain an energetic flow from the sky to the ground was the very one by which Luigi Galvani first recognized that currents existed in the sky. His elevated copper masts were the very first aerials, the methodic "drawing down" of various energetic currents being attended by a most fascinating series of semi-electrical phenomena. In this regard Dr. Galvani recognized two distinct varieties of current, the one a vitalizing variety; the other, a deadly strain. Before Dr. Franklin ever dreamed of launching forth his famed kite-string-and-key combination, Dr. Galvani had already routinely engaged the several distinct currents with which he was principally fascinated.

Thereafter, the world would seek the mysteries of the skyfire by direct contact: through lightning rods and other highly elevated conductors. Aerial terminals of various kinds were tested throughout the latter Eighteenth and Nineteenth Centuries, a period of intense experimentation with otherwise deadly forces. Lightning Rod patents flood the patent archives, a magnificent display of remarkable designs whose operative success predicated their receiving official license. Each such design had to prove its effectiveness in protecting against the rogue behaviors of lightning discharges. This meant that the designs had to be tested and witnessed. Heavy wooden blocks were the test mounts for these designs, well placed on the tops of rocky crags. A shower of lightning blasts, and the shrapnel of inferior rods were tossed aside. Those capable of withstanding the blast were granted patent.

It was later found in these regards that the presence of electricity was not limited to the upper regions of the atmosphere, certainly not to clouds alone, but to every part of the aerial strata immediately above the ground. Therefore many individuals began discovering that power, tremendous power, could be obtained by the use of several different kinds of "collectors". For this purpose, the inventors of aerial batteries each empirically developed various systems for the methodic accumulation and storage of the "atmospheric current". In none of these patents do we find the inventors referring to these energetic sources as anything but potent. Indeed, each of the designs were fitted with several lightning arresters. These were used, not so much for the storm conditions which would invariably bring in several accidental lightning bolts, but for the fair weather electrical discharges which appeared with equal and repetitive strength.

The "Electric Apparatus" of H. C. Vion (1860) was stated to be a device for obtaining natural electricity for Industrial Applications. His most powerful embodiments were exceedingly long metallic screens, well insulated from the mountain ridges on which they placed. These screen collectors were interspersed by very tall metallic masts, also well insulated, each sharpened and protruding into the mountain air. The system of Vion brought in a prodigious and dangerous supply of usable current. In his words, the system was an electrical "pile of considerable strength". A device perfected by W. H. Ward (1872) took the bizarre form of a very large funnel-like turret. Placed atop a very tall peak, and capable of being turned so as "to drive in an aerial current of electricity". This supply was stored in capacitors and batteries, and used to operate a telegraphic system. M. Dewey (1889) raised a very tall mast, fitted with a large and multi-spiked capacitor hood and drew off sufficient electrical power to run motors and charge storage batteries. Other designs utilized metallic-studded balloons, apparatus capable of bringing in a very powerful surge of current (Palinscar 1901, Pennock 1909).

Experiments with these "passive" designs were gradually moved to very high alpine lands. In addition, it was found that these conditions were most favorably and readily obtained in regions which were as far north as possible. These two requirements, elevation and northern latitude, and the supply of electricity was found to be enormous.

## LEMSTROM

A strange and forgotten series of experiments were conducted in Lapland by Professor Selim Lemstrom as early as 1882. Professor Lemstrom arranged an insulated array of pointed aerials atop a mountain ridge. These were connected with a mile of cable along the mountain ridge. Surging auroral streamers above succeeded in producing corresponding low level auroras, which visibly rose as a white streamer of light. As these covered both the mountain ridge and the geophysically coupled apparatus, the sizzling of millions of electrical watts could be both seen and heard. On December 22, 1882, Dr. Lemstrom succeeded in attracting an auroral streamer, one whose visible corona extended for some 400 feet. This pivotal experiment in deriving vast quantities of electrical energy from the auroral process was the probable inspiration for much of what Nikola Tesla sought in his large scale tests with space energies. Such experiments having been the subject of intense mystery for Tesla, it was his greatest pleasure to write an occasional column for The Electrician Magazine on these wonderful subjects. Tesla consistently shared his fascinations concerning those artificial laboratory simulations of auroral streamers and other such phosphorescent displays, experiments performed in Northern Europe by Bjerknes, Birkeland, Stormer, and others. The Experimental Station of Nikola Tesla in Colorado (1899), is the probable result of applications learned through these exposures.

The vast and critical difference between what Tesla did with the Lemstrom experiment require only appreciation for the fact that Tesla was stimulating a very special light-like non-electric current. The essential difference in approach however was that Tesla applied an active agency in his large elevated capacity terminals. All the pervious experiments were passive systems, limited to a passive process of absorption. Tesla was the very first to stimulate the aerial capacity with an active signal. Despite the fact that his energies were nonelectric, he was the originator of all systems termed "active". Tesla viewed the terrestrial atmosphere as one under continual bombardment by a dense pressure of rarefied ætheric gas, an incoming flood which bombarded the air and rock, manufacturing electrons in the process. As we have seen, his aims were not to generate electricity, but to secure a usable stream of the otherwise elusive æther flow. The aurora was a polar manifestation of the incoming æther, an interaction between æther, manufactured electrons, and the geomagnetic field. In this view, the polar Auroras were special cases of a general principle; by which Tesla believed he could draw in an equivalent streamer anywhere beyond the pole.

Tesla successfully arranged the very same conditions through the use of his high voltage electrostatic impulse system. The active capacity terminal drew in a prolific enough stream of æther to sustain the continuous white fluidic discharges seen in his numerous photographs for long time periods after the initiating power has been withdrawn. These experiments proved the ability of his system to stimulate aurora-like streamers at very much greater distances from the Arctic Circle than normally thought possible. With this apparatus he was incidentally able to produce the flame-like discharges and variable colorful flashes which characterize the auroral streams; a phenomenon successfully reproduced by no experimenters beside Eric Dollard. Although requiring far more activating equipment than that of Dr. Lemstrom, the geophysically coupled demonstration in Colorado Springs made it possible for Tesla to derive continuously powerful aurora-like energies from outer space at any location below the pole. Tesla later reconfigured his apparatus for operational effectiveness in Wardenclyffe, Long Island.

During solar peak emissions, this pole-concentrated circulating ring, the auroral electrojet, represents a current of well over 300,000 Amperes at a charging potential of 200,000 Volts. The potential power of the auroral ring current is thus some 60 Gigawatts! Awe inspiring accounts may be found throughout the literature; those instances when the aurora "descended" and wandered freely just above or even along the ground. The events where such streamers make their way to ground have always evoked the greatest sense of awe and mystery. Eskimaux legends tell that when the auroral streamers walk along the ground, people are taken from the earth. In one such case, a geophysicist saw the aurora playing among poplar tress and flimmering along the ground. He ran out into the display in order to experience the power. He felt nothing, remarking that the whole area around him was sparkling. In this fortunate case, the plasma was neutral. But this is not the only condition in which the aurora can present itself. Auroral surges have historically resulted in groundward lightning strokes, incidents which defy reason and yet persist in the accounts of highly credible witnesses throughout the literature. Reports of " sheet lightning and luminous auroral masses" (1821), "horizontal flash of lightning followed by an aurora" (1888), "spectacular aurora followed by a violent thunderstorm" (1915), "aurora followed by intense lightning...flashes arcing through the zenith...more auroral activity after thunderstorm" (1952).

Indeed, auroral-like discharges are constantly occurring everywhere on earth, but are most prevalent from elevated peaks in the northlands. It has long been known that the ground is a prolific source of electrons, a process which Nikola Tesla studied with greatest interest. In this respect, ground charge reserves vary in time. High ground electron concentrations precede lightning strokes. When ground electron concentrations meet auroral columns, dangerous conditions are produced. The strongly biased ground proliferates a state not unlike lightning, though obviously in a more vast extent. Negative charges flow furtively up the auroral column, eventually reaching the lowest strata of the auroral body. This effectively gives the upward charges a huge capacity into which they may powerfully surge. In such cases auroral lightning has been observed, the activity of which is horrifying and awesome. But these instances are, very fortunately, rare occurrences.

Auroras do touch ground on their own with greater regularity than most imagine. Although this condition is not rare in the natural process, it is rare for human observers of its mystifying dynamics. A great many professional persons of gifted observational skills chanced to experience the rare effects of terrestrial electricity and "close auroral encounters". Mountain climbers in all parts of the world began reporting instances of "mountain bourdonnement", the vibration and ringing resonance of mountain rock bursting with glowing electrical currents (H. de Saussure, 1865). Others observed the explosive emergence of fireballs between mountain peaks, tall spark-like columns projecting out from mineral rich lands, ball lightning of various volumes and colors, and a veritable host of auroral displays which yet defy ordinary explanation (Corliss). A balloonist descended on a European mountain peak, some 1300 meters in height, and saw auroral rays through a thin mist, and heard a "muttering" sound (1870). Several observers told of the electrical sensation produced by a low level flickering aurora (1883). Observers in the polar areas observed arrays of "dancing streamers having prismatic colors...a swishing sound as they moved" (1901).

In New York State an aurora touched down "not thirty rods from us...a curtain of auroral light passing through the valley", the stated height from the ground was some 30 feet (1852). In Northern Ireland, a chemist examined several solutions which had become fluorescent in a darkened laboratory, the auroral storm playing all around the building (1858). On the Yukon River, an astounded witness saw an auroral arch come "right over the water's edge" (1906). A radio engineer in the Northwest Territory told that he, along with several others, saw an auroral curtain come down to within 4 feet of the ground, a pale green curtain through which he actually walked (1925). In Abisco Sweden, an observer reported an auroral streamer which came "below a completely cloudy sky" (1929).

There are so many of these accounts that one is literally forced into realizing that auroral process engages in a consistent ground-touching flow of its fluidic streams. Neither Reichenbach nor Tesla never equated the Aurora Borealis with electricity per se. Each recognized that the Aurora itself was a neutral æther flow, whose interactions with the terrestrial atmosphere produced electrons and positive ions, the result of successive and resistive bombardments. This is why the beautiful colorations could flow and change with every second, impossible to explain in quantitative terms. Varying electrical voltages and currents alone do not explain the sudden color changes supposedly the result of gas activations. Atmospheric gases are in an absolute state of admixture, and cannot so easily be isolated and activated by such influences to produce the magnificent and multicolored displays, that which the ancients perceived to be the beautiful responses of a quasi-living entity.

## POWERPOINT

Dr. Lemstrom showed the possibility of drawing auroral energy down through passive systems. His apparatus did not produce consistent available outputs of the energy, a frustrating attribute. Dr. Tesla showed the active means by which energies which produce the auroras could be drawn from outer space at lower-than-polar latitudes. These effects have not been duplicated. However, there have been strange effects produced by shortwave transmitters which have accidentally stimulated certain auroral dynamics, effects which produced anomalous radio echoes and other such "energy storage" phenomena within the auroral envelope. Several noteworthy observers noted the "long-delay echoes" produced when north latitude shortwave transmitters were keyed. In this phenomenon, signals which were being sent out, each "returned" to their transmit site after several seconds of time. These delays could not be rationalized by those models which modelled the ionosphere as a variable altitude series of fixed shells. Three dots were sent out, the time between echoes counted. Echoes exceeding 12 seconds were repeatedly demonstrated, a path of 12 light-seconds (Hals, Stormer, van der Pol, 1928).

The echoes were always strong, clear, and coherent. Considering the speed of radiowave propagation, these shortwave echoes required that signals were being launched along tremendous arcs through interplanetary space. A signal path of 12 light-seconds is a path exceeding 84 earth circumferences. The distances represented here are truly astronomical, requiring a reflective layer averaging some 6 times further away than the moon! But there were complications to the notion that this was a fixed reflective shell which the signals had managed to reach. The successive testing of the LDE (Long Delay Echo) effect did not produce clock-consistent results. Echoes returned at varied intervals, always longer than 3 seconds, but not always of the same interval. These experiments were conducted with some consistency within a small period of time, so it is unlikely that the "shell" notion would represent a viable model. No reflective shell could vary its concentrated density that much to produce such echo-variations.

Where did these signals go, and how did they return with such strength, clarity, and coherence? Were they somehow "stored" within the geomagnetic field, launched along such a line and stored in an interplanetary plasma? An auroral plasma? Each instance of the effect required a north polar proximity, locations which placed the transmitters in that zone where geomagnetic field lines emerge from the ground and depart toward deeper space. Such is not the case at lower latitudes, where the geomagnetic field lines are nearly parallel with respect to the ground surface. Extraordinary radiowave signals launched from an equatorial city might take a circumferential orbit, requiring perhaps one or two tenths of a second to "echo-return". But the phenomenon of signal storage is an important one to the devising of modern means for an experimental derivation of auroral energy.

There have been accidental instances in which applied radio "pumping action" has actively influenced the aurora itself. The action begins when a high latitude radio station of very moderate power is broadcasting during an auroral condition. Each alternation from the station carrier exerts a strong deforming action on the aurora. Passing overhead like a band across the sky, these deformations produce a "bunching action" in the auroral body, not unlike that action which occurs in Klystron Tubes (see CHAPTER 5). VLF stations often displayed peculiar amplifying phenomena, where applied signals were mysteriously strengthened by an unknown energetic source. These amplifications always occurred when VLF transmissions were "immersed" in auroral activity, the obvious effects of solar-derived pressures. VLF modulation is regularly exercised between poles, where VLF signals at Siple Station, Antarctica creates audio disturbances at Roberval, Quebec (Brett).

Transmitter impacts are stored in this plasma, the successions reappearing over the transmitter sites within a given period of time. The auroral clustres maintain their relative disposition as they pass overhead. Signals thus directed to the auroral ring current, are stored there as charge clustres. The auroral electrojet is a hypersonic plasma body which travels around the pole with regularity. These successive returns over the station offer an opportunity for energy absorption. These deformations will grow with continued carrier pumping action. Each deformation is stored in the auroral electrojet. As this rapidly advancing auroral plasma streams repeatedly over the station, successive previous deformations reappear. These deformations can be distorted to the point that the auroral streamers can actually and forcibly be drawn down to the transmitter. The literal "drawing down" of the aurora requires a repetitive application of force with the overhead appearance of each previous deformation, each previous clustre. When sufficient deformations are applied with periodicity, auroral streamers can touch ground. It is at this point that usable power may be drawn from the aurora.

## MODULATOR

Once a significant deformation in the auroral electrojet has been stimulated, the very pressure of the solar wind exaggerates the deformation. The clustre is pushed down to a lower altitude. If a significant succession of these is applied to the auroral ring current, then energetic streaming toward the ground will continue. Absorbing incoming energy, absorbing incoming momentum from the solar wind, these travelling waves feel an enormous pressure which drives them groundward. If each radio pulse draws the electrojet down in successions, and if the "pull" frequency is timed just right, then the auroral current will begin flowing groundward. In their rapid orbit about the geomagnetic pole, the deformations fall into a literal tornadic stream toward the transmitter. This amplification effect continues until "contact" is made between the auroral stream and the transmitter site. Once contact is made, once charges begin streaming down from the auroral ring current, the transmitter site becomes recipient of an avalanche phenomenon which grows in magnitude beyond imaginable bounds. This dynamic MHD phenomenon is one in which applied wave radio forces are stored as charge clustres in a fluidic stream until a steady leakage has been achieved. The solar wind then "blows through" this leakage zone, providing an endless and incalculable current.

Early wireless operators and shortwave aficionadi had long observed the "fading" and "swinging" of strong radio signals because of undetermined natural variables. In certain strange cases of signal "swinging" or fading, stations were modulated by other, much smaller transmitters. Later investigation proved that these stations were conjugately aligned near the Arctic Circle. These furtive activities have been well documented in old radio journals. It was believed that the phenomenon could be used for the derivation of enormous energies directly from the auroral electrojet. Sounds impossible?

This very effect has been responsible for the several radio modulation phenomena which are completely reliant on the fluidic auroral ring current for their effect. The effect occurs in the northern latitudes. Because of auroral "immersion", small radio stations have accidentally modulated the transmissions of much larger stations at great distances. Widely spaced along the same latitude lines, completely opposite in power output, and widely divergent in operating frequencies, two such transmitters will appear to have "superimposed" their signals. What has occurred is a simple result of force application from the weak transmitter, to a mobile auroral fluid which contains the signals of the much larger transmitter. The smaller transmitter, usually never heard beyond a few miles distance, exercises a "valving action" on the auroral fluid. As a result, one hears the stronger signals with the weaker transmitter signal superimposed.

These amplifications can begin as nearly insignificant signals. Substantially immersed in the effect of an auroral current, an insignificant current can grow to very large and very influential proportions. The stimulating signal does not have to be strong at all in order to attract an auroral streamer to the ground. The modulations of powerful radio signals by small near-polar transmitters revealed the aurora as a dynamic energy amplifying stratum. An incredible incident occurred in Norwood, Ontario during the winter of 1929. The operation of a large radio receiver was suddenly and abruptly brought to a halt. Though the tubes were bright, the aerial sure, and the ground secure, reception very suddenly "went dead". The gentleman went to a window in order to inspect his aerial, when he noticed that a bright aurora was in progress. Going outside to observe the aurora, he was shocked to find that an auroral streamer had completely surrounded his house, though maintaining a distance of several feet. It became a veritable curtain of streamers, many colors being simultaneously visible. The curtain appeared unsteady, its scintillating appearance continually "snapping". In a visible display of enormous significance, the curtain was continually and visibly sparking to ground. Here was the source of his radio "disturbance". The receiving oscillator, weak and insignificant, had successfully drawn an auroral streamer down to ground (Corliss).

To engineers and analysts, the DP is a straightforward application of commonly understood radio principles. It is a massive HF array, an immense 33 acre field of separate vertical towers. How these applications have been combined to form a distinct technology is not well perceived or suspected by engineers. Until the several noteworthy accidents which occurred in radio stations throughout the early part of the century, confidence that the aurora itself could be accessed as a very realistic natural energy source was viewed as insanity itself. Throughout the time span between World War II and the Cold War years, powerful back EMF effects were noted in certain near-polar radio stations when auroras soared overhead. The notion of tapping this natural immensity as a reservoir gradually developed in the minds of inspired engineers. The enormous current represented in the auroral ring may be drawn down from its seemingly fixed aerial throne. To bring down...Valhalla.

## VALHALLA

The conclusions lead us to consider the strong possibility that the DP is being used to test the possible modulation of the auroral ring for purposes altogether different than stated. The DP may not be a device whose modulating effects on the aurora are for signalling at all, but for the derivation of power. In the absence of all other evidence, and in the balancing of all which has been deduced, one is compelled to consider the thought that the DP is a an experimental device designed to draw power from the aurora directly. If this is really so, then HAARP has been designed to assess the potentials of a new energy generating technology; and has done so on behalf of a corporate megalith. We are compelled to consider the various social and technical directions of its commercial implementation. The notion of the DP represents a new venture frontier in energy technology, of which Raytheon may hold but the smallest thread. All of the other possible reasons for HAARP have largely been eliminated. Advanced Power Technologies is the subsidiary assigned to the HAARP Project. The entire bureaucratic array is completely dominated by Industry, one of the largest defense contractors in the nation.

The routine modulation of the auroral ring could become the energy future of the northern hemisphere. But what are the necessary theoretical overviews which can enable an understanding of such a completely surprising notion? There are several techniques which employ different electrodynamic force symmetries to achieve deformation and groundward conductive flow in the auroral ring. The aim of each such technology is to "draw down the fire". Each depends upon the fact that the sun supplies an enormous plasma flow. Once this flow enters the northern polar region, geomagnetism separates the plasma flow into two opposed current flows of opposite charge. Electrons and protons flow in opposite directions, the electrons moving with far greater mobility and being the significant charge carriers. Static electrical field applications from the ground cannot influence this plasma because dielectric field lines diverge before they reach the requisite spaces. This explains the inconsistent operation of "passive" auroral attractors.

The most efficient use of this applied field energy requires that the site be based near the Arctic Circle. In this technique, the actual applied radiowave energy need not be very great at all. Timing is the secret. Pulsation rhythms provide the critical factor. Geophysicists have made extensive surveys of resonant responses in the auroral ring. These resonances represent a continuum which begin in the ULF range, extending well into the Radar Bands. We have reviewed the mechanism whereby consecutive applications of radioelectric influence produce significant deformations of the auroral ring charges. It is a process which relies on the permanence of auroral deformation, and the quasi-cohesive rotation of the auroral ring around the pole. Deformations have a ponderance, a permanence which maintains shape in travel within the whole ring current. Cyclic appearances of these deformations over a station site can be resonantly timed to amplify each previous deformation.

Successions of ever increasing deformations produce cyclonic spiralling of auroral charges toward ground sites. Auroral columns of charge begin reaching the station within a specified time. This flow of charge must be appropriated in proper absorbers. In order to appropriate auroral energy, one needs a VERY LARGE absorption area. Preparation for this flowing charge requires a substantially large metallic terminal. The absorber is one which necessarily is possessed of a very large area. It must be made of very heavy and highly conductive gridwork. The DP is equipped with just such a grid. It is a crosshatched gridding of very heavy gauge copper cable, perhaps one inch in thickness. The gridwork appears to have been wired and welded together.

The various means for achieving this kind of condition differ only in the electrical field symmetries which are applied to the auroral ring. Each experimental ground transmitter be designed to test these radiowave varieties. One scheme employs simple vertically oriented radio pumping action. This ground based influence exerts a pulling action upon the ring, a stimulation which pulls down on the ring current as it surges over the station. These powerful "tugs" are strong enough to produce downward movements in the ring current. Once the conductive path has been established, the vast flowing power of the auroral stream can be used.

In another variation of this method, asymmetrical pulsations are applied to a tall antenna of large capacity. The results of this method exceed those obtained with high frequency alternating energies. Although better designs can be developed, a simple field of antennas will serve well in developing the experimental functions. Only the size of the absorptive terminal, into which the auroral stream is made to flow, will limit or liberate the amount of available energy from the auroral ring current. This technology utilizes a wide variety of technologies which we have already discussed. In its action on the auroral ring, the DP functions like a valve, the auroral ring current as a Klystron current of enormous volume. The absorptive screen is the passive component, resembling the passive capacities of Galvani, Vion, Ward, Dewey, and Lemstrom. In its active components, the DP seeks to mimic impulse technology.

A distinct variety of resonant technique is being developed in Gakona. The

DP is designed to induce rhythmic HF pulsations of circular polarization in the Auroral Electrojet. The DP applies this energy as a focussed beam. The large receiving area spreads out the incoming power. The secondary function of the vast insulated copper screen is to act as absorber. Downflowing electrical energy is safely absorbed in this highly conductive screen. The DP utilizes a circularly polarized beam, the result of whole array phase shifting. Cross dipoles conduct HF radio energy with a phase difference of 180 degrees. The resultant radiant field rotates like a screw into the auroral plasma. This energy is focussed by a superimposed system of phasing which bends the outermost beams toward a central point. If the rotations are timed properly then swirling energy reaches the auroral ring, bunching electrons. The method produces long travelling waves of charge so immense it staggers the imagination. In the DP, auroral charge bunching is consistently concentrated and deformed toward the ground site. Timed pulsations in the station maintain the resonant pulling on these successive bunches, which soar overhead in a steady supply. All of these schemes seek duplication of the Teslian ætheric methods, a task for which neither academes, military managers, nor engineer-designers are equipped to achieve. These endeavors do not engage the æther, neither can they do so. These designs engage the by-products of æther, the high aerial strata of electrons and ions which ætheric bombardments manufacture, otherwise known as "the ionosphere".

Once this energetic ion flow has been secured, the auroral streamer can be modulated to the need of any load. There is moderation, control over this groundward ion stream. Such pulsating power under control may be rectified and used. In fact, such power can be sold. Sixty Gigawatts of natural, non-polluting energy at no cost for those who own the system. And this could be tapped from a single large terminal base. Several such stations would vastly amplify the amount of induction energy. Pulsations of power derived directly from the aurora. If it were possible to handle such an output of energy, whole regions could be supplied with electricity for centuries. But who would outline such a proposal? Who would benefit from such a venture? The Military itself? No. The Military takes orders from its rulers. Once the initial phases of such an experiential station have been assessed, then proper parameters can establish a first model commercial station.

## IMPACT

For the informed, the DP is a convoluted admixture of several much older technologies. It may be strongly suggested, on logic alone, then that the DP is serving none of the functions which have been demonstrated in the past. Because all the prior uses of such an array had already been established through historical progression, we are all too easily compelled to and eliminate those possibilities on the very basis of that progression. But the pursuit of truth may not be one which can be based on the movements which we consider "progressive" or "reasonable". Technology, of the kind which we see in Gakona, is not always subject to the natural dictates of true progress. Technology of this kind is subject to the whims and fancies of a superior directive, whose supply of capital literally decides the progressive line. The natural progress and funded progressions do not always coincide. In fact, they oftentimes clash in oppositions which defy our natural sense of reason and of progress. In truth then HAARP, and projects like HAARP, serve best as focal points on which we may test both our thought process and our world-models.

In assessing the DP, we have coordinated several resources abilities. Among these we count a fundamental knowledge of radio principles, access to an extensive bibliography, and an unerring logical guidance. In our lengthy analysis we have considered the great many possible functions of the DP, and have by that study, determined what the experiment cannot be. But all of our considerations have presupposed the fact that military is operating by processes of advancement. By processes of logic. But here may be our very source of error! It may be, in the very furthest stretch of our imagination, that military has actually been directed to pursue a regressive progress; degenerating to a more primitive state of technical utility. If this is so, then its cause can find no reasonable source except in the superior dictates of an socio-interruptive agency. A geopolitical agency. The interruptive and frustrating manipulations of geopolitical rulership are not unknown in social history. In this bleak scenario we may comprehend some of the absolute technological reversals taken throughout our Century; steps which have witnessed the eradication of revolutionary energy technology, and the substitution of the same with inferior technology.

Were the DP experiments directed toward development of newer trans-ionospheric beaming systems, designs which possibly launch signals along vast geomagnetic loops, then we will find our logical process completely defeated.

This extreme possibility represents the absolute reversal of reasonable thematic progression. If this is indeed the reality behind HAARP, then none of its stated functions have any connective relationship with things believed to be reasonable. But such a deflating, depressing, and utterly disappointing theme, a negative progression, defies the newest evidence. Those patent documents which have recently been uncovered support the positive theme. The overwhelming evidence that technological advancement is, yet very much the thematic direction of technology, strongly supported by the shocking evidences recently found in the Patent Archives. These evidences, official patent documents, prove that a newer technology is available for the achievements of unheard military objectives. It is in the consideration of each of these patents that we will find the thematic progression of technology very much intact, a progression which has powerful repercussions in every other related discussion.

Geopolitical issues become more complicated as efforts to achieve domination of world resources intensify. In the regime of weapons proliferation between warring oligarchies, both the United States and the Soviet Union were driven to the point of economic failure. Amid the proliferation of high-tech weapons systems and erudite scientific research, an obsolescent commodity was insidiously elevated above the limits of reason. Petroleum became the focus of world capital and capital transactions. Petroleum is the accessible power, the practical resource which has fueled the engines of oligarchic labor. Having far fewer requirements than uranium reactors, having far less hazardous aftereffects than nuclear means, oil has been the very blood pumping in the oligarchic heart. The supposed new order is really a defined and very obvious recapitulation of a former Old World Order, one whose themes demand a complete return to simplistic technological methods. It is here that we discover the reversals of otherwise natural progress in dictated directions, the source of a prolonged obsolescent world state. But these directives do not exist in a vacuum. Indeed there are other Houses, and Houses war against one another.

The revenues reaped through the total domination of any utility are not the empowering influence behind oligarchic ascents. It is the control of utilities which brings elevations. When once the world utility market has been made completely subservient to and dependent upon a fueling source, any House which holds that source will ascend. The revenues are secondary and even tertiary considerations to those for whom control is the central theme. The various reversals in thematic direction, throughout the last one hundred technological years, have represented those instances in which the geopolitical influence interrupted natural progress. Progress and social improvement through technology, working class themes of reason and logic, does not exist for those who wish control and mastery of world conditions. Any system judged to have potential for the greatest proportion of supply and demand, a system which offers highest control potentials, will be aggressively sought by Oligarchies; and sought, regardless of thematic working class notions of progress. In the minds of oligarchs, progress is a condition which their manipulations establish. For these personages progress is an ephemeral, an expendable and arbitrary fluctuation in a world state which they repeatedly demonstrate ability in producing.

This is why we have seen the complete reversal, from futuristic nuclear industries to obsolescent oil industries, in the very years when nuclear perspectives were being espoused with greatest social force. Oligarchs assessed each emerging technology against a central theme of control. POWER IS HAD IN THE CONTROL OF THINGS MADE NECESSARY. When once it was realized that technology ran on fuels, then oligarchs strove to own and ration that fuel. The control was the means through which power came, not the money earned. If a system required a rationed fuel, that system became the "universal" proliferation, the addiction by which working class society was enslaved. Whenever new technologies emerged, having no dependence on rationed supply, that technology was destroyed.

Fuel and energy themes have historically proven themselves to be the central focus of necessity, the lever in the hand of the powerful. In this latter part of the Twentieth Century, petroleum has been the fuel on which technology has been made dependent. Ownership of oil is control only because of the cup which one wields to mete it out. The price of oil is insignificant. It is the cup which holds the control. Fuel and Energy drive the relentless wheels of Industry, and maintain the precious Control. Energy is the demand, oil the rationed supply. Energy is the single valuable commodity. And of all energy supply, the rationed supply of oil is the power. How fitting, that rock sludge should be the earthly claim to power! But petroleum does not exist for its own sake.

One observes the fact that 65 percent of the world petroleum supply finds itself focussed in Saudi Arabia, a remarkable statistic. The common misconception is that the Arabian Peninsula contains an exclusive excess of petroleum; a supply otherwise unsurpassed in the world. But this preponderance of supply is based solely on the geopolitical exploitation of this region. Indeed there are reserves throughout the territories of the world which dwarf those of the Arabian Peninsula, a fact which appears all the more strange when one considers the sheer richness of oil reserves in several other locales. What made this region more attractive to oligarchic development had much to do with the original inaccessible nature of the locale. When first engineered to produce its supply, certain highly attractive features brought the investments of a single House at the turn of the century. Inaccessible, isolated, easily acquired, and geopolitically unchallenged. This fact alone became all too evident during the First World War, when a cluster of national alignments revealed the significant Houses originally desirous of controlling the region. To this day, the Arabian Peninsula commands the attentions of a major House. Perhaps it is before the dictates of this world dominating House that all Houses have too long done obeisance. But from where is the perceived power of petroleum derived?

Petroleum is not valuable for the wealth which it brings. Petroleum is valuable for the control which it brings. This required a complete world proliferation of fuel-dependent technology, a feat accomplished throughout the early Twentieth Century by several originally competing Houses. For petroleum to acquire a control potential, one requires a utility which relies on petroleum. In the latter part of the Twentieth Century, petroleum was coupled to the generation of electrical power. Thomas Edison was used to achieve this control factor. The social dependence on utility is a need which has been addicted to electricity. The need of those who wish electric light is now withheld by those who hold the oil. It is thus that the power of cruel mastery is transformed into need. Earthly power moves through phases, from willful intent to electric light. Earthly power now flows back from the needy to the cruel. It is a 60 cycle rhythm by which the subservient draw light from cruel masters, while cruel masters draw life from the subservient. An alternating current.

## OUTSIDE

Oil has not become the cause of worldwide oligarchic elevations. This is obvious when observing the world geopolitical condition. Those who go to war for oil, are not those who delegate its rations. In this, many Houses serve but one. Observe that oil sources are not universally available to all geopolitical Houses in equal measure. Several Houses have the technological engineworks, but only one House has the fuel to drive those engines. The total domination of oil sources and oil refineries has been the result of a single House rule. Oil is obviously not the power base of the NAO (North American Oligarchy). Abundant proof of this is found in the opened forum which the media has granted. Displaying every oil-acquiring military operation, we have recently witnessed countless occupations of underdeveloped oil-rich territories by the local House Rule.

Imagine a geopolitical scenario in which the total domination of petroleum resources by a single Oligarchic House has grown so uncontrollable that its power now holds every other existing House captive. Now suppose that the other oligarchies have realized a means for destabilizing their common foe. The flow of logic may be something like this: Oil does not exist in a socio-technological vacuum. There is a reciprocal agency which weakens the power of controlling oil. Because its worth is so bound up in the electrical generating technologies, the control-value of oil is now dependent on the continued existence of those very technologies. Here is a variable which has devastating importance for those Oligarchs empowered to use the option. Since the electrical technologies are worldwide systems, a takeover of their supply of current would amount to a world power shift. Electrical technologies can be "fueled" by alternative means besides oil, the problem is to establish a system large enough and powerful enough to achieve the change. Replacing the obsolescent fuel with another supply would represent a world power shift of enormous significance.

Recall what geopolitical region first developed the nuclear reactor technology. The hope of controllable, limitless electrical supply was championed in North America, Great Britain, and Canada. The revolution seemed to spell defeat for that House left with major world control of petroleum. Despite each movement toward a petroleum-free technology in this geopolitical zone, there has tenaciously followed an insistent demand that oil be the only supply. It is not therefore strange to understand the quest for controlled fusion in the same two national clustres. The ZETA Project, ASTRON, STELLARATOR, and the DCX began a desperate search for a controllable nuclear fusion source. In

1966, this goal was indeed fulfilled in the hands of Dr. Philo Farnsworth. His methodic and systematic development of an electrostatic containment system, the patented FUSOR machine, successfully produced a self-sustained thermonuclear fusion reaction, and a consequent electrical output of enormous value. These effects were witnessed by credible professionals. The subsequent suppression of this major work, couple with the elimination of the truly great Dr. Farnsworth was the direct result of a superior directive which used ITT as its bureaucratic agent of eradication.

In the past, patent examiners were directed by privateers to screen all energy devices. The motive during that purge was the maintenance of strict control, the method was elimination. The continual rejection of energy devices forced the nation to become addicted to a continual supply of inferior technologies. Simultaneous to this action was the proliferation of fuel-dependent technologies. Addiction to the supply of the supplier provided the greatest power making ploy of the millennium. Oligarchies fell behind the shadow of one House, whose dominating ambitions ruled the other rulers. Suppose that the powerful enemies of this dominating House have recognized the essential weakness in petroleum as a fuelstuff. Perhaps the eradication of revolutionary energy technologies is no longer profitable or now capable of supplying geopolitical power. Have the combined efforts of several Houses found a new energy venture which will dethrone oil and supply them with untold earthly power? But why the DP, so large and seemingly obsolescent? In comparison with the more refined energy devices of the suppressed technologies, the DP seems so unnecessarily huge; almost like a Marconi Station.

For energy devices to have geopolitical utility, the heart of control and regulation must be established. Power generating installations must be large, costly, distant, and inaccessible. They must involve systemologies which can easily be represented as impossible to reproduce without the sheer size. Propaganda through education then blocks those who would seek to miniaturize the system, a gradually less likely possibility with time. The secrets of such a science need not be too erudite, just physically unfeasible and inaccessible. Technological creation of new markets has not always being pursued by world major oligarchies. Stability and status quo has been the theme of all investors for nearly a centuries. Investments are made and secured. They are not tested in the fields of venture. But technology is the "wild card". Technology destabilizes the status quo. Irrepressible technological progress has not been permitted to fulfill its expression in the world. Those who demanded a halt to progress managed to silence the wonder for a time. Now however, a situation has now presented itself where even the oligarchies have demanded a world revolution in technology.

The dissolution of the obsolescent need by a new system can replace the petroleum ration along with the agency which supplies that ration in a single technological leap forward. This spells defeat for the dominating supplier, as all the threatened oligarchies may have already banded together to develop a new and superior substitute. This explains why the DP has had so much cooperation among the several bureaucratic agencies of Industry, Military, and Academia. If this model proves correct, we can expect major announcements on the successive breakthroughs of the DP soon. Those who direct the development of devices such as the IRI, if indeed our assumptions prove correct, will reap and divide the acquired power of that dominating House. If the IRI is an attempt to drive technology backward, then this redirected relapse in progressive technological sequence will defy the very existence of the new weapons and communications technologies which have filled the Patent Archives. Indeed these recently retrieved technologies, which cover the Cold War Years until SDI, would then stand as yet more monumental witnesses, documents proclaiming the existence of superior and insidious directives.

Are petroleum markets being driven toward an ultimate destiny, one which conforms with plans to eliminate it as the principle world fuel? Contrary to public belief, there is adequate motivation for the destruction of the petroleum trade among those who have been kept on the periphery of this powerful arena. Petroleum outsiders seek new ventures now. To successfully dethrone the petroleum insiders would be a decisive strike against the principal House which rules that market. Such a maneuver would require an incredible revolution in energy production. The utter rage of petroleum outsiders has perhaps mobilized a singular effort which we now may be seeing in its initial experimental phases. An alternative to oil may have thus been found in the IRI. Not one of the outsider Houses would refuse to support such a petroleum-destabilizing venture now, a strong inducement to empower such an energy utility. Requiring the sheer size and access which only a monopoly can own and operate, the IRI venture may be offering these House rulers a perfect opportunity to achieve this very thing.

# CHAPTER 8
## Orbital Reconnaissance and Radiation Technology

### VISIONARIES

The opening decades of the Twentieth Century were years yet carried by the visionary winds of a previous new awakening. Accompanied by forty years of the most intense auroral demonstrations ever observed in this millennium, the "Victorian" storm first penetrated the social mind with new and thrilling advancements in consciousness. The subsequent effects of this new awareness took the form of extraordinary and unexpected developments in technology. Primarily transacted as a new awareness of visionary potentials, working class persons found themselves receiving imagery and means for achieving their dreams. Representing an eidetic upheaval of long forgotten archane power, visionary writers and experimenters suddenly provided new future dreamlines; into which society could and would move. Those who have no power might at least have vision. Recall that technology, especially technology of a biodynamic nature, represents a conundrum to the rulership.

Technology of the kind to which we refer, has great power. It is not easily eliminated. It generates power at a working class level. Primary technological discovery cannot be "poised" within the superstructure by bureaucrats, regulated by decree, or employed by aristocrats. The conundrum which this kind of technology poses to the whole pyramidal gantry disturbs the structure, bringing the geopolitical structure and all of its synthetic authorities into proper proportion and poise within the natural hierarchy. To see the weak points in rulership and in the bureaucratic superstructure is to know exactly where to direct specific kinds of technological conundrums. Recall that the flow of power which best serves civilization is that which flows from the base to the point.

Jules Verne wrote extensively on the topic of space travel, his great adventure tales fulfilling part of the powerful Victorian tide which was then sweeping the world of the Northern Hemisphere. "From The Earth To The Moon" (1865), and "Around The Moon" (1870)) each stimulated such a degree of excitement, that experimenters everywhere immediately began seeking means for imitating the space travel theme. In 1869, E. E. Hale described an artificial moon which could be used as a manned military base, a story entitled "The Brick Moon" which appeared in Atlantic Monthly. The idea was taken with the seriousness usually ascribed to dreamers and their dreams. But the imagery of space and space travel was so strong, so compelling, that a great number of practical researchers began seeking the means to accomplish the objective.

Hermann Ganswindt (1891) lectured in Berlin on rocket-propelled vessels for interplanetary travel.

Konstantin Ziolkovsky wrote a great number of aeronautical works which included "The Theory of Dirigibles" (1885), a 480 page tome containing over 800 formulas and descriptions of lighter than air craft. This was followed by "The Possibility of Constructing A Metal Dirigible" (1890), and "Maneuverable Dirigibles" (1892). Turning his mind toward greater heights, Ziolkovsky wrote the first technical treatises on space travel. "Dreams About Earth and Skies", "On The Moon", and "Gravitation As a Source of Cosmic Energy", were all written in 1894. These were followed by his classic "Investigation of Cosmic Reactive Machines" (1898), which engages a detailed description of propellants such as liquid oxygen and liquid hydrogen. In these works, Ziolkovsky also discussed the problems of life support in long space journeys, offering possible solutions in closed reservoir systems. In each of these engineering areas, Ziolkovsky opened the realistic engineering dialogues which yet remain the foundation of rocketry and life support as we know it. His wonderful model crafts illustrate the use of external sensors and signal lights, as well as the detailed design of both cabin and engine structures. This he achieved with neither the benefit of formal education nor the much needed funding which would have taken his theoretics into the realm of physical reality. Besides later having suffered the loss of his small basement workshop by fire, Ziolkovsky the pure researcher, was beset by many personal handicaps and frustrating resistances. Completely deaf, often hungry and ill, deprived of personal necessities, and never encouraged or supported by colleagues, he remained enthralled by transcendent realms of vision and revelation until death; the resolution of genius to limitations whenever encountered.

Victorian science-based fantasy stories written by H. G. Wells ("War of The Worlds and "First Men In The Moon", 1898 and 1901 respectively) and sagas written Edgar Rice Burroughs ("The Princess Of Mars", 1917) voiced the strong mythical themes associated with space travel and the discovery of alien civilizations of the day. Fueled with these themes of wonder, society began seeking the means for achieving the dreams. This preoccupation suddenly reemerged as an engineering proposal. In 1913 Rene Lorin patented a ramjet powerplant. The next major work on space travel was a technical description "On A Means For Reaching High Altitudes", published in the Smithsonian by Robert H. Goddard (1920). Professor Hermann Oberth (1922) wrote a thesis dealing with chemical rockets and their potential use as engines for travelling into interplanetary space. In his "Die Rakete zu den Planetenraumen" ("The Rocket Into Interplanetary Space") Professor Oberth wrote of multi-staged "step-rockets", instrument-carrying probes, orbital manned stations, and interplanetary vessels for carrying research crews. His wonderful and visionary descriptions told of permanent space stations, manned space satellites. Serviced by a continual stream of shuttle rockets, whose regular visits would bring supplies and fresh space crew members, such a manned station would be but one step closer to achieving a lunar landing.

Dr. Oberth advanced the notion that a trip to the moon could be well achieved by the establishment of successive high orbital and interorbital manned stations. Short shuttle jumps between each station, journeys well supplied and sufficiently prepared, could bridge the relatively long distance to the moon with ease. Dr. Walter Hohmann published "The Attainment of the Celestial Bodies" (1925), a discussion of interplanetary vehicles and interplanetary ventures. He detailed the engineering calculations required in fueling proposed ventures from Earth to Venus. He provided remarkable instructions on life support systems and materials required for such journeys. Dr. Hohmann devoted much of his writings to a consideration of various orbits, their characteristics, and the probable best selection of interplanetary pathways. All of these technically oriented books provided an inestimable stimulus to designers and engineers. Dr. Goddard began designing and testing small chemical rocket engines in 1926. These first launches rarely achieved altitudes exceeding the height of rooftops, but did serve as validation of the essential notion concerning liquid fuel propellants and valved rocket engines. Working afterhours in his self-funded machine shop, his later designs would form the basis of all future rocket technologies.

The German Society for Space Travel (1927) was comprised of engineering students whose passion for space travel reached heights far greater than their actual achievements. Building their own rockets from private funds, launching these, and following each launch with wonderful picnics of wine, women and song, formed the heart of these largely visionary journeys. Nevertheless, there were a few member for whom the desire to reach for space was much more than a personal afterhours hobby, a pursuit of dreams with only picnics and dancing as their reward. Friedrich Stamer piloted the first German-made rocketplane to 4000 feet in 70 seconds (1928). Dr. Oberth published his "Means for Space Travel" (1929), and Hermann Noordung described artificial satellite and space station designs (1929).

By now, the challenge to create bigger and better rockets became a decision which a few now demanded. The perfection of this craft was their goal, a serious step into professional rocket engineering. Indeed these demands became realities, with greater precision in designs. More thrilling results were the outcome of this pursuit of excellence. The craft of rocket making was rapidly losing its visionary lure, and becoming an engineering theme. This lunge forward marked a defined line between those who wished the preservation of a hobby, from those who wished the development of an engineering profession. Some members of the German Rocket Society who wished more serious outcomes began seeking more serious funding. This small group of engineers, whose passion for space travel reached wonderful experimental perfections, decided to approach various governmental agencies. Seeking funds through patents and royalties, the notion of utilizing rocketry in the delivery of mail was proposed; a system which worked, but found no utility at the time.

But these wonderful dreams also stimulated some toward the use of rocketry in the art of devastations. Next in line of governmental contacts was the military, a very obvious application of their rocket technology in national defense. German military officers, who early discerned the use of rocket systems in weapons delivery application, were surprised to discover that the Berlin Rocket Club had advanced to such a degree on personal funding alone. Receiving an enthused reception, the military hierarchy ultimately rejected the rocket system in favor of large and more dependable field artillery. This original introduction of their research work, an endeavor with visionary objectives, was a contact with peacetime military leaders; a contact which later proved disastrous when the totalitarian Nazi rule had rooted itself in the nation. Those same military figures who now feared the ravings of Adolph Hitler, sought to fulfill his demands for "vengeance weapons". Recalling every strange and curious system developed in the previous decade by arduous experimenters, these officers began reaching into the civilian population to find those weapons. In 1929, the German Army became more than interested in the rocket developments of the Rocket Club, but considered having the more serious work more fully developed through established Industrial groups. This consideration soon lost its appeal, when the high security risk of such an Industrial undertaking was realized.

Nazi forces recruited members of the Rocket Club, conscripting their service toward those vengeful objectives. In this single sweep of the rich German community of experimenters, the world was acquainted with yet a new source of fear and woes. In 1931 their Office of Weapons Development organized a private research group, largely taken from members of the little Club whose merits were well approved. Friedrich Schmiedl, an Austrian, conducted commercial rocket mail shots between 1931 and March 1933, when his work was unexpectedly destroyed. By 1935, the American Dr. Goddard regularly launched rockets which attained altitudes of 7500 feet. In the very same year, Russian rockets reached an unparalleled 6 miles, a truly amazing technical demonstration. Each of these developments were viewed by the Nazi regime as dangerous foreign military potentials requiring ready answer.

Then Captain Walter R. Dornberger (later General), Wernher von Braun and Heinrich Grunow formed the core of this rocket research team. Somewhere in all the threats, the screaming, the pressures, the fear, these visionaries were coerced into perverting their work for the now "inevitable" war. By 1939, the Peenemunde Research Institute was designing, building, and launching tactical weapons. Rockets, originally known by the engineers as the A-4 and the A-5, later became weapons of mass destruction. How easy it was to press the launch trigger and forget the fate of those whose lives lingered under the Damocles Sword of the V-2. The early V-2 designs dwarfed all the previous records set by rocket research teams around the Northern World. Each successful V-2 launch reached as much as 118 miles (1942). Having devastating consequences for their English neighbors, ramjet powered V-1 cruise missiles, and V-2 ballistic missiles, brought down a rain of death.

For those living in London and Antwerp, a demonstration of rocket power in military hands removed all of the vision, all of the wonder, and all of the beauty which once flooded the dreams of space travel. Misunderstood from their very start, the visionary presentation of space travel did not require the excessive engineering applications which subsequently developed. Archetypal and potent, the dream of other worlds and their parallel developing civilizations reaches further back into the forgotten past, where archane science understood the true nature of metadimensional worlds (Michel, Bergier). Now the only floods were floods of flame, of dust, of ruin, and of tears. A man and a close friend went out one clear English night by chance, and endured an unexpected rain of vengeance weapons by hiding in the London subways. "What of London, Father?", one of them asked a priest who had stood watch in the dark tunnels all night long. "Oh my son, London...London is no more". Upon returning, they found a crater where once their boarding house and its dear tenants enjoyed the sunlight.

## SPACE CAPTURE

Technology is the greatest invader of nations. It is insidious in its approach and conquest, emerging from social sectors usually not considered by those in power. From its unknown haunts in countless cellars or garret laboratories, technology changes the whole world structure; a relentless campaign which assails, re-configures, and redefines the flow of world power. Technology is the conqueror. Furthermore, the movements of Technology cannot be traced, plotted, predicted, or diminished by any ruler regardless of totalitarian completeness. Technology is especially unpredictable when it derives from biodynamic foundations. But there are Technologies whose nature is not derived from the deeper, more biodynamic energy reservoirs of Nature. Certain such technological "applications" represent superficial, more inert aspects of Nature. They can therefore be twisted into a mere exercise of force. Depending entirely on the hand of those who wield them, such "technological applications" provides brute force and exhibitions of power in a negative slant. Unfortunately, movements in the biodynamic directions of thought and technology would not rule the exploration of space, or determine the direction of space technology. The military potentials of space were immediately recognize by those who had recalled the medium range ballistic V-2 devastations of London. In the race toward achieving more military objectives, military bureaucracies were given authority to pursue these research endeavors. The ideal dream of exploring space was suddenly being forcefully changed into a scheme of "capturing space.

First in military priority was the capture of the V-2 missiles. With collapse of the Nazi regime, a plethora of technologies were carved up among the Allies, and carted off to each national intelligence group for study and exploitation. V-2 rockets were shipped to North American shores, components to manufacture some 75 such rockets. Though managing to sack a far greater quantity of rocket components than did the Soviet agents, the NAO did not obtain the very best technology which the Peenemunde Institute had to offer. The mighty A-9 reappeared on October 4, 1956 when the Soviets launched Sputnik I. A hybrid rocket system having an enormous thrust potential per unit volume, the A-9 repeatedly worked its wonders for Soviet space initiatives. The mystery which so confounded NAO spaceward efforts was the sheer power of the A-9, a craft standing little over 3 stories in height. Able to launch incredibly heavy payloads into orbit, the A-9 outperformed all of its predecessors. The sidestrapped boosters were clustered around the main stage, a conical form of diminished height, but undiminished power. It was known by western agents that certain German science prisoners enabled Soviet efforts in achieving their continuous series of space spectaculars. The A-9 reemerged as the Soviet R-7, a redesign by Sergei Korolev.

The testing of these captured missiles required specialists, a necessity which produced "Project Paperclip". This repatriation of Nazi scientists under the aegis of various Intelligence Agencies was rationalized by bureaucrats who viewed these obvious contradictions as necessary evils, the maintenance of some vague "national security". Cloaked in this oft-misused phrase, one peers beyond the bureaucracy and into the true source of those contradictory but superior directives. The very rockets which murdered the precious and valiant lives of thousand upon thousand souls were thus imported for study and future use. Designations of the rockets were changed from "Vergeltungswaffe" (retaliatory weapon) to "Viking", a seemingly venturesome. The NAO was enthralled. Some 67 Viking rockets were tested repeatedly at White Sands, a project known as HERMES. Tests were conducted between April 1946 and June 1951. These rockets demonstrated a new and unlimited means for achieving the world-ambitious goals of rulership. Tactical ballistic missiles promised a new arena in which to wage war and win. Missiles of these kinds could threaten any hostile House, acquiring new territories without contest.

This new notion of "seizing...taking...capturing" the space potential was the aggressive venture of military authority, whose first priority recognized the defensive needs of the oligarchy. Civilian and Industrial space applications would not be a viable enough purpose to require such expenditures of labor and capital. Once the North American Oligarchy (NAO) was made to recognize these realities, it would be moved in their behalf yet again. Indeed from thereon, the famed "Race For Space" ceased existing as a peacetime altruistic venture. It was no longer a visionary pursuit. The space endeavor was now very evidently a military venture, and has been dominated by the military presence since that time.

In the engineering community, new and thrilling uses for rocketry began to emerge. Theoreticians, well aware of both the engineering aspects and visionary goals, began to meld each discipline together into a new tapestry of dreams. The October 1945 issue of Wireless World published a short treatise on the possibility of rocketing communications relay stations into orbit, a then very controversial topic. In his article, Arthur C. Clarke discussed he theoretical requirements for a telephonic exchange satellite, an unmanned "space relay". Clarke described the inefficiency of long-range radio communications relay systems, the relative absorptivities and reflectivities of the ionosphere for various kinds of communications waves, and the variable ionospheric responses to VHF, UHF, and SHF signals. Anticipating both the increased demand for intercontinental communications, as well as the social proliferation of television, Clarke explained the need for high frequency exchange systems; an impossibility for existing ionospheric relay methods. The impossibility of using ionospheric techniques to reflect such high density signals to distant locales would not be much helped by the use of land RADAR relays.

Mr. Clarke had previously explained (1935) that ground based RADAR relay chains would be of exceeding cost, while prohibiting intercontinental communications. Bouncing signals from the lunar surface was a scheme which his analysis proved impractical. The heart of his thesis centered about the use of an "artificial satellite", an orbital relay station permitting the intercontinental exchange of high density signals; the key to an impending communications dilemma. In his classic Wireless World article he proposed the use of three satellites in geosynchronous orbits, each orbiting at 22,300 miles, as a means to maintain intercontinental communications between television, radio, and telephonic exchange centers. But, though the access and potential was certainly very evidently available, the technology of space would not be seized by civilian based Industry. Six months after Mr. Clarke's article appeared, the US Army Signal Corps bounced a very moderately powered RADAR signal from the moon. Civilian experimenters could have done as much, but did not.

## SPACE STATIONS

Shortly after these events, the megalithic RAND Corporation released a most remarkable and advanced Air Force sponsored portfolio. RAND was the direct recipient of highly classified data on captured V-2 rockets. It was not therefore a profound extrapolation when, in their "Preliminary Design Of An Experimental World-Circling Spaceship" (1946), RAND outlined a project in which a 500 pound spacecraft would be rocket-lifted into orbit by 1951. RAND projected the total cost of this endeavor at 150 million dollars, then a fantastic sum of money. The report alerted authorities to both the military and scientific potentials of such a spaceship, also informing their bureaucratic readership of the remarkable reconnaissance attributes which such a ship would offer. RAND explained why such a vehicle would well be the single most potent tools of the Twentieth Century for both military applications and scientific research. In addition, they were quick to point out that such a spacecraft would so "inflame the imagination of humankind" that its "repercussions in the world would be comparable to the explosion of the atomic bomb".

In this, RAND virtually quoted each forgotten statement heard in the previous decades by Dr. Nikola Tesla, who described the "increase of human energy" as a venture which would literally "inflame the imagination of humankind". By this, meaning the increase of human consciousness through Radiant Energy applications, Tesla would have directed social consciousness up into new transcendent states through his new psychotronic technologies. But neither RAND nor bureaucracy was interested in magnifying human consciousness. While the application of nuclear weaponry to this space proposal was not then evident, RAND blatantly proposed the manipulation of Cold War hysteria by their space station project. Diverting social attention from the magnified nuclear threat of a military station in space, RAND inferred that proper public relations and media manipulations could convince society that the venture was actually altruistic! RAND seemed to infer that the social impact of any space venture could raise expectations while hiding a superior directive.

Progress in rocketry was rapidly approaching a state of art difficult to ignore. But only military applications of rocketry were being viewed, the newest mean for deploying nuclear weapons across vast intercontinental distances. Had they not feared that the Nazi regime would accomplish this very thing? Soon thereafter, the Viking Project BUMPER tested two stage rocket systems, reaching 250 miles (1949). This project used a four stage system comprised of a liquid fueled Redstone first stage, and three successive solid fuel rocket stages. Each solid fuel stage was placed within the next, the fourth stage propelling the equipment payload into orbit. Contemplating the thought of world destruction, Cold War humanity recoiled with every subsequent nuclear test. Pounding the earth in a long series of weapons improvement experiments, military seemed uninterested in the civilians who surrounded their test sites. Society began to assimilate the fear of nuclear holocaust with a deep resentment for all those in authority. Born of fear and the sense of divorce from those holding the nuclear secrets, these social fixations were beginning to concern those in authority. A growing reactionism was flooding deeper levels of the working class with an assurance concerning the real intent of those in power. Citizens everywhere began sensing themselves the victims of totalitarian controls, couched in a democratic setting. The growing uneasiness was once again cultivating a new counter-consciousness in the working class which, in the next decade, exploded in a wave of new intolerance and penetrating awareness.

These proposals remained unheeded. RAND again proposed the establishment of reconnaissance satellites (1951), a plan having great appeal with certain key members of the CIA. RAND was then provided with funds toward the feasibility of actually accomplishing such a task (1952). Wernher von Braun then published a collection of articles entitled "Across The Space Frontier" (1952), describing a space station which offered ruling authorities with "a superb observation post"...where technicians would use "specially designed telescopes attached to large optical screens, radarscopes, and cameras". The space station would "keep in constant inspection every ocean, continent, country, and city". Dr. von Braun also stated that "even small towns will be visible...nothing will go unobserved". But this totalitarian expression would find its rationale in some "national security". Dr. von Braun saved his reputation by stating that "because of the telescopic eyes and cameras of the space station, it will be practically impossible for any nation to hide warlike preparations for any length of time", a concession to those who detected that residual fascist streak in his proposals.

The von Braun proposal carried weight which is not commonly appreciated. He had already alerted bureaucratic channels of the dangers inherent in procrastinating the NAO sponsored space program. The potentials of space were as dangerous as those having to do with the development of nuclear weaponry. A strange pressure was now forcing bureaucracies out toward space. Coupled together, the marriage of nuclear weaponry with space technology would indeed pose a world threat of unquestioned magnitudes. First in this venture would be the establishment of an unmanned reconnaissance station, one which could first be deployed to assess the potentials of the Soviet military threat.

RAND next produced a report "An Analysis of the Potential of an Unconventional Reconnaissance Method", a complete discussion of the advantages of espionage satellites (March 1954). CIA majority viewed all these schemes as furtive, and chose more practical aeronautic alternatives. Meanwhile, military suffusion of each supposed "scientific research project" showed itself to the naive public throughout the early years of the space initiative. The all too obvious military launch vehicles were routinely employed in the orbital launching of sometimes dubious instrument packages. Launching vehicles were all military: Vanguard (Navy), Redstone (Army), Thor (Air Force), Sergeant (Army), and Scout series (Navy, Air Force). Equipped with the only powerful such means, the actual engineworks to attain space, the military had effectively again attempted the concentration of bureaucratic power among themselves. The bureaucratic power struggle between military and Industry proved to be a futile tautology, in which one thought the other inferior. In truth, the NAO was simply studying and observing the tension, while assessing the technological capabilities of each faction. The establishment of military priority in space then became the main thrust of all subsequent industrial effort. Project ORBITER (1954) attempted the orbiting of a satellite system. The joint Army-Navy project proved unsuccessful.

The repetitive military inability to demonstrate proficient use of power and funding from the higher levels eventually provoked an unexpected twist in the bureaucratic delegation of authority. Both because of the successive failures of military rocket projects, and the prior demonstration of disloyalty in regards to the nuclear weapons issue, a new delegation of power was issued. The first priority was a defensive priority. This necessarily involved the military. It was necessary to develop defensive systems in space, the obvious next nuclear battlezone. Fixed into their singular objectives, military laboratories were never as prolific, competitive, or diversified as Industrial laboratories. Military systems personnel had not the excessive experimental and developmental prowess of Industry, whose diversified objectives afforded them a far greater capability with new variables. Now, Industry was given the rulership of research, development, and deployment. Military would cooperate with Industry to achieve the necessary tactical results.

In the decades following World War II, certain North American Industries would gradually find themselves in possession of new authority. Delegated from the uppermost levels of the geopolitical pyramid, the new initiative did not immediately make itself apparent until 1958. The later rocket giants and their successive models: the Jupiter (Juno), Saturn, Atlas, Delta, Agena, and Titan. These were all Industry hybrids of military designs. In 1955, Dr. J. R. Pierce of Bell Telephone Laboratories published an article in "Jet Propulsion" magazine, the monthly periodical of the American Rocket Society. In this article, Dr. Pierce amplified on the general theories of Arthur Clarke, providing technical information on transmission frequencies and other technical problems related to the operation of large-capacity communications satellites. He discussed the differences between simple orbital reflectors (passive) and true orbital communications relays (active). Active satellites receive, amplify, and retransmit signals beamed to them. The process provides the clarity necessary in establishing high resolution televisual communications. The "direct rebroadcaster" was a theoretical system, not then in existence. This system would receive signals, amplify them, and rebroadcasting them directly into the population. Here they could be received by small units, placed atop the homes of those equipped to appropriate the signals. While altruistic, the existence of corporate "middlemen" has interrupted this ideal view of broadcasting to the global village free of charge.

Project Vanguard (1955) continually failed. Shot after public shot continued to evidence the serious lack of technical expertise in the military-dominated space venture. Soviet space endeavors seize worldwide attention in 1957 with Sputnik I. In 1958, US military efforts succeeded in orbiting both Explorer I and Vanguard I. On December 18, 1958 Project SCORE (Signal Communication Orbit Relay Equipment) was placed in earth orbit by the US Air Force. It was the upper stage of a military rocket, the Atlas. The instrument package within this stage contained a "delay rebroadcaster", absorbing signals onto magnetic tape and rebroadcasting them a short time later. The Soviet DAYDREAM (Metachta) package (1959) was sent into a transsolar orbit, taking it between Earth and Mars every 444 days. The Soviet rocket system KOSMIK Rocket II struck into the moon on September 12, 1959; a 35 hour journey. The TIROS (1960) supposed weather satellite was followed by the TRANSIT 1B (1960) a supposed navigational aid system.

On August 12, 1960, the passive satellite named ECHO was placed into orbit, a 100 foot diameter mylar balloon having an anodized surface. While radiotelephonic signals were vastly improved by this method, television signals remained blurred and distorted. ECHO was the direct result of directives placed on the Space Agency, a Federal Bureau. The Army was developing its own communications satellite, an active system capable of serving the Army Signal Corps. Shortly thereafter, the COURIER active communications satellite system was completed. The launch proved unsuccessful, demanding the destruction of the entire package. Two months later, on October 4, 1960, a second version was launched. COURIER 1B operated successfully for a period of 18 days before it failed. On January 19, 1961 the ATT project TELSTAR was placed in orbit by a Thor-Delta rocket system. TELSTAR used nickel-cadmium batteries charged by solar cell panels.

The great success of TELSTAR prompted a volley of similar systems. RELAY (1962) and SYNCOM (1963) followed. With only minor periodic adjustments, these Industry deployed systems continued to operate as planned. The glaring differences between Industry and Military deployments of space technology began to be noticed. By now, the obvious success of each Industry-developed space venture loomed over the failure of nearly every military space project with a disturbing poise. Ruling powers made the decisive movement, delegating authority to Industry, while conscripting military to its service. The needs of defense initiatives notwithstanding, Industry was given bureaucratic contract to develop new military systems in advance of possible hostilities from foreign competitors. Thereafter the "Space Agency", a bureaucratic conglomerate which contracts Industrial laboratories, successfully launched a series of military satellites.

## SPACE CAMERAS

Born of nuclear fear, a new regime of reconnaissance technology was contemplated. The development of space technology was first predicated on the deployment of reconnaissance and possible weapons platforms. This was the sole theme behind the over propagandized "Race for Space". The thought that hostile foreign forces might use these very potentials so threatened NATO that an immediate development of reconnaissance satellites took first place in the Agenda of the NAO. The actual use of rocketry specifically for reconnaissance began in Germany. Alfred Maul, in Dresden (1912), launched special rockets containing small automatic cameras. Others employed various aeronautic means to achieve high clarity, high resolution photographs of landscape. G. W. Goddard (1925) used high resolution cameras for night photography, trailing gliders which had been filled with explosive flares for lighting. Dr. R. Goddard (1929) placed automatic cameras in the payloads of his liquid fuel rockets. Sidney Cotton (1939) was a privateer who took aerial photographs of Europe in anticipation of World War II, believing that peacetime reconnaissance would prepare against wartime. His tenets were well taken during the war, where high-speed stroboscopic flash systems were synchronized to special high sensitivity cameras.

After the Second World War, reconnaissance became a priority. The right arm of defense being weaponry, reconnaissance formed the left arm. One had to know what the antagonist was doing in order to be completely secure. In anticipation of Soviet attack under a dictatorial Stalin, NATO stepped up its reconnaissance operations. The least favored source of espionage-derived information was that obtained through human agents. CIA director A. F. Dulles distrusted human agents, preferring the hard data of photographs. The weak link in this chain of reasoning directly involved those whose task it was to interpret photographs thus obtained. This task increased in both difficulty and importance, especially as increasingly elevated aerial reconnaissance became necessary.

Boeing B-47 turbojets were converted and used in reconnaissance (RB-47), gathering photo intelligence (PHOTINT), and electronic intelligence (ELINT). These flights were low speed, high altitude recon missions. Vulnerable to enemy fire, F-86 Sabrejets were then equipped for reconnaissance (RF-86). These were capable of extremely high speed recon missions, growing increasingly vulnerable to enemy heat-seeking missile fire. The fear of Soviet manned long-range bomber attack began with the first Soviet fissile bomb (1949), and grew to frenzied proportions with the first Soviet hydrogen bomb (1953). In March 1954 RAND presented CIA with a two volume study on "An Analysis of the Potential of an Unconventional Reconnaissance Method". Bureaucrats were intrigued, but were consumed with the notion of more immediate and practical reconnaissance methods.

General Eisenhower, turned President Eisenhower established the Technological Capabilities Panel (1954), also known as the Surprise Attack Panel. This Panel was divided into three project teams, three subcommittees, each studying and solving the various new problems associated with offensive, defensive, and reconnaissance arts in the Nuclear Age. Each of these subcommittees reached engineering conclusions, having engineering solutions. Their directives have deployed unmentioned technologies whose combined use has effectively rendered obsolete all of the previous military systems which many yet consider indispensable. First NAO response was the establishment of the Distant Early Warning (DEW) Line of radar stations throughout the Alaskan and Canadian Arctic, a new level of territorial surveillance. Next came the development of special reconnaissance aircraft.

## JETSTREAM

Intelligence subcommittee Project Three was led by Edwin Land, inventor of the Polaroid Camera System. The RAND study which dealt with cameras in space found its place under a study on conventional aerial reconnaissance systems. RAND was directed to produce a study on high flying unmanned reconnaissance systems, and considered the use of stratospheric balloons. These systems, GOPHER and GENATRIX, were ground launched so that their aerial ascent would assume a trajectory directly driving into the jetstream. Jetstream propelled camera systems hurtled over Soviet territories, and were actually recovered. Edwin Land supported the GENATRIX project, informing the government on the state of his new high-resolution reconnaissance photography. High Altitude Balloons Weapon System 461-L, using high resolution photographic techniques (W. Levison), and air recovery.

After the somewhat inadequate results of these balloon missions, Project Three decided that only a manned overflight could obtain much needed data on Soviet military installations. CL-282 craft designs were referred to as "Utility-2" or, "U-2". The U-2 aircraft was discussed under Project name "Aquatone", code name "Idealist". The U-2 was viewed as an interim measure, a more immediate means until the deployment of a working spacecraft could be achieved. The U-2 aircraft was fitted with cameras and ELINT detectors. The Hycon Camera Corporation built the optical systems for the U-2, a camera (B-2) of resolving power 100 lines to the millimetre. The B-2 was capable of reading the labels from cigarette packages at 8 miles aerial elevation; and could, at 13 miles elevation, produce the print from a newspaper page without difficulty. Land suggested that the Lockheed U-2 be the vehicle of choice (1954). CIA overseers, A. F. Dulles and R. Bissel (Marshall Plan), directed Air Force Authority to use the U-2. Dulles and Bissel ordered 22 spy planes, a total cost of approximately 8 million dollars. These spy plane ventures carried inherent international hazards, a failed mission possibly resulting in a declaration of war. War in this scenario could have erupted into tactical nuclear deployments, the end of the known world for all rulerships.

Throughout this time frame, the CIA sponsored the Air Force issued design requirements for a military satellite system. Otherwise known as the Strategic Satellite System, designation WS-117L (Weapons System-117L), several agencies had already begun building workable space technologies. Of the three Industrial bases competing for the contract, Air Force chose the Lockheed design, called the AGENA (see figure). The AGENA spacecraft was 19 feet in length, 5 feet in diameter, occupied by a Bell Aerospace "Hustler" rocket engine and its fuel tanks (see figure).

*The Agena*

## THE CORONA PROJECT

Weapon System 117-L was to be a space based "reconnaissance platform" equipped with television systems. Images of Soviet territory would be stored on tape and slowly converted to signals in facsimile manner. The Lockheed Agena (Project code name "Pied Piper") was to be thrust into polar orbit by an Atlas booster rocket. This televisual transmission plan was independently pursued by the Air Force during the next few months. While the Agena system was itself flawless, the engineering problem focussed upon the state of television art. RAND analysts viewed the problem of obtaining high resolution images from an orbiting satellite station in typical ill-informed style. The several optoelectronic applications of Dr. Farnsworth, special image storage devices, were completely ignored. These astounding Farnsworth devices could have absorbed and stored any image with greatest resolution and definition. Quickly dissected and transmitted to ground bases in NATO regions, such a system would have prevented the next almost impossible consideration which RAND advised. In a technological mismaneuver, RAND analysts published their "Physical Recovery of Satellite Payloads: A Preliminary Investigation" (1956). This report declared that a "recoverable satellite system" would be the best means for obtaining reconnaissance photographs of Soviet territories. This totally unfeasible project was code-named "Project CORONA", which was publicly known as DISCOVERER. The Discoverer series was a CIA project.

Aerial reconnaissance was interrupted by a new invader, the first artificial satellite Sputnik I (1956). Sputnik I emitted a distinct facsimile signal, a fact discovered by a British school teacher. Sputnik I was found to be a surveillance system, one whose images were transmitted in facsimile photographs. This compelled CIA directors toward ordering a relentless series of U-2 flights deeper into Soviet airspace, a decision which ultimately led to the capture of U-2 pilot, Gary Powers (1960). But the message was out. Space was the new warzone where ultra-aerial photographs were free for the taking. The ITEK Company designed all CORONA camera technology. Agena launches from Vandenburg Air Force Base would place the recoverable satellite into polar orbit, the Pacific range offering a security factor in emergency launch mishaps (see figure).

The film loaded camera was now designed to dislodge from the Agena, fire a retro-rocket, and fall to earth. Parachute deployed, a specially equipped C-119 would then be used to "scoop" the falling satellite while yet in its atmospheric descent. Highly practiced aerial capture methods were therefore of primary importance to the entire mission, a pitiful regression. Project CORONA was known to the public as "Discoverer". The Discoverer launches were an incredible series of failures and mishaps. Eisenhower, Dulles, and Bissel were furious over the entire affair. Discoverer I ("Flying Yankee"), Discoverer II ("Early Time"), III ("Gold Duke"), IV ("Long Road"), V ("Fly High"), VI ("Hurry Up"), VII ("Cargo Net, Livid lady, and XIII ("Foggy Bottom") were a sorry trail of missile malfunctions, satellite failures, camera failures, and failed recoveries. Discoverer XIV was successful. Discoverer XV sank. Those launches which worked, successfully mapped and studied USSR and China. Discoverer XVI and XVII worked well, a string of successes finally managing to surpass the early failures. CORONA system clarity from orbit was astounding, recovered film gave within 6 feet optical resolution.

The Air Force WS-117L project continued pursuing the televisual scan technology, and in 1960 was given the designation SAMOS (Satellite and Missile Observation System). SAMOS 2 successfully photographed strategic sections of Soviet Russia, enabling realistic estimates of military installations. Reconnaissance satellites gradually became larger and more equipped to obtain minute details. New designations were given to a growing population of "Key Hole" (KH) satellite recon systems. Area-survey satellites (KH-5), and close-inspection satellites (KH-6), infrared reading area-surveys (KH-7), and multispectral close-looks (KH-8), were to have been eventually followed by the MOL (Manned Orbital Laboratory). This military reconnaissance outpost was cancelled in 1970. Soon thereafter, the KH-9 was launched (1971). This satellite was 50 feet in length, 10 feet in diameter, weighed 29,000 pounds, and was equipped with cloud-piercing RADAR. KH-11 (1976) was 64 feet in length, 10 feet in diameter, weighed 30,000 pounds, and utilized Farnsworth technology. The photomultipliers used starlight to see night views with the clarity of full sunlight. Their digital imaging systems provided extraordinary detail.

DSP (Defense Support Program) satellites are placed in opposed geosynchronous orbits which provide continual watch over world events. Each contains a 12 foot Schmidt telescope, and 2000 IR detectors. DSP satellites can detect missile launches within 60 seconds, rendering the DEW line obsolete. DSP satellites are vulnerable however. Their sensors can easily be destroyed by the single flash of any powerful ground based laser system. Indeed, there were developed a series of satellite-destroying weapons; rail guns, shrapnel bombs, and high-pulse laser systems. ASAT (Anti Satellite Weapons) systems can be guided into orbital proximities of enemy satellite packages and directed to completely disable them. It was during this time frame that extremely sensitive gamma ray detectors were developed, sensors designed to locate such sources in orbit or on the ground from orbit. The degree of sensitivity in these sensors is extraordinary, permitting several much publicized X-Ray and Gamma Ray geophysical profiles. These public relations "disclosures" are nothing less than admissions, security leaks of the military potential for which these satellite sensing systems have been deployed. Able to focus on the most minute ground movements of radioactive material, such systems constantly survey political "hot spots" which may stimulate the development of nuclear arsenals among third world territories.

TRW was contracted to devise and deploy radiation-detecting satellite systems (1961) VELA ("watchman") satellites were launched in 1963. Nuclear detectors were placed aboard DSP satellites in 1970. DSP satellites detected two separate 2 kiloton nuclear shots over the Antarctic in 1979. South Africa was accused of testing nuclear weapons, an allegation which their Prime Minister promptly denied. These satellite systems also function to watch space for the deployment of orbital nuclear materials, probable weapons packages. The likelihood that nuclear weapons are in orbital positions was so high that Space Shuttle Program was initiated. Reconnaissance satellites had already observed the deployment of several satellite packages which seemed especially radioactive. It was noted that, contradicting their agreement to halt the proliferation of orbital nuclear materials, the Soviet KOSMOS 954 rained radioactive debris across Canada when it abruptly and uncontrollably fell from orbit (1978). In fact, Intelligence Agencies suspected that the large Soviet SLAR RADAR orbital systems (Side Looking Airborne RADAR) utilized nuclear reactors to fuel their exorbitant energy needs. NASA development of the Shuttle and the Strategic Defense Initiative were not coincidental events. Indeed, they were the final phase of the RAND survey which had been initiated in 1946.

There are tactical applications of each satellite system, an application which cannot be denied. NAO directed ITSS (Integrated Tactical Surveillance System) actively tracks and reports ship movements through RADAR scanning methods. Piercing cloud cover and the darkness of night, these sea-scanning systems watch more than surface movements. TEAL RUBY satellites are equipped with extremely sensitive IR equipment, utilizing active cooling agents to maintain their sensitivity. These satellites can discern the actual identity of aircraft and missiles at the moment of their launch. But while these methods enable a tracking of surface movements and some IR detectable subsurface movements, there are means now available for "seeing through" ocean water with unerring accuracy. Orbital Gamma Ray detection systems can track the movement of nuclear weapons-bearing submarines despite their excessive depths. Gamma Rays are not deterred in passage through seawater. In the eyes of these special new Gamma Ray sensors, deeply submerged nuclear submarines appear as bright as spotlights. This singular fact propels us into the final phase of our discussion, one whose unquestionable implications are enormous in scope and ramifications.

SPACE EXCHANGE

The state of art required by military "watchers" was a reliability factor only obtained through the hard precision afforded by machines. Only robotic machines, ELINT and PHOTINT systems, could be depended upon to provide continuous reconnaissance of selected geopolitical regions. Toward these objectives, the great number and diversity of reconnaissance satellites emerged. Designed, developed, and launched in great throughout the days of SDI, the function of certain newer systems have not been addressed. The real function of most new satellite systems is not immediately recognized by those having no access to the Patent Archives. Why has the espionage of space become the absolute mainstay of modern military arts? Certainly for their clarity, access, detail, and geopolitical insulation, space espionage systems can achieve objectives which human agents cannot. But are there deeper reasons, reasons which only patent access can truly redefine and illuminate?

Military intelligence once relied absolutely on the hissing and crashing waves received through transcontinental relay stations and Ionospheric Backscatter systems. Complete reliance on wave energy applications maintained a completely inefficient communications systemology, even as Tesla stated. The development of space technologies, more specifically the development of communications satellites, replaced the cumbersome overland relay stations and mammoth Ionospheric Backscatter systems within a decade. The military usually dismantles its installations as quickly as it assembles newer state of art technologies. To fall behind the state of technological art is a defense weakness, an inherent failure in primary defence initiatives which cannot be tolerated among superpowers. All world Houses have been enslaved to the dictates of technology, a headlong pursuit into the dictates which technological potentials alone direct. International military groups are in fierce competition.

DSCS (Defense Communications Satellites) support military communications. MILSTAR coordinates military branch communications and weapons deployments under command. GPS (Global Positioning System) or NAVSTAR can pinpoint target positions to within 50 feet from orbit. TDRSS (Tracking and Data Relay Satellite System) are military communications satellites which exchange data among themselves through space in the even that ground-based communications are destroyed or interrupted. Even as the ineffective "over the horizon" and other such "back-scatter" RADAR techniques were replaced by satellite systems, so the RADAR communications exchange among satellites was also replaced. Each discovery of a new communications system provoked he antagonistic development of hostile systems whose function was to disrupt and interfere. Opposing forces have forever developed "jamming techniques", a military advantage against antagonists. Each countermeasure in turn seeks new continua, undisturbed communications technologies. Indeed, this search for completely new continua is forever pursued by newer interference techniques. Each communications continuum is always balanced by a countermeasure technology. These neutralizing countermeasures find their limitations however, when communications continua of excessive energetic potentials are secured; a state of art which we will now examine.

# RADIATION TECHNOLOGIES

This problem of continua and interference technologies began in the later years of World War I, when antagonistic forces discovered the multiwave spark-broadcasting technique which killed wave radio communications in the battlefield. "Jamming" became a radio communications countermeasure of unprecedented importance. Systems whose deliberate purpose was the radiation of broadband noise were developed in secrecy. Along with these countermeasures came the need for maintaining communications despite the static of jamming apparatus. Naval engineers reinvoked the art of signalling by light. Photophonic signalling soon replaced the use of telegraphic code with vocal transmissions. Designs perfected by several inventors soon permitted secret vocal communications between ships through both ultraviolet and infrared "darklight" beams (Zickler, Case, Coblentz). Though these tests actually proved the viability of point-to-point darklight communications across several miles of space, the systems suffered because their light sources diverged with optical path length.

Each of the early satellite systems relied on the directed RADAR beam method for exchanging signals between command centers and satellite stations. But the use of radio jamming techniques provoked the demand for an uninterruptible or unjammable form of communications between ground command and satellites. The LASER, an unexpected development in optical communications, suddenly provided a potent exchange system which could not easily be interrupted by natural or hostile military agencies. The large military tracking dishes and their cumbersome worldwide line of relay stations were all replaced by point-to-point LASER signalling systems. In this arena, radiowave communication has become obsolete. Whether military or commercial, the future of all orbital communications systems is found in luminal energies. Comprised of two components, the LASER and the SATELLITE, luminal communications exceed the radio art by immeasurable factors of clarity, reliability, and security. Please recall that EMP strikes, whether nuclear or RADAR induced, offered no interruptive hazards for optical channels. Potential EMP environments demanded the development of optical communications systems, a technological line which led to a wide diversification of military applications. But there were those who had observed that beyond optical spectra, there existed a realm of energetic continua whose penetrating power could not be resisted, and would not sustain interference except by exceptional means. The possible implementation of radiant transmission means other than wave radio is more than a theoretical possibility. It is a documented fact.

In 1932 a "Ray Aviation Compass" was developed by S. L. Weber, a working guidance system which provided beacon light in the X-Ray spectrum for aircraft and seagoing vessels. Employing an extremely sensitive fluorescent screen, the Ray Compass system proved invaluable during inclement conditions ordinarily prohibitive to aircraft. In 1946, several remarkable radiative sensor technologies were applied to military operations. While the "Submarine Detecting Method and Apparatus" (E. McDermott) used extremely sensitive detectors for tracking the "heat wakes" of deeply submerged vessels, an early IR system, other more esoteric systems began appearing. "A Method And Apparatus For Locating Objects" (J. H. Demming) is a system for sighting radioactive sources from great heights, no doubt an early reconnaissance means for determining the development of nuclear arsenals. The "System For Directing The Movements of Air and Marine Craft" (W. T. Weber) describes a tested means by which thin X-Ray beams are projected "either as continuous beacons or as periodically interrupted code". Utilizing this system, convoys and air squadrons could maintain unjammed communications in transport, maintaining position and direction with absolute precision. This technology also enabled the precise directing of aircraft to the decks of large carriers at sea, permitting an excellent safety margin regardless of weather or time of day.

This trend in ultra-radiative beam technology, initially developed during World War II, was neither viewed as excessive or impractical. Indeed technology of this variety continued appearing throughout the Cold War. The number of military applications for nucleonic energies represents a formidable assortment, means for tracking and tagging enemy movements, as well as directing the movements of operational forces. An "Angle of Attack Indicator, Using radioactive Source and Detector" (E. D. Jernigan, 1967) utilizes a nucleonic radiative source to project a thin weak scanning beam of Gamma Rays out into space. Designed to track supersonic aircraft, sensors read the scattered Gamma Ray "echoes" resulting when supersonic shock waves and flow lines are encountered by the Gamma Ray beam. The "Radiation Generator providing Amplitude Modulation" (R. Kaminskas, 1971) has as its assignor the AEC. It is an aircraft landing system which uses Gamma radiation interferometry to direct supersonic aircraft, a Gamma Ray analogue of RADAR.

Most of the engineering community associates RADIATION TECHNOLOGY with "radiant" LASER technologies. To a military obsessed with weapons and communications supremacy, the potentials represented in Ultraviolet, X-Ray, and Gamma Ray technologies were truly tantalizing. Was it any wonder then that a flood of patents, producing powerful coherent radiations in each of these spectra, were produced throughout the last thirty years? LASER technology began reaching heights of perfection never before dreamed, luminal channels rapidly becoming available across the spectrum for communications, detection, and weapons applications. While the optical LASER was the first coherent optical device, it has not remained the sole variety of coherent radiant technologies.

## QUANTUM WEAPONS

RADAR marked a new technological breakthrough which was soon applied to weaponry. The use of super pulse RADAR as a lethal weapon became especially feasible with the development of large multicavity Magnetrons such as the Planotron of Kapitza, and the MASER system. Coupled with megawatt pulse systems, experiments using RADAR as a beam weapon were briefly entertained. The rumors of killed RADAR technicians, unfortunates who chanced to be caught in the beam of the intense pulsed output, are not rare. Service men continue to report these incidents. Cold War initiatives called for new such non-nuclear weapons deployments. This twofold potential became a directive guidance for industrial research teams throughout the last fifty years. Target irradiation techniques reached a state of unsuspected perfection in the hands of military developers during the Cold War, a breed of hybrid NUCLEONIC weapons. These combined radioactive sources, targets, and electronic pulse techniques to produce an astounding diversity of heinous killing weapons.

The "X-Ray Source" (L. Reiffel, 1957) is a beam weapon, a device which can utilize a small and compact linear accelerator to produce extremely tight beams of hard X-Rays and Gamma-Rays. The device utilizes a long conical shaped rod of Strontium-90, one which tapers to a sharp point (see figure on following page).

Impacted by high energy electrons, the rod releases a needle of intense and deadly quanta, a radiation thread which can propagate for miles in a straight line. The "Device For Collimation of A Ray Beam" (W. Gschleiden, 1959) utilizes a Cobalt-60 source in a ray-tight box. Active matter baffle plates amplify, refine, and collimate the beam for projection. The list of isotopic radiation sources is lengthy, and represents a passive form of radiation beam projectors. The advent of MASER and LASER technology opened a new regime of beam weapons.

The "Coherent Gamma Ray Emitter" (J. W. Eerkens, 1966) uses Mossbauer isotopes in magnetic fields to produce high-yield Gamma Ray pulses, yields which indeed force the material to decay faster than the supposedly immutable half-life. Such a weapon is deadly, and "clean". With the press of a switch, a coherent killing beam emerges, a quantum flux in the Gamma Ray spectrum of penetrating power. The patents describe a formerly undeclared phenomenon in great detail, one in which matter can be completely converted into Gamma Rays by sufficiently powerful and abrupt sonic impulse. This device is small, compact, and requires very little supportive equipment. Such a design could easily be packaged and placed in a hundred different orbits. The "Apparatus For Generating Frequencies Higher Than Those of Light" (G. Gould, 1967) represents a patent for a hard Ultraviolet and X-Ray LASER system. The "Gamma Ray Laser and Closed Resonating Cavity" (Pieckenbrock, 1968)

June 25, 1957 — L. REIFFEL — 2,797,333
X-RAY SOURCE
Filed July 24, 1953

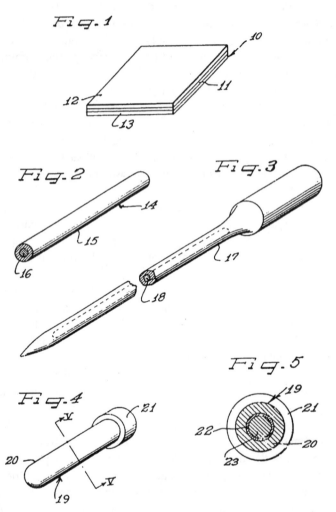

Inventor
LEONARD REIFFEL
by Hill, Sherman, Meroni, Gross & Simpson
Attys.

is a system which utilizes an unnamed crystalline material, a Gamma ray source, having stated coherent Gamma Ray potentials in excess of 30 Gigawatts. These exceedingly small packages could render more lethal devastation than any heavy metal fissile weaponry (see figure).

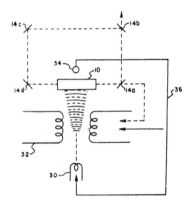

The radiant beam and target technique was used to produce a series of super pulse X and Gamma Ray LASER Systems. In the announcement made by Dr. Edward Teller, during the closing years of SDI, an explosive Gamma Ray LASER system was widely described throughout the public media. The Teller system was a large bathysphere-shaped weapon, studded with pointed metal prongs. This weapon, a thing of which the acrid Dr. Teller seemed proud to describe, combined a neutron bomb and long pointed targetable beam collimator rods. These projection rods were identical to the "X-Ray Source" of L. Reiffel (1957). The design represented a launch weapon, capable of being deployed by missiles. Each rod could be locked onto target-cities while in flight. The system obviously self-destructed after ignition, but not before the high yield Gamma Ray blasts were directed through the pointed beam collimators. The weapon which Teller claimed was a "new height" in the nuclear arts is a hideous device of even greater death potential than his Hydrogen Bomb.

Thereafter, a new regime of disposable material, or "single shot" repeater systems made their way into the technology of tactical LASER weaponry. The "Method And Means For Producing Coherent X-Ray and Gamma-Ray Emissions" (J. A. Viecelli, 1973) uses a natural radioactive source to produce a dense and collimated ion flux. This current is bombarded by an incident LASER pulse, and produces instantaneous X and Gamma Ray quantum states at greatly elevated power levels. The "X-Ray LASER" (L. Wood, 1973) flash heats thin wire rods of radioactive isotopes with a high power IR LASER pulse, releasing a coherent quantum beam of deadly power. The wire rods vaporize and are replaced, a LASER cannon. This notion of disposable shot Gamma LASERS (technically termed GRASERS) also utilized metal foil technologies, the "slapper detonator" principle being used to produce instantaneous coherent quantum pulses in the Gamma Ray spectrum. "Producing X-Rays" (Mallozzi, 1972) uses alternate foil layers of unnamed "heavy metals". The sudden shock impact of a powerful optical LASER pulse into such multiplanar target foils successfully releases coherent X-Rays of 100 Gigawatts potential.

Other systems employ variations of metals and foils to produce Gamma Ray beams of equivalent strengths. In the patent text one reads that the apparatus is fully able to "weld, cut, and melt metals". Indeed such energies, when super pulsed, can punch holes through metal walls several feet thick, rupture stone barriers of greater thickness. Mounted in a satellite station, these devices do not violate nuclear ban treaties, being the realization of Cold War weapons objectives. With such weapons in place, nuclear weaponry is made obsolete. Gamma Ray LASERS can be applied on command, at the flick of a switch. Deactivated, they remain inert, covert, and insidious. Military reliance on special radiant energies is the most recent misinterpretation of Tesla Radiant Energy Technology.

## QUANTUM COMMUNICATIONS

Satellite to ground performance relies on ionospheric conditions. What is needed is communications links which remain unaffected and uninterrupted by natural and hostile military deformations. The result of this inconsistency became a desperate need for sustained secure-communications systems; one which neither could be disturbed by ionospheric conditions, nor fulfilled by existing LASER systems of the day. Optical LASER beams, regardless of coherent power, are blocked by cloud cover and distorted by ionospheric disturbances. Events leading up to SDI necessitated the development and deployment of entirely new communications continua. The use of Ultraviolet LASERS would not fare well in linking satellites with ground command, those spectral lines being rapidly absorbed in transit through small sections of atmosphere. Infrared LASERS of specific spectral content are able to penetrate deeper levels of the atmosphere, but may become distorted through voluminous water vapor currents. They are therefore not completely reliable for military communications links. Clearly some other spectral bands must be sought if space-to-ground or even space-to-sea communications are to become absolute.

Examination of early photophone and radiophone patents suggested communications diversity in several distinct spectra. The notion of communicating along an X-Ray beam at first presents a bizarre impression. Yet one finds that the plausible use of modulated X-Ray sources is not without merit. Any sufficiently powerful X-Ray beam will pass, unhindered through most materials. The passage of such a beam through the entire volume of a column, from orbit to ground, or from deep-sea to orbit is not therefore so impossible. In addition, X-Ray beams can and do penetrate sea water, and are also capable of reaching certain submerged vessels without difficulty. Furthermore, there is no known way to "jam" such beams, cannot be blocked by variable weather conditions, and do not rely upon the ionosphere for long range propagation. While these considerations seem to be pure fantasy, more like science fiction, one is shocked and amazed to find a sizable patent bibliography in the art.

The "Communication System" (DeLoraine, 1947) describes a complete Gamma Ray communications system, one by which vocal signals may be transmitted over a Gamma Ray beam, received at a great distance, and accurately reproduced with great definition and clarity. The system uses a Gamma Ray emitting isotope, mounted on a fine wire in a resonant cavity. Applications of vocal energy through magnetic fields so vibrate this wire as to produce corresponding vibrations in the source material. This produces measurable variations in the Gamma Ray emission, a variation which is transmitted a s a disturbance along the beam. A high pressure Argon gas ionization chamber is used to demodulate the Gamma Ray fluctuations. The high pressure receiving tube behaves much like a miniature spark chamber, relying on the gaseous discharge currents which are stimulated between a great number of close-spaced charged capacitor plates. These discharges vary with the incoming Gamma Ray variations, and resolve the beam fluctuations into clarified vocal signals. The "Space Communications System" (H. R. Chope, 1961) uses electrostatic or magnetic fields to modulate emanations from radioisotopes, such as Strontium-90 or Krypton-85. These emanations are directed to special targets, whereupon they become a very penetrating beam of hard X-Rays. This beam is intelligently modulated to carry coded or vocal information, and is designed to provide secure-communications between space stations and ground command, as well as among space craft (see figure).

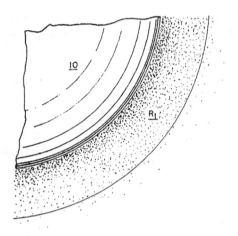

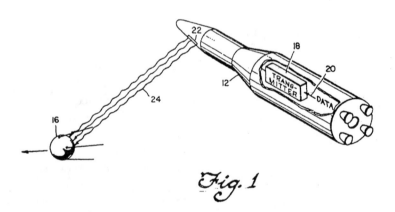

Fig. 1

While there exist numerous X-Ray radiophones and communications patents, most of the Cold War designs which hold our interest are those which engage and modulate Gamma Ray beams. A great many of these devices flood the declassified patent archives. It is probable that a great many more remain yet classified. The engineering problems associated with the concept of modulating a Gamma Ray source is enormous, only if we accept that view which supposes the immutability of radioactive half-life and the unchangeable nature of radioactive materials. Indeed, ordinary Gamma Ray sources cannot be "turned off and on" like switches. Their radioactive emissions remain constant.

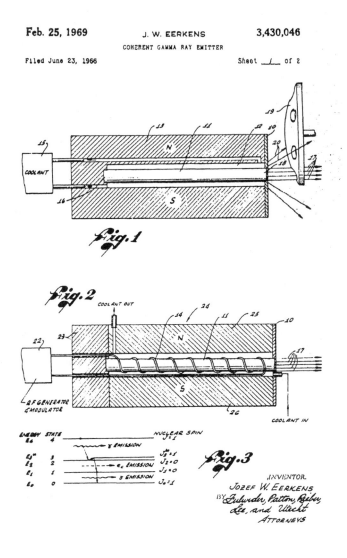

The numerous patents which describe means for producing a pulse coded Gamma Ray beam represent an important first engineering dialogue on the use of Gamma Ray carriers. These systems employed rapid shutters by which otherwise constant Gamma emanations could be gated. Each of these shuttered systems provided a lightweight communications system having inherent code-signal limitations. The advent of LASER technology provided the very first intimation that Gamma Ray modulations might actually carry vocal intelligence. Apparatus in which the modulated generation of Gamma Rays was stimulated through applied signal energies provided a means by which such radiations could be modulated at the very instant of their formation. Not limited to the use of constant Gamma Ray sources, not by isotopic sources, the Gamma Ray LASERS tested well in these communications channels. Each such system produces modulated Gamma Ray beams. By far the most remarkable of these patents must include the "Coherent Gamma Ray Emitter" (J. W. Eerkens, 1966) which uses long classified aspects of the otherwise well-known Mossbauer Effect to achieve the unexpected. This system achieves a powerful modulation of coherent Gamma Radiations capable of carrying vocal signals by actually forcing certain isotopes to radiate Gamma Radiation in smooth coherent modulations.

Both the phase modulation of Mossbauer Gamma Ray emissions, and the resonant absorption of the same in identical isotopes, permits a new form of communication never before conceived in realms of the art. Except for the excessive hazards associated with the quantum continuum so engaged, the potential of a Gamma Ray Communications system is virtually unlimited. There are those radiation imaging systems by which static images and printed data may be coded, scanned, transmitted along a Gamma Ray beam, received, and resolved at the reception site. Indeed one finds X-Ray video scanners by which even live video images can be converted into modulated X and Gamma Ray beams, decoded in receivers, and converted into live images. The "Display Device" (R. D. Kell, 1960) is an electrified imaging system which converts X-Ray beams into visual images. The "Radiation Modulation Apparatus" (R. S. Jensen, 1973) is a LASER scanning technology which can modulate X-Ray energies with video information. Each of these are weak analogues of the Teslian Televisual System.

## CONCLUSIONS

Of all the coherent species, Gamma Ray beams may be excessively thin in cross-section while maintaining their power. Coherent Gamma Ray beams do not de-cohere with greatest distance, neither are they capable of being disturbed by material interruption. Gamma Rays are neutral particles. Neutral particle beam communications are never subject to natural interference, and cannot be artificially jammed. The only manner by which a Gamma Ray signal may be interrupted or distorted is by directed volleys of equivalent radiation, and that would be an excessive nuclear exposition. A highly directed and continuous Gamma Ray beam would indeed disrupt such a communications channel, but this would constitute an act of war. Gamma Rays are highly directional and can be of minute cross section. It is possible to maintain the tightest control on Gamma Ray beams, directing their threadlike channels between ground and space points without the slightest divergence. Gamma Ray beams maintain their collimation across incredible distances. Most important, these penetrating rays easily pass through halls, walls, waters, and clouds. Deeply submerged vessels can, by Gamma Ray communications links, communicate directly with an orbital relay station. No depth of seawater can adequately hinder or distort Gamma Rays.

These considerations open the field of radiation detectors into a much wider perspective now, it being recognized that the vast majority of such devices can actually serve in the reception of modulated radiation broadcasts. The several notably declassified patents which describe both X-ray and Gamma Ray Detectors represent critical clues in this inference. Orbital detectors can do more than scan space for nuclear warheads. They can read the coded messages beamed up from beacons however deeply submerged. In like manner, such detectors empower submerged craft to read the ocean penetrating coded signals beamed down from orbit. In such systems, Gamma Ray detectors form the very heart of receivers, responding to each pulsed transmission with unerring accuracy. Analogous in every manner to those photophones of the Victorian Epoch, and the radiophones of Post World War I decades, Gamma Ray communications technologies represent a new state of art which is both unexpected and unsuspected.

The onboard equipment required in implementing these penetrating rays is minuscule when compared with the equivalent radio transmitters and required aerial trailers. The modulated use of Gamma Ray quanta represents a technology which renders the frail Art of Radio Wave Communications obsolete. Passing through several thousand feet of seawater, Gamma Rays suffer neither dispersions nor diminutions of strength. For Gamma Rays, water and steel may represent extremely weak refractions, but for coherent Gamma Rays, these substances are transparent. Coded, vocal, and video communications over a pulsating beam of Gamma Rays! Normal scrambling processors may be employed with these systems, a revolutionary comlink which cannot be stopped. Current state of art military deployments in space enlist the combined aid of several such key components; Gamma Ray beam weapons and Gamma Ray beam communications technologies representing the known apex of the art. These space poised components collectively form a mighty world communications system of far reaching military potentials. With this system now in active placement, military personnel can access and execute commands literally from any point on or "under" the world.

When taken in their various combinations, these state-of-art components excel radiowave communications systems. Such communications systems provide effortless access to and from normally unbreached boundary zones. Used in pulsed mode, both X-Ray and Gamma-Ray systems form encrypted secure communications links. Each of these have demonstrated their effectiveness in connecting submarines, at extreme depths, with orbital communications satellites. We have thus discovered the numerous components of systems which render radiowave communications obsolescent. Compact, portable, easily powered, and highly directional, such X and Gamma Ray communications systems are a military dream come true. Using these beams as connective links, military command centers are easily joined with personnel on the ground, in the air, and deep within the sea via high orbital satellites. Gamma Ray switching satellites therefore serve as a perfect relay exchange center for all terrestrial military communications. Moreover, there are nonnuclear weapons which have now been placed in selected deep space orbits. Therefore, we realize that unique weapons and communications systems are already in place, an armada of super pulse Gamma Ray LASER systems and communications links. Regularly monitored by now habitual Space Shuttle missions, these orbital fortresses have effectively rendered obsolete every terrestrial weapon and communications technology. The orbital arsenal.

The very obvious transfer of military systems, from terrestrial to orbital positions, provokes a line of reasoning which few technology analysts have addressed. Since space orbital positions are the most advantageous locations for military applications, and since space deployments perform their functions with imminently greater efficiency than even ground based installations, why would military require terrestrial systemologies at all?

It is suddenly realized that the very rationale which directs the construction of ground based military installations stands in question. The reason for building a SANGUINE/SEAFARER system is to enable communications between central command and submerged fleet vessels. Yet since a truly invincible means now exists, then the very use of ELF becomes cumbersome and redundant. The superior directive which commanded the development of "nuclear solutions" had a twofold purpose. The first phase demanding deployment of a space poised reconnaissance system. The second and final phase demanded deployment of space poised weapons platforms. Nonnuclear weapons.

Oligarchic rulerships each now seek supremacy in orbital space. They are not interested in interplanetary space at all. Mastery over the planet is what each House desires, the theme of ambitions and acquisitions. For social working class personalities, there is a new credibility gap which now extends out into orbit. Archimedes declared "give me a lever...and a place on which to stand...and I will move the very earth itself". Indeed, the fulcrum of that lever once sat squarely on the ground, in thrones of power which ruled openly. The withdrawal of rulers into the shadows marked the retreat of power up into a virtual pyramid, whose vertex rose up in virtual directions skyward. Geopolitical regions were mastered and manipulated from these virtual points, points which have very mysteriously now become physical realities. Power over terrestrial regions has literally raised itself above the planet, an arrogant pride in which overseers who gather and disperse power have promoted themselves heavenward. In their attempt to force the terrestrial fulcrum skyward, they have reversed the traditional order, but not changed its themes. Space fulcrums now rule the earth with wide leverages, and our attentions are therefore caught between systems visible and systems invisible. It is no longer the Nuclear Age.

The Cold War space directive, that which was issued in 1946, was accomplished with the successful establishment and continued improvement of orbital reconnaissance systems, a technology which remains unsurpassed in its abilities. But SDI marked the second phase of the thirty year directive, the deployment of nonnuclear orbital weapons platforms. The threat of nuclear holocaust, itself the horror which destroyed the known world, has been done away. Now there is only a sublime space: "The Space Age". Yet for all the bureaucratic promises of unlimited and endless horizons, we find ourselves and our geopolitical zone unable to rise above the ground. But this may be a secret and mysterious blessing, for power appears among those who receive dreams and passions while laboring on the ground. Indeed, the distance between earth and space has now taken on two completely separate meanings for us. One defines the oligarchic powerlines out to a limiting vertex. The other follows a dreamline into endless translations and metaphysically beauteous spaces. And it will be into those who dream and who love vision that the real power will continually flow.

# BIBLIOGRAPHY

My sincere thanks to M. Theroux for all of his efforts in editing, reconfiguring, and preparing this document for its public presentation.

FORTHCOMING COMPANION TEXT:
*COLD WAR TECHNOLOGY PATENT COLLECTION*

[VC designates Vril Compendium Volumes published by Borderland Sciences Research Foundation]

**Abrams, Dr. Albert.**
"Abrams Method In Practice", Dr. B. Swayze, *Pearson's Magazine*, August 1922.
*Certain Body Reflexes*, 1926. Borderland Sciences Research Foundation Reprint.
*Disease: Its Cause and Cure*, Dr. Strong. Borderland Sciences Research Foundation Research Reprint.
*The Electronic Reactions of Abrams*, Dr. F. Cave, Boston 1922. Borderland Sciences Research Foundation Research Reprint.
*Human Energy*, Dr. Abrams, San Francisco, 1914. Fifth Edition. Borderland Sciences Research Foundation Research Reprint.
"Abram's Methods of Diagnosis and Treatment", Sir James Barr, *British Medical Journal*, July, 1912. Borderland Sciences Research Foundation Research Reprint.
*New Concepts in Diagnosis and Treatment*, Dr. A. Abrams, San Francisco, 1922. Borderland Sciences Research Foundation Research Reprint.
"The Electronic Reactions of Abrams", *International Clinics*, Vol. 1, Series 27, 1917. Borderland Sciences Research Foundation Research Reprint.

**ÆTHER Studies:**
"The Ether Drift Experiment", D. C. Miller, *Reviews of Modern Physics*, No. 5, pp 204-241, July 1933, Borderland Sciences Research Foundation Research Reprint.
*The Ether Ship Mystery*, Meade Layne, Borderland Sciences Research Foundation, 1946.
*The Ether of Space*, Sir Oliver Lodge, Harper and Brothers, New York 1909, Borderland Sciences Research Foundation Reprint.
"Etherion Gas", Dr. Charles Brush, *Science*, No. 8, pp 485-494, 1898.
*Relativity and Space*, Dr. K. P. Steinmetz, Borderland Sciences Research Foundation Reprint.

**Ainsworth, Chester D.**
"Electric Wave Detector" (Radioactive), Patent 1.145.735, 6 July, 1915.

**Alexanderson, Ernst**
"Antenna", Patent 1.360.167, 23 November, 1920.
"Antenna", Patent 1.360.168, 23 November, 1920.
"Antenna", Patent 1.360.169, 23 November, 1920.
"Transoceanic Radio Telegraphy", *American Inst. Electrical Engineers*, 1920.
    [VC 11 - Military ELF]
"Electron Discharge Device" (Magnetron copy), Patent 1.535.082, 21 April, 1925.
    [VC 10 - Electric Ray Projectors]

**Appleton, Dr. E. V.**
"Retardation of Short Wave Signals", Wheatstone Laboratory, *Nature*, No. 122, 8 December, 1928.

## AURORA
"Abnormal Earth Currents", B. Grandy, *Electrical Engineer*, 8 June, 1892.
"Auroral Disturbances", *Nature*, 29 April, 1886.
"Earth Currents", B. Grandy, *Electrical Engineer*, 29 March, 1893.
"Earth Currents", W. Finn, *Electrical Engineer*, 16 November, 1892.
Earth Currents, W. H. Preece, Nature, 12 April, 1894.
"How the Aurora Affects Telegraph Lines", H. Gernsback, *Electrical Experimenter*, January 1918.
"Registering Apparatus for Earth Currents", *Science*, 29 June, 1883.
"Recent Observations on Earth Currents", *Electrical Engineer*, 29 August, 1894.
"Telegraphs", J. D. Caton, *Scientific American*, 11 September, 1862.
"Terrestrial Electricity", *Nature*, 1874.
[All above taken from VC 1 White Ray Conductors]
"Aurora on the Ground", J. H. Johnson, *Nature*, No. 127, 341, 1931.
"Walking Into Aurora", Dr. S. Chapman, *Nature*, No. 127, 342, 1931.
"Walking Through An Aurora", F. C. Kelley, *Nature*, No. 133, 218, 1934.
"Auroras and Thunderstorms", J. E. Davidson, *Nature*, No. 47, 582, 1893.
"Auroras In Daytime", A. Paulsen, *Journal of the British Astronomical Association*, Volume 73, 234, 1963.
"Auroral Columns Touching Earth", R. H. Bonneycastle, *American Journal of Science*, No. 1, 32: 393, 1837.
"Barium Cloud Auroras", *Nature*, No. 267, 135, 1977.
"Measuring Auroral Voltages", *Modern Wireless*, pg. 475, January 1926.

**Aspden, Dr. Harold**
*Physics Without Einstein*, Sabberton, University of Cambridge, 1969 (Aether Physics).

**Austin, L. W.**
"Radiotelegraphy", Bureau of Standards, *Washington Academy of Sciences*, Vol. 16, pp 398-410: 19 August 1926.
"Radiotelegraphy", Bureau of Standards, *Washington Academy of Sciences*, Vol. 16, pp. 457-460: 18 October, 1926.

**Bearden, T. E.**
"Tesla's Secret", US Psychotronics Association Video Essay, 1987.

**Branly, Edouard**
"Absorption of Electric Waves", *Comptes Rendus*, No. 128, pp. 879-882, 1899.
    [VC 9 - Aerial Radio]

**Brasch, Arno**
"Impulse Generator", Patent 1.957.008, 1 May, 1934. [VC 11 - ELF Devices]

**Braun, Ferdinand**
"Signals Over Surfaces", Patent 750.429, 26 January, 1904. [VC 8 - Ground Radio]

**Brett, James S.**
*The Whistler Serenade*, Stonehenge Viewpoint, pp. 16-19, 1995.

**Brush, Dr. Charles**
"Kinetic Theory of Gravitation", *Nature*, 23 March 1911.
"Kinetic Theory of Gravitation", *Proc. American Philosophical Society*, Volume 67, 1928, pp. 105-117.
"Persistent Generation of Heat in Some Rocks", *Proc. American Philosophical Society*, Volume 66, 1927, pp. 251-266.

**Case, T. W.**
"Infrared Rays Used For Signalling", *Wireless World*. [VC 10 - Electric Ray Projectors]

**Chope, H. R.**
"Detecting and Identifying Remote Objects", Patent 3.358.602, 19 December, 1967.
"Space Communication System", Patent 3.123.714, 3 March, 1964.

**Coblentz, Dr. William**
"The Black Light Radio", S. R. Winters, *Popular Radio*, 1920.
"Radiophone", Patent 1.345.586, 6 July, 1920. [VC 10 - Electric Ray Projectors]

**Corliss, William R.**
*Lightning, Auroras Nocturnal Lights and Related Luminous Phenomena*, Sourcebook Project, Glen Arm, MD 1985.
*Unusual Natural Phenomena*, Arlington House, New York, 1986.

**Dalessio, Gerald**
[Private conversation 23 July 1995 at Twin Lights New Jersey, concerning Marconi Station artifacts recently unearthed on New Brunswick seacoast]

**De Loraine, E. M.**
"X-Ray Communication System", Patent 2.546.984, 3 April, 1951.

**Dement, J.**
"Nuclear Explosive Light Generator", Patent 3.715.596, 6 February, 1973.

**De Moura, Roberto**
"Wireless Telegraph", Patent 775.846, 22 November, 1904.
[VC 10 - Electric Ray Projectors]

**Demming, J. H.**
"Locating Objects", Patent 2.401.723, 11 June, 1946.

**De Saussure, Henri**
"Observations on Mountain Resonance", translated from *Comptes Rendus*, Smithsonian Institute, tome 44, 1867. [VC 1 - White Ray Conductors]

**Dewey, Mark W.**
"Method of Utilizing Natural Electric Energy", Patent 414.943, 12 November, 1889
[VC 1 - White Ray Conductors]

**Dolbear, Dr. Amos**
"Mode of Electric Communication", Patent 350.299, 5 October, 1886, [Dolbear newspaper articles in VC 7 - Dendritic Ground Systems]

**Dollard, Eric**
*Dielectric and Magnetic Discharges*, Borderland Sciences Research Foundation.
*Symbolic Representation of the Generalized Electric Wave*, Borderland Sciences Research Foundation, 1986.
*Transverse and Longitudinal Electric Waves*, Borderland Sciences Research Foundation Video, 1985.
*Condensed Intro to Tesla Transformers*, Borderland Sciences Research Foundation, 1985.
*Theory of Wireless Power*, Borderland Sciences Research Foundation, 1986.
*Tesla's Longitudinal Electricity*, Borderland Sciences Research Foundation Video, 1985.

**Drown, Dr. Ruth**
*Theory and Technique of the Drown Homovibraray*, Hatchard and Company, London, 1939, Borderland Sciences Research Foundation Reprint.
*The Ray of Discovery - Medical Radionics*, Borderland Sciences Research Foundation Video, 1988.
*Drown Radiovision and Homovibraray Instruments*, Los Angeles, 1940, Borderland Sciences Research Foundation Reprint.
*Science and Philosophy of the Drown Radio Therapy*, Los Angeles 1938, Borderland Sciences Research Foundation Reprint.

**Eerkens, Josef W.**
"Coherent Gamma Ray Emitter", Patent 3.430.046, 25 February, 1969.

**Farnsworth, Dr. Philo**
"Multipactors" [Patent Collection and Personal Laboratory Notes]
"The Farnsworth Cold Cathode Electron Multiplier", A. H. Halloran, *Radio*, October 1934.
[both in VC 10 Electric Ray Projectors]
*Distant Vision*, E. G. Farnsworth, Pemberley-Kent, Salt Lake City, 1989.
*Polytubes*, J. Resines, Borderland Sciences Research Foundation, 1990.

**Fessenden. Dr. Reginald**
"Wireless Telegraphy", *Electrical Review*, Vol. 58, 11 May, 1906.
"Wireless Telegraphy", Patent 706.738, 706.739 (Wave Chutes), 12 August, 1902.
[VC 9 - Aerial Radio]
"Wireless Telegraphy" (Rays), Patent 974.762, 1 November, 1910.
"Wireless Transmission and Reception" (UHF System), Patent 1.617.242, 8 February, 1927.
[VC 10 - Electric Ray Projectors]

**Gati, Bela**
"Telegraphy" (Rays), Patent 799.555, 12 September, 1905.
[VC 10 - Electric Ray Projectors]

**Gosztonyi, Adam**
"Invisibility At Last", A. L. White, *Electrical Experimenter*, October 1936.
[VC 10 - Electric Ray Projectors]

**Gould, Gordon**
"Generating Radiation", Patent 3.388.314, 11 June, 1968.

**Grindell-Matthews**
"Diabolic Rays", H. G. Matthews, *Popular Radio*, 1922.
"Carrier Rays That Kill" (photograph with caption) [VC 10 - Electric Ray Projectors]

**Grotz, Toby**
"Wireless Transmission of Electrical Power", 1987 lecture tape L23A, US Psychotronics Association.

**Gschlieden, Wilhelm**
"Collimating Ray Beam", Patent 2.904.692, 15 September, 1959.

**Heising, Raymond**
"Directive Radio Transmissive System", Patent 1.562.961, 24 November, 1925.
"Oscillation Generator", Patent 1.240.206, 18 September, 1917.
[VC 11 - ELF Devices]

**Hendershot, Lester**
"The Hendershot Motor Mystery", compiled by T. Brown, Borderland Sciences Research Foundation Reprint.

**Hennelly, Edward**
"Amplifier" (Magnetron Tube), Patent 1.530.364, 17 March, 1925.

**Hettinger, John**
"Aerial Conductor For Wireless Signaling", Patent 1.309.031, 8 July, 1919.
"Wireless Transmission of Power Now Possible", T. Benson, *Electrical Experimenter*, 1919. [VC 10 - Electric Ray Projectors]

**Highton, Henry**
"Telegraphing Long Distances", *London Society of Arts*, 1872.
"Biographic Sketch of Henry Highton", *Pioneers of Wireless*, Ellison Hawks.
[VC 8 Ground Radio]

**Hodowanec, Gregory**
"Gravitational Impulses", *RE Experimenters Handbook*, private publication.
"Gravitational Waves", *Radio-Electronics*, April 1986.
*Investigations in Electro-Gravitation*, private publication, 1985.
*Rhysmonic Cosmology Æther Physics*, private publication, 1985.

**Houston, Edwin**
"On A New Connection For The Induction Coil", *Scientific American*, 1872.
[VC 9 Aerial Radio]

**Hughes, David Edward**
"Professor Hughes and Wireless", historical account. [VC 8 - Ground Radio]

**Hull, Albert W.**
"Magnetron Tube", *Journal American Institute Electrical Engineers*, pg. 715, September 1921.

**Hulsmeyer, Christian**
"Improvement in Hertzian Wave Projection", British Patent 13.170, 10 June, 1904.
[VC 10 - Electric Ray Projectors]

**Hunt, Dr. Valerie**
"Human Aura", US Psychotronics Association, 1985.

**Jernigan, E. D.**
"Angle of Attack Indicator", Patent 3.557.366, 19 January, 1971.

**Jensen, R. S.**
"Radiation Modulation Apparatus", Patent 3.818.222, 18 June, 1974.

**Kaminskas, R.**
"Radiation Generator Providing Modulation", Patent 3.818.221, 18 June, 1974.

**Kell, Ray D.**
"Display Device" (X-Ray Imaging System), Patent 3.064.134, 13 November, 1962.

**Kelvin, William Thompson**
"On The Generation of Longitudinal Waves In The Ether", *Nature*, 12 March, 1896.

**Knight, Chester R.**
"Magnetron Amplifier", Patent 2.546.033, (Magnetron Tubes in tandem).

**Le Bon, Dr. Gustav**
*Evolution of Forces*, London, Dryden House, 1908, Borderland Sciences Research Foundation Reprint.
*Evolution Of Matter*, Walter Scott Publishing Co, 1906, Borderland Sciences Research Foundation Reprint.

**Lemstrom, Dr. Selim**
"Artificially Induced Auroras", *Science*, No. 4, p. 465, 1884.

**Lindsay, ??**
"Pioneers of Wireless", Elliston Hawks, *Wireless World*.
Mechanics Magazine, Vol. 13, First Series, p. 182 [VC 2 - Telegraphy]

**Longoria, Prof. Antonio**
"Death Ray", *Popular Science*, pg. 114, February 1940.

**Loomis, Dr. Mahlon**
"Improvement in Telegraphing", Patent 129.971, 30 July, 1872.
[Personal Papers and Drawings, Government Documentation, Historical accounts, VC 7 - Dendritic Ground Systems]

**MacFarland-Moore, Daniel**
"Electrical Control of Devices At A Distance", Patent 723.176, 17 March, 1903.
"Radio Generator That Blew Up Bombs", *Popular Radio*.
[VC 10 - Electric Ray Projectors]
"Peaked Wave Wireless Transmission", Patent 755.305, 22 March, 1904.
[VC 11 - ELF Devices]

**Mallozzi, Phillip J.**
"Producing X-Rays", Patent 4.058.486, 15 November, 1977.

**Marconi, Marquese Guglielmo**
"Directional Radiation of Waves", *Proceedings of the Royal Society*, 22 March, 1906.
[VC 10 - Electric Ray Projectors]
"Transmitting Electrical Signals", Patent 586.193, 13 July, 1897. [VC 9 - Aerial Radio]
"Variations of VLF Signals", *Proceedings of the Royal Society*, Volume 77, June 1906.

**Mateucci, Charles**
"On The Electrical Currents Of The Earth", Smithsonian Institute.
[VC 1 - White Ray Conductors]

**McCullough, Frederick**
"Directive Transmission of Electromagnetic Waves", Patent 1.403.700, 17 January, 1922.
"Radiotelegraphy" (Radiant Location), Patent 1.471.406, 23 October, 1923.
[both in VC 10 - Electric Ray Projectors]

**McDermott, E**
"Submarine Detecting Method", Patent 2.412.165, 3 December, 1946.

**McElrath, Hunter B.**
"Electron Tube" (Radioactive), 2.032.545, 26 October, 1931.

**Meissner, Alexander**
"Oscillations By Shock Excitation", Patent 1.007.733, 4 November, 1913.
[VC 9 - Aerial Radio]
"Directional Antenna System", Patent 1.740.950, 24 December, 1929.
[VC - 11 ELF Devices]

**Mendeleev, Dmitri**
*A Chemical Conception of The Ether*, Longmans Green and Company, London, 1904.

**Meucci, Antonio**
[Personal Papers, Complete Biography in VC 5 - Connection]

**Michel, John**
*The New View Over Atlantis*, Harper and Row, San Francisco, 1983.

**Moray, Dr. Thomas Henry**
*Beyond The Light Rays*, Moray, Salt Lake City, 1930.
"Electrotherapeutic Apparatus", Patent 2.460.707, 1 February, 1949.
"Ore Enrichment by High Energy Bombardment", (Lecture) 68th National Western Mining Conference, Denver, CO, 4 February, 1965.

*Recovery Of Minerals*, Research Institute, Salt Lake City, 1965.
*Talk On Radiant Energy*, Moray, Salt Lake City, 1962. Borderland Sciences Research Foundation Reprint.
*The Complex Secret of Dr. T. H. Moray*, J. Resines, 1989, Borderland Sciences Research Foundation Reprint.
*Treatise on Alpha, Beta, and Gamma Rays*, Moray, 1946.

### Morse, Samuel
"Conducting Power and Galvanic Power of The Earth", *Silliman's Journal*, Volume 35, pp. 253-267, 1839.
"Mode of Crossing Broad Rivers", Dr. Morse, Letter to House of Representatives, 23 December, 1824.
 [all accounts collected in VC 2 - Telegraphy]

### Murgas, Fr. Josef
"Constructing Antennæ", Patent 860.051, 16 July, 1907.
"Wireless Telegraphy", Patent 915.993, 23 March, 1909.
 [Biography and Patents, VC 8 - Ground Radio]
"Ground Telegraphy in War", H. Gernsback, *Electrical Experimenter*.
"Radiation And Reception With Buried Antenna", *IEEE*, AP-11, No. 3, pp. 207-218 (Relates Murgas to PANGLOSS).
"Subsurface Radio Propagation Experiments", Tsao and deBettencourt, Raytheon Company, 1965. [VC 11 - Military ELF]

### Musits, Sigmund
"Apparatus For Wireless Telegraphy", Patent 777.216, 13 December, 1904.
 [VC 8 - Ground Radio]

### Napolitano, Richard
[private conversation on geopolitical regions, 13 September, 1996]

### Nelson, J. H.
"Astronomical Shortwave Signal Disturbances", *Electrical Engineering*, 71: 421, 1952.
"Lunar Influence on Shortwave", *Nature*, No. 159: 396, 1947.

### Nipher, Dr. Francis
"Can Electricity Destroy Gravitation?", *Electrical Experimenter*, March 1918.

### Ohl, Russel S.
Ultrahigh Frequency Generator, Patent 1.656.987, 24 January, 1928.
 [VC 10 - Electric Ray Projectors]

### Palinscar, Andor
"Apparatus for Collecting Atmospheric Electricity", Patent 674.427, 21 May, 1901.
 [VC 1 - White Ray Conductors]

### Paneth, Dr, Fritz
"Helium and Neon in Vacuum Tubes", *Nature*, No. 90, 13 February, 1913.
"Hydrogen and Electrical Discharge", *Nature*, No. 118, p. 526, 1926.
"Hydrogen into Helium", *German Chemical Society*, No. 59, 1926.
"Palladium and Hydrogen Discharges", *Science*, No. 54, October 1926.

"Transmutation of Hydrogen into Helium", *Nature*, No. 119, pp 706-707, 14 May, 1927.

### Patterson, James A.
"System For Electrolysis", Patent 5.494.559, 27 February, 1996.

### Pennock, Walter I.
"Apparatus for Collecting Atmospheric Electricity", Patent 911.260, 2 February, 1909, [VC 1 - White Ray Conductors]

### Persinger, M. A. et al
"Psychophysiological Effects of ELF Fields", *Perceptual and Motor Skills*, Vol 36, 1973.
"Global Geomagnetic Activity", *Neuroscience Laboratory*, Laurentian University, 1985.

### Pickard, G. W.
"Oscillation Detector" (Crystal), Patent 904.222, 17 November, 1908.
"Oscillation Receiver" (Crystal), Patent 924.827, 15 June, 1909.
"Oscillation Detector" (Crystal), Patent 1.118.228, 24 November, 1914.
"Rectifier" (Crystal), Patent 1.225.852, 15 May, 1917.

### Pieckenbrock, Lawrence J.
"Gamma Ray LASER", Patent 3.557.370, 19 January, 1971.

### Poulsen, Valdemar
"Highpower Radio Arcs", Federal Telegraph Company.
"Generator of High Frequency Currents", Patent 1.214.214, 30 January, 1917.
"The Poulsen Arc", *Modern Wireless*, April 1923.
"The Poulsen Arc Generator", C. F. Elwell, London, 1923.
"The Poulsen Selective System of Wireless Telegraphy", A. J. Collins.
[Article Collection VC 11 - Military ELF]

### Preece, Sir William
"Recent Progress In Telephony", *British Association Reports*, 1882.
"Electrical Induction Between Wires", *British Association Reports*, 1886.
"Signalling Through Space Without Wires", *Proc. Royal Inst.*, London, 1897.
"Aetheric Telegraphy", *Society of Arts*, 3 May, 1899.
"Aetheric Telegraphy", *Inst. Electrical Engineers*, 22 December, 1898.
"Aetheric Wireless Telegraphy", *Proc. Inst. Electrical Engineers*, London, 1898.
[Collections VC 8 Ground Radio], [Collections VC 9 Aerial Radio]

### Puthoff, Harold E.
"Remote Viewing of Natural Targets" (with R. Targ), Stanford Research University, Research in Parapsychology, 1975, p. 33.
"Precognitive Remote Viewing" (with R. Targ), Stanford Research University, Research in Parapsychology, 1975 p. 35.
"A Perceptual Channel for Information Transfer", *Proceedings IEEE*, No. 64, March 1976, pp. 329-354.
*Mind-Reach*, R. Targ and H. Puthoff, New York, Delacorte Press, 1977.

### Reich, Dr. Wilhelm
*Bion Experiments*, Octagon, New York, 1979.
"Cosmic ORGONE Energy and Ether", *Orgone Bulletin*, Vol. 1, No 4, 1949.

*Cosmic Pulse of Life*, T. J. Constable, Borderland Sciences Research Foundation, 1993.
*Cosmic Superimposition*, Noonday Press, New York, 1973.
*Discovery of The ORGONE*, Rangeley, 1948.
*Etheric Weather Engineering on the High Seas*, T. J. Constable, Borderland Sciences Research Foundation Video.
*Fury On Earth: Biography of Wilhelm Reich*, Myron Sharaf, Andre Deutsch Publishers, England, 1983.
"ORGONE Energy", T. J. Constable, *National Exchange*, Vol 3 No 1, September 1978.
*ORGONE Energy Accumulator*, Rangely, 1951
*ORGONE Engineering*, Dr. Reich, Rangeley, July 1954.
Letters by Dr. Reich to The National Research Council (1952-1953).
"ORGONE Luminous Phenomena", *Orgone Energy Bulletin*, No. 1, Vol 1, 25 March, 1948.
*The ORANUR Experiment*, Reich Institute, Rangely, 1951.
"Reich Technology and Nuclear Systems", Dr. R. L. Clark, San Diego, 1982.
"Soft Particle Physics Experiment", Dr. R. L. Clark, San Diego, 1982.
Private correspondenc on The ORANUR Experiment, Dr. R. McCullough, Borderland Sciences Research Foundation.

### Reichenbach, Baron Karl von
*Letters on Od and Magnetism*, Stuttgart, 1858.
*Odic Glow*, Vienna, 1867.
*Physico-Psychological Researches*, Stuttgart, 1850.
*The Sensitive*, Stuttgart, 1858.
*Somnambulism & Cramp*, Stuttgart 1855.
*World of Plants and Sensitivity*, Vienna, 1858.

### Reiffel, Leonard
"Resonant Absorption of Gamma Rays", Patent 3.193.683, 6 July, 1965.
"X-Ray Source (LASER)", Patent 2.797.333, 25 June, 1957.

### Reno, Conrad
"Transmitting Energy Without Wires", Patent 1.504.974, 12 August, 1924.
[short newspaper biographies, VC 10 - Electric Ray Projectors]

### Rife, Dr. R. Raymond
"Rife Research Laboratory", J. Crane, Borderland Sciences Research Foundation Video.
*Royal R. Rife Report*, Borderland Sciences Research Foundation Video.

### Righi, Augusto
"Pioneers of Wireless", Ellison Hawks, *Wireless World*.
 [VC 9 - Aerial Radio]
"Inventors of Radio", D. S. Bartlett, Righi Biography.
 [VC 10 - Electric Ray Projectors]

### Rogers, James Harris
"America's Greatest War Invention", H. W. Secor, *Electrical Experimenter*, 1919.
"Ground Wires and Shortwaves", Lieut. Comm. H. A. Taylor, *Proceedings of the Institute Radio Engineers*, Volume 7, Number 4, 1919.
"Longwaves and Strays on Rogers Antennæ", Lieut. Comm. A. H. Taylor, *Electrical Experimenter*, 1920.

"Radiosignaling System", Patent 1.303.730, 13 May, 1919.
"Submarine Signaling System", Patent 1.395.454, 4 November, 1921.
"Submarine Wireless", P. R. Coursey, *Wireless World*, 27 November, 1920.
"The Rogers Underground Aerial for Amateurs", J. H. Rogers, *Electrical Experimenter*, 1920.
"Underground Wireless System", *Electrical Experimenter*, March 1919.
[Patent Collection, VC 8 - Ground Radio]

## SANGUINE/SEAFARER
"Earth Conduction Experiments", H. W. Dodge.
"Finding Mines By Radio", *Popular Radio*, September 1924, pp. 238-245.
"Grounding System For New High Power Stations", *The Marconigraph*, September 1919, pp. 548-549.
"Subterranean and Submarine Antennas", A. H. Taylor, *Institute Radio Engineers*, August 1919.
"Underground Radio Telegraph", S. R. Winters, *Popular Radio*, May 1924, pp. 490-492.
[Articles in VC 8 - Ground Radio]
"Electronic Countermeasures for ELF", J. A. Mullen, *IEEE*, 6 December 1973, Raytheon Company.
"ELF Propagation Measurements Along A 4900 Kilometer Path", L. Ginsberg, *IEEE*, 5 December 1973.
"Influence of Ionospheric Phenomena on ELF Propagation", J. R. Davis, *IEEE*, 6 December 1973, NRL sponsored.
"Nighttime Variations Of ELF", Bannister et al, *IEEE*, 6 December 1973.
"Propagation of ELF Waves", Dr. J. R. Wait, *IEEE*, 6 December 1973.
"Resistive Surveying In SANGUINE Site Selection", Davidson et al, *IEEE*, 17 September 1973, US Navy.
"SANGUINE Biological Research", Valentino et al, *IEEE*, 6 December 1973, US Naval Electronics Systems Command.
"SANGUINE Biological Research", Bennedick and Greenburg, *IEEE*, 19 November 1973, US Naval Electronics Systems Command.
"Wisconsin Test Facility", Bannister et al, *IEEE*, 6 December 1973.

## Scheller, Otto
"Multiple Antenna", Patent 1.595.166, 10 August, 1926. [VC 9 - Aerial Radio]

## Schauberger, Viktor
*Implosion, The Secret of Victor Schauberger*, Borderland Sciences Research Foundation, 1985.
*Nature Was My Teacher*, Borderland Sciences Research Foundation Video, 1991.
*Man-Made UFO's*, Renato Vesco, Adventures Unlimited Press, Kempton, IL.
*Secret of the Schauberger Saucers*, Jorge Resines, Borderland Sciences Research Foundation.
*Water-Element of Life*, Theodore Schwenk, op.

## Steinheil, C. A.
*On Telegraphy and Galvanic Craft*, Munich, 1898.
*History of Wireless Telegraphy*, Fahy, — Steinheil account taken from.
[all accounts VC 2 - Telegraphy]

**Stormer, Dr. Carl**
*Electron Paths and Geomagnetism*, Archives de Sciences, Geneva 1907.
"Short Wave Echoes", *Nature*, p. 681, 3 November, 1928.
"Short Wave Echoes and the Aurora", *Nature*, Vol. 122, 8 December, 1928.

**Stubblefield, Nathan**
"Electrical Battery", Patent 600.457, 8 March, 1898.
Personal Papers, Patents. [VC 4 - Archeforms]
Earth Batteries Patent Collection. [VC 4 - Archeforms]

**Tesla, Dr. Nikola**
"Apparatus For Transmitting Electrical Energy", [VC 9 - Aerial Radio]
"Coil", Patent 512.340, 9 January, 1894, [VC 9 - Aerial Radio]
*Colorado Springs Notes*, Nolit, Beograd, 1978.
*Discharges, Waves, Impulses, and Other Transients*, K. P. Steinmetz. Borderland Sciences Research Foundation Reprint.
"Dissipation of Energy From Hertz Resonator", *Electrical Engineer*, Dec 1892.
[VC 9 - Aerial Radio]
"Dr. Nikola Tesla's Achievements", *Electrical Experimenter*, February 1917.
"Electricity And The War", (Ray Televisor), W. H. Secor, *Electrical Experimenter*, 1919,
[VC 10 - Electric Ray Projectors]
"Electrical Transformer", Patent 593.138, 2 November, 1897.
[VC 8 Ground Radio]
*Inventions, Researches and Writings of Nikola Tesla*, Thomas Commerford Martin, The Electrical Enginneer 1894.
*Tesla - The Lost Inventions*, G. Trinkhaus, High Voltage Press, Claremont, CA.
"Magnetic Disrupter", Lecture to Institute of Electrical Engineers, London, February 1892.
"Method of Using Radiant Energy", Patent 685.958, 5 November, 1901.
[VC 10 - Electric Ray Projectors]
"Method of Signalling", [VC 9 - Aerial Radio]
*The Ray of Discovery - Nikola Tesla*, Borderland Sciences Research Foundation Video.
"Radiant Energy From Carbon Button Lamps", Lecture to Institute of Electrical Engineers, London, February 1892.
*Radio Tesla*, G. Trinkhaus, High Voltage Press, Claremont, CA.
"Signaling System" (spiral loops), Patent 725.605, 14 April 1903.
[VC 9 - Aerial Radio]
*The Ray of Discovery - Tesla's New York*, Borderland Sciences Research Foundation Video.
"Transmitting Electrical Energy", Patent 1.119.732, 1 December, 1914.
[VC 9 Aerial Radio]
"Transmitting Through Natural Mediums", Patent 787.412, 18 April, 1905.
[Patents, VC 8 - Ground Radio]
"Utilizing Effects Through Natural Media", Patents 685.956, 685.957, 5 November, 1901.
[VC 10 - Electric Ray Projectors]
*Vacuum Tubes of Tesla*, J. Resines (forthcoming publication).
"Wireless Light", *Electrical Engineer*, May 1894.
"Wireless Light", *Scientific American*, May 1894.
[VC 10 Electric Ray Projectors]

**Thomson, Elihu**
"Curious Effects of Hertzian Waves", *Electrical Engineer*, 4 July 1894, Vol. XVII, number 322. [VC 9 - Aerial Radio]

**Tommassina, T.**
"Carbon Coherers", *Comptes Rendus*, No. 128, pp. 666-667, 1899.

**Trowbridge, John**
"The Earth As A Conductor of Electricity", *American Academy of Sciences*, 1880.
[VC 9 Aerial Radio]

**Turpain**
Does Radio Cause Explosion? Popular Radio 1924
[VC 10 Electric Ray Projectors]

**Ulivi, Giulio**
"Ulivi's Experiments With Exploding Bombs", *Scientific American*, 4 July, 1914 (see also) "Electricity And The War", W. H. Secor on Dr. Tesla.
[VC 10 Electric Ray Projectors]

**Van Der Pol**
"Capacity Aerials", *Proc. Phys. Society*, 15 June, 1917.
"Echoes From The Depths of Space", R. T. Beatty, *Wireless World*, 28 November, 1923.
"Long Delayed Radio Echo Phenomena", Villard et al, QSR 53: 38, May 1969.
"Long Delayed Radio Echoes", *Nature*, No. 122, p. 878, 1929.
"Long Radio Echoes" (H. L. Rasmussen), *Nature*, p. 257:36, 1975.

**Viecelli, James A.**
"Coherent X-Ray And Gamma Ray Emissions", Patent 3.813.555, 28 May, 1974.

**Vion, H. C.**
"Improved Method of Utilizing Atmospheric Electricity", Patent 28.793, 19 June, 1860.
[VC 1 - White Ray Conductors]

**Von Arco, Count Georg**
"Aerial Conductor", Patent 959.100, 24 May, 1910. [VC 9 - Aerial Radio]
"Radiotelegraphic Station", Patent 1.082.221, 23 December, 1913.
[VC 8 - Ground Radio]

**Vreeland, Frederick**
"Production of Undamped Oscillations", Patent 829.934, 28 August, 1906.

**Ward, William**
"Improvement in Collecting Electricity", Patent 126.356, 30 April, 1872.
[VC 1 White Ray Conductors]

**Weber, S. L.**
"Ray Aviation Compass", Patent 1.948.552, 27 February, 1934.

**Weber, W. T.**
"Directing The Movements of Air Or Marine Craft", Patent 2.411.400, 19 November, 1946.

**PROJECT WESTFORD**
"Needles In The Sky", Tony Reichhardt, *Space World News*, 1984.
[VC 11 - Military ELF]

**White, Dr. George S.**
*Cosmo-Electric Culture*, Los Angeles, 1929.
*Finer Forces of Nature*, Los Angeles, 1929, Borderland Sciences Research Foundation Reprint.
*New Light on Therapeutic Energies*, M. L. Gallert, Borderland Sciences Research Foundation Reprint.
*Story of The Human Aura*, Los Angeles, 1928, Borderland Sciences Research Foundation Reprint.

**Winkelmann, Louis**
"Radioactive Vacuum Tube", patent 1.466.777, 4 September, 1923.
"Vacuum Tube" (Radioactive), Patent 1.650.921, 29 November, 1927.

**Wood, L. L.**
"X-Ray LASER", Patent 3.823.325, 9 July, 1974.

**Zickler, Carl**
"Telegraphy by Means of Electric Light", Patent 625.823, 30 May, 1899.
[VC 10 Electric Ray Projectors]

# INDEX

Acorn tubes 201
Aerial batteries 260
Æther 39-44, 262, 264, 270
   Dangers 78
   Electroneutrality of 86
   Electrostatic 78, 91, 111
   Engines 76
   Geology 69, 72, 78, 220, 235, 272
   Gravitation 63, 79, 84, 85
   Interstellar 40, 68
   Mendeleev 40, 43
   Pressure 29, 31, 37, 41, 43, 46, 49, 55, 62-68, 86
   Solar 68, 71, 75-76
   Space 34, 36, 38, 40
Arecibo 256, 264-265
ARGUS 178-180, 215, 219, 233
Atomic 41, 58-59, 70, 141, 146
   Aftermath 146, 161-165
   Atomic Energy 163
   Atomic energy 155-156, 172, 192
   Blast 169
   Fallout 163, 182
Aurora 56, 111, 178-188, 250, 252-253, 259-270

Biodynamic
   Coupling 171, 177-180
   Environment 66, 70-71 277, 281
Biosensors 188-189
Blackout 214-217, 231, 249-250

CALUTRON 151, 154
Clarke, Arthur C. 283
Coblentz, Dr. William 206, 231, 295
Colorado Springs 80, 82, 86, 262
Conspiratists 5, 6, 238, 245, 248
Critical mass 152, 183
Crookes, Sir William 46, 59, 131, 158
   Scrying tubes 63

Developmental prototype (DP) 256, 257
Dielectricity 49, 181, 213, 215
Dischargers
   Carbon 47, 48, 215 228
   Disruptive 26, 42, 47, 54
   Fluidic 35, 42, 171, 262, 266
   Magnetic 34-36, 47-50
   Nitrogen 47-50
   Whitefire 48, 83, 88
Dolbear, Dr. Amos 96
Dollard, Eric 25, 35, 38, 41, 43, 51, 55-56, 262

Electrons 38-39, 42, 44, 48-56, 63, 67
   Geoprocess in 230
   Manufacture of 44, 55, 67, 70-71, 78, 82-85
   Separation from 50, 173
Elettra 119, 120
ELF 17, 136-137, 172, 206, 213, 220, 233-238
   Jamming 206, 213, 217, 238
   Monopoles 238
   Physiological effects of 64, 238-241
EMP 172-181, 206, 209-219, 231-233, 249-250, 254, 295-296
   Cannon 175, 181
   Nuclear 169, 171, 173
   RADAR 175, 179, 201

Farnsworth, Dr. Philo 114, 202-204, 275, 290, 292
   Multipactor 203, 204
Fessenden, Dr. Reginald 105, 111-112, 120, 135, 198, 224-225
Fuchs, Klaus 159, 160
Fusion research 169, 275

Galvani, Luigi 43, 49, 260, 270
Gamma ray bomb 185-186
Gammatron 214

Governments 12, 15, 129
Grindell-Matthews, Dr. H. 139, 215, 250

HAARP 5-9, 16-17, 142, 244-260, 268, 271
Hamer, Armand 159-160
Hammond, Dr. John 22, 89
Hanford 149-151
Henry, Dr. Joseph 30-31, 49
Hettinger, John 114, 139, 215, 250
HIPAS 256
Hydrogen bomb 165, 288, 300
Hysteria 6-9, 188, 239, 245, 248, 257, 284

IGY 177
Impulses 26, 28, 34-46, 55-56, 63-64, 73, 79, 83, 90, 92, 103, 109, 174, 206-208, 216, 240
  Backrushes 29
  Unidirectional 29, 32-39, 44, 54, 76
Ionoscatter 210, 215, 254
Ionospheric Research Instrument 16, 249, 256-257

Jim Creek 232, 234

Klystron 202, 211, 265, 269

Le Bon, Dr. Gustav 53, 60, 67, 145-147, 182, 190, 192
Lemstrom, Dr. Selim 105, 261-264, 270
Lighthouse tubes 201-202
Lightning rods 260
Lodge, Sir Oliver 35-37, 40, 46, 96, 97, 131, 198-199, 220
Long Delay Echoes 265

Magnetron 202-209, 214, 218, 230, 297
Marconi 35, 40, 57, 69, 89, 95-124, 129, 132, 134-143, 194, 196, 198, 211, 218, 220-230, 236, 243-244, 257, 275
Military 5-6, 10, 16-21, 47, 57, 62, 93, 94, 97, 115, 126, 128-129, 133-142, 145, 153-179
  Coups 159, 160
  Privatization 11, 155, 194, 226
  Models 9-19, 245, 271
  micropatterns 15
  similacra 14
Mossbauer Effect 186-187, 297, 304
Murgas, Fr. Josef 135-136, 229, 235-236

Neutron bomb 181, 183, 299
New Brunswick 112
Nonnuclear weapons 306
NRL 137, 149, 189, 231, 233, 257

Oakridge 150
Oil 26, 31, 99, 119, 198, 207, 235, 272, 274-276
Old World 126, 144-145, 159-161, 247-248, 272
Oligarchy 128, 139, 143, 144, 146-161, 167, 206-212, 247-248, 274, 283
Optoexplosives 183-184
ORANUR Experiment 190
Orgone Energy 189-190

Paneth, Dr. Fritz 145, 192
PANGLOSS 231, 233. *See also* RCA
Photonuclear reactions 145
Piezonuclear reactions 187
PLOWSHARE 182-184
Poulsen Arcs 107, 109, 214, 228, 230
PROJECT WESTFORD 217

RADAR 147, 171-175, 214-219, 232, 242, 254, 260, 283, 292-297
  highpower 147, 172, 205, 208-210, 214, 217
  longwave 200, 211
  pulse 172, 175
Radiant Energy 34, 42-44, 52-54, 59-68,

71, 85, 101, 103, 109, 115, 117, 131, 172, 207, 218, 220, 243-244, 284, 300
Radioactive tubes 148
Radioactivity 44, 58, 63, 69, 90, 147, 161, 191
  neutralization of 190-191
  Tesla model of 44, 58, 63, 90
Radiocartography 122
Radiophones 231, 303, 305
RAND Corporation 283-293
Rays 30, 34, 43, 50-51, 57-68, 103-104, 114, 129, 132, 170, 183-186, 207, 240, 264, 293, 296-297
  beamrays 55, 61, 64, 66
  darklight 51, 57
  lightlike 30, 42
  televisual 286, 290-292, 304
RCA 89-90, 123-124, 232-237. See also PANGLOSS and Tesla 89
Reich, Dr. Wilhelm 189-192
Rogers, James Harris 136-137, 229, 234-237

SANGUINE-SEAFARER 137, 220, 234-241, 250, 251, 306
Schauberger, Victor 85
Shadowgraphs 51
Soundwaves 25, 31, 186
  electrical 25
  Standing waves 82-87, 240, 251
Space stations 279, 283, 303
STARFISH 179-180, 215, 219
Stubblefield, Nathan 96, 222, 229
Submarine communications 61, 100, 229-230, 234, 238, 293, 306
Symbols 8-15
  models 9, 11
  subconscious 8-9, 16
  symbolists 6-8

TEAK 178
Tellurian explosives 183, 184

Tesla 19-117, 120-121, 124, 129, 130-139, 143, 146, 147, 172, 173, 177, 192, 195-199, 206-211, 218, 220, 223-225, 229, 238-245, 254-258, 262-263, 284, 294, 300
  and electric automobile 92-93
  and Heinrich Hertz 25-26, 34
  and Lee De Forest 93
  and Rockefeller 89
  and Sarnoff 89
  and shockwaves 26, 29, 31, 36
  compact power receiver 57
  German experimenters 103
  lost papers 21
  Polyphase 22, 24-25, 73, 112
  The "Tesla Rule" 244-245
Thomson, Elihu 30, 97
Thyratron 207, 214

U-2 289, 291
Uranium 58, 145-151, 154-155, 167, 176, 182, 187, 272
  armor piercing darts 187
  isotopic separation 149-151
  purifying 168

Van Allen 177-179
Vion, H.C. 105, 261, 270
VLF 17, 105, 107, 109-114, 118, 121, 123-124, 136, 179, 197-198, 206, 219-234, 242, 253, 266

Wardenclyffe Station 79, 88, 106
Wireless 73, 95-104, 114-117, 122-124, 129, 134-136, 207, 220, 223-229, 267, 283
  Loomis aerial 95, 100, 119
  shortwave 119, 121
  subaqueous 95, 136, 229
  subterranean 95, 136, 206, 220, 229, 235-236